PEARSON CLASSICS *in* POLITICAL SCIENCE

Party Politics in America

Fifteenth Edition

MARJORIE RANDON **HERSHEY**

Indiana University

Foreword by

JOHN H. **ALDRICH**

D0970766

PEARSON

Boston   Columbus   Indianapolis   New York   San Francisco   Upper Saddle River   Amsterdam
Cape Town   Dubai   London   Madrid   Milan   Munich   Paris   Montreal   Toronto   Delhi
Mexico City   São Paulo   Sydney   Hong Kong   Seoul   Singapore   Taipei   Tokyo

Executive Editor: Reid Hester
Editorial Assistant: Emily Sauerhoff
Senior Marketing Manager: Lindsey Prudhomme
Production Project Manager: Clara Bartunek
Project Coordination, Text Design, and Electronic
Page Makeup: Integra Software Services, Pvt. Ltd.
Cover Design Manager: Jayne Conte
Cover Designer: Karen Noferi
Cover Art: Alamy.com
Printer/Binder/ Cover: STP Courier Companies

Library of Congress Cataloging-in-Publication Data
Hershey, Marjorie Randon.
    Party politics in America/Marjorie Randon Hershey.—15th ed.
        p. cm.
    Includes bibliographical references and index.
    ISBN-13: 978-0-205-25177-3 (alk. paper)
    ISBN-10: 0-205-25177-3 (alk. paper)
    1. Political parties—United States.   I. Title.
JK2265.H477 2013
324.273—dc23

                                          2011044529

10 9 8 7 6 5 4 3 2 1—CRW—16 15 14 13

ISBN 10:   0-205-25177-3
ISBN 13: 978-0-205-25177-3

DETAILED CONTENTS

CHAPTER 8
Parties and Voter Turnout   149

FOREWORD

Why should you be interested in studying political parties? The short answer is that virtually everything important in American politics is rooted in *party* politics. Political parties are at the core of American democracy and make it what it is today—just as they have virtually from the Founding.

Why should you use this book to guide you in the search for understanding democratic politics in America? The short answer is that this book is the best guide you can have, and it has been the best guide in this search for quite a long time. Now, let's turn to the longer answers.

I first encountered this text at the same stage in my life you are in now: as an undergraduate, although in my case that was back in the 1960s. At that point, the book was authored by an up-and-coming scholar named Frank Sorauf. Following on the heels of his important study of the effect of political parties on the Pennsylvania legislature,[1] *Party Politics in America* established him as arguably the leading scholar of political parties of his generation. In those days—less so today—it was common for a "textbook" (i.e., a book designed to be used in class) to do more than just tell you what others had written about its subject. Rather, books written for undergraduates were also designed to make a coherent argument about its subject matter—to engage you, the reader, intellectually. So it was then, and with this book, so it remains today.

In the sixth edition, published in 1988, Frank brought in Paul Allen Beck as coauthor. Paul took over the authorial duties beginning with that edition, and Marjorie Randon Hershey did so beginning with the ninth edition in 2001, leading to the book that you are about to read today. Each did so with considerable respect for the substance and the perspective that characterized the previous editions. This has brought a high degree of intellectual continuity to *Party Politics in America*. There are several important continuities. First, Sorauf, Beck, and Hershey very effectively use a three-part division in the discussion of political parties. More specifically, they divide the political party into its electoral, governing, and organizational roles. These three aspects of a party create a coherent system that (sometimes loosely, sometimes more tightly) provides a degree of integration to the diverse workings of any one political party.

When Sorauf first wrote, the three pieces were rather loosely integrated. Partisanship in the public, for example, was nearly as strongly held as today, but the party in government was deeply divided, especially the Democrats (into North and South, or pro- and anti-civil rights) but also the Republicans (into "Wall Street" and "Main Street," or urban vs. suburban and rural). Today, partisanship is as strong as always, but Democratic officeholders are much more strongly united, and Republicans are, if anything, even more so. In addition, the party organizations are stronger and more effective (and vastly better financed), making them able to hold together the other two parts. However, even with a highly polarized party system (as this homogeneity among fellow partisans and differentiation from the opposition is called), there are serious strains among the various parts. What, for example, would you do if you were an adviser to the Republican Party faced with the following choice? There is a policy stance that will help your presidential nominee win votes from undecided (typically moderate) voters and thus perhaps help your party win the presidency. That same stance, however, will hurt your party's candidates for the U.S. House of Representatives in their fund-raising campaigns and thus put at risk the narrow majority they currently hold in the House. Is it more important to hold a majority in the House or to hold the presidency? Should you risk losing potential support from moderate voters to maintain close ties with more extreme groups key to your organizational strength in fund-raising?

The second continuity is that Sorauf, Beck, and Hershey see the two major political parties in the United States as a *system*. The two-party system has long played a central role in the historical evolution of American politics (see especially Chapter 7). Although this two-party system has important implications for the dynamics of American politics, they also see the two-party system as a part of the intermediary groups in society. By this, the authors mean that the parties serve as points of contact between the public and its government (see Figure 1.1, a figure that I believe has graced this book for fourteen editions now).

The third continuity is that each author is a terrific scholar of political parties, and although these continuities have allowed this book to keep its unique intellectual stamp, the transition among authors has also allowed each to bring to the work his or her particular strengths. In the end, this has made the fifteenth edition of the book richer and stronger than ever before. As I noted earlier, Frank Sorauf used his expertise to explain the role of the political party in government. Since then, he became one of the nation's leading experts on the role of money in politics and in later editions reflected that increasingly important but perennially controversial subject.[2] Paul Beck brought a distinguished career of scholarship, examining the role of political parties in the electorate and adding nicely to Frank's expertise about the governing role.[3] Paul is, like Frank and Marjorie Hershey, an expert on American politics. However, Paul is also, more than most of us who study American politics, genuinely knowledgeable about comparative politics.

Marjorie Randon Hershey, through her expertise, has made important contributions to one of the most difficult questions to study: How do candidates and their campaigns shape and are shaped by electoral forces?[4] This interaction links the two most important components of the party, elections and governance, into a more coherent whole. It has allowed her to bring clarity to what has become an increasingly confused portion of the field. Marjorie also has closely studied the role of gender in politics, a dimension of party politics that not only has been of long-standing importance from at least the granting of women's suffrage but has also become especially critical with the emergence and growth of the "gender gap."[5] Finally, she has made a long series of contributions to help us understand how to bring meaning to complex events.[6] One special feature of this book is the increased use of narratives from well-known and little-known party figures alike, narratives that serve to bring the subject matter to life.

Not only does each author add a unique and innovative understanding to political parties as they join the continuity of leading scholars who have shaped this book, but also each edition adds new life to the text by considering the politics of the time. This fifteenth edition is not an exception. Here then are some of the facets of particular relevance to contemporary politics that I find particularly worth considering (by you that is).

One issue that is critical to all who study American politics is the way that an understanding of politics matters in your life. This is your government, and the political parties are ways in which you can help shape what your government and elected officials do. This is one of the most important meanings of American political parties. They, and the government that they create, are the consequences of you and your political actions. So saying allows me to move more directly to the longer answer about the study of political parties themselves.

At the outset, I mentioned that you should want to study political parties because they are so important to virtually everything that happens in American politics and because political parties are so central to the workings of any democracy. Great, but you are probably asking, "So what questions should I keep in mind as I read this book? What questions will help me understand the material better?" Let me propose as guidelines three questions that are neither too specific nor too general. We are looking, that is, for questions somewhere in between "Are parties good?" on the one hand and "Why did the Senate Minority Leader Mitch McConnell (Republican, Texas) say about the coming Senate term, 'The single most important thing we want to achieve is for President Obama to be a one-term president,' "[7] on the other.

You are well aware that today politicians can appear magnanimous and statesmanlike if they say that they will be nonpartisan and if they call for Congress to "rise above" partisan politics to be bipartisan. Yet essentially every elected official is a partisan, and essentially every elected official chooses to act in a partisan way much of the time. Why do politicians today, you might ask, speak as if they are of two minds about political parties? Perhaps they actually are. Even if you dismiss this rhetoric as just words, it is the case that the public is of two minds about parties, too. This book, like virtually all written about American political parties, includes quotes from the Founding Fathers warning about the dangers of party and faction, often quoting such luminaries as John Adams, Thomas Jefferson, and James Madison. Yet these very same men not only worried about the dangers of party but they were the founders and leaders of our first political parties. So the first question is "why are people—leaders and followers, founders and contemporary figures alike—both attracted to and repulsed by political parties?"

Let me suggest two books that might give you additional ways to think about this question. One is Richard Hofstadter's *The Idea of a Party System: The Rise of Legitimate Opposition in the United States, 1780–1840* (Berkeley: University of California Press, 1969). This book is a series of public lectures that Hofstadter gave in which he roots political parties deeply in the American democratic tradition, arguing that they represent the outward manifestation of a change in philosophic understanding of the relationship between citizens and leaders in this, the world's first practicing democracy. Austin Ranney, in *Curing the Mischiefs of Faction: Party Reform in America* (Berkeley: University of California Press, 1975), connects Hofstadter's view of the role of philosophic ideas and American democratic practice from our first 60 years to the contemporary era. Ranney was a leading scholar of political parties, but in this case he was also writing this book in reflection upon his time spent as a member of the so-called McGovern-Fraser Reform Commission, which revised the rules for the Democratic Party and advocated the reforms that led to the current presidential primary system. Thus, there is both a theoretical and practical dimension to this work.

This question of the purpose of parties in our democracy, both theoretical and practical, leads easily to a second major question that should be in your mind as you work through this book and your course: "How does the individual connect to the political party?" There are two aspects to this question. One is fairly direct—what do parties mean to the individual and how, if at all, has this changed over time? The great work that laid out this relationship in the modern era is *The American Voter* by Angus Campbell, Philip E. Converse, Warren E. Miller, and Donald E. Stokes (New York: John Wiley & Sons, 1960). Many argue that this connection has changed fundamentally. At one extreme, Martin P. Wattenberg has written about the declining relevance of political parties to the voter, such as in his *The Decline of American Political Parties, 1952–1996* (Cambridge, MA: Harvard University Press, 1998), using such striking evidence as a dramatic decline in the willingness or ability of citizens to say what they like or dislike about either of our two major political parties. Others disagree with Wattenberg. Larry Bartels, and in a completely different way, Green, Palmquist, and Schickler, for example, has shown that partisanship remains as influential in shaping the vote as ever.[8] It is certainly the case that today we hear people say, "The government, they ...," and not "The government, we ...." I suspect that few of us think that way. It is certainly common to hear politicians call for a tax cut by claiming that doing so will give the people back their money. Such a statement would not make sense if we thought of the government as being composed of us, ourselves, and thus thought of *our* taxes as using *our* money to work in *our* government, doing *our* bidding by enacting *our* preferences into legislation selected by *our* representatives whom *we* chose. The question can, however, be cast even more broadly, asking whether the people feel removed from social, cultural, economic, and political institutions, generally, with political parties and the government therefore only one more symptom of a larger ill. This is certainly a part of the concerns that motivated Robert D. Putnam in his *Bowling Alone: The Collapse and Revival of American Community* (New York: Simon & Schuster, 2000). Today that sometimes comes out in the sense that the debate among the politicians in Washington seems to be more about scoring points over the partisan opposition and less about working in the public's interest. This sense of remove peaked this summer of 2011 in the debate over whether to raise the debt ceiling, in which the elected figures in each party appeared to put the country's economic recovery at risk merely to win their side of a policy dispute.[9]

The change from a trusting, supportive, identified public to one apparently dramatically less so is one of the great changes that took place in American politics over the past half century. A second great change is "polarization," a growing distance between the elected officials of the two parties. That is, compared with 50 years ago, today the Democrats are more liberal and consistently more so than Republicans, who in turn are much more conservative. Although this is not to say that there is anything close to an identical set of beliefs by the members of either party, there is a greater coherence of opinion and belief in, say, the congressional delegations of each party than in earlier times. Even more undeniable is a much clearer divergence between the policy interests and choices of the two parties in Washington than, say, 50 years ago. You might refer to *Polarized Politics: Congress and the President in a Partisan Era* (Washington, DC: CQ Press, 2000), edited by Jon R. Bond and Richard Fleisher, for a variety of fairly early indications of this fact. The question then is not whether there is greater polarization today; the question is whether this relative clarity of polarization matters. As usual, there are at least two ways to understand the question. One is simply to ask whether a more polarized Congress yields policies very different from a less polarized one. The readings in Bond and Fleisher generally support that position. Others, for example, Keith Krehbiel and David W. Brady and Craig Volden argue that the Founders' creation of checks and balances makes polarization relatively ineffectual in shaping legislation due to vetoes, compromises necessary between the two chambers, and so on.[10] Even more generally, however, David R. Mayhew has argued that our system generates important legislation regardless of which party is in control or whether they share power under divided partisan control of government.[11] As you might expect, there has been considerable interest in the challenge that Mayhew, Krehbiel, and Brady and Volden have raised. One set of responses can be seen in the Bond and Fleisher volume, another can be found in *The Macro Polity*.[12]

However, this returns us to one of the original questions: Just how closely does the party in the electorate align with the party in government? On this, too, there is considerable disagreement. On the one hand, Alan Abramowitz argues that the partisan public follows only at a degree of lag the polarization of the partisan elite in Washington, while on the other hand, Morris Fiorina argues that the public remains primarily, even overwhelmingly, moderate, and sees the polarization in Washington, but does not follow it. There is, in his words, a "disconnect," presumably caused by political parties and their leaders.[13] As you can see, we have now reached the point of very recently published work. That is, we are asking questions that are motivating the work of scholars today and problems that are motivating the public and its leaders today. So, let's get on with it and turn to the book and the study of political parties themselves.

JOHN H. ALDRICH
DUKE UNIVERSITY

PREFACE

WHY SHOULD YOU USE THE NEW EDITION?

Creating a new version of a book about party politics every two years has costs, not only for the students who will buy it, but also for the instructors who will assign it and even for the person who researches and writes it! So why do it? Because American political life changes quickly. We elect a new Congress every two years, and each election tells us something new about the American parties. The last edition of this book portrayed American political life in the early months of the Obama presidency. At that time, the Democratic Party had just hit the trifecta; Democrats controlled the White House, held a big majority in the U.S. House, and had the supermajority in the Senate required to end any filibuster. Some prominent analysts were asking whether the Republicans would ever recover. The health care reform bill had not yet been considered. The Tea Party had not yet formed. Osama bin Laden was alive and well and living in Pakistan.

Then, things changed. A month before the fourteenth edition reached bookstores, a Republican underdog, Scott Brown, beat a Democratic stalwart to take over Ted Kennedy's Senate seat in bright-blue Massachusetts. Soon after, the Supreme Court told corporations in the *Citizens United* ruling that they could now spend unlimited funds on campaign advertising right up to Election Day. Within a few months after the book's publication, organized and spontaneous protests against the Democratic health care reform legislation commanded news coverage throughout the nation. Little more than a year later, in the election of 2010, Democrats lost control of the House, barely hung on to a majority in the Senate, and gave up large numbers of state governorships and legislatures to the quickly-recovered Republicans. It seemed like a long time since the 2006 and 2008 Democratic wave elections. The magnitude of the change surprised even many Republican strategists.

The current, fifteenth edition completely updates every chapter to include data on the 2010 midterm elections and the start of the 2012 race and traces the nature and meaning of these changes. But it does much more than that. Among the new features are focuses on:

- The development and impact of the Tea Party (in Chapters 1 and 3): Is it a new political party, a lasting movement in American politics, or simply an intense faction of the Republican Party?
- The growth of income inequality and battles over the rights of public employees' unions (Chapters 1 and 3)
- Re-introduction of the idea of a "party network" (in Chapters 3 and 4)
- A new section on voter intimidation (in Chapter 8), to join those on the parties' roles in the voter ID and proof of citizenship controversies

- The impact of early voting and vote-by-mail, now used by increasing numbers of states (Chapter 8)
- Rules changes for the 2012 presidential primaries and caucuses (in Chapter 10)
- Effects of the *Citizens United* case and Super PACs on congressional and presidential campaigns (in Chapter 12): Does the term "campaign finance regulation" still have meaning?
- Partisan sorting and greater ideological extremism (in Chapters 7, 13, and 15)
- The two parties' long-term prospects in view of racial and other demographic changes in the electorate (in Chapters 6 and 16) and shifts in partisanship since 2005 (Chapters 6 and 7)

Even with all these changes, however, the aims of the book are the same as they have always been. Frank J. Sorauf, a pioneer of modern political science, had the vision to create *Party Politics in America* in 1968, and Paul Allen Beck brought the book into the late 1980s and 1990s, with the intellectual mastery and comparative perspective that has marked his research on parties and voting behavior. Their goal for each new edition was to provide students with the clearest, most comprehensive and engaging understanding of political parties and partisanship, which in turn are key to understanding the workings of elections, public opinion, policy-making, and leadership. They succeeded so well that *Party Politics in America* has long been known as the "gold standard" of political parties texts.

This edition contains new and updated versions of the features that were so well received in recent editions. The boxes titled "A Day in the Life" tell the personal stories of individuals whose experiences help to illustrate recent changes in the parties. Many of my students see political parties as remote, abstract, and a bit underhanded—something that might interest elderly people, but not teens and twentysomethings. I hope these compelling stories—for instance, that of a college student striving to win votes for Obama in the rural areas and small towns of Appalachia—can show readers why studying party politics is worth their time.

In other chapters, the feature titled "Which Would You Choose?" presents students with major debates about party politics: for instance, whether encouraging greater voter turnout would help or harm American democracy (see Chapter 8). These summaries, using the point–counterpoint format with which undergraduates are familiar, could serve as the basis for classroom debate on these and many other fundamental concerns.

As in previous editions, I've tried to make the reader's job easier by putting important terms in boldface and clearly defining them, emphasizing the central points even more, and making some of the long tables into figures or shorter, clearer tables. In addition, for instructors, I have worked to make sure that each chapter can stand alone, so that teachers can assign chapters in any order they choose without leaving their students puzzled because relevant concepts were explained elsewhere.

Textbooks have constituents, just as political parties and elected officials do. However, as elected officials know, it is hard to be accountable to constituents without getting detailed information about what they want—in this case, what readers like and don't like about a book. I have very much appreciated the reactions I've received from some faculty members and students who have read *Party Politics in America*, but I would like to receive many more. How about you? You can reach me at hershey@indiana.edu; I'll be happy to respond.

ACKNOWLEDGMENTS AND THANKS

Throughout these editions I have received generous help in researching, writing, and revising this book: from my graduate and undergraduate students; present and former colleagues at Indiana University, particularly Ted Carmines and Bob Huckfeldt, Bill Bianco, Eileen Braman, Mike Ensley, Yanna Krupnikov, Elinor Ostrom, Leroy Rieselbach, Regina Smyth, John Williams, and Jerry Wright; and departmental staff members Fern Bennett, Amanda Campbell, Steve Flinn, Marsha Franklin, Sara Huntsman, Sharon LaRoche, Jan Peterson, James Russell, and Deb Speer, and Jessica Williams.

Austin Ranney, Leon Epstein, Jack Dennis, and Murray Edelman were most responsible for my interest in party politics and for my training in political science. Murray Edelman deserves special mention in that group, not only as a mentor and model for so many of us but also as a much-beloved friend. John Aldrich, one of the most insightful and systematic analysts of political parties, has been kind enough to write the Foreword to the book. I've learned so much as well from Bruce Oppenheimer, Gerry Pomper, Larry Bartels, Paul Beck, Tony Broh, Tom Carsey, Richard Fenno, John Green, John Hibbing, Jennifer Hochschild, Robert Jackman, Anthony King, John Kingdon, Mike Kirn, Geoff Layman, Burdett Loomis, John Petrocik, Brian Silver, Jim Stimson, Brian Vargus, and John Zaller. Many others provided valuable help with this edition, including Alan Abramowitz, Melody Crowder-Meyer, Audrey Haynes, Christian Hilland, Scott McClurg, Chuck Prysby, Doug Roscoe, Megan Trusnik, Brad Warren, Richard Winger, and especially my terrific research assistant, Nate Birkhead.

The political scientists who reviewed the previous edition—Craig Brians of Virginia Tech, David Darmofal of the University of South Carolina–Columbia, Scott McClurg of Southern Illinois University, and John McGlennon of the College of William and Mary—offered lots of useful comments, which helped me continue adapting the book to meet students' and instructors' needs. And it remains a pleasure to work with the people at Pearson Longman: Editor Reid Hester, editorial assistant Emily Sauerhoff, and the other members of the production team, and with Moganambigai Sundaramurthy at Integra.

Most of all, I am very grateful to my family: my husband, Howard, and our daughters, Katie, Lissa, Lani, and Hannah. Everything I do has been made possible by their love and support.

MARJORIE RANDON HERSHEY

Parties and Party Systems

To many college students, government is for old people. Politics is a negative term, they think, relating somehow to corruption or, at the least, boredom. What a surprise it must be when these students discover that, in fact, government is at the very center of their lives.

Who decides how old you must be to drink beer legally and what the penalty is if you get caught with a fake ID?

Who decides whether the pizza you recently ordered was prepared in a sanitary kitchen, and what "sanitary" means in practice?

What determines how much money will be taken out of your paycheck for taxes and Social Security?

It's government that makes these decisions and thousands more that affect your life every day. In fact, you would have to look very hard to find an aspect of your life that is *not* affected by government action. The federal government determines whether the lettuce in your salad needs to be tested for contamination and the maximum interest rate you can be charged for your student loan. State governments have decided which sex acts can be prosecuted and whether your high school had to teach you the theory of evolution, the Biblical story of creation, or both. Local governments choose when to fill potholes and how aggressively to prosecute drug and alcohol crimes. It is the political system that plays the most important role in deciding, as a famous political scientist put it, "who gets what, when, how."[1]

Because government decisions affect almost everything we do, large numbers of groups have mobilized to try to influence these decisions, as well as the selection of the men and women who will make them. In a democracy, the political party is one of the oldest and most important of these groups. Parties have a lot of competition, however. Organized interests such as the National Rifle Association and the National Gay and Lesbian Task Force also work to get the government policies they want, as do pro-life groups, National Organization for the Reform of Marijuana Laws (NORML), and People for the Ethical Treatment of Animals. Even organizations whose main purpose

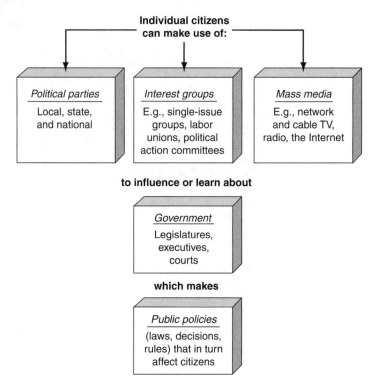

| FIGURE I.1
Parties and Other Intermediaries Between Citizens and Government.

is nonpolitical, such as universities, Walmart, and MTV, try to influence the government decisions that affect them.

All these groups serve as *intermediaries*—links between citizens and the people in government who make the decisions that affect our lives (Figure I.1). They raise issues that they want government to address. By bringing together people with shared interests, they amplify these people's voices in speaking to government. They tell people what government is doing. They keep an eye on one another's behavior as well as on the actions of public officials.

Different intermediaries specialize in different political activities. Parties focus on nominating candidates, helping to elect them, and organizing those who win. Most organized interests represent narrower groups; they are not likely to win majority support so they try instead to influence the views of candidates who do win office—and of appointed officials, such as bureaucrats and judges. Groups like these in other democracies may play different roles. The American parties, for example, tend to concentrate on election activities, whereas many parties in Europe have been more committed to spreading ideologies and keeping their elected officials faithful to the party's program.

The competition among these intermediary groups is fierce. Parties, of course, compete with one another. They vie with interest groups for money, expertise, and volunteer help and then, with those resources in hand, for the support of individual citizens and elected officials. Getting people's attention and support is difficult in an age when TV and the Internet soak up the free time of so many prospective activists and voters. Parties must even fight for a major role in political campaigns; the American parties are not nearly as dominant in the business of campaigning as they were a century ago. In many newer democracies, such as those of post-Communist nations, parties face even greater competition from "party substitutes" such as governors' nonpartisan political machines, which also provide money and services to candidates.[2]

Adding to their burden, the American parties fight for power in a culture that claims to hate partisanship. Parties have been the targets of suspicion and ridicule since the nation began. James Madison and the other founders were very wary of organized factions in their new republic. A century later, the Progressive movement—reformers intent on rooting out political corruption and returning power to middle-class people like themselves—worked to combat the parties' "boss rule." Disgust with party power in the 1960s and 1970s led to another series of party reforms that has helped to reshape current politics. Many Americans today are not only fed up with the Republicans and Democrats but hostile even to the idea of political parties.[3]

Public hostility has led state legislatures to pass waves of restrictions on how parties can organize and what they can do. Parties have adapted to these rules over time by changing their organizations and activities. The political parties of the 2010s would hardly be recognizable to politicians of a century ago, and the parties that we know today may change dramatically in the coming decades.

The aim of this book is to explore the American parties: how they have developed, how they affect us, and what they are capable of contributing to a democratic politics. Given the rise of blogs, the growth of single-issue groups, and the many other ways in which we can learn about and affect government, are political parties really as essential to the survival of a democracy as many have assumed? Are they a benefit to both candidates and voters, or do they deserve the distrust with which so many Americans—and probably you yourself—view them?

What Are Political Parties?

A Republican presidential candidate charges that President Obama has anti-American views. A Democratic member of Congress calls some Republicans "unscrupulous, foot-dragging, knuckle-dragging Neanderthals." This is not exactly the type of high-minded rhetoric that we would like to hear from our nation's leaders, but it has become as common as reality TV. Why, people ask, can't we all just get along?

"The main reason it is so hard for Democrats and Republicans in Washington to cooperate," one analyst argues, "is not that they don't like each other, but that they disagree profoundly about the major issues facing the country."[1] Not only in Congress but also in state legislatures and even courtrooms, Democrats often disagree strongly with Republicans about the economy, abortion, same-sex marriage, taxes, immigration, and other issues that animate Americans. These differences among elected officials have grown dramatically in the past three decades. The gulf between the parties in government is now so wide that the U.S. House elected in 2010 was the most polarized in American history.

The result is that a shift from Democratic to Republican control of Congress and the White House can now lead to a fundamental change in public policies. In 2008 and 2009, the Democratic-majority House was the most liberal in the past three decades. Yet, just a year later, the Republican swing in the 2010 elections produced the most conservative House in that period.[2] These party conflicts on issues are often painful to watch, but they help to clarify voters' choices and hold elected officials accountable to the people—a vital set of functions for a democracy.

Why, then, do so many Americans see political parties as meaningless and, perhaps, even as harmful? Their suspicion of parties has long roots; George Washington declared in his Farewell Address that "the spirit of party" was the "worst enemy" of popular government. Parties, he feared, would encourage people to pursue their narrow self-interest at other people's expense, seek domination over others, and cause jealousy, division, and revenge. Without parties, in this view, we'd be more likely to get noble and uncorrupted leaders who could speak for the nation as a whole, in a spirit of unity and mutual benefit.

Washington was expressing a widely shared dream but one difficult to put into practice. Most people are not very interested in politics, so how would they decide on a candidate without the guidance that party labels provide? Will they spend hours researching the experience and issue stands of dozens of candidates, or will they choose the candidate with the most attractive personality?

Without parties, how would we choose a president? In the absence of party primaries and caucuses, who would be able to trim down the thousands of presidential wannabes to the very few who will run in the general election? Could members of Congress make that decision? Not in a system designed to separate legislative from executive powers. How about nomination by the nation's mayors and other elected officials, as happens in France? A new version of the television series *Survivor*? The answer is not obvious, though it is obviously critical to the nation's future.

Strong party organizations bring voters to the polls. Without political parties, would voter turnout, already lower in the United States than in most other industrialized democracies, drop even further? How would members of Congress elected as individuals, with no party loyalties to guide them, put together majorities for packages of legislation?

What is this political organization that is so needed and yet so distrusted? Does the concept of party include only the politicians who share a party label when running for and holding public office? Does it also include the activists who work on the campaigns and the citizens who vote for a party's candidates? Or is a party any group that chooses to call itself a party, whether Republican or Tea?

THE THREE PARTS OF PARTIES

Most scholars would agree that *a party is a group organized to nominate candidates, to try to win political power through elections, and to promote ideas about public policies.* To the analysts quoted in the box "What Is a Political Party?" on pages 6–7, the central figures in a political party are the candidates and elected officials who share a party's label (see, for example, Edmund Burke's and Anthony Downs's definitions). Many parties in democratic nations, including the United States, began as groups of political leaders who organized to advance certain policies.

Most observers, however, see the American parties as including more than just candidates and officeholders. As John Aldrich's definition reminds us, parties are organizations—institutions with a life and a set of rules of their own, beyond that of their candidates. Interested individuals can become active in them and help set their goals and strategies, just as one would do in a sports team or a church youth group. These activists and organizations are central parts of the party, too. They can link the party to a network of "policy demanders" in organized interests such as pro-life, pro-choice, business, or labor groups.[3]

It is tempting to close our definition at this point and to view the American parties solely as teams of political specialists—elected officials, candidates, party leaders, activists, and organizations—who compete for power and then exercise it. That leaves the rest of the population on the outside of the parties, a position that many citizens may prefer. Yet this would ignore an important reality: Parties are rooted in the lives and feelings of citizens as well as candidates and activists. Even though the American parties do not have formal, dues-paying "members," most voters develop such strong and enduring attachments to a particular party that they are willing to tell a pollster, "I'm a Democrat" or "I'm a Republican." Further, when writers refer to a "Democratic surge" or a "Republican suburb," they see parties that include voters and other supporters as well as officeholders, office seekers, and activists.

The Progressive movement of the late 1800s and early 1900s, which promoted voter registration and the practice of nominating candidates in primary elections, strengthened the case for including a citizen base in a definition of American parties. Voters in primary elections make the single most important decision for their party: who its candidates will be. In most other democracies, only the party leaders and activists have the power to make this choice.

Because American voters have the right to nominate the parties' candidates, the line that separates party leaders from followers in most other nations becomes blurred in the United States. American voters are not only consumers who choose among the parties' "products" (candidates) in the political marketplace but also managers who decide which products will be introduced in the first place. Making consumers into managers has transformed political parties, just as it would revolutionize the market economy. Taking this into account in our definition of parties, as do the definitions by Chambers and Key in the box on page 7, makes for a messier concept of political party, but a more realistic one in the American political environment.[4]

What Is a Political Party?

A party aims to promote certain policies:

> [A] party is a body of men united, for promoting by their joint endeavors the national interest, upon some particular principle in which they are all agreed.
>
> *Edmund Burke (1770)*

It works to gain power in government:

> In the broadest sense, a political party is a coalition of men seeking to control the governing apparatus by legal means...[through] duly constituted elections or legitimate influence.
>
> *Anthony Downs (1957)*

It is an organization with rules and durability:

> Political parties can be seen as coalitions of elites to capture and use political office.... (But) a political party is...more than a coalition. A major political party is an institutionalized coalition, one that has adopted rules, norms, and procedures.
>
> *John H. Aldrich (2011)*

It inspires loyalty among voters:

> [A] political party in the modern sense may be thought of as a relatively durable social formation which seeks offices or power in government, exhibits a structure or organization which links leaders at the centers of government to a significant popular following in the political arena and its local enclaves, and generates in-group perspectives or at least symbols of identification or loyalty.
>
> *William Nisbet Chambers (1967)*

A political party is all of the above:

> Within the body of voters as a whole, groups are formed of persons who regard themselves as party members.... In another sense the term party may refer to the group of more or less professional political workers.... At times party denotes groups within the government.... Often it refers to an entity which rolls into one the party-in-the-electorate, the professional political group, the party-in-the-legislature, and the party-in-the-government.... In truth, this all-encompassing usage has its legitimate applications for all the types of groups called party interact more or less closely and at times may be as one.
>
> *V. O. Key, Jr. (1958)*

In short, the major American parties are composed of three interacting parts. These are the *party organization*, which includes party leaders and the activists who work for party causes and candidates; the *party in government*, composed of the men and women who run for and hold public office on the party's label; and the *party in the electorate*, or those citizens who express an attachment to the party (see Figure 1.1).[5] We explore each of these parts separately, keeping in mind that the character of the American parties is defined by the ways in which they interact.[6]

The Party Organization

Party organizations are made up of people who hold party jobs with titles—the national and state party chairs and other officers; the county, city, ward, and precinct leaders and committee people (see Chapters 3 and 4)—and other supporters who are devoted enough to volunteer their time, money, and skills to advancing the party's aims (see Chapter 5). These groups are charged with

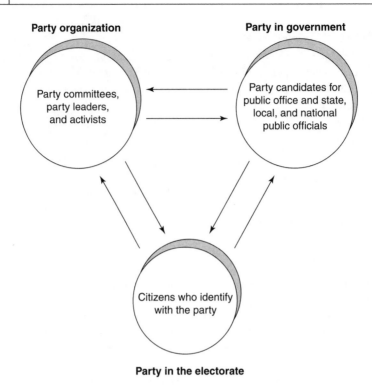

Party organization

Party committees, party leaders, and activists

Party in government

Party candidates for public office and state, local, and national public officials

Citizens who identify with the party

Party in the electorate

FIGURE 1.1
The Three Parts of American Political Parties.

promoting *all* of the party's candidates and its stands on major issues, not just an individual candidate or two. Some party leaders or activists may be waiting for the right time to run for public office (and thus cross over into the party in government); others have been pressed into service as candidates for Congress or city clerk when nobody else wants the job. Many party activists prefer the tasks of meeting volunteers and making phone calls from the party headquarters, however, rather than the frenzied days and anxious nights that are the life of a political candidate.

The Party in Government

The party in government consists of the candidates for public office and those who hold office, whether elected or appointed, who share a party label (see Chapters 13 and 14). The major figures here are presidents, governors, judges, Congress members, state legislators, bureaucrats, mayors, and other local officials who hold the same party affiliation.

Members of the party in government do not always have smooth relationships with people in the party organization. They often work together to meet shared goals, but they may have different priorities in reaching those goals. A senator, for example, may be trying to raise as much campaign money as possible in order to win big and boost her chances of running for president later. At the same time, the party organization's leaders may be hoping that some of her campaign contributors will support other, more vulnerable party candidates instead, so the party can get or keep a majority in Congress.

These two parts of the parties also contend for leadership of the party as a whole. When reporters want to get a "Democratic view" on an issue, they will often interview a source in the White House, if the president is a Democrat, or a Democratic leader in Congress; these members of the party in government are often assumed to speak for the party. Leaders of the party's organization, such as the chair of the Alabama state Democratic Party, might want to put a different spin on the issue. But presidents and congressional party leaders do not have to clear their pronouncements with the party organization, nor can they be controlled by it. These tensions, and the competition for scarce resources, show why it is helpful to treat the party organization and the party in government as separate parts of the party.

The Party in the Electorate

The party in the electorate consists of the women and men who *see themselves* as Democrats or Republicans: citizens who feel some degree of loyalty to the party, even if they have never set foot in the party's headquarters or met its candidates. We call them *partisans* or *party identifiers.* Many of these partisans declared themselves to be a Democrat or Republican when they registered to vote; more than half of the states require citizens to register by party. Others see themselves as partisans even if they do not register to vote under a party label or even if they do not vote at all.

Partisans are usually inclined to support their party's candidates and issue stands, but nothing forces them to do so. In general elections, they may vote for one of their party's candidates and reject another; in primaries, they may decide to saddle the party with a candidate that the organization can't stand. However, they are vitally important as the core of the party's electoral support; without this reliable base, the party would have to work much harder to win and keep power.

This relationship between the party organization and the party in government, on the one hand, and the electoral party, on the other, is one of the most striking characteristics of the major American parties. Other political organizations—interest groups such as teachers' unions and oil companies—try to attract supporters in addition to their members, but these supporters remain outside the group's organization. In contrast, in the American parties, the party in the electorate is not just an external group to be mobilized. In addition to its power to choose the parties' candidates by voting in primaries, in many states the electoral party selects local *party* officials, such as precinct committee leaders. Thus, the major American party is an open, inclusive, permeable organization. The extent to which citizens can affect the choice of its leaders and candidates sets it apart from parties in most other democracies.

WHAT PARTIES DO

Political parties in every democracy engage in three sets of activities to at least some degree. They select candidates and contest elections; they try to educate citizens about issues important to the party; and they work to influence government to provide certain policies and other benefits.[7] Parties and party systems differ in the degree to which they emphasize each of these activities, but no party can completely ignore any of them.

Electing Candidates

Parties often seem completely absorbed by their efforts to elect candidates. The activity of the American party follows the cycles of the electoral calendar, with activity reaching a peak at election time and falling off between elections. Parties are goal-oriented, and in American politics, achieving goals depends on winning elections. The need to elect candidates is the main link connecting the three parts of the parties. Party leaders and activists committed to a particular elected official often join with other members of the party in government and with party identifiers to return that official to office. After the election is won or lost, they frequently drift apart again. These groups of individuals from different parts of a party, drawn together to elect a particular candidate, are like the nuclei of the party.[8]

Educating (or Propagandizing) Citizens

Parties also try to teach or propagandize citizens. (If you like their message, you might call it "voter education." If not, it may sound like propaganda.) They work to focus voter attention on the issues that bind the party together and downplay issues that might split their adherents. The Democrats and Republicans do not promote all-inclusive ideologies like those of a fundamentalist Islamic party. They do, however, represent the beliefs and interests of the groups that identify with and support them. In this sense, the Republicans are usually linked with business and conservatives, and Democrats are often seen as the party of labor and the disadvantaged.

Governing

Almost all American national and state elected officials ran for office as either Democrats or Republicans, and their partisan perspectives affect every aspect of the way government works. The legislatures of 49 states[9] and the U.S. Congress are organized along party lines. On some issues, party cohesion may break down. Yet, in general, there is a surprising degree of party discipline in voting on legislation. In executive branches, presidents and governors usually choose cabinet officers and agency heads of their own party. Even the courts show evidence of the guiding hand of parties, though in more subtle ways.

The American parties, however, do not have a monopoly on educating citizens, working to elect candidates, or governing. They compete with interest groups, other political organizations, and even the media in all these areas. Although the parties organize state legislatures and Congress, they vie with interest group lobbyists and legislators' own beliefs to influence legislators' votes. In elections, especially at the local level, other groups, such as those backing or opposing a new sports stadium or a smoking ban, also try to influence primaries or urge candidates to run.

Because the American parties' activities center on electing candidates, the party in government dominates the party to a degree unusual among Western democracies. In parties more strongly committed to educating citizens about the party's ideology—European Marxist parties, for instance—party organizations are more likely to be able to dictate to the legislative parties, telling them what to emphasize and holding them accountable for their votes.

THE EFFECTS OF PARTY ACTIVITY

How do these party activities affect American politics? First, parties help people make sense of the complexities of politics. Most of us don't pay much attention to government. Parties simplify issues and elections for us; thus, people can make sensible choices in politics even when they don't have a lot of political information, by using their party attachment as a guide for evaluating candidates and issues. By making it easier for citizens to form political judgments, parties ease the way for people to become politically active. They educate Americans by transmitting political information and values to large numbers of current and future voters.

Second, the American parties help aggregate and organize political power. They put together individuals and groups into blocs that are powerful enough to govern. So in the political world as well as within the individual, parties help to focus political loyalties on a small number of alternatives and then to build support for them. Parties also provide an organized opposition. That is not a popular role to play; the behavior of a constant adversary may seem like that of a sore loser. But an organized opposition is vital to a democracy because it has a natural incentive—its own ambition—to serve as a watchdog on a powerful government. Few of us would be willing to devote the time and effort to play this important role on our own.

Third, because they are so focused on contesting elections, the parties dominate the recruitment of political leaders. Large numbers of legislators, political executives, and even judges entered public service through party activity. Because they are constants in the election process, parties help to make changes in government leadership more routine and orderly. In nations where parties are not stable from one election to the next, leadership changes can be much more disruptive.

Finally, the parties help pull together a divided American political system. The U.S. government was designed to fragment political power, to make sure that no single group could gain enough of it to become a tyrant. The division between the national government and the states, multiplied by the separation of powers at each level, does an impressive job of fragmenting power. The challenge is to make these fragmented units work together to solve problems. The two major national parties can provide a bridge over the separation of powers, a basis for cooperation within a government marked by decentralization and division.

HOW DO PARTIES DIFFER FROM OTHER POLITICAL GROUPS?

We have seen that parties have a lot of competition as intermediaries in politics. *All* political organizations, not just parties, try to educate at least some citizens and mobilize their supporters either to win public office or to influence those who do win. The parties maintain close working relationships with a variety of organized interests who share their concerns: labor unions, environmental and feminist groups for the Democrats and the NRA, small business groups, and conservative Christian organizations for the Republicans.[10] How do parties differ from these other political organizations?

Parties are Paramount in Elections

Above all, a party can be distinguished from other political organizations by its role in structuring elections. In most elections, candidates are listed on the ballot as "Democrat" or "Republican"; they are not listed as "friend of the oil companies" or "gay rights activist." It is the major parties that normally recruit the election clerks and the poll watchers, not the Chamber of Commerce. The parties are paramount among political groups in contesting elections.

They Have a Full-Time Commitment to Political Activity

The major American parties are fully committed to political activity; it is the sole reason for their existence. Interest groups and other political organizations, in contrast, move frequently from political to nonpolitical activities and back again. The Steelworkers' Union, for example, is fundamentally concerned with collective bargaining for better pay and working conditions. It may turn to political action to oppose unfriendly candidates or to lobby Congress against antiunion legislation, but its interests are rooted in the workplace. Parties live entirely in the political world.

They Mobilize Large Numbers

An interest group, such as an organization that lobbies for a tax break for energy companies, does not need millions of supporters to persuade Congress to pass a bill; it may be able to succeed with only a few strategists and a well-mobilized clientele. However, because winning elections is so vital to parties' goals, parties must mobilize an enormous range of supporters to win large numbers of races. The result is that in a system such as that of the United States, a major party cannot afford to represent only a narrow range of concerns.

They Endure

The American parties are unusually stable and long lived. Most business, environmental, and single-issue groups are mere juveniles by comparison. Both major American parties can trace their histories for more than 150 years, and many of the major parties in other Western democracies also have impressive life spans. This remarkable endurance adds to their value for voters. The parties are there as points of reference year after year, election after election, and candidate after candidate, giving continuity to the choices Americans face and the issues they debate.

They Serve as Political Symbols

Finally, political parties differ from other political organizations in the extent to which they operate as symbols, or emotion-laden objects of loyalty. For tens of millions of Americans, the party label is a social identity, like that of an ethnic or religious group. It is the chief cue for their decisions about candidates or issues; it relates their values to the real options of American politics.

Remember, however, that the differences between parties and other political organizations are differences of degree. Interest groups do become involved in elections, and the larger organized interests serve as political symbols, too. Groups such as the AARP can recruit candidates, promote their endorsed candidates to their members and friends, and get their supporters to the polls on Election Day. Other nonparty groups may do the same (see box on page 14). Interest groups also promote issue positions, try to influence officeholders, and give money to campaigns. But candidates are listed on the ballot as representatives of a party, not of an interest group.

In some respects, the major parties have more in common with some of the larger interest groups, such as the Chamber of Commerce and the AARP, than they do with minor or third parties. Most minor parties are electoral organizations in name only. Most of their candidates are in no danger of needing a victory speech on election night. They may have few or no local organizations. Their membership base may be just as narrow as that of most interest groups. However, minor parties may qualify to be listed on the ballot, and their candidates can receive public funding where it is available and where they can meet the criteria for it. In these ways (and sometimes *only* in these ways), they can be more like the major parties than the large interest groups.

Is the Tea Party a Party?

Soon after taking office, President Obama proposed to help homeowners who were about to default on their mortgage payments. This outraged CNBC correspondent Rick Santelli; he saw it as a case of big government forcing responsible people to pay their "loser" neighbors' mortgages. We need a new "tea party," he said, similar to the American colonists' protest against British rule by throwing highly taxed British tea into Boston Harbor. Santelli's call was answered. In the summer of 2009, groups of conservatives flocked to their Congress members' town meetings objecting to the Democratic health care reform program and insisting on smaller government. By 2011, polls showed that about one in five Americans—mainly older, white, Republican conservatives—still supported the Tea Party movement, and prominent Republicans such as Sarah Palin championed its cause. Tea Partyers focused much of their anger on President Obama and government-funded social services to people they defined as "undeserving," including younger people and illegal immigrants (though not on Social Security and Medicare, which many Tea Party supporters receive). In several 2010 Republican primaries, Tea Party–backed conservatives defeated mainstream Republican incumbents.

If the Tea Party has some national leaders, local supporters, and a deeply felt issue, then is it a political party? At this time, no. Most Tea Partyers continue to identify as Republicans, though many have criticized Republican congressional leaders for not doing enough to shrink government. Political parties differ from other political organizations in that only the party has the power to nominate candidates. In 2010, very few voters saw the "Tea Party" label on their ballots; the two major parties have long made it very difficult for any group except Democrats and Republicans to get their names and candidates on the ballot. Thus, Tea Party activists had to educate their followers as to which Republican candidates favored the group's principles. So although the Tea Party's colorful and angry protests have grabbed a lot of media attention, the group has functioned more as a movement within the Republican Party than as a party in its own right. To grow into a political party, the movement's adherents would need to do the intensive work of achieving ballot access and backing candidates from the local to the national level, developing more of an organizational structure, and agreeing on a platform.

Sources: Kate Zernike and Megan Thee-Brenan, "Poll Finds Tea Party Backers Wealthier and More Educated," *New York Times,* April 15, 2010, p. A1; and Christopher F. Karpowitz, J. Quin Monson, Kelly D. Patterson, and Jeremy C. Pope, "Tea Time in America?" *PS: Political Science and Politics* 44 (2011): 303–309.

HOW THE AMERICAN PARTIES DEVELOPED

The world's first political parties were created in the United States. For more than 200 years, the development of the American parties has been closely interrelated with the expansion of popular democracy. At times during their history, the party in government, then the party organizations, and then both the parties in government and in the electorate have taken the dominant role within the parties.[11]

The Founding of American Parties

Although the founders of the American government despised the idea of factions, they nevertheless began taking sides and moving in the direction of creating rudimentary political parties soon after the new government began its work. The dominant group, led by the ambitious young treasury secretary, Alexander Hamilton, believed that the nation's economic survival required centralized (federal government) control over the economy. These *Federalists* championed a central banking system and high tariffs to protect newly developing American industries (see box on page 16).

Thomas Jefferson, James Madison, and others objected. Hamilton's proposals, they felt, made the federal government too powerful and threatened states' rights. Each group gathered in meetings, called "caucuses," to plan how to get their ideas adopted. During the 1790s, these alignments took a more enduring form. Their differences, as is the case now, were both principled and personal; as historian David McCullough reports, the animosity between Hamilton and Jefferson "had reached the point where they could hardly bear to be in the same room. Each was certain the other was a dangerous man intent on dominating the government."[12]

These early parties, then, were formed primarily "from the top" by their party in government. They focused at first on issues that concerned the national leaders who formed them—not surprisingly at a time when most Americans played only an indirect role in politics. At this time, in almost every state the vote was restricted to free men who could meet property-owning or taxpaying requirements. Even these relatively small numbers of voters had limited power, as the writers of the Constitution intended. The president was chosen not directly by the voters, but indirectly by the Electoral College. Although members of the House of Representatives were selected by a direct popular vote, state legislatures were given the right to choose their state's U.S. senators. This cautious start for democratic self-government produced very limited political parties.

Because Jefferson's supporters were in the minority in Congress, their main hope of passing legislation was to elect more Jeffersonians. To do so, they began organizing like-minded activists and other voters in states and localities in the early 1790s. Sympathizers at the grassroots level joined in "committees of correspondence" between national and local leaders. Each side established one or more newspapers to propagandize for its cause. As early as the middle of that decade, less than 10 years after the Constitution was adopted, almost all national politicians had aligned with either the Jeffersonian *Democratic-Republicans* (often called just Republicans) or Hamilton's Federalists, and these incipient parties had taken sides on the major issues facing the new government.[13]

The American Major Parties

There have been only five major political parties in more than two centuries of American history:

1. **The Federalist Party, 1788–1816.** The champion of the new Constitution and strong national (federal) government, it was the first American political institution to resemble a political party, although it was not a full-fledged party. Its strength was rooted in the Northeast and the Atlantic Seaboard, where it attracted the support of shopkeepers, manufacturers, financiers, landowners, and other established families of wealth and status. Limited by its narrow electoral base, compared with that of the Democratic-Republicans, it soon faded.

2. **The Democratic-Republican (Jeffersonian) Party, 1800–1832.** Many of its leaders had been strong proponents of the Constitution but opposed the extreme nationalism of the Federalists. It was a party of small farmers, workers, and less-privileged citizens, plus southern planters, who preferred the authority of the state governments to that of the national government. Like its leader, Thomas Jefferson, it shared many of the ideals of the French Revolution, especially the extension of the right to vote and the notion of direct popular self-government.

3. **The Democratic Party, 1832–Present.** Growing out of the Jacksonian wing of the Democratic-Republicans, it was the first really broad-based, popular party in the United States. On behalf of a coalition of less-privileged voters, it opposed such business-friendly policies as national banking and high tariffs. It also welcomed the new immigrants (and sought their votes) and opposed nativist (anti-immigrant) sentiment.

4. **The Whig Party, 1834–1856.** This party, too, had roots in the old Democratic-Republican Party, but in a faction that opposed the Jacksonians. Its greatest leaders, Henry Clay and Daniel Webster, stood for legislative supremacy and protested the strong presidency of Andrew Jackson. For its short life, the Whig Party was an unstable coalition of many interests, among them nativism, property, and business and commerce.

5. **The Republican Party, 1854–Present.** The Republicans formed largely to oppose slavery. As the Civil War approached, the new party came to stand for the Union, the North, Lincoln, the freeing of slaves, victory in the Civil War, and the imposition of Reconstruction on the South. From the Whigs it also inherited a concern for business and industrial expansion.

The more elitist Federalists could not keep up, however, either in organizing at the grassroots or in legislative victories. The Federalist candidate for president, John Adams, was defeated by Jefferson in 1800, and the Federalists faded into history during the next decade. In short, the pressures for democratization were already powerful enough by the early 1800s to scuttle an infant party whose leaders in the government could not adapt to the need to organize a mass electorate. Yet the Federalists gave a historic gift to American democracy. They accepted Adams's defeat in 1800 and handed control of the presidency to their Jeffersonian rivals.[14]

The Democratic-Republicans, who were the party of agrarian interests, the less privileged, and the frontier, then held a one-party monopoly for almost 20 years. They dominated American politics so thoroughly by the time of James Monroe's election in 1816 that the absence of party conflict was called the "Era of Good Feelings." Despite the decline of one party and the rise of another, however, the nature of party politics did not change much during this period. It was a time when government and politics were the business of an elite group of well-known, well-established men, and the parties reflected the politics of the time. Without party competition, leaders felt no need to establish larger grassroots organizations, so the parties' further development was stalled.

American politics began to change markedly in the 1820s. By then, most states had eliminated the requirement that only landowners could vote; the suffrage was extended to all white males, at least in state and federal elections. The growing push for democratization also led governments to make more and more public officials popularly elected rather than appointed.[15]

One big change at this time was the emergence of an aspect of the presidential election process that has lasted to this day. The framers of the Constitution crafted an unusual arrangement for selecting the president, known as the Electoral College. Each state, in a manner selected by its legislature, would choose a number of presidential voters (electors) equal to the size of its congressional delegation. These electors would meet in the state to cast their votes for president; the candidate who received a majority of the states' electoral votes was the national winner. If no candidate received a majority, the president was to be selected by the House of Representatives, with each state casting one vote.

This Electoral College was an ingenious invention. By leaving the choice of electors to the state legislatures, the framers avoided having to set uniform election methods and voting requirements, issues on which they strongly disagreed (and which involved, of course, the explosive question of whether and how to count slaves). This also eliminated the need for federal intervention in a question on which the states had previously made their own decisions and which might have produced state opposition. Requiring electors to meet simultaneously in their respective states helped prevent a conspiracy among electors from different states to put forward their own choice for president. At first, states used a variety of methods for selecting presidential electors, but by the 1820s, popular election was the most common method.[16]

This growing enthusiasm for popular control also raised doubts about whether the party's congressional caucus should have the power to nominate a presidential candidate. Some criticized caucus nominations as the actions of a small and self-appointed elite. At the same time, the caucus system began to fall apart from within. In 1824, the Democratic-Republicans' attempt to nominate a presidential candidate ended in chaos. No candidate won a majority in the Electoral College, so the House of Representatives had to choose among John Quincy Adams, William H. Crawford, and Andrew Jackson. Although Jackson was the front-runner in both the popular and electoral votes, the House chose Adams. Jackson, in turn, defeated Adams in 1828. The congressional party caucus, then, was losing its role as the major force within the parties as the nation entered a new phase of party politics.

A NATIONAL TWO-PARTY SYSTEM EMERGES

The Era of Good Feelings gave way to a two-party system that has prevailed ever since. The Democratic-Republicans had developed factions that chose divorce rather than reconciliation. Andrew Jackson led the frontier and agrarian wing of the Democratic-Republicans, the inheritors of the Jeffersonian tradition, into what is now called the ***Democratic Party***. Another faction of the old Democratic-Republicans who had promoted Adams for president in 1824 and 1828 later merged with the ***Whigs*** (an old English term referring to those who opposed the dominance of the king, by whom they meant Jackson). That created two-party politics in the United States.

Just as important, the parties developed a much bigger nationwide grassroots (citizen) base. Larger numbers of citizens were now eligible to vote, and the presidential campaigns became more concerned with reaching out to the public; new campaign organizations and tactics brought the contest to many more people. As the opposition to the Jacksonians formed, presidential elections became more competitive, and voter turnout increased. Party organization in the states and localities also expanded, with the help of improved roads and communications. Candidates for state and local office were increasingly nominated by conventions of state and local leaders, rather than by the narrower legislative caucuses. By 1840, the Whigs and the Democrats were established in the first truly national party system and were competitive in all the states.

During the 1840s and 1850s, the bitter issue of slavery increasingly affected both parties. The Whigs fractured on the issue and then collapsed. Antislavery activists created the ***Republican Party*** to demand that slavery be abolished. The Republicans then adopted the Whigs' commitment to protect American businesses with high tariffs and to levy high taxes to subsidize industrial development: roads, railroads, and settlement of the frontier. The party organized throughout the nation, except in the South and the Border States, which were Democratic strongholds, and won the presidency in 1860. To a great extent, the party system and the nation broke into North and South.

In short, modern political parties similar to those we know today, with their characteristic organizational structures, bases of loyal voters, and lasting alliances among governmental leaders, had developed by the mid-1800s.[17] The

American parties grew hand in hand with the early expansion of the electorate in the United States. Comparable parties did not develop in Great Britain until the 1870s, after laws were passed to further expand the adult male electorate.

The Golden Age of the Parties

As the parties were developing, they received another massive infusion of voters from a new source: European immigrants. Hundreds of thousands of Europeans, the majority from Ireland and Germany, immigrated to the United States before the Civil War. The newcomers were welcomed by the Democratic Party, which sought their votes. However, their large numbers worried others, and an anti-immigrant minor party, the American Party (the so-called Know-Nothing Party), sprang up in response in the 1850s.

The tide of immigration was halted only temporarily by the Civil War. After the war ended, new nationalities came in an almost constant flow from 1870 until Congress closed the door to mass immigration in the 1920s. More than 5 million immigrants arrived in the 1880s (equal to one-tenth of the 1880 resident population), and 10 million more came between 1905 and 1914 (one-eighth of the 1900 resident population).

The political parties played an important role in assimilating these huge waves of immigrants. The newcomers gravitated toward the big cities where industrial jobs were available. It was in the cities that a new kind of party organization, the urban "machine," developed in response to the immigrants' needs and vulnerabilities. These party machines were like social service systems that helped the new arrivals cope with the challenges of an urban industrial society. They softened the hard edge of poverty by helping needy families with food and funds, smoothed the way with government and the police, and taught immigrants the customs of their new home—all in exchange for the immigrants' votes for the party's candidates at election time. With those votes, a party machine could gain and keep control over the city's government. The machines were the means by which the new urban working class won control of the cities from the largely Anglo-Saxon, Protestant elites who had governed for so long.

The period of the late 1800s and the early 1900s was the "golden age" of the American parties: the high point of their power and influence. Party organizations, now the dominant segment of the party, existed in all the states and localities and flourished in the industrial cities. Party discipline reached a record high in Congress and most state legislatures. Parties ran the candidates' campaigns for public office; they held rallies and torchlight parades, canvassed door-to-door, and brought voters to the polls. They controlled access to many government jobs ranging from sewer inspectors to members of the U.S. Senate. They were an important source of information and guidance for a largely uneducated and often illiterate electorate. As a result, the highest voter turn-outs in American presidential history were recorded during the latter half of the 1800s. The parties suited the needs and limitations of the new voters and met the need for creating majorities in the rapidly industrializing nation.[18]

The Progressive Reforms and Beyond

The drive to democratize American politics continued into the 1900s. Passage of the Seventeenth Amendment gave voters, rather than state legislatures, the right to elect U.S. senators. Women and then blacks finally gained the right to vote. As popular democracy expanded, a movement arose that would impose major changes on the parties.

The period that parties saw as their "golden age" did not seem so golden to groups of reformers. To Progressive crusaders, party control of politics had led to rampant corruption and inefficient government. Because the Progressives saw party power as the culprit, they tried to weaken the control that the parties, and especially the party organizations, had achieved by the late 1800s. The reformers attacked party "boss rule" by pressing for primary elections (see Chapters 9 and 10), which took the power to choose the parties' candidates out of the hands of party leaders and gave it to voters instead. Presidential nominations were made more open to the public by establishing presidential primaries in the states. Many state legislatures wrote laws to define and limit party organizations.

The reforms did weaken the party organizations and their power in elections. When the party in the electorate gained the right to nominate the parties' candidates, the party organizations and leaders lost their most important function. Candidates, who could now appeal directly to primary voters, became more independent of the party organizations. The effect of the Progressive reforms, then, was to undercut the dominance of the party organization within the party as a whole. Therefore, the expectations of a democratic society, which first made the parties more public, more decentralized, and more active at the grassroots level, later turned on the party organization, leaving it less capable of the important role that it once played in American politics.[19]

More recently, however, the party organizations and their leaders have created new sources of power for themselves. Beginning in the 1970s, first the Republicans and then the Democrats expanded the fund-raising capacity of their national party organizations and used their new money to provide more services to candidates and to increase the capabilities of state party organizations. In the past four decades, the Democratic Party, through its national committee and convention, has created rules for state Democratic Parties to follow in nominating a presidential candidate. Both of these changes have strengthened the national party organizations; in fact, the national organizations probably have more of a presence within the two major parties, relative to the state and local party organizations, now than at any other time in American history. (Chapters 3 and 4 say more about these changes.)

In short, the parties have changed dramatically and continue to change. Yet they remain the leading organizations of popular democracy. They grew with the expansion of the right to vote and the increasing role of citizens in electoral politics. They are the channel through which voters come together to choose representatives and ambitious people gain positions of power. They help to clarify the alternatives on such challenging issues as abortion, taxes, and terrorism. They amplify the voices of some groups in making demands on public policy and dampen the voices of others.

WHAT DO THE PARTIES STAND FOR?

The parties have changed their stands on many issues over time, even major issues. The national Democratic and Republican Parties, for example, have shifted their positions dramatically over the years on the question of civil rights for black Americans. The traditional decentralization of the American parties (discussed in Chapter 2) has meant that party organizations in some states or local communities have taken stands different from organizations of the same party in other areas.

Yet there have been times of clear party differences on big policy questions. The current period is one of those times. Although some would argue that the parties' issue stands are simply a means to attract votes, the ongoing competition between the Democrats and Republicans has always been more than just a story of raw ambition. Ever since the parties began, they have organized to gain power in order to achieve particular policy goals. Changes in the electorate and the growing strength of the national party organizations in the past three decades have encouraged *party polarization*: greater agreement on policy stands *within* each party and sharper policy differences *between* the Democrats and Republicans.

If you explore the Republican National Committee's Web site, the party platform, or the votes of Republicans in Congress, you will find that the Republican Party has long believed in a strong business sector. It has opposed government action to remedy individual inequalities by creating welfare programs or redistributing income. Former president George W. Bush referred to the Republican vision as an "ownership society," in which individuals will have more opportunities to build up their own wealth and to free themselves from the heavy yoke of government intervention.

These principles can be seen in the party's stands on many current issues (see Table 1.1). Tax cuts for individuals and businesses rank high on the party's agenda; lower taxes shrink the government's revenue and, therefore, its ability to create new programs—a strategy that some conservatives call "starving the beast" (government).[20] The tax cuts should favor those who are better off, many Republicans would argue, because that helps the economy grow. The party has traditionally argued for protecting property rights, which also limits the government's ability to interfere in the economic decisions of its citizens.

Republican positions on other issues also demonstrate these commitments to private rather than governmental solutions to problems and to state and local rather than national and international authority. On the environment, for example, the party wants businesses to have greater flexibility in complying with environmental laws. On defense, the Republican tradition defines a strong national defense as requiring a powerful military rather than as giving priority to international agreements on arms control and other matters.

Over time, Republicans have been more likely than Democrats to draw their party leaders and candidates from the business community. The party has long favored restricting labor unions' power because unions, they feel, are an artificial barrier to the working of the free market. As a result, the relationship between labor unions and the Republican Party is somewhere between strained and nonexistent, as could be seen in state legislative battles over the rights of public employee unions in 2011. Recent polls report that only 18 percent

TABLE 1.1

Party Differences in the 2010s, Issues and Core Supporters

Democrats	Republicans
Core belief	
A strong government provides needed services and remedies inequalities	A strong government interferes with business and threatens freedom
Biggest exception	
Government should stay out of people's decisions on such issues as abortion and gay rights	Government should regulate people's behavior in such matters as abortion and homosexuality
Issue agenda	
Social services, health, education	Strong military, tax cuts
Environmental protection	Property rights
Emphasizes	
Fairness, especially for disadvantaged groups	Individual success, not group rights
Relations with labor unions	
Close and supportive	Distant and hostile
Core supporters	
Northeast, West Coast	South
Minority groups	Caucasians
Secular individuals	Conservative Christians
Teachers, trial lawyers	Business people

Source: Compiled by the author from materials including the 2008 party platforms and the American National Election Studies *Guide to Public Opinion and Electoral Behavior* (at http://www.electionstudies.org).

of Republicans hold a positive image of unions, compared with almost half of Democratic identifiers.[21] Core groups of Republican supporters include conservatives (conservative Christians in particular), white southerners, and people living in rural and exurban areas.

The Democratic Party represents a different tradition. To Democratic activists, government is a valuable means of redressing the inequalities that the marketplace can cause. These activists believe that needed social services should be provided by government rather than be privatized. Tax cuts, they argue, limit the ability of government to provide these services. Any tax cuts, they say, should be directed toward helping the needy rather than those who are more affluent. Whereas Republicans believe that the purpose of government is to promote greater individual economic achievement, even at the cost of economic inequality, Democrats feel that fairness requires reducing economic inequality, and that it is government's job to offer a safety net to those who need it.

During the past half-century, the national Democratic Party has favored using government to enforce civil rights for black Americans, and during the past 30 years, it has been the party of abortion rights and environmental action. If property rights get in the way of environmental protection, Democratic activists contend, then property rights must usually give way. The party's stand on education, similarly, stresses the need to invest in public schools and aim for equality of opportunity. That is one reason why the Democrats are more likely to draw their candidates and activists from among teachers and trial lawyers. The core of Democratic support comes from liberals, lower-income people, those living in the Northeast and West Coasts, minorities, and labor unions.

These party differences were crystal clear in the parties' responses to the economic slowdown in 2011. Characteristically, the new House Republican majority moved to reduce the federal deficit by cutting government social services, such as aid to lower-income people, and environmental regulations. House Democratic leaders, just as characteristically, opposed the cuts and demanded greater regulation of business. A Gallup poll showed that 72 percent of Democrats said they trust government more than they trust businesses to solve the nation's economic problems; 64 percent of Republicans said they placed greater trust in businesses.[22]

Yet, even today, neither party is a model of consistency on issues. In particular, as Table 1.1 shows, the parties seem to switch core beliefs on some "values" issues. The Republican Party, which usually opposes government interference, asks for government action to limit abortions and homosexual behavior and to support conservative family values. And the Democrats, the party that sees government as an ally for the needy, often want government to stay out of individuals' lives on issues such as abortion and homosexuality. Perhaps because "values" issues affect people differently from economic issues, individuals' attitudes toward abortion and homosexuality do not always correlate with their preferences for a strong or a weak government.

This party difference on traditional values could be seen in a dramatic series of events in 2005. Terri Schiavo, a seriously brain-damaged woman in a persistent vegetative state, had been kept alive by a feeding tube for 15 years. Her husband wanted to have the feeding tube disconnected, saying that his wife had expressed a desire not to be kept alive by extraordinary means. Her parents disagreed and, with the support of pro-life groups, sought to have her feeding tube reconnected. After several state judges sided with the husband, national Republican leaders pushed hard for federal authority to override the state courts, citing the need for a "culture of life." The Republican efforts failed and Schiavo died, but the scenario of Republicans arguing for federal intervention and Democrats opposing it brought this inconsistency in the parties' stands into sharp relief.

These twists and turns in party principles can sometimes stem from a party's efforts to pick up additional support. In the case of traditional values, for example, some conservative Republicans in the 1970s became aware that the pro-life and antigay rights stands of the Christian Right were much more engaging to swing groups of voters (including, at that time, many conservative white southerners) than were some of the conservative wing's economic proposals and moved to attract these voters by adopting their causes. Over time, as more of these voters became enthusiastic Republican activists, their issues rose to a leading place on the party's agenda.

These changes also grow out of the powerful impact of their environment on the parties' development. The Republican Party could begin life as a party of both business interests *and* big government because the expanding businesses of the 1800s needed government help. The building of roads and other means of transporting products, large-scale communications networks, and high tariffs to protect American-made goods could be done much more efficiently by the national government than by the states or the businesses themselves. Once American business became well established and the needed infrastructure was in place, however, a strong national government could become a threat to businesses—as it did in responding to the Depression of the 1930s—because it could regulate their operations and raise their taxes to help fund social programs.

PARTIES ARE SHAPED BY THEIR ENVIRONMENT

Throughout their history, then, the nature of the parties' activities, their issue positions, and their organizational form have been influenced by forces in their environment, and they have affected that environment in return. A major task of this book is to explain those impacts. One of the most important of these forces has been the nature of the electorate: Who has the right to vote?

Voters and Elections

As we have seen, the expansion of the right to vote has helped shape the parties' development. Each new group of voters entering the electorate challenges the parties to readjust their appeals as they vie for the group's support. Parties in states where black citizens finally gained the right to vote, for example, learned to campaign differently from the days when they needed to appeal to an all-white clientele. The increasing numbers of Latino voters are affecting the strategies of both parties now.

The parties' fortunes are also bound up with the *nature* of American elections. If you were a party leader in a state where conventions of party activists used to nominate candidates for governor, your life would change when your state switched to primary elections and you needed to appeal to a much larger and more varied set of people choosing your party's candidate. Even relatively minor differences in primary laws from state to state—for instance, whether a state's primary is held early or late in the nomination season—affect the parties. These electoral institutions set the rules within which the parties compete for votes and thus affect parties' efforts and organization.

Political Institutions

The two main "rules" of American politics, federalism and the separation of powers, affect the parties profoundly. Consider, for example, the impact of the separation of powers. Nationally and in the states, American legislators and executives are elected independently of one another. That makes it possible and, in recent decades very likely, for the legislature and the governorship or the presidency to be controlled by different parties. Most other democracies, in contrast, have parliamentary systems in which the legislative majority chooses the officials of the executive branch from among its own members. When that parliamentary majority can no longer hold, a new government must be formed. In contrast, in the American system, legislators can vote against a president or governor of their party on key issues without fearing that they will bring down the government and force new elections. As a result, American legislative parties can rarely achieve the degree of party discipline that is common in parliamentary systems.

The federal system, in which states have a number of independent powers (rather than being "branch offices" of the national government), has also left an imprint on the American parties. It has permitted the survival of local political loyalties and traditions. It has spawned an awesome range of public offices to fill, creating a system of elections that dwarfs that of all other democracies in size and diversity. These local traditions and loyalties have nurtured a large set of semi-independent local parties within the two national parties.

Laws Governing Parties

No other parties among the world's democracies are as regulated by laws as are the American parties. It was not always this way. Before the Progressive reforms a century ago, American parties were self-governing organizations, almost unrestrained by state or federal law. For most of the 1800s, for example, the parties made their own rules for nominating candidates and also printed, distributed, and often—with a wary eye on one another—even counted the ballots. Since then, the "Australian" (or secret) ballot gave the responsibility for running elections to government. The arrival of the direct primary in the early 1900s and recent reforms of the presidential nominating process have also severely limited the parties' freedom to govern themselves.

The existence of 50 different sets of state laws governing the parties has produced 50 different varieties of political parties. State laws control the forms of their organization and even define the parties themselves, often by defining who has the right to place candidates on the ballot. Most states try to regulate party activities such as finances and campaign practices. More recently, the federal government has added burdens of its own, including rules governing parties' campaign finances.[23]

Political Culture

A nation's political culture is the set of political values and expectations held by its people. One of the most persistent components of the American political culture is the feeling that party politics is an underhanded, dirty business. A 2011 Gallup poll showed that only 42 percent of respondents held a favorable opinion of the Democratic Party and only 43 percent were favorable toward the Republicans—close to the record lows for each party.[24]

These and other elements of the political culture help shape what the parties can do. Public distrust of parties encourages candidates to campaign as individuals rather than as members of a party team. The widespread view that legislators ought to vote based on their local district's interests can make it harder to achieve party discipline in Congress and state legislatures. Even the question of what we regard as fair campaigning simply reflects the values of large numbers of Americans. Whether a strongly worded campaign ad—for instance, "Congressman X has taken thousands in pay raises for himself while refusing to support our troops"—is seen as "mudslinging" or as "hard-hitting and informative" depends on cultural values, not on some set of universal standards. These cultural values affect the parties' appeals to voters, their fund-raising, and their selection of leaders.

The Broader Environment

Parties' environment is broader than their *political* environment. Changes in the nature of the mass media have profoundly affected the parties' development. With increasing media use, people no longer had to depend on the parties to get information about candidates and issues. Candidates can now contact voters directly as individuals through the Internet, and in larger audiences through TV, rather than having to depend on the parties to carry the message for them. That weakened party control over candidates' campaigns. To add insult to injury, media coverage tends not to pay much attention to the parties themselves. Because television attaches great importance to visual images, it is much more likely to cover individuals—candidates and public officials—than to cover institutions, such as parties, that do not have a "face."

Economic trends in the nation as a whole can greatly affect the parties. Income inequality—the gap in income between the wealthy and the poor—has increased in recent decades.[25] That increases the ability of wealthy people to contribute to parties and campaigns. Income inequality is also affected by the core beliefs of the two major parties. When the Democrats hold power, the party is likely to respond to this inequality with government-funded social services for needy people. When power moves to the Republicans, we are more likely to see tax cuts for the wealthy, with the intended aim of putting more money into the hands of people who can create jobs.

In this chapter, we have explored the nature of parties, what they do, and how they have developed in and been shaped by their environment. These themes will continue to guide us throughout the book. The next chapter tackles one of the biggest puzzles that students of parties face when comparing the American parties with those in other nations: Why does the United States have two major parties, rather than several, or only one?

The American Two-Party System

Most Americans believe that party politics comes in twos: two parties, two candidates for each office, two sides of an issue. A two-party system has been in place for almost two centuries of American history, so it seems as though all democracies must work that way.

Except that they don't. The United States is one of the few democracies with a two-party system. Some democratic nations, such as Mexico, have had extended periods of one-party rule. Many more democracies, including most of those in Europe, have long supported multiparty systems with three, four, or even more parties. (In Tunisia's first democratic election in 2011, 117 parties contested for 199 legislative seats.) In these nations, it often happens that one single party cannot win a majority of the votes, so two or more parties put together a coalition in order to govern.[1]

In the United States as well, some states and cities have had a long tradition of one-party rule; in other areas, several parties have flourished at certain times. Minor ("third") parties and independent candidates continue to affect elections on occasion. Green Party candidate Ralph Nader took just enough votes in key states from the Democrats in 2000 to tip the presidential election to Republican George W. Bush.[2] As an independent presidential candidate in 1992, Ross Perot actually ran ahead of both major parties' candidates in polls early in the race. At the state level, comic country singer Kinky Friedman ran for governor of Texas as an independent candidate in 2006 with the campaign slogan, "Kinky: Why the Hell Not?" (After a well-publicized start, he lost, with 13 percent of the vote.)

These campaigns are fun to watch; Friedman, for instance, may have been the only candidate to support both school prayer and gay marriage and had written a book titled *Kill Two Birds and Get Stoned*. Minor party and independent candidacies are rarely successful, however. For most of American history, since the Era of Good Feelings ended in the 1820s, only two parties have had a realistic chance of winning any given national election and of governing. Even the rapid rise of the most successful third party in American history, the Republican Party, shows the power of two-party politics in the United States. The party was founded in 1854, but instead of competing with the existing Democrats and Whigs, it replaced the Whig Party within two short years.

Why has American politics remained a two-party system for so long, when most other democracies have more than two competitive national parties? In this chapter, we look at the level of competition between the parties, the major theories as to how the two-party system developed, and the efforts by minor parties and independent candidates to break the two-party mold.

THE NATIONAL PARTY SYSTEM

Over this remarkably long period of two-party politics, the two major parties have been close competitors, at least at the national level. Since 1868, the great majority of presidential elections have been decided by less than 10 percent of the vote. It has been a quarter of a century since a presidential candidate—Ronald Reagan in 1984—won by more than 10 percentage points in the popular vote. Although the Democrats seemed to be on the ropes after the Republican congressional sweep of 1994, they recovered quickly enough to keep the presidency in 1996 and regain it in 2008. Similarly, the GOP (or Grand Old Party, a nickname the Republican Party developed in the late 1800s) was able to rebound from the Watergate-related losses of the mid-1970s and the Obama victory in 2008. Some of the closest presidential contests in American history have taken place in the past decade. The 2000 election was a virtual tie.

Congress was a different story for the last half of the 1900s, when Democrats dominated both houses most of the time. However, since 2000, the two parties have exchanged control regularly. After Republican successes in 2000 and 2004, Democrats won back both houses of Congress in 2006. The Democrats' big gains in 2006 and 2008 led one expert analyst to title a blog post in 2008, "Are the Republicans Still a National Party?" Yet two years later, in the 2010 midterm elections, Republicans came back with an extremely strong net gain of 63 House seats—bringing the party totals in Congress nearly back to what they were in 2004.

If we average election results by decade during the past 70 years, we find that the percentage of the two-party vote cast for all Democratic candidates has not differed much from the percentage cast for Republicans (see Table 2.1). Both parties have a voice at the state level as well. In 2011, 17 states had divided party control (as opposed to unified control, in which one party controls the governorship and both houses of the state legislature), 11 were fully Democratic controlled, and 21 were Republican controlled. (The remaining state legislature, Nebraska's, is nonpartisan.) The two major parties, then, have shown a great deal of resilience over time. Media coverage may suggest otherwise because it trumpets the events of the moment. But whenever one party has had a string of big wins, the other party has been able to restore the balance.

> ▶ **TABLE 2.1**
>
> **Percentage of the Two-Party Vote Won by Republican Candidates for President and House of Representatives, 1940–2010**
>
> | | Presidential Elections | | House Elections | |
> | --- | --- | --- | --- | --- |
> | Decade Average | Republican Share of Two-Party Vote (%) | Difference Between Republican and Democratic Vote (%) | Republican Share of Two-Party Vote (%) | Difference Between Republican and Democratic Vote (%) |
> | 1940s | 46.3 | 7.5 | 49.8 | 5.9 |
> | 1950s | 56.6 | 13 | 48.1 | 3.9 |
> | 1960s | 46.3 | 7.9 | 46.6 | 6.7 |
> | 1970s | 55.4 | 12.8 | 44.6 | 10.9 |
> | 1980s | 56.1 | 12.3 | 46.3 | 6.7 |
> | 1990s | 45.9 | 8.1 | 49.5 | 4.4 |
> | 2000s | 49.1 | 3.4 | 48.9 | 5.4 |
> | 2010s | — | — | 53.4 | 6.8 |
>
> *Sources:* Calculated from Norman J. Ornstein, Thomas E. Mann, and Michael J. Malbin, *Vital Statistics on Congress 2001–2002* (Washington, DC: AEI Press, 2002), p. 63, for House elections through 1998; Census data for House elections from 2000–2010; and Dave Leip's "Atlas of U.S. Presidential Elections," at www.uselectionatlas.org for presidential elections (accessed October 29, 2011).

THE 50 STATE PARTY SYSTEMS

Interestingly, however, this pattern of close competition at the national level has coexisted for a long time with one-party dominance in many states and localities. Georgia, for example, chose Democratic governors in 50 consecutive gubernatorial elections, starting before the end of Reconstruction, until finally electing a Republican in 2002.[3] Georgia is still largely one-party today, though the dominant party is now the Republicans.

How can we measure the level of competition in the 50 state party systems? There are many questions to answer in building an index. Should we look at the vote for president, governor, senator, statewide officials, state legislators, or some combination of these? The competitiveness of a state's U.S. Senate seats may be strikingly different from that of its state legislative races. Should we count the candidates' vote totals, the number of offices that each party wins, or something else?

Measuring State Party Competition

The approach used most often to measure interparty competition at the state level is an index originated by Austin Ranney.[4] The Ranney index averages three indicators of party success during a particular time period: the percentage of the popular vote for the parties' gubernatorial candidates, the percentage of seats held by the parties in each house of the legislature, and the length of time plus the percentage of the time that the parties held both the governorship and a majority in the state legislature.

Like any other summary measure, the Ranney index picks up some trends more fully than others. One reason is that it is based wholly on state elections. This protects the measure from being distorted by landslide victories and other unusual events at the national level. Yet those national events may foreshadow what will happen in voting for state offices. In the South, for example, growing GOP strength appeared first in competition for national offices and only later worked its way down to the state and local levels. In these states, for a time the Ranney index showed less interparty competition than really existed. Nevertheless, its findings provide an informative picture of state party competition.

Figure 2.1 presents the calculations for the Ranney index for the period 2007–2011. It shows what appears to be more balanced party competition at the state level than had been seen in these calculations earlier in the years since World War II. Note especially that no state is classified as fully one party. The driving force in this change has been a regional transition in party strength, especially in the South and New England. For years a solid Democratic region, southern states have become largely Republican in recent decades, with the tipping point occurring in 1994 (see Chapter 7). As this Republican trend has continued, we have recently seen states such as South Carolina moving from "competitive" to "modified one-party Republican." The New England region has shifted dramatically in the opposite direction; although moderate Republicans won most congressional elections in these states until fairly recently, only two Republicans were elected to the U.S. House from a New England state in 2010. So, although the Ranney index shows greater two-party

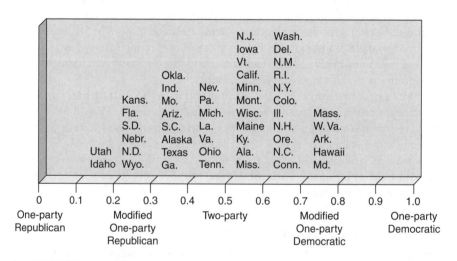

FIGURE 2.1

Interparty Competition in the States, 2007–2011.

Source: Thomas M. Holbrook and Raymond J. La Raja, "Parties and Elections," in Virginia Gray, Russell L. Hanson, and Thad Kousser, eds., *Politics in the American States,* 10th ed. (Washington, DC: CQ Press, 2012), Table 3-4.

competitiveness in the early 2000s, this may reflect the ongoing movement from one pattern of regional party strength to a different, but even more polarized, pattern.

Limits on Competitiveness: Incumbency

There is even less party competition below the statewide level. For example, although the House of Representatives as a whole has often been closely divided, most House candidates are elected with a comfortable margin of victory. In 2008, more than two-thirds of House candidates won with relative ease, getting at least 60 percent of the total vote. Although the number of "marginal" House winners rose substantially in the Republican wave election of 2010, the great majority of House seats remained safe for the incumbent (or the incumbent's party). At the state legislative level, in recent years, fewer than two-thirds of the races had even the bare minimum needed for competition: both a Democratic and a Republican candidate.[5]

What keeps the relatively close party competition at the national level from infiltrating congressional districts to a greater extent? One brake on competition in these districts has been the electoral value of incumbency. Although there was a lot of party turnover during the 1800s, and the fates of candidates from politically competitive areas depended on the national or statewide forces affecting the parties, members of Congress have had greater electoral security in the past half-century. Since 1964, the average success rates for incumbents seeking reelection were 93 percent in the U.S. House of Representatives—as high as 98 percent in three recent elections—and 82 percent in the Senate.[6] These rates are somewhat inflated by the fact that incumbents who think they might lose the next election may decide voluntarily not to run again, but they are impressive indeed.

There have been occasional elections when incumbents' job security was at greater risk. In the early 1990s, for instance, a well-reported scandal and a resulting crop of especially strong challengers dropped the success rate of House incumbents to "only" between 88 and 90 percent. The Republican sweep in the 2010 midterm elections cut the House reelection rate to a 40-year low of 87 percent. In an election year when national conditions heavily favor one party, the "wave" will carry into office candidates who win in districts that normally support the other party. These "exposed" candidates will then be at risk in the next election. But in a more typical election year, most congressional incumbents may be as likely to be hit by an SUV in Washington, DC, traffic as they are to lose reelection. Incumbents in most state legislatures have been just as likely to keep their jobs.[7] In fact, the incumbency advantage has increased in elections for all types of executive and legislative offices.[8]

There are many reasons why incumbency came to be such a valuable resource in congressional elections. Incumbents learned how to benefit from the "perks" of holding office—their name recognition and the attention they receive from the media, the services they can provide to constituents, the greater ease with which they can raise campaign money, as well as their experience in having run previous successful campaigns, all of which discourage potentially effective candidates from running against them. These add up to what can be called the *personal* incumbency advantage, which was especially strong in the 1970s and 1980s.[9]

...And Other Reasons for Limited Competitiveness

Researchers have found, however, that although most House seats have remained safe, the *size* of the average House incumbent's advantage in winning reelection has declined since the early 1990s. Therefore, the personal incumbency advantage can't fully explain why most congressional races are not competitive.

Another explanation often cited is that during the past decade, state legislators have been able to use sophisticated computer programs to redraw legislative district lines for themselves and for U.S. House members. Thus, they make their districts safer by "choosing their own voters." Redistricting after the 2000 census reduced the number of competitive House seats by making three-fourths of these districts safer for one party.[10] Yet redistricting can't be the only reason for safer districts because incumbents are also doing better in elections for offices that are not redistricted, such as local and statewide offices.

Bruce Oppenheimer has suggested an alternative: New patterns of residential mobility are a major cause of declining party competition. As people have become more mobile, they are more able, and more inclined, to move to areas where like-minded people live. As a result, areas become more homogeneous—and, thus, congressional districts are more likely to be dominated by one party.[11] This ideological "sorting" has added to the growing geographic divergence in party loyalties. An analyst found that although the 2000 and 1976 presidential elections were both won by narrow margins, almost twice as many of the voters in 2000 lived in counties where one candidate or the other won by a landslide. This suggests, he argues, that there has been a "voluntary political segregation" in the United States.[12] Alan Abramowitz and others show that the declining ability of challengers to raise campaign money also reduces the competitiveness of House elections.[13] The result is that in recent decades, when we have seen lively party competition in the nation as a whole, it has been built not on a lot of highly competitive House, state legislative, and other districts, but rather on the fact that the large number of fairly safe districts for one party has been closely matched, over time, by the number of fairly safe districts for the other party.

Political competition is vital in a democracy. To the extent that incumbents continue to be reelected because they work hard to serve their districts, then their constituents may be well represented.[14] And the recent drop in public approval of Congress will probably hold down House incumbents' reelection rates for a while. But when an officeholder expects to win reelection easily, he or she has less incentive to pay close attention to voters' needs. In particular, the needs of disadvantaged citizens are more likely to be ignored (because advantaged citizens have other means, in addition to voting, to make their voices heard in government).

WHAT CAUSES A TWO-PARTY SYSTEM?

We have seen that the American parties are durable and that, at least at the aggregate level, when one party has had a run of dominance, the other party has been able to bounce back. Why have we had a two-party system for so long, when most other democracies do not? There are several possible explanations.

Institutional Forces

The most frequent explanation of the two-party system ties it to the nature of American electoral institutions. Called *Duverger's law*,[15] it argues that plurality elections in single-member districts (and no runoff elections) tend to produce two-party systems. A *single-member district* means simply that one candidate is elected to each office, and a *plurality election* is one in which the candidate with the largest number of votes wins, even if not a majority. Finishing a close second, or third or fourth, brings no rewards. The American election system is, for most offices, a plurality election system with single-member districts; it offers the reward of winning an office only to the one candidate who gets the most votes. Thus, the theory suggests that minor parties will see no point in running candidates if they don't have a shot at winning.

The flip side of Duverger's law is that proportional representation in multimember constituencies results in multiparty systems. A system with multimember constituencies is one in which a particular legislative district will be represented by, say, three or four elected legislators rather than one.[16] In proportional representation (PR), each party prepares a slate of candidates for these positions, and the number of party candidates who win is proportional to the overall percentage of the vote won by the party slate (see box on pages 33–34). Because a party may be able to elect a candidate with only 15 or 20 percent of the votes, depending on the system's rules, smaller parties are encouraged to keep competing.

Plurality Versus Proportional Representation: How It Works in Practice

Does it matter whether an election uses plurality or proportional representation (PR) rules to count the votes? To find out, let us compare the results of one type of American election in which both rules are used. In presidential primaries—the elections in which party voters choose delegates to the national parties' presidential conventions—the Democrats use PR to select delegates (with at least 15 percent of the vote needed for a candidate to win delegates) and the Republicans can use some form of plurality election (also called winner-take-all).

Imagine a congressional district that will send four delegates to the national convention, in which candidates A, B, C, and D get the following percentages of the vote.

(continued)

(continued)

The candidates would win the following numbers of delegates, depending on whether the plurality or PR rule was used:

		Delegates Won	
	Vote (%)	Plurality	PR
Candidate A	40	4	2
Candidate B	30	0	1
Candidate C	20	0	1
Candidate D	10	0	0

With the *plurality* (winner-take-all) rule, candidate A, who received the most votes, wins all the delegates at stake in that district. So in a typical Republican primary using the plurality rule, only the leading candidate will emerge with delegates; the other candidates win nothing. Under most circumstances, the less successful candidates will find it hard to stay in the race very long when they are not winning any delegates in return for their efforts. In 2008, for example, all of John McCain's rivals for the Republican presidential nomination had left the field within the first two months of the five-month primary season, after a series of narrow McCain victories gave him an overwhelming lead in delegates. Under *PR* rules, in contrast, *three* candidates win delegates in rough proportion to their popular support. Therefore, in a typical Democratic primary, the less successful candidates are encouraged to stay in the race longer because the PR rules permit them to keep winning at least a few delegates.

The contrast is even clearer when we compare British elections with the multimember district systems of most European legislative elections. The use of PR in the European elections promotes multiparty politics and coalition governments in which two or more different parties often share control of the executive. In the British parliamentary system, on the other hand, single-member districts operating under plurality rules typically produce a parliamentary majority for one party, giving it sole control of the executive, even if it does not win a majority of the popular vote. In the 2010 British parliamentary elections, a minor party (the Liberal Democrats) did gain enough votes to force its way into the governing coalition. Nevertheless, the plurality system still took its toll; although the Liberal Democrats got almost a quarter of the popular vote, they won less than 10 percent of the legislative seats.

However, a puzzle remains. Single-member district systems with plurality elections exist in some other democracies that support more than two parties. Shouldn't the United States, with its great diversity, do the same? To some analysts, the nature of the American presidency helps to sustain Duverger's law. The presidency is the most visible single-member district in the United States. It is the main prize of American politics, and only one person is elected to that office at a time. Many other democracies, using a parliamentary system, have a governing "cabinet" as the executive authority. This cabinet is made up of a number of officeholders, so it can be a coalition that includes representatives of several parties, including smaller parties.

In a system with a single executive, minor parties will be weakened because they do not have a realistic chance to compete for the presidency.[17] Even the minor parties strong enough to elect candidates in their own localities usually find it unrealistic to run a candidate for president. That denies a minor party the national attention that major parties get. Add to that the uniquely American institution of the Electoral College. To win, a presidential candidate must get an absolute majority of electoral votes—so far, at least, an impossible task for a minor-party candidate. Because the presidency is so prominent in American politics, the argument goes, it shapes the politics of the system as a whole. Because minor parties have no chance of winning the presidency, they will not thrive.[18]

Some minor parties try for the presidency anyway. In 1996, the Reform Party focused primarily on the presidential race. But its leader, Ross Perot, a billionaire willing to spend tens of millions on his presidential campaign, was clearly not typical of most minor parties' candidates, no matter how much they may dream of such an opportunity. Thus, the importance of the single, indivisible executive office in the American system strengthens the tendency toward two-party politics.

Political scientist Leon Epstein has identified another institutional factor, the direct primary, as a force that prevented the development of minor parties in areas dominated by one party.[19] Primaries, which allow voters to choose the parties' nominees, have become the main method of selecting party candidates in the United States. When disgruntled groups have the opportunity to make their voices heard within the dominant party through a primary and may even succeed in getting a candidate nominated, the resulting taste of power will probably discourage them from breaking away to form a third party. Thus, in the one-party Democratic South of an earlier era, where traditional animosities kept most people from voting Republican, factional disputes that under other conditions would have produced one or more minor parties were contained within the Democratic Party by the use of primary elections.

"Dualist" Theories

Some theorists believe that there is a basic duality of interests in American society that has sustained the two-party system. V. O. Key, Jr. argued that tension between the eastern financial and commercial interests and the western frontiersmen stamped itself on the parties as they were forming and fostered two-party competition. Later, the dualism shifted to North–South conflict over the issue of slavery and the Civil War and then to urban–rural and socioeconomic divisions.[20]

We can see tendencies toward dualism even in multiparty systems, in that some parties will join together to construct a governing coalition and the other parties will find themselves in opposition. In the 2007 French presidential race, for example, the Socialists and other leftist parties, and the various conservative and rightist parties, all competed against one another in the election's first round, but then came together along largely ideological lines to contest the runoff election. So, the argument suggests, there is a natural dualism within democratic institutions: government versus opposition, those favoring and opposing the status quo. What distinguishes two-party from multiparty systems, in short, may be whether this basic tendency toward dualism is expressed in every aspect of the electoral process or only in the creation and functioning of a government.

Party Self-Protection

Once a two-party system has developed, the two dominant parties are highly motivated to protect it. The two major parties will support election systems (such as plurality elections and single-member districts) that make it hard for minor parties to do well. Through their control of Congress and state legislatures, the Democrats and Republicans have manipulated the rules to keep minor parties from qualifying for the ballot. The major parties have no interest in leveling the playing field so that their minor-party competitors can take a shot at replacing them.[21] Further, after the two-party system was launched, it created loyalties within the American public to one party or the other.

The two parties' openness to new groups and adaptability to changing conditions—qualities rare among democratic parties—have also undermined the development of strong minor parties. Just when a third party rides the crest of a new issue to the point where it can challenge the two-party monopoly, one or both of the major parties is likely to absorb the new movement. In the 2004 campaign, for example, the Democrats worked hard to appeal to the nearly 3 million voters who supported Ralph Nader's Green Party candidacy in 2000.[22]

The most important of these explanations for a two-party system is the institutional arrangement of American electoral politics. Without plurality elections, single-member districts, the Electoral College, and an indivisible executive, it would have been much easier for minor parties to break the near-monopoly enjoyed by the Republicans and Democrats. Other Anglo-American democracies such as Britain and Canada, which share many of the American institutional arrangements, also tend to be dominated by two parties, although minor parties are more successful in these nations than in the United States.

EXCEPTIONS TO THE TWO-PARTY PATTERN

As we have seen, there are pockets of one-party politics in states and localities within the American two-party system. Some areas have even developed a uniquely American brand of no-party (nonpartisan) politics. Minor parties or independent candidates have occasionally made their presence felt. Where do we find these exceptions to two-party politics, and what has been their impact?

Nonpartisan Elections

One of the Progressive movement's most treasured achievements was to restrict the role of parties by removing party labels from many ballots, mostly in local elections. About three-quarters of American cities and towns, including Los Angeles, Chicago, Miami, and Atlanta, conduct their local elections on a nonpartisan basis. Many states elect judges using a nonpartisan ballot. Nonpartisanship adds to the parties' burdens; even the strongest local parties have to work much harder to let voters know which candidates are affiliated with their party.

Removing party labels from the ballot has not usually removed partisan influences where parties are already strong. A resourceful party organization can still select its candidates and persuade voters when party labels are not on the ballot. Even where local elections are nonpartisan, local voters are still affected by the partisan content of state and national elections. Typically, however, the reform took root in cities and towns that already had weak parties and for offices, such as judgeships and school boards, where the traditional American dislike of party politics is most deeply felt. Most northeastern cities, where strong party machines were the main targets of the Progressives, were able to resist the reforms and to continue holding partisan local elections.

Beyond adding to the difficulties faced by party organizations, what difference does it make if an election is nonpartisan? Researchers had long believed that nonpartisan elections gave an advantage to Republican candidates, who were more likely to have the financial resources to attract voter attention in the absence of party labels. More recent research suggests, however, that it is the minority party in an area that benefits, because the nonpartisan ballot takes away the party cue that would otherwise remind the majority's voters to choose the majority party's candidates.[23] Nonpartisan elections have also been found to reduce voter turnout. The party label is an important and low-cost shortcut for voters to use in elections; without it, fewer people make the effort to vote.[24]

In an ingenious experiment, one group of researchers compared the behavior of state legislators in Nebraska, who are selected in nonpartisan elections, with those in partisan Kansas. The legislators in both states took clear stands on major policy issues. But legislators' votes on bills were not as clearly structured in Nebraska as they were in Kansas. That made it harder for Nebraskans to predict how their representatives will behave and to hold them accountable.[25] Therefore, nonpartisan elections can weaken the policy links between voters and their legislators—a result that would have greatly disappointed the Progressives.

Areas of One-Party Monopoly

In the past, the states of the Deep South were the nation's best-known examples of one-party domination. Today, one-party politics can still be found in thousands of cities, towns, and counties in which a mention of the other party can produce anything from raised eyebrows to raised tempers.

Where do we find these one-party areas? For most of their history, the major parties, especially in national elections, have divided the American voters roughly along social-demographic lines. (More about this can be found in Chapter 7.) A local constituency may be too small to contain the social diversity that supports both Democratic and Republican politics. Thus, we can find "safe" Democratic congressional districts in the poorer, older, and black neighborhoods of large cities and "safe" Republican districts in small town and rural, heavily white, Christian and southern areas. The less diverse its people are, at least in terms of the demographic characteristics that typically divide Republican from Democratic voters, the more likely the district is to foster one-party politics.

Alternatively, there may be some local basis of party loyalty so powerful that it overrides the relationship between socioeconomic status and partisanship. In the classic one-party politics of the American South for many decades, racial fears, white hatred of Republicans as the party of abolition and Reconstruction, and laws and practices preventing blacks from voting long outweighed the factors that were dividing Americans into two parties in most of the rest of the country.

Once one party has established dominance in an area, the weaker party may have a hard time overcoming the dominant party's advantages. These advantages begin with enduring party loyalties. Many voters are not easily moved from their attachments to a party, even though the reasons for the original attachment are long past. A party trying to become competitive may find itself caught in a vicious circle. Its inability to win elections limits its ability to raise money and recruit attractive candidates because, as a chronic loser, it offers so little chance of achieving political goals. For much of the 1900s, for example, the Republican Party in the South found that the Democrats had recruited the region's most promising politicians and claimed its most powerful appeals. Now, in many parts of the South, it is the Democrats who face this same disadvantage.

The weaker party's ability to attract voters locally is also affected by media coverage of its national party's stands. If the Democratic Party is identified nationally with the hopes of the poor and minority groups, its appeal in an affluent suburb may be limited, no matter how attractive its candidates are. Thus, a nationalized politics may rob the local party organization of the chance to develop strength based on its own issues and candidates. To the extent that party loyalties grow out of national politics, as Democrats in the South have learned, competitiveness may be beyond the reach of some local party organizations.

And as noted earlier in this chapter, redistricting can make it harder for the weaker party to bounce back. Majority parties have found effective ways to redraw legislative district lines that preserve their advantage, so the minority party in an area must compete in districts drawn by the stronger party. This is why parties are especially concerned with winning state legislative majorities in years ending in zero, when district lines must be redrawn.

Minor Parties

Minor parties, often called "third" parties, have a long history in American politics, but they rarely win elections. Only seven minor parties in all of American history have carried even a single state in a presidential election. The recent high point of third-party strength was Ross Perot's run as the Reform Party candidate for president in 1996, when he won just over 8 million votes. In 2008, all third-party presidential candidates combined won less than a quarter of that number.

Minor-party successes below the presidential level are as uncommon as they are fascinating. Of more than a thousand governors elected since 1875, fewer than 20 ran solely on a minor-party ticket and another handful ran as independents.[26] Perhaps the best known was former professional wrestler Jesse "The Body" Ventura's election as governor of Minnesota in 1998. Ventura's Reform Party candidacy got enormous media attention precisely because it was so unusual, but Ventura stepped down from the governorship in 2002 after having been largely ignored by the state legislature, and the next candidate of his party attracted only 16 percent of the vote.[27] Nationally, minor-party and independent candidates won more than 4 million votes for governor in 2010, plus another 400,000 in 2008, but only one—Lincoln Chafee of Rhode Island, formerly a Republican senator—had enough support to win office.

The Libertarian Party has been the strongest vote getter of any minor party in the past quarter century. Libertarian candidates received more than a million votes for U.S. House seats in 2010 (see Table 2.2), though no Libertarian candidate won. A handful of other minor party and independent candidates were elected to state legislatures that year, and a few were successful in local races; in 2011, three Constitution Party candidates were elected to county office in Nevada, and there was a Green Party county collector in Arkansas and a Libertarian township board member in Indiana.

TABLE 2.2

Voting for Independent and Minor-Party Candidates for U.S. House, 2010

Party	Votes
Libertarian (candidates in 32 states)	1,074,189
Conservative Party (New York only)	267,939
Green (candidates in 14 states)	256,307
Constitution Party (candidates in 18 states)	251,741
Working Families (Connecticut, New York, South Carolina)	202,762
Independence Party of New York	118,540
Independence Party (Minnesota)	84,816
Tea Party (Florida and New Jersey)	38,790
Peace and Freedom (California only)	30,714
Other minor parties	79,159
Total votes for minor party candidates	2,404,957
Total votes for independent (nonparty) candidates	829,909

Note: Democratic U.S. House candidates received a total of 38.7 million votes in 2010, and Republican U.S. House candidates received 44.5 million votes.

Source: Richard L. Winger, *Ballot Access News*, January 1, 2011, at www.ballot-access.org/2011/02/08/ballot-access-news-january-2011-print-edition/ (accessed October 29, 2011).

More significantly, a minor party has sometimes shifted the balance in an important race. In 2008, the Minnesota Senate race was so close that a lengthy recount was required. The Democrat, Al Franken, finally won. The stakes were high: Franken's win gave the Senate Democrats 60 seats—in theory, enough to quash a Republican filibuster. An Independence Party candidate took 15 percent of the vote in the Minnesota Senate race; if only a tiny proportion of minor-party voters had chosen the Republican candidate instead, the Minnesota seat would have gone to Franken's Republican opponent, and the Senate Republicans would then have been assured of enough votes to block almost any Democratic legislation. However, for every example of minor-party success, there are thousands of races with no minor-party candidate. The two major parties have monopolized elections even more fully in the states and cities than at the national level. (See "A Day in the Life" on pages 40–41.)

> **A DAY IN THE LIFE**

Competing Against the "Big Guys"

The Democrats and the Republicans, Brad Warren says, have a "death grip" on the American political process. Warren, a tax attorney in Indianapolis, is a Libertarian Party activist who ran for the U.S. Senate under that party's banner. "If I need a new pair of socks," he points out, "I can go to dozens of stores and pick from several different brands and dozens of colors—for something as insignificant as socks. But when it comes to politics, which has a monopoly on the lawful use of force in our society, we have only two choices. That is tremendously scary! How do you hold them accountable? If you get angry with the incumbents, you can throw them out, only to reelect the nasty incumbents you had thrown out in the previous election. Four years from now, you'll be throwing out the incumbents you elected today. There's no choice."

Minor-party activists such as Warren must compete against the "big guys"—the two major parties—on an uneven playing field. A major problem for a minor party is simply to get its candidates' names on the ballot. The Indiana state legislature used to require any minor party to win just half of 1 percent of the vote for secretary of state in order to get its candidates on the state ballot automatically in later elections. The Libertarians met that goal in 1982. The result? The legislature raised the hurdle to 2 percent. Ballot access requirements differ from state to state, making it difficult for a minor party to appear on the ballot in all 50 states.

"Even once you have ballot access," Warren argues, "you will still be excluded from any *meaningful* participation in the election. In practice, we run elections on money, not on votes, and in presidential elections, the Republicans and Democrats divide up hundreds of millions of federal dollars among themselves."

The worst problem for minor parties, Warren feels, is getting noticed after the major parties hold primary elections. "I got pretty good media coverage up to the primary

(continued)

(continued)

election. After the primary, I was nobody. Even though the primary doesn't elect anybody to any office, it *seems to*. Primaries are a government-funded means of anointing the two major parties' candidates as the "real" candidates and delegitimizing all the others. The media say we have no chance to win, so they won't cover any candidates except the [major] party-anointed ones. The debates typically don't include third-party candidates. Why? Because the commissions that decide who's going to be allowed to participate in debates are 'bipartisan' commissions, made up entirely of Republicans and Democrats, just like the legislatures that write the ballot access laws and the judges who interpret them. A party that has gotten on the ballot in all 50 states, like the Libertarians, deserves to be heard."

"The two major parties won't give you any choice," Warren contends, and "if you continually vote for the lesser of two evils, what you get is evil." So what is the role of a minor party? To Warren, "It's like that of a bee: You rise up, you sting, and then you die." ■

Minor parties in the United States vary greatly in their purposes, origins, and levels of activity:[28]

Differences in Ideology   Most minor parties are driven by issues and ideologies, but they differ in the nature and scope of that commitment. The New York State Right to Life and the Christian Liberty Parties are very specific and targeted: the former in wanting to ban all abortions and the latter in favoring Christian principles in politics. At the other extreme are socialist parties whose programs demand sweeping changes, including an end to capitalism and class privilege. The Libertarian Party wants government to involve itself only in national defense and criminal law and to turn over all other programs, from Social Security to education, to private efforts.[29] In sharp contrast, Green Parties argue for extensive government programs on behalf of the environment, peace, and social justice.

Difference of Origins   Minor parties differ, too, in their origin. Some were literally imported into the United States. Much of the early Socialist Party strength in the United States came from the freethinkers and radicals who fled Europe after the failed revolutions of 1848. Socialist candidates did well in cities such as Milwaukee, New York, and Cincinnati because of the concentrations of liberal German immigrants there. Other parties, especially the Granger and Populist Parties, were homegrown channels of social protest, born of social inequality and economic hardship in the marginal farmlands of America.

Some minor parties began as splinters or factions of one of the major parties. For example, the Progressives (the Bull Moose Party) of 1912 and the Dixiecrats of 1948 objected so strenuously to the platforms and candidates of their parent parties that they ran their own slates and presented their own programs in presidential elections. In fact, the Dixiecrats, an anti–civil rights faction within the Democratic Party, substituted their own candidate for the one chosen by the party's national convention as the official Democratic presidential candidate in several southern states. If Tea Party activists were to nominate their own candidates for office, rather than try to influence Republican primaries, then they, too, would become a minor party.

Differing Purposes Finally, minor parties differ in their intentions. Some of these parties aim to educate citizens about their issues; getting votes is merely a sideline. They run candidates because their presence on the ballot brings media attention that they could not otherwise hope to get. Many of these parties serenely accept their election losses because they have chosen not to compromise their principles to win office. The Prohibition Party, for example, has run candidates in most presidential elections since 1872 with unflagging devotion to the cause of banning the sale of alcoholic beverages but without apparent concern for the fact that its highest proportion of the popular vote was 2 percent, and that came in 1892. Other minor parties are serious about trying to win office. Often, their goal is local, although today they find it difficult to control an American city, as the Socialists once did, or an entire state, like the Progressives.

What Difference Do They Make? Some argue that minor parties deserve the credit for a number of public policies—programs that were first suggested by a minor party and then adopted by a major party when they became politically popular. A possible example is the minimum wage, which was advocated by the Socialist Party for more than two decades before the minimum wage law was enacted in the 1930s by a Democratic Congress. Did the Democrats steal the Socialist Party's idea, or would they have proposed a minimum wage for workers even if there had been no Socialist Party? There is no way to be sure. Major parties usually propose a new policy once a large number of Americans has accepted the idea, so the party can gain votes. However, the major party might have picked up the new proposal from any of a number of sources in addition to the Socialists.

If the impact of minor parties is so limited, then what attracts some voters to them? There aren't many such voters; the self-fulfilling prophecy that a vote for a third party is a wasted vote is very powerful in American politics.[30] Yet some voters do cast minor-party ballots. To Steven Rosenstone and his colleagues, this results from the failure of major parties "to do what the electorate expects of them—reflect the issue preferences of voters, manage the economy, select attractive and acceptable candidates, and build voter loyalty to the parties and the political system."[31] So, minor parties tend to gain support when they promote attractive ideas that the major parties have ignored, or because of public dissatisfaction with the major party candidates, rather than because many voters believe in a multiparty system as a matter of principle.

The Rise of Independent Candidates

In recent elections, dissatisfaction with the two major parties has also produced several notable independent candidacies—those who run as individuals, independent of any party organization. The most successful was Ross Perot, who mounted a well-funded independent candidacy for president in 1992 before running as the Reform Party candidate in 1996. The story of Perot's two candidacies, one as an independent and the other as a third-party candidate, helps us understand some of the advantages and disadvantages of each choice.

In his race as an independent candidate in 1992, Perot and his supporters built a remarkably strong national organization. Through its efforts, Perot got on the ballot in all 50 states. He ended the race with 19.7 million votes—a larger share of the popular vote than any "third" candidate in history who was not a former president. In fact, he outdrew the combined total of all his minor-party opponents in that race by more than 19 million ballots. The key ingredient in his success was money; Perot invested more than $65 million of his own funds in his campaign. That financed organizational efforts at the grassroots level and bought large blocks of expensive television time. Even so, Perot failed to win a single state, and much of his support came from voters who were more dissatisfied with the major-party candidates than they were attracted to a long-lasting commitment to another party or candidate.[32]

Three years later, Perot organized the new Reform Party and sought to qualify it for the ballot in all 50 states. That was harder than qualifying to run as an independent. In California, his toughest challenge, Perot had to get at least 890,000 signatures on a petition by October 1995 to win a place on the state's ballot 13 months later. He failed. Using a different mechanism, Perot finally qualified in California and in all other states but found it difficult to recruit acceptable Reform candidates for other offices. On Election Day, Perot got less than half as many votes as a Reform Party candidate than he had four years earlier as an independent.

Why was his minor-party effort less successful? Many factors were at work. One reason may have been simple familiarity; at times, a candidate does not benefit from letting voters get to know him or her better. Perot spent much less of his own money in 1996 than he had four years earlier. In addition, it is harder for an organization to support many candidates rather than just one. In the 2000 presidential campaign, for example, conflicts among Reform Party activists became so intense that the party's national convention disintegrated into a fistfight and the party split.

Ralph Nader's experience as a presidential candidate in 2000 and 2004 was very different from Perot's. In 2000, Nader won access to 43 state ballots fairly easily because he ran as the Green Party candidate, which had already qualified for ballot access in those states. In 2004, Nader struggled to get on those same ballots as an independent candidate. Democratic activists filed lawsuits to try to keep Nader off state ballots, because his candidacy was expected to hurt Democrat John Kerry more than Republican George W. Bush.

Want to Run for Office as an Independent? Good Luck!

If you want to run for the U.S. House of Representatives as an independent (nonparty) candidate in Georgia, Montana, or North or South Carolina, you will have to get more than 10,000 people to sign a petition for you. (As a result, no independent candidate for the House has ever appeared on a government-printed ballot in either North or South Carolina.)

If you'd prefer to run as an independent candidate for president, then you must get a total of almost a million valid signatures on petitions. Each state has its own requirements, which you will have to unearth and follow. In Texas alone, you'd need to get 80,778 signatures from registered voters during a 75-day period, which ends in May of an election year, and none of the signers can have voted in the most recent party primaries. In Florida, you must have 112,174 signatures from registered voters by July 15 of the election year. (You'll actually need about three times as many signatures, because Democratic and Republican election clerks can disallow any signatures they don't regard as valid.)

Paid signature gatherers usually earn about $2 for each signature collected, so unless you are able to recruit a small army of volunteers, you'd pay at least $2 million just to get the petitions signed and much more for the lawyers in each state who will be needed to defend your petitions against legal challenges from other candidates or parties. These are examples of ways in which state legislatures, made up almost entirely of Democrats and Republicans, have protected the two major parties by passing laws making it much tougher for minor party and independent candidates to get on the ballot.

Sources: Richard L. Winger, *Ballot Access News,* November 1, 2011, p. 5 (on presidential candidates) and Winger, personal communication (on House candidates).

Even when a minor party meets the difficult challenge of maintaining its line on the ballot, it will still face the enormous hurdle of recruiting candidates for thousands of state legislative seats and county offices as well as for president. The Greens and the Libertarians have made real efforts since 2000 to establish themselves as organizations that contest offices from the top to the bottom of the ballot. If history is any guide, however, that is a battle they are likely to lose. The result is that when voters consider alternatives to the major parties, independent candidates (especially if they happen to be billionaires, such as New York mayor Michael Bloomberg, who considered running for president as an independent in 2012) will continue to have advantages over those who try to form fully elaborated minor parties.

WILL THE TWO-PARTY SYSTEM CONTINUE?

This look at two-party politics and its alternatives leads to two main conclusions. First, in important respects, the two-party system is secure in the United States. Minor parties are not gaining ground. Third-party members of Congress, common in the early decades of the two-party system, have been very rare in the past century and especially in recent years. Since 1952, only three members of Congress have been elected on a minor-party ticket. Four have recently served as independents, but all have aligned themselves with one of the major parties' caucuses. Minor-party candidates have also fared poorly in state legislative contests during this period.

The barriers to ballot access for minor-party and independent candidates are not as high now as they once were. And quirks in some states' election laws continue to support a few minor parties. New York is a good example; several minor parties, notably the Conservatives and the Working Families Party, survive because state law allows them to nominate candidates of a major party to run under their own parties' labels as well.[33] But in most cases, candidates other than Republicans and Democrats must still jump substantial hurdles to get on state ballots and satisfy a patchwork of differing state laws to qualify for the ballot nationwide (see box on page 44). Even when courts have overturned laws that discriminate against these candidates, the decisions have been limited, requiring petitioners to mount a challenge in each state.[34]

In addition, independent and minor-party candidates still face huge financial disadvantages. Although candidates don't need to be Democrats or Republicans in order to reach voters throughout the United States with television and the Internet, the enormous cost of modern campaigns probably restricts this opportunity to only a few highly visible or personally wealthy individuals. Minor-party presidential candidates can receive public funding for their campaign (as they do in other democracies, such as Canada and Australia) if they win at least 5 percent of the popular vote. However, in 30 years, the only campaign to qualify was that of Perot's Reform Party in 1996. That assured the Reform Party's 2000 presidential candidate of receiving $12 million in federal funds for his campaign. The money no doubt increased the attractiveness of the party's presidential nomination; yet the eventual nominee, Patrick Buchanan, earned less than half of 1 percent of the popular vote.

Independent candidates for president and governor have made some elections less predictable. But running by themselves, with no other candidates on their "tickets," they are not likely to create a lasting challenge to the Democrats and Republicans. To make a sustained challenge that could fundamentally transform the American parties, these independents would need to organize to confront the major parties from the top to the bottom of the ballot. Those who try soon realize that the two-party system may not be greatly beloved, but it is very well entrenched.

How would a multiparty system change American politics? Proponents could cite a number of benefits. Voters would have more choices. A greater variety of views would be able to find expression through a party platform. Smaller parties, speaking for identifiable segments of society, might give citizens in these groups more confidence that their voices are being heard.

On the other hand, when the threshold for ballot access is lowered, extremist parties are better able to compete. In a system where the government will probably be a coalition of several parties, voters need to anticipate the compromises that their preferred party will make in order to form a government and perhaps, in order to influence that compromise, vote for a party whose views are more extreme than their own.[35] Votes are more directly translated into leadership in a majoritarian two-party system, though American politics, with its separation of powers, limits that direct translation now. Coalition governments can be unstable. And a multiparty system would likely require major changes in American electoral institutions, such as the single-member presidency and plurality elections. But these advantages and disadvantages are a moot point because of the durability of American two-party politics.

The second major trend that we have seen in this chapter is an especially intriguing one. The Democratic and Republican Parties are highly competitive at the national level; presidential elections are won by relatively small margins, and both parties have had recent runs of dominance in Congress. When we look beneath the aggregate level at individual House and state legislative districts, however, close competition becomes more rare. The intense party competition at the national level is often built on the backs of fairly equal numbers of safe Democratic and safe Republican congressional and lower-level seats.[36]

Officeholders elected in districts that are relatively safe for their party may not feel as great a need to appeal to voters of the other party as they would if the district were more competitive. Incumbents in safe districts face more of a threat from within their own party, in the primary election, than from the other party. These primary threats usually come from the ideological extremes of their party. As Chapter 13 shows, then, safe incumbents can take more partisan stands in order to ward off a primary challenger, knowing that they are not likely to suffer for it in the general election. Party polarization in Congress, state legislatures, and among politically involved citizens has accompanied this process. Even in a relatively stable two-party system such as that in the United States, moderation in political debate can be in short supply.

The Political Party as an Organization

When you hear the term "party organization," what comes to mind? For many Americans, the image is of a few older white guys, party "bosses," dividing up the spoils of winning in a smoke-filled room. That image may have been accurate a hundred years ago. It isn't now. But because the party organization is less visible than the party's candidates, it remains mysterious even to many partisans. The next three chapters will examine the formal *party organization*— the set of party committees and volunteers who work at all the levels at which Americans elect public officials: precincts, townships, wards, cities, counties, congressional districts, states, and the federal government—and the informal groups of activists who give life to these organizations. How do the party organizations work, and how have they changed over time? What kinds of people become party activists? These internal characteristics influence the party's ability to act effectively in the larger political system.

American party organizations vary tremendously, from powerful and elaborate structures to empty shells. Compared with those of other Western democracies, however, most American party organizations would be considered fairly weak. Shackled by state laws, the party organizations have rarely been able to exercise much influence over the other two parts of a party: the party's candidates and officeholders (the party in government) and the party in the electorate.

The three parts of any party differ in their goals. In an election, for instance, the party organization and party activists hope to support as many of the party's candidates as possible, whereas each individual candidate wants as much of the party's money as he or she can get, and party voters are concerned instead with taxes or same-sex marriage or cheaper college tuition. Each seeks control of the party to achieve its own ends. In the American system, the party organizations find it difficult to hold their own in this competition and to get the resources they need to influence elections and promote policies. American party organizations can't translate their platform planks into law; they must depend on the members of their party in government to do that. Party organizations must work hard to court and mobilize the party electorate, who may be loyal party voters at some times but more fickle at others.

This lack of integration among the party's component parts is typical of *cadre parties*—one of two terms often used to describe the nature of party organizations. Imagine that party organizations are arranged along a continuum. At one end is the cadre party, in which the organization is run by a relatively small number of leaders and activists with little or no broader public participation. These officials and activists make the organization's decisions, choose its candidates, and select the strategies they believe voters will find appealing. They focus largely on electing party candidates rather than on issues. Thus, the party becomes active mainly during campaigns, when candidates need their party organization's help the most. The cadre party, then, is a coalition of people and interests brought together temporarily to win elections, only to shrink to a smaller core once the elections are over.

At the other end of this scale is the *mass-membership party*, a highly participatory organization in which all three parts of the party are closely intertwined. In this type of party, large numbers of voters become dues-paying members of the party organization and participate in its activities year-round, not just during campaigns. A mass-membership party concentrates on promoting an ideology and educating the public as well as on winning elections. Its members decide what the party's policies should be as well as choose its organizational leaders. Members of the party in the electorate are so integral to the party organization that the party may even provide them with such nonpolitical benefits as insurance and leisure-time activities. Because the membership-based party organization has great power over candidate selection—it does not need to give less involved voters the right to choose party candidates in a primary election—it can also exercise much greater control over the party in government.

In important ways, the major American parties can be considered cadre parties. The great majority of local and state party leaders and activists are not paid professionals but volunteers, whose party activities ramp up around election time. These organization leaders do not try hard to control the party's candidates and elected officials, nor are they likely to succeed. Most party identifiers in the United States are not involved at all in the party organization.

They do not fit the cadre mold perfectly; in practice, parties have a tendency to slip out of precise definitions.[1] For example, party leaders contact their supporters in the electorate more frequently now than they did a few decades ago, and the state and national party organizations are active year-round. Nevertheless, these changes have not made the major American parties into mass-membership organizations. The major parties concentrate on electing candidates more than on educating voters on issues.

Why does it matter whether party organizations are strong or weak, cadre or mass membership? Because party organizations are at the very core of the political parties. They are the sector of the parties that can provide continuity, even as the party's candidates, elected officials, and identifiers come and go. A strong party organization can hunt for the resources needed for long-term election success and can present a united, persuasive approach to issues. So the development of a stronger party organization can change the character of politics and elections. In fact, as American party organizations have become more robust in recent years, they have altered our politics in ways ranging from campaign fund-raising to the nature of political debate. Chapter 3 begins by exploring the party organizations closest to home: state and local parties.

The State and Local Party Organizations

A century ago, many party organizations were described as "machines," with the power to control city governments and mobilize large numbers of activists. Just a few decades later, most of these machines were gone. A variety of forces had drained the strength of state and local parties, and most party organizations at the state and local levels were described as weak and inactive. Since that time, party organizations have revived at all levels and moved into the Internet age. State and local parties, in short, have been on a wild ride during the past century—demonstrating how capable they are of adapting to changes in the American political environment.

What difference does it make if a party organization is vibrant or weak? As the Introduction to Part II noted, in many ways, the party organization is the foundation of a political party. It gives the party a way to endure, despite a changing cast of candidates and elected officeholders. More than the party in government or the party identifiers, the party organizations are the keepers of the parties' brands—the unifying labels and ideas that give candidates a shortcut in identifying themselves to voters and that give voters a means to choose among candidates. Without this organization, a party becomes only an unstable alliance of convenience among candidates and between candidates and groups of voters—too changeable to accomplish the important work that parties can perform in a democracy.

In this chapter, after considering how to measure "party strength," we will explore the reality of state and local party organizations as they adapt to their environments. Next, we will turn to the local party organizations, tracing their path from the fabled political machines that dominated a number of eastern and Midwestern cities beginning in the last half of the 1800s to the fall and rise of local parties more recently. Finally, we will see how the state parties grew from weakness to greater strength in the closing decades of the twentieth century.

WHAT IS A "STRONG" PARTY?

How can a "strong" party be defined? Many researchers measure a party's vigor by examining its organizational features. Stronger parties would have larger budgets and more full-time, paid staff members. That can be termed *party organizational strength.*

There are other ways to measure party strength. A strong party would work effectively to register voters, tell them about party candidates, and get them to the polls on Election Day. It would be successful in filling its ticket with attractive candidates. Its candidates would win more races than they lose. We could even measure whether the party is able to get its platform enacted into law (as we will see in Chapter 15).

In order for a party to do these things—and especially to register voters, canvass, and get out the vote—it needs money, staff, and other forms of organizational strength. We will look at most of these measures of party strength in this chapter but focus mainly on party organizational strength.

STATE REGULATION OF THE PARTIES

Americans' traditional suspicion of political parties has led most states, especially during the Progressive Era of the late 1800s and early 1900s, to pass large numbers of laws restricting their party organizations. Party committees are regulated "lightly" in only about a third of the states, most of them in the South, Plains states, and upper Midwest.[1] At the other extreme, in 15 states—including California, New Jersey, and Ohio—lawmakers have thought it necessary to control even the smallest details of state party activity, such as the types of public buildings in which parties must hold their conventions.

These extensive state rules have not necessarily weakened the parties; some of the strongest party organizations in the nation are also the most tightly regulated. In fact, all these state laws help prop up the Democratic and Republican Parties against competition from minor parties. However, they do give state governments a set of tools for keeping an eye on their parties. They also indicate that state law does not view the parties simply as private groups. As Leon Epstein argued, the parties are seen as public utilities that can be subject to a great deal of state direction.[2] And federal campaign finance regulations since the 1970s have built a substantial body of national law that affects party organizations and candidates.

States do not have complete freedom to decide how to regulate the parties. Federal courts have frequently stepped in to protect citizens' voting rights (see Chapter 8), to keep the states from unreasonably limiting minor-party and independent candidates' ballot access (see Chapter 2), and to acknowledge the parties' right to control their internal affairs. In the 1980s, for example, the Supreme Court ruled that the state of Connecticut could not prevent the Republican Party from opening up its primary to independents if it wanted to. Soon after, the Court threw out a California law saying, among other things, that parties could not endorse candidates in primary elections. A 2000 Supreme Court decision overturned a California state initiative setting up a "blanket primary" on the grounds that it violated the party organization's First Amendment right to decide who votes in its primaries.[3] Even so, American party organizations are more heavily regulated than are their counterparts in other democracies.

LEVELS OF PARTY ORGANIZATION

The party organizations created by the states follow a common pattern. Their structure corresponds to the levels of government at which voters elect office-holders. This structure is often pictured as a pyramid based in the grassroots and stretching up to the statewide organization. A pyramid, however, gives the misleading impression that the layer at the top can give orders to the layers below. So picture these party organizations, instead, as they fit into a geographic map (Figure 3.1).

Local Party Committees

The county is the main unit of local party organization in most states, because so many important local officials are elected at the county level, and usually in partisan elections: sheriffs, prosecutors, county attorneys and clerks, judges, council members, treasurers, assessors, surveyors, coroners, and more. These officials control vital functions ranging from policing the area and prosecuting those accused of crime to assessing and collecting property taxes. Party organizations exist in almost all of the nation's counties to at least some

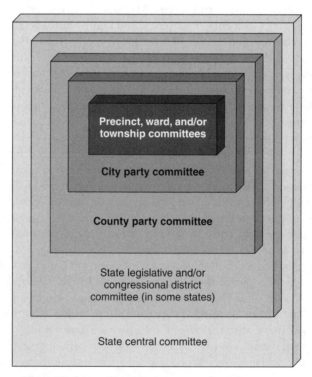

FIGURE 3.1
The Party Organizations in a Typical State.

degree. These are the parties' "grassroots," where a lot of the activity of party volunteers takes place.

In most areas, counties are divided into smaller units called precincts. Each precinct (or town, township, or ward, in some areas) in theory has a party leader—a committeeman and/or committeewoman—to conduct the party's activities in that area. Because there are about 193,000 precincts in the United States, it would be easy to imagine a vibrant party base made up of at least 200,000 committed men and women. However, this exists only in the dreams of party leaders; in reality, up to half of these local committee positions are vacant because nobody volunteers to serve in them.

When these (unpaid) positions do get filled, it generally happens in one of three ways. Most committeemen and women are chosen at local party caucuses (meetings) or in primary elections, but in a few instances, higher party authorities appoint them. In states that use caucuses, parties hold meetings in the precincts and wards that are open to any voters in the area who declare themselves attached to the party. These local party supporters then elect the precinct committee leaders and often elect delegates to county and/or state conventions as well. In states that choose precinct committeemen and women in the primaries, any voter may nominate himself or herself for the job by filing a petition signed by a handful of local voters. If, as often happens, there are no nominees, the committeeman or woman may be elected by an even smaller handful of write-in votes. These local committee positions, in short, are not normally in great demand, especially in the weaker party in an area. Therefore, the local parties are far from being exclusive clubs; their "front doors" are often open to anyone who chooses to walk in.

What do these precinct and county party leaders do? Their three most important jobs are registering new voters, going door-to-door (called "canvassing" or "d2d") to tell potential supporters about the party's candidates, and getting voters to the polls (known as "GOTV," or "get out the vote"). They need to recruit volunteers to help with these labor-intensive tasks and to help staff the party's headquarters. County party leaders may also try to raise money to support local candidates. And when there are vacancies on the party ticket—offices for which nobody chose to run in the primary election and for which the party has not been able to recruit candidates—then the local party committees may be responsible for appointing a candidate to run. In the less active local parties, the committeemen and women may do little more than show up at an occasional meeting and campaign for a party candidate or two.

The precinct committeemen and women usually come together to make up the next level of local party organization, or they elect the delegates who do. In some states, the next level is the city party committee; in others, it may be the town, county, or state legislative and congressional district committees. Usually, however, there is greater activity at the county level than in any other layer of the local party.

State Central Committees

At the state level, the party organization is usually called the state central committee. The state parties typically help to recruit candidates for statewide offices (for instance, state treasurer or attorney general) and state legislative seats, assist in training them, and raise money to support their campaigns. They may also work with local parties on the crucial tasks of voter registration, canvassing, and GOTV.

State law usually gives party central committees a number of other important powers: the responsibility for calling and organizing party conventions, drafting party platforms, supervising the spending of party campaign funds, and selecting the party's presidential electors, representatives to the national committee, and some of the national convention delegates. Some other states give these powers to the party's statewide convention instead. In a few states, such as Indiana, the party's state convention actually nominates candidates for some statewide offices, a reminder of the power that party conventions held in the days before primary elections.

These are the formal organizational structures that state law creates for the state and local parties. From them, we can draw three important conclusions. First, the levels of party organization have been set up to correspond to the voting districts in which citizens choose public officials in that state (e.g., county and congressional districts), and the main responsibility of these organizations under state law is to contest elections. State laws, then, see the party organizations as helpers in the state's task of conducting nominations and elections—tasks that before the turn of the twentieth century belonged almost entirely to the parties alone.

Second, the laws indicate that state legislators are ambivalent about what constitutes a party organization. Many of these laws treat the parties as cadre organizations (see page 48) run by a small number of party officials. Yet, when they specify that the party's own officials, including local committeemen and women, must be chosen in a primary election, this gives party voters— and potentially, any voters—a vital, quasi-membership role in the party organization. So state laws help to create a party that is semipublic, rather than a genuinely private group whose active members choose its leaders and set its direction.

Finally, the relationships among these state and local party organizations are not those of a hierarchy, in which the lower levels take their orders from the higher levels. Instead, through much of their history, the parties were best described as "a system of layers of organization,"[4] or as a "stratarchy,"[5] in which each of the levels has some independent power. In fact, power has traditionally flowed from bottom to top in the local and state parties, as opposed to a hierarchy, where power would be centralized at the top.[6] Party organization is a system of party committees growing from the political grassroots. Thus, the party organizations remain fairly decentralized and rooted in local politics, even in the face of recent trends toward stronger state and national committees.

THE LEGENDARY PARTY MACHINES

The high point of local party organizational strength in the United States occurred in the late 1800s and early 1900s, when the urban political "machine" reached its peak of power. At this time, by some accounts, a large majority of American cities were governed by machines.[7] The party machine was a disciplined organization that controlled the nominations to elective office. It had the hierarchical structure that today's local parties lack. It relied on material incentives—giving out jobs and favors—to build support among voters. Above all, it controlled the government in a city or county.

Yet, for all their power in shaping how we think of party organizations, the great urban machines were not found in all cities, and they gradually disappeared. The decline began in the 1930s, and almost all were gone by the 1960s and 1970s. These "traditional party organizations"[8] were brought down by a number of forces. Some party machines, such as those in Pittsburgh and New York, never recovered from election upsets by middle-class reformers. Others, including those in Philadelphia and Gary, Indiana, lost power when racial tensions overshadowed the old ethnic politics.[9]

How the Party Machines Developed

In the late 1800s, large numbers of the immigrants arriving in major American cities had urgent economic and social needs. These newcomers were poor, often spoke no English, and faced a difficult adjustment to their new urban environment. Party leaders in many of these cities—usually Democrats, reflecting that party's history of openness to immigrants—saw the opportunity for a mutually profitable exchange. The immigrants needed jobs, social services, and other benefits that a city government could provide. The party leaders needed large numbers of votes in order to gain control of city government. If the party could register these new arrivals to vote, their votes could put the party in power. In return, the party would then control the many resources that the government had available and could give the new voters the help they needed so desperately.

Jobs ranked high among the newcomers' needs. So the most visible of the benefits offered by party machines were *patronage* jobs in the city government—those awarded on the basis of party loyalty rather than other qualifications. During the glory days of the machine, thousands of these patronage positions were at the machines' disposal. By giving patronage jobs to party supporters, the party's leaders could be assured that city workers would remain loyal to the machine and would work to help it win elections by delivering not only their own votes but those of their family, friends, and neighbors as well. After all, if the party lost the election, then the city workers would lose their jobs.

For example, in its prime, the Chicago Democratic machine controlled an estimated 35,000 patronage jobs in government and influenced hiring for another 10,000 jobs in the private economy. Adding the families and friends of these jobholders, the party machine could deliver 350,000 motivated voters at election time. Local party workers also won voter loyalties by finding social welfare agencies for the troubled or by providing Christmas baskets or deliveries of coal for the poor. Machine leaders, called "bosses," attended weddings and wakes, listened to job seekers and business executives, bailed out drunks, and helped the hungry and homeless.

The machine had favors to offer local businesses as well. Governments purchase many goods and services from the private sector. If a bank wanted to win the city's deposits, it could expect to compete more effectively for the city's business if it were willing to contribute to the party machine. Insurance agents and lawyers who wanted city contracts, newspapers that printed city notices, and even suppliers of soap to city bathrooms were motivated to donate money or services to the party machine. In addition, city governments regularly make decisions that affect individuals' and businesses' economic standing, such as building permits and health inspections. If you were helped by one of these decisions, you could expect the machine to ask for your thanks in the form of contributions and votes. A political leadership intent on winning support in exchange for these so-called preferments can use them ruthlessly and effectively to build political power.

How Machines Held On to Power

The classic urban machine, then, was not just a party organization but also an "informal government," a social service agency, and a ladder for upward social and economic mobility. In some ways, it looked like the local organization of a European mass-membership party, except that the American machine had little or no concern with ideology. Its world was the city; it focused on the immediate needs of its constituents, and its politics were almost completely divorced from the issues that animated national politics.

An important source of the machines' strength was their ability to appeal to ethnic loyalties. Although there were party machines in cities without large immigrant populations, the rise and fall of the American political machine is closely linked to changes in ethnic-group migration to the big cities. The machine was a method by which ethnic groups, especially the Irish, gained a foothold in American politics.[10]

Machines were capable of creating a "designer electorate" by using force and intimidation to keep their opponents from voting. Because the party machines controlled the election process, it was possible, in a pinch, to change the election rules and even to count the votes in a creative manner. One of the indispensable tools of rival party workers in Indianapolis, for example, was a flashlight—to locate ballots that did not support the dominant party's candidates and happened to fly out of the window at vote-counting headquarters in the dark of night.

Machine politics was most likely to flourish in the big cities, but American party machines took root in other areas as well. The conditions that led to the development of machines, especially a large, parochially oriented population with immediate economic needs, were also found in small southern and one-company towns. Even some well-to-do suburbs have spawned strong machine-style party organizations. In the affluent Long Island suburbs of New York City, for example, a Republican Nassau County political machine controlled local government "with a local party operation that in terms of patronage and party loyalty rival[ed] the machine of the famed Democratic mayor of Chicago, Richard J. Daley."[11] The Nassau machine, which was generations old, was dominated by Italian Americans and provided jobs just like the big-city machines of old before losing its power in the 1990s. However, in nearby Queens, the local Democratic organization rebounded from scandal and continues to control primaries and elect candidates.

We cannot be sure how powerful the party machines really were, even at their strongest. A Chicago study found, for example, that in 1967 and 1977, the party machine distributed public services mainly on the basis of historical factors and bureaucratic decision rules rather than to reward its political supporters.[12] In New Haven, researchers reported that ethnic loyalties seemed more important to a party machine than even its own maintenance and expansion. The machine, led by Italian Americans, distributed summer jobs disproportionately to Italian kids from nonmachine wards, who rarely took part in later political work, and not to kids from strong machine areas.[13]

Regardless of how well they functioned, there is no doubt that the conditions that helped sustain party machines have been undercut. Economic change and political reform took away the machine's most important resources. Most city jobs are now covered by civil service protection, so the number of patronage jobs that can be used to reward the party faithful has been greatly reduced. Federal entitlement programs, such as welfare and Social Security, have reduced the need for the favors that party machines could provide. Economic growth has boosted many Americans' income levels and reduced the attractiveness of the remaining patronage jobs; the chance to work as a sewer inspector or on garbage pickup just doesn't have the allure that it once may have had. Higher education levels have increased people's ability to fend for themselves in a complex bureaucratic society. And in many areas, racial divisions have overwhelmed the machine's ability to balance competing ethnic groups.

LOCAL PARTY ORGANIZATIONS DECLINED AND THEN REBUILT

After the machines failed, local parties' organizational strength dropped dramatically in many areas. By the mid-1900s, many city and county parties were starved for leadership, money, and volunteers. Then the local organizations began to rebuild. However, the new local parties were no longer as capable of *running* campaigns as the traditional machines had been; instead, they tended to focus on providing services to candidates.

Local Parties in the 1970s

We got the first comprehensive look at the nature of local party organizations in a 1979–1980 survey of several thousand county leaders (see Table 3.1).[14] The results showed the distinctive fingerprints of cadre parties, and fairly weak ones at that.

> ### TABLE 3.1
>
> #### Changes in Local Parties' Organizational Strength, 1980s–2010s
>
> | The local party organization has (in percent) | Democrats | | | Republicans | | |
> |---|---|---|---|---|---|---|
> | | 1980 | 1996 | 2010 | 1980 | 1996 | 2010 |
> | A complete or nearly complete set of officers | 90 | 95 | 89 | 81 | 96 | 92 |
> | A year-round office | 12 | 17 | 25 | 14 | 25 | 24 |
> | A telephone listing | 11 | 27 | 33 | 16 | 30 | 29 |
> | A Web site | — | — | 70 | — | — | 70 |
> | Some paid staff members | | | | | | |
> | Full time | 3 | 4 | 6 | 4 | 4 | 7 |
> | Part time | 5 | 6 | 8 | 6 | 7 | 7 |
> | A regular annual budget | 20 | 26 | 34 | 31 | 34 | 34 |
> | A campaign headquarters | 55 | 60 | 54 | 60 | 60 | 61 |
> | *Campaign activities* | | | | | | |
> | Door-to-door canvassing | 49 | 55 | 73 | 48 | 57 | 59 |
> | Organized campaign events | 68 | 81 | 79 | 65 | 82 | 77 |
> | Arranged fund-raising events | 71 | 74 | 75 | 68 | 76 | 77 |
> | Contributed money to candidates | 62 | 75 | 57 | 70 | 78 | 59 |
> | Distributed posters or lawn signs | 59 | 93 | 84 | 62 | 93 | 81 |
> | Used public opinion polls | 11 | 13 | 11 | 16 | 15 | 14 |
>
> *Note:* 1979–1980 figures are based on responses from 2,021 Democratic and 1,980 Republican organizations to a mail survey; 1996 figures are from mail surveys of all county party chairs in nine states (Arizona, Colorado, Florida, Illinois, Missouri, Ohio, South Carolina, Washington, and Wisconsin), with responses from 340 Democrats and 335 Republicans; 2010 data are from an Internet survey of local party chairs in 49 states, with responses from 543 Republicans and 672 Democrats. Note that the 1996 data are not from a national sample.
>
> *Sources:* John Frendreis and Alan R. Gitelson, "Local Parties in the 1990s," in John C. Green and Daniel M. Shea, eds., *The State of the Parties*, 3rd ed. (Lanham, MD: Rowman & Littlefield, 1999), pp. 138–139 (for 1980 and 1996); Douglas D. Roscoe and Shannon Jenkins, "State and Local Party Organizations in the 21st Century," paper presented at the 2010 annual meeting of the American Political Science Association, pp. 34–36 (for 2010).

The researchers found that most county organizations were headed by a volunteer party chair and executive committee; almost none received salaries for their efforts, and only a few had a paid staff to assist them. Not many of these local party leaders had even the most basic forms of organizational support, such as a regular budget, a year-round office, or a listing in the phone book. Most did meet regularly, had formal rules to govern their work, and, together with a few other activists, raised funds and sought out and screened candidates. However, their activity was not constant; it peaked during campaigns.

Democratic local parties didn't differ much from Republican local parties in terms of the overall strength of their organizations during the 1970s. States differed a great deal, however, in the organizational strength of their local parties. Some states in the East and Midwest had relatively strong local organizations in both parties, while others—Louisiana, Georgia, Alabama, Kentucky, Texas, and Nebraska—had weak parties at the county level. In a few states, such as Arizona and Florida, one party was considerably stronger than the other party at the local level. Most often, strong organizations of one party were matched with strong organizations in the other party.[15]

There is persuasive evidence, however, that the county party organizations in 1980 were in the middle of a growth spurt. In a 1980 survey, by asking county party chairs about the changes in their parties since 1964, researchers found that, on average, local parties had become much more involved in the nuts-and-bolts activities of registering voters, raising money, and publicizing candidates. When the researchers checked in again with these county organizations in 1984, they saw further development, and a national survey in 1988 indicated even higher levels of local party activity.[16]

Local Parties Today: More Active, More Structured

Local parties have continued to develop as structured organizations, though they still depend on unpaid volunteer activists to accomplish their goals. Especially in urban areas, more county parties had the basic ingredients for a viable party organization (a permanent office, a budget, a telephone listing, a staff) in 2010 than had been the case in 1980.[17] Most of these county parties report that they organize campaign activities, run voter registration and canvassing drives, contact voters by phone, and distribute lawn signs and posters; and again, more local parties report conducting most of these activities now than they did in 1980. In particular, the county parties are increasing their use of Web sites and e-mail as well as free social media such as Twitter and Facebook.

Other forms of campaigning, such as using public opinion polls and buying radio or TV time for candidates, are less common. Not very many of these local parties put a priority on mobilizing young voters.[18] Relatively few county parties are active year-round, raising funds and holding events at times when no campaigns are going on. Nevertheless, it seems clear that more local parties have been energized and are providing choices to voters.

Michigan's Democratic Party provides an example of this increase in party organizational strength. Michigan Democrats, long the minority party, were in sorry shape for the first half of the 1900s, after machine politics had faded. By the end of the 1940s, more than half of the state's counties had no Democratic county committees. Then, labor unions, led by the United Auto Workers, stepped in to bring volunteer and financial support to the Democrats. Within two years, there was a Democratic Party organization in almost every county in the state. After internal conflicts took their toll in both parties during the 1960s and 1970s, organized labor moved again to rebuild the Democratic organization. By the late 1990s, the great majority of local Democratic Parties were raising money and contributing to candidates, buying ads, and distributing literature. The county organizations have now become the backbone of the state Democratic Party.[19]

Local party leaders in many areas of the country have recently stepped up their efforts regarding absentee and early voting. By 2008, most states had relaxed their requirements for casting an absentee ballot. Large numbers of registered voters can now vote by mail or in person before Election Day. To take advantage of these changes, many local parties—those in Washington state, for example—now mail absentee ballot requests to all known party voters. By working to "bank" as many loyalists' votes as possible, the party organization can protect itself against last-minute campaign surprises or Election Day thunderstorms that might depress the party vote. Local parties can spread their GOTV efforts over several weeks and then focus their Election Day activities on mobilizing less involved voters. The downside is that because absentee voting is much harder to monitor than voting at the polls, parties need to find ways to keep the other party from delivering absentee ballots that have been filled out illegally or with "help" from overzealous party workers.

Local parties are also expanding their efforts to recruit candidates.[20] One study found that more than a third of people regarded as potentially strong candidates for Congress in 1998 had in fact been contacted by local party leaders and that those contacted were more likely to run.[21] In another study, almost half of all state legislative candidates reported that local party leaders had encouraged them to run.[22] County party leaders can improve their chances of recruiting candidates when, as in Ohio, they can endorse candidates in primaries and fill vacancies in elections. Keep in mind, however, that it is not yet clear whether being recruited by a local party organization, as opposed to being a "self-starter," helps a candidate win the general election.

In sum, we have good evidence that county party organizations are stronger and more active now than they were a generation ago. It is harder to determine whether county parties now are as effective organizationally as were the old city machines, because there are so few reliable records prior to the 1960s. But it is possible that many counties now have more robust party organizations than they have ever had.

At the same time, however, the nature of the local parties has changed. From organizations that once were at the very center of election activity, county parties have become service providers to candidates who often have several other sources of help. So the challenge for the local parties is this: In an age of largely candidate-centered campaigns, does this growing county organizational presence matter as much as it would have a few decades ago?[23]

THE STATE PARTIES: GAINING MONEY AND SERVICES

State parties have been the poor relations of American party politics. Throughout the parties' history, the state committees rarely had significant power within the party organizations. There have been exceptions; some powerful, patronage-rich state party organizations developed in the industrial heartland in the late 1800s.[24] But in most states, most of the time, the state committee was the weak link in the party organization.

In recent years, however, state parties have grown in importance. They are richer, more professional, and more active now than they have ever been before. There has been some centralization of activity throughout the party structure. Let us start the story in the years before this change began.

Traditional Weakness

State party organizations were traditionally weak for several reasons. They began as loose federations of semi-independent local party chairs. These local parties within a state differed from one another in many ways: rural/ urban, regional, ethnic, and religious differences, loyalties to local leaders, and conflicts between more liberal and more conservative interests. If one of these factions gained control over the state party organization, the others would be seriously threatened. So this threat was often avoided, in the past, by keeping most of the party's resources out of the hands of the state organization. Power was decentralized, collecting in the most effective of the local organizations.

Progressive reforms in the early 1900s also weakened the state party organizations. In particular, the introduction of the direct primary (see Chapters 9 and 10) limited the influence of state parties on campaigns for state offices. Candidates could win party nominations in primary elections without party organization support, raise money for their own campaigns and, thus, run them without party help. Even today, relatively weak state party organizations are still found in the states where the Progressives and Populists had greatest strength—the western states, especially the more rural ones.[25]

Beginning in the late 1960s, the national Democratic Party adopted reforms that greatly increased the number of primaries in the presidential nominating process. That reduced the state party's role in selecting a presidential candidate. The voters, rather than the state party organization, choose most convention delegates now, and most of the delegates come to the convention pledged to a particular candidate rather than controlled by state party leaders. Further, extensions of civil service protections and unionization eroded the patronage base for many state parties. In what may have been the final indignity for patronage politics, some courts have even prevented the firing of patronage workers when the governing party changes.

One-party dominance in several states during the first half of the 1900s also kept a number of state parties weak and conflict-ridden. Southern Democratic Parties were a notable example. When a single party dominates a state's politics, the diverse forces within the state are likely to compete as factions within that party; the state party organization has neither the incentive nor the ability to unify, as it might if it faced a threat from a viable opposition party. For all these reasons, many state party organizations were described as "empty shells" in the 1940s and 1950s.[26]

Increasing Strength in Recent Decades

Since the 1960s, however, state party organizations have become stronger and more active. The state parties began to institutionalize—to become enduring, specialized, well-bounded organizations—during the 1960s and 1970s. In the early 1960s, for example, only half of a sample of state organizations had permanent state headquarters; two decades later, by 1980, that was true of 91 percent. The number of full-time, paid state party chairs doubled during this time, as did the number of full-time staff employed by the parties in non-election years. These resources—full-time leaders and a stable location—are vital to the development of parties as organizations.[27]

As with local parties, the state organizations have continued to expand since then. More than half of the state parties surveyed in a 1999 study had full-time party chairs, research staff, and public relations directors. Three-quarters had a field staff, and 91 percent employed a full-time executive director, perhaps the most crucial position in a state party organization. A number of state parties have created internship programs for college students. In California, the Republican Party set up a task force in 2009 to apply leading-edge technologies, including the next generation of computer applications that will come after Facebook, Twitter, and YouTube, to all aspects of party work. The empty shells are being filled.

Fund-raising   State parties have put special effort into developing fund-raising capabilities. By 2000 (see Table 3.2), almost all of the state parties surveyed raised money at events and by direct mail. They used the money to support a variety of races; party candidates for governor, state legislature, and the U.S. Senate and House received contributions from more than four-fifths of these parties. Over 90 percent of the parties made efforts to recruit candidates for state races; the parties' new fund-raising skills can be very useful in convincing attractive prospects to run for an office.[28]

The parties are especially active in recruiting and helping fund candidates for the state legislature.[29] These state legislative candidates rely on various levels of party committees for different kinds of help. State legislative parties' campaign committees[30] often recruit and train candidates and provide fund-raising support, advice on consultants, and liaison with political action committees, whereas the local parties are thought to be more helpful in traditional grassroots activities such as GOTV drives.[31]

The increase in state parties' election-year fund-raising since 1980 fairly leaps off the page in Table 3.2. National party committees played an important role by transferring increasing amounts to the state parties and candidates. The transfers peaked in 2000, when the national party organizations gave a whopping $430 million to parties and candidates at the state level, many times the amounts that the national parties had infused into the state organizations just a few years earlier.[32] Collectively, the state parties were able to spend $53 million raised in large sums, called "soft money" (see Chapter 12), on voter mobilization and GOTV activity in the 2000 campaigns.[33]

Just as important for the development of strong party organizations, fund-raising during nonelection years was growing as well. The nonelection-year budgets of the state parties climbed from an average (in absolute dollars) of less than $200,000 in 1960–1964 to more than $800,000 by 2000. The result is that at that time "most state parties are multimillion-dollar organizations with experienced executive directors and knowledgeable staffs."[34]

TABLE 3.2

Increasing Organizational Strength Among the State Parties

Party Strength and Activity	1979–1980	1999–2000	Difference
Typical election-year budget	$340 K	$2.8 mil.	+$2.46 mil.
Typical election-year full-time staff	7.7	9.2	+1.5
Off-year budget	$337 K	$812 K*	+$475 K
Off-year staff	7.2	7.6*	+0.4
Conducted campaign seminars	89%	95%	+6%
Recruited a full slate of candidates	—	91%	—
Operated voter ID programs	70%	94%	+24%
Conducted public opinion polls	32%	78%	+46%
Held fund-raising event	19%	98%	+79%
Contributed to governor candidate	47%	89%	+42%
Contributed to state legislator	47%	92%	+45%
Contributed to state senator	25%	85%	+60%
Contributed to U.S. congressional	48%	85%	+37%
Contributed to local candidate	—	70%	—

Note: Data for 1979–1980 are from a mail survey of state parties. Data for 1999 come from a mail survey by John H. Aldrich and associates of 65 state party chairs (39 Democrats, 26 Republicans), and data for 2000 from a mail survey by Raymond La Raja of 37 Republican and 37 Democratic state party executive directors.

*Data from La Raja's 2000 survey.

Sources: For the 1999 data, see John H. Aldrich's "Southern Parties in State and Nation," *Journal of Politics* 62 (2000): 659. For 2000, see Raymond J. La Raja, "State Parties and Soft Money," in John C. Green and Rick Farmer, eds., *The State of the Parties,* 4th ed. (Lanham, MD: Rowman & Littlefield, 2003), p. 141. The 1979–1980 data are from James L. Gibson, Cornelius P. Cotter, and John F. Bibby, "Assessing Party Organizational Strength," *American Journal of Political Science* 27 (1983): 193–222.

Passage of new campaign finance legislation in 2002 (the Bipartisan Campaign Reform Act, or BCRA, discussed in Chapter 12) took away the national parties' ability to transfer soft money to the state parties. Although that was a blow to the state parties' finances, BCRA did allow state parties to spend federally regulated money (which the national parties could transfer to states without limits) on federal campaign activities and to raise a certain amount of soft money themselves (up to $10,000 per donor) for grassroots mobilization and party-building. These, added to the high stakes of polarized politics, helped the state parties to maintain active fund-raising. In 2003, after the end of the soft money transfers, state Democratic and Republican Parties raised a total of $189 million—more than they had in 2001.[35] Since that time, collective state party receipts and media buys by state parties have not matched their pre-BCRA levels, but party spending in some states, including Missouri and Indiana, has gone up considerably. State parties, then, have become more effective fund-raisers and most have learned to cope with the BCRA reform rules.

Campaign Services To run a competitive campaign, state legislative and statewide candidates need consultants, voter lists, and computers, and they often turn to the state party organizations to provide these services. With their increased organizational resources, the state parties have been able to comply. All the parties surveyed in a study by John H. Aldrich operated voter identification programs to determine which voters were most likely to support their party's candidates and took part in GOTV drives. Most provided campaign training seminars, and almost four-fifths conducted public opinion polls in the late 1990s.[36] Since then, however, the BCRA rules have limited state parties' ability to run coordinated campaigns, in which a variety of candidates share campaign services.

Republican Advantage Unlike the situation at the county level, Republican state organizations are stronger than their Democratic counterparts. The Republican parties surveyed by Aldrich had much larger budgets and bigger and more specialized staffs. Because they are bigger and richer, they can provide more services to their candidates. For example, Republican state parties have been more likely to conduct polls, employ field staff and researchers, and contribute to local parties than the Democrats are.[37]

But Democratic state parties are catching up. Howard Dean was elected Democratic National Chairman in 2005 by promising state party chairs that he would give every state, not just the closely-fought "battleground states," enough resources to hire at least three or four field organizers and access to a party database of voters. Many of the party's Washington-based consultants opposed this "50-state strategy," asking why an increase in the party staffs in small states would help Democrats nationally. But after major Democratic gains in the 2006 and 2008 elections, Dean's expensive efforts to build strong state parties were acclaimed by some as "visionary."[38] (For more on this program, see Chapter 4.)

Allied Groups Labor unions, especially teachers' and government employees' unions, have worked closely with their state Democratic Party organizations to provide money, volunteers, and other services to party candidates. For 15 years, for instance, the New Jersey A.F.L.-C.I.O. has run a "boot camp" training program for first-time legislative and local candidates, most of them Democrats, to help them with fund-raising, media, and messages, and, then, campaign support. State Republican Parties have close ties to allied groups as well. Small business groups, manufacturing associations, pro-life groups, and Christian conservative organizations often provide services to Republican candidates. As the state parties gain strength, these constituency groups often try to increase their influence on, or even take over, state party organizations. Christian Right and Tea Party groups, in particular, have come to dominate or have substantial influence on a majority of state Republican Parties (see box "How to Take Over a State Party Organization" on page 65).[39]

Because of the close association between parties and activists from these allied groups, it is possible to think of the parties as networks of organizations, which include the interest groups, consulting firms, and "think tanks" (research groups) that offer their resources and expertise to a party.[40] For party leaders, these allied groups can be a mixed blessing, of course; labor unions and religious groups have their own agendas, and they can be as likely to try to push the party into locally unpopular stands as to help elect party candidates.

How to Take Over a State Party Organization

Just as groups of evangelical Christians worked to dominate several state Republican Party organizations during the 1990s, Tea Party supporters tried to do the same in 2010. In Michigan, the local party meetings that elect delegates to the state Republican convention are normally poorly attended. So when Tea Party activists flooded these local meetings, they were able to elect about 20 percent of all the state convention delegates. At the convention, they succeeded in influencing the state party platform and the selection of some statewide candidates. In Maine, a group of Republican delegates with Tea Party connections, frustrated with the moderation they saw in the state Republican organization, changed the party platform to include Tea Party stands such as eliminating the U.S. Department of Education and the Federal Reserve and calling for an investigation of "collusion between government and industry in the global warming myth." A coalition including Tea Party supporters in the Idaho Republican convention passed a platform that recommended ending the public election of U.S. Senators. A Michigan Tea Party activist explained, "This is about wrestling with the very devil himself, if we have to, for the soul of the Republican Party."

These events demonstrate that the state and local party organizations are *permeable*. Party organization officials are usually elected by party activists and the volunteers they recruit. So groups within (or even outside of) the party structure can take over the party organization if they can gather sufficient numbers to win party elections. In fact, Tea Party and other conservative activists created the National Precinct Alliance to urge like-minded people to become Republican local activists for just this purpose.

Sources: Kathy Barks Hoffman, "Michigan Tea Partiers Launch Surprise Push," August 26, 2010, at news.yahoo.com/s/ap/20100826/ap_on_re_us/us_tea_party_clout (accessed August 27, 2010); Colin Woodard, " 'Tea Party'-backed Platform Sails Through Maine GOP Convention," *Christian Science Monitor*, May 10, 2010, at www.csmonitor.com/USA/Politics/2010/0510/Tea-party-backed-platform-sails-through-Maine-GOP-convention" (accessed March 21, 2011).

It is not easy to build a powerful state party organization. It requires having to overcome the localism of American politics, widespread hostility toward party discipline, and conflicts among party supporters. Strong and skillful personal leadership by a governor, a senator, or a state chairman helps.[41] So does a state tradition that accepts the notion of a unified and effective party. State law makes a difference as well. More centralized party organization has flourished in states that make less use of primary elections, so the party organization has more control over who the statewide and congressional candidates will be.

The Special Case of the South The most striking instances of party organizational development have occurred in the formerly one-party Democratic South. As the national Democratic Party showed greater concern for the rights of African Americans in the 1960s and 1970s, and particularly as the Voting Rights Acts increased the proportion of African American voters in southern states, conservative southern Democrats became increasingly estranged from their national party. Southern whites support for Republican candidates grew, first in presidential elections, later in statewide and U.S. Senate races (as you will see in Chapter 7).

In the 1980s, state legislative candidates could sense the opportunity to run and win as Republicans. By 1994, Republicans were contesting as many as one-third of the state legislative seats in the South and winning two-thirds of the seats they contested. Since 1994, Republicans have won the governorship of all but one southern state at least once, as well as a majority in at least one house of the state legislature in most of these states. Republicans are now surpassing Democrats in state elections—this in a region where, just a few decades before, it was often more socially acceptable to admit to having an alcoholic than a Republican in the family.[42]

Along with these electoral gains, southern Republican Parties grew stronger organizationally. North Carolina's state Republican Party, for example, was only minimally organized in the early 1970s. It started in earnest to recruit state legislative candidates during the mid-1980s. By the 1990s, with a much expanded budget and staff, the party focused on attracting experienced candidates for targeted districts, producing direct mail and radio ads, and helping candidates with training and research. Even the Florida Republicans, still not very strong organizationally, have come a long way since the years when state party chairs had "portable offices" in their homes or businesses.[43] Democrats have had to respond, so the strength of both parties' organizations has been increasing since the 1990s.[44] Southern parties, long among the weakest and most faction ridden, have become some of the strongest state party organizations in the past two decades.[45]

National Party Money An important ingredient in strengthening the state party organizations has been the national parties' party-building efforts. The full story of these efforts is told in Chapter 4, but the central point is that the national parties, with more energetic leadership and more lavish financial resources than ever before, infused a great deal of money into the state parties, and at least some of the money was directed toward helping build the state parties' organizational capacity. State parties have also become effective fundraisers in their own right, and the BCRA rules have spurred them into finding new ways to support themselves. Thus, the state parties, so recently the poor relations of the party organizations, have come into money.

SUMMING UP: HOW THE STATE AND LOCAL PARTY ORGANIZATIONS HAVE TRANSFORMED

There have been dramatic changes in party organizational strength at the state and local levels. The high point of *local* party organizations may have been reached a hundred years ago, when some parties could be described as "armies drawn up for combat" with an "elaborate, well-staffed, and strongly motivated organizational structure."[46] Although this description did not apply to party organizations throughout the nation even then, it would be hard to find a local party organization that could be described in these terms today.

Local parties were buffeted by a variety of forces since then. Progressive reforms adopted in the early 1900s undermined party organizations by limiting their control over nominations and general elections as well as their valued patronage resources. A number of other factors—federal social service programs, economic growth, a more educated electorate, and even racial conflict—also undercut the effectiveness of the local parties.[47]

Yet local parties have come a long way toward adapting to these changes. County parties have moved to fill at least some of the void created by the decline of the urban machines. New technologies such as Web sites and social networking are enabling these county parties to expand their activities. Local party organizations, in short, are demonstrating again their ability to meet the new challenges posed by a changing environment—a resilience that has kept them alive throughout most of American history.

The state party organizations have followed a different route. Traditionally weak in all but a handful of states, state party organizations have grown much more robust and professional in recent years. They are providing campaign and organizational services to candidates who, in an earlier era, would not have dreamed of looking to their state headquarters for help. In fact, the recent flow of money, resources, and leadership from the national party to the state party, and in turn from the state to the local parties, helped to modify the traditional flow of party power. Through most of their lives, the American parties have been highly decentralized, with power and influence lodged at the grassroots. The parties were hollow at the top, depending on the base for whatever influence and resources they had. Because of the death of urban machines and the birth of vigorous state and national party organizations, we no longer see this extreme form of decentralization. The nationalization of American society and politics has affected the party organizations as well, leading to a greater balance of power among party organizations at different levels.

Yet ironically, although they are much stronger now, the state and local party organizations probably have less impact on our politics than they once did. One reason is that they have much more competition for the attention of voters, candidates, and the media. The campaign communications sent out by the parties merge into a flood of Internet, television, and direct mail fund-raising and advertising by citizen groups, corporate and labor political action committees, and nonprofit groups, all of whom try to influence voters' choices. Many of these groups encourage individuals to run for office. They can offer candidates money and a means to reach voters independent of the party organization. They have campaign expertise rivaling that of the party's experts.

Second, although most state parties have become better able to raise funds, the party's resources are still dwarfed by those of other actors in elections. In state legislative campaigns, for example, this new party money has accounted for only a small fraction of the funds received by most candidates. Campaigners are happy for every dollar, of course, but these relatively small sums, even with the helpful services that accompany them, may not be enough to entice candidates to listen carefully to the party on legislative matters or any other concerns.

So the increasing organizational strength of the state and local parties has helped them adopt modern campaign skills and recapture a role in candidates' campaigns. However, it is not a *dominant* role—not in the way it could have been if party organizations, rather than voters in primaries, selected party candidates. Party organizations rarely *run* the campaigns; instead, their new resources give them more of a chance to compete for the attention of those who do—the candidates—at a time when other competitors (organized interests, consultants, and others) have become more effective as well.

Does this mean that the increases in party organizational strength are unimportant? Not at all. In a very competitive political environment, there is little doubt that it is better to have a stronger organization than a weaker one and to have more resources rather than fewer. In the end, however, despite all the changes in party organization during the past few decades, their most basic structural features have not changed. The American state and local parties remain cadre organizations run by a small number of activists; they involve the bulk of their supporters mainly at election time. By the standards of parties in other democratic nations, American state and local party organizations are still weaker—more limited in their activities and authority and more easily dominated by a handful of activists and elected officials. But by the standards of American politics, the state and local organizations are more visible and active than they have been in some time.

The Parties' National Organizations

S everal decades ago, the national organizations of both major parties were like many college students: chronically short of cash and searching for new housing. Their small staffs moved back and forth between New York and Washington, and their activity was visible mainly during presidential campaigns. Leading students of the national committees could accurately describe them as "politics without power."[1] The real power in the party system was decentralized, collected in the local party organizations.

There is good reason why the parties have long been decentralized, as Chapter 3 indicated. Almost all American public officials are chosen in state and local elections; even the voting for president is conducted mainly under state election laws. In years past, most of the incentives parties had to offer, such as patronage jobs, were available at the state and local levels, and the state governments have been the chief regulators of parties. All these forces have given the parties a powerful state and local focus that can restrain any centralization within the party organizations. So state and local party organizations have chosen their own officers, taken their own stands on issues, and raised and spent their own funds, usually without much interference from the national party.

In recent years, however, both parties have responded to the powerful nationalizing forces that have affected most other aspects of American politics. Since the 1970s, the two parties have reacted to a series of challenges by strengthening their national committees. Their resources and staffs have grown; both the Democratic National Committee (DNC) and Republican National Committee (RNC) are now multimillion-dollar fund-raising and candidate-support operations. They have taken on new activities and influence, and the Democrats have limited the independence of state and local organizations in selecting delegates to the parties' national conventions.

The change has been remarkable. Only in the earliest years of the American parties, when presidential candidates were nominated by congressional caucuses, were the national parties as important in American politics. Although the local pull remains strong, the distribution of power among the national, state, and local parties is now more balanced than ever before. This chapter will examine the effects of this increase in national party power.

THE NATIONAL PARTIES

What is the national party? Officially, each major party's supreme national authority is the *national convention* it holds every four years to nominate a presidential candidate. However, the convention rarely does more than to select the presidential and vice-presidential nominees and approve the party's platform and rules. Between conventions, the two parties' main governing bodies are their national committees.

The National Committees

Each party's *national committee* is a gathering of representatives from all its state parties; its leaders run the national party on a daily basis. Their main focus is to help elect the party's presidential candidate. They also distribute polls and policy information, work with state parties, and assist in other races by recruiting and training candidates and helping them raise money. Both national committees have a long history: The Democrats created theirs in 1848 and the Republicans in 1856. For years, every state (and some territories, such as Samoa and Guam) was represented equally on both national committees, regardless of the size of its voting population or the extent of its party support. California and Wyoming, then, had equal-sized delegations to the national party committees, just as they do in the U.S. Senate, even though California has a population of about 37 million and Wyoming's is about 550,000. That system overrepresented the smaller states and also gave roughly equal weight in the national committees to the winning and the losing parts of the party. In practice, this strengthened the southern and western segments of each party, which tended to be more conservative.

Since 1972, when the Democrats revised the makeup of their national committee, the parties have structured their committees differently. After briefly experimenting with unequal state representation in the 1950s, the Republicans have kept their traditional confederational structure by giving each of the state and territorial parties three seats on the RNC. In contrast, the DNC, now almost three times the size of its Republican counterpart, gives weight both to population and to party support in representing the states. California, for example, has 21 seats on the DNC, and Wyoming has 4. This change reduced the influence of conservatives and moderates within the DNC.

The two national committees also differ in that the Democrats give national committee seats to representatives of groups especially likely to support Democratic candidates, such as blacks, women, and labor unions—a decision that shows the importance of these groups to the party—as well as to associations of elected officials, such as the National Conference of Democratic Mayors. National committee members in both parties are chosen by the state parties and, for the Democrats, by these other groups as well.

National Party Chairs

The national committee's chair and the staff he or she chooses are the heart of the national party organization. Members of the full national committees come together only two or three times a year, mainly to call media attention to the party and its candidates. Officially, the national committees have the power to select their own leaders. By tradition, however, a party's presidential candidate can name his or her party's national chair for the duration of the presidential campaign, and the committee ratifies this choice without question. The national chair chosen by the winning presidential candidate usually keeps his or her job after the election, at least until the president picks someone else. Thus, in practice, only the "out" party's national committee actually selects its own chair.[2] In both parties, fund-raising is the chair's most important job (see box "Show them the Money" on this page).

Show Them the Money

The main responsibilities of a national party chair are to raise lots of money for the party and build or maintain an effective campaign apparatus. Michael Steele, the first black Republican National Committee chair (2009–2011), served during a period of exceptional election success for Republicans. But that wasn't enough to make up for Steele's weakness in fund-raising. He raised much less money than had previous RNC chairs and burned through those funds quickly with lavish spending, raising charges of mismanagement. He also alarmed party activists by criticizing Rush Limbaugh, expressing pro-choice views (in opposition to his party's platform), and stepping on congressional party leaders' toes. Several of the RNC's biggest donors warned that they would not keep raising money if Steele continued in office. So when Steele campaigned for a second two-year term in 2011, the RNC said no. Reince Priebus, the former Wisconsin Republican chair, was elected instead. His first challenge was to pay off the $24 million debt the RNC had incurred under Steele's leadership. Priebus understood his mandate; he raised $3.5 million in his first two weeks on the job and promised to focus on rebuilding relationships with major donors.

Priebus's counterpart at the Democratic National Committee was former Virginia Governor Tim Kaine, a close associate of President Obama, who appointed him to the post. Kaine's tenure earned better reviews than Steele's; he traveled frequently and held fund-raisers in most states. Although he was criticized by some for his unwillingness to go on the attack, his cooperative style helped to smooth relationships when the Obama grassroots campaign organization, "Obama for America," was renamed "Organizing for America" (OFA) and moved into the DNC. Some state party leaders worried that OFA would operate independently of the state party structure, but Kaine managed a fairly peaceful transition, in which the DNC took on many of the characteristics of OFA. Kaine resigned in 2011 to run for an open U.S. Senate seat, and Obama appointed U.S. House member Debbie Wasserman Schultz, a highly skilled fund-raiser, to replace him.

Sources: See Jeff Zeleny, "G.O.P. Elects a New Chairman as Steele Drops Out," *New York Times*, January 15, 2011, p. A1; and Ben Smith, "Tim Kaine," *Politico*, October 26, 2010, at http://hamptonroads.com/2010/10/tim-kaine-dnc-chair-nice-guy-nasty-time (accessed March 22, 2011).

Presidents and Their National Parties

Presidents came to dominate their national committees early in the twentieth century and especially since the 1960s. In the president's party, then, the national committee's role is whatever the president wants it to be. James W. Ceaser cites the example of Robert Dole, RNC chair from 1971 to 1973, who was quickly fired by the president when Dole tried to put a little distance between the party and the president's involvement in the Watergate scandal: "I had a nice chat with the President ... while the other fellows went out to get the rope."[3] Some presidents have turned their national committees into little more than managers of the president's campaigns and builders of the president's political support between campaigns. Other presidents, such as George W. Bush, have used their control to build up the national committee to achieve party, not just presidential, goals.

When their party does not hold the presidency, the national party chair and committee have the freedom to play a more independent role in national politics. At these times, the "out" party's national chair becomes one of several people (including past presidential nominees and congressional leaders) who may speak for the party and its policies. He or she will also need to help pay any debts from the losing presidential campaign, energize the party organization around the country, and—always of prime importance—raise as much new money as possible for the party.

Because of changes in campaign finance rules (see Chapter 12), the national committee has had to work separately from the presidential candidate's own campaign organization in presidential elections. To play this more autonomous role, national chairs have recruited staffers with extensive experience in raising money, managing databases, and mobilizing organizers and grassroots supporters.

OTHER NATIONAL PARTY GROUPS

Several other party organizations are normally included in the term "the national party," even though they work independently of one another and often compete for donors, resources, and other sources of power.

Congressional Campaign ("Hill") Committees

The most important of these related groups are each party's *House and Senate campaign committees*, called the *"Hill committees"* (because Congress is located on Capitol Hill) or the CCCs (Congressional Campaign Committees). The House committees were founded in the immediate aftermath of the Civil War; the Senate committees came into being when senators began to be popularly elected in 1913. The Democratic Congressional Campaign Committee (DCCC) and the National Republican Congressional Committee (NRCC) are concerned entirely with House elections, and the Democratic Senatorial Campaign Committee (DSCC) and the National Republican Senatorial Committee (NRSC) fund Senate races.

Although incumbent House and Senate members control these committees, they have resisted pressures to work only on behalf of incumbents' campaigns; they also support their party's candidates for open seats and challengers who have a good chance of winning. In short, they concentrate their money where they think they are likely to get the biggest payoff in increasing their party's representation in Congress. During the past four decades, the Hill committees have developed major fund-raising and service functions, independent of the DNC and RNC. They provide party candidates with a wide range of campaign help, from get-out-the-vote (GOTV) efforts to hard cash (see box "How to Target a Congressional Campaign" on page 74). For House and Senate candidates, the Hill committees are more influential than their parties' national committees.

Democratic and Republican Governors' Associations

State governors have long had a powerful voice in their national parties, for several reasons. They have won statewide elections for prestigious offices. Many lead or, at least, are supported by their state party organization, and some will be considered potential presidential candidates, such as former governors George W. Bush of Texas, Bill Clinton of Arkansas, Mitt Romney of Massachusetts, and Ronald Reagan of California. Governors' organizational influence in the national parties tends to be greatest, like that of the national committee chair, in the power vacuum that occurs when the other party holds the presidency. The Republican Governors' Association was especially prominent in fund-raising for the 2010 elections, to help make up for the RNC's financial troubles. State party leaders have also recently formed the Republican State Leadership Committee (RSLC) and the Democratic Legislative Campaign Committee (DLCC) in order to help fund state legislative and statewide campaigns. The RSLC made a big splash in 2010, spending $31 million in a coordinated nationwide effort.

Women's and Youth Groups

For a long time, both the Democrats and Republicans have had women's divisions associated with their national committees.[4] The importance of these women's divisions has declined markedly in recent decades as women have entered regular leadership positions in the parties.

On campuses, the College Republican National Committee (the CRs) and the College Democrats (whose Web log or "blog" is named Smart Ass, in honor of the party's donkey mascot) have experienced big increases in membership and numbers of chapters in the 2000s. Both these groups train field representatives to recruit volunteers for campaigns at all levels. The CRs have been closely associated with a number of conservative nonparty groups. The Young Democrats of America and the Young Republican National Federation also work actively among high school and college students as well as other young adults.

Party Networks

Just as state and local parties do, the national party committees work closely with a network of allied groups. For the Democrats, these include labor unions, environmental, women's rights, and civil rights groups, and other liberal organizations. Organized labor in particular has supplied the volunteer canvassers and callers so vital to Democratic campaigns. The national Republican network includes small business groups, the National Rifle Association, and groups of conservative Christians. In competitive races, these allied groups often run parallel campaigns to those of the candidates—as do the parties themselves—providing independent media ads, canvassing, and other forms of electioneering,[5] as you'll see in Chapter 12. Several other groups outside of the formal party structure act as "idea factories" for the party in government. For the Democrats, the leftist Center for American Progress and the more moderate Progressive Policy Institute and Third Way serve this function. On the Republican side, groups such as the conservative Heritage Foundation and the more libertarian Republican Liberty Caucus try to affect party policy.

How to Target a Congressional Campaign

The parties' Hill committees hope to support all their congressional candidates to at least some degree, but they target a few candidates for much more intensive help. The most important criteria for choosing which campaigns to target are the competitiveness of the district and candidate quality, as measured by the amount of money the candidate has been able to raise (or contribute to his or her own campaign) by June 30 of the election year. Candidates, then, raise money not only to run their campaigns but also to leverage even more money by impressing the party operatives. In giving money directly to candidates, Hill committee targeters also ask, Is the candidate's organization capable of spending the money effectively? Has he/she effectively generated media coverage? How expensive are the district's media? Targeting decisions can change daily as the election approaches, depending on movement in the candidates' poll numbers and on the parties' finances. The Hill committees can offer these services to targeted candidates:

- Candidate recruitment and help with hiring and training campaign staff, choosing consultants, and making strategic decisions
- Development of campaign messages, information about issues, and "oppo" research on the opponent's strengths and weaknesses
- Advice on making effective television and radio ads at low cost (though the production is done mainly by party-related private consultants)
- Commissioning poll data to gauge the campaign's progress and measure responses to particular issues and messages

(continued)

(continued)

- Contributor lists given to selected candidates on the condition that these candidates give their own contributor lists to the party after the election
- Fund-raising events in Washington and party leaders' visits to candidate events, to help candidates raise money and attract votes
- "Hard-money" direct contributions to campaigns*
- "Coordinated spending" to buy polls, media ads, or research for a candidate*
- Independent spending on ads in the candidate's district* and help in raising money from political action committees (PACs), other political groups, and individuals.

*Explained in Chapter 12.

Sources: Paul S. Herrnson, *Congressional Elections*, 5th ed. (Washington, DC: CQ Press, 2008), pp. 90–131; and Victoria A. Farrar-Myers and Diana Dwyre, "Parties and Campaign Finance," in Jeffrey E. Cohen, Richard Fleisher, and Paul Kantor, eds., *American Political Parties: Decline or Resurgence?* (Washington, DC: CQ Press, 2001), pp. 143–146.

TWO PATHS TO POWER

The national parties have traveled two different roads to reach these new levels of effectiveness. The Republicans have followed a service path by building a muscular fund-raising operation that pays for needed services to their candidates and state parties. The Democrats, in contrast, first followed a procedural path, strengthening their national party's authority over the state parties in the selection of a presidential nominee.

The central element in both national parties' continued development, however, was their ability to attract thousands of small contributions through mass mailings to likely party supporters. This gave the national parties, which formerly depended on assessments provided by the state parties, an independent financial base. Ironically, then, at a time when some were warning that the parties were in decline, the national party organizations were reaching levels of strength that had never been seen before in American politics.

The Service Party Path

A party organization that supports campaigns with money and other help, as opposed to running the campaigns itself, can be thought of as a *"service party."* The foundation for a service party was laid during the 1960s, when RNC Chair Ray Bliss involved the committee to a much greater degree in helping state and local parties with the practical aspects of party organizational work. Chair William Brock continued this effort in the mid- to late 1970s as a means of reviving the party's election prospects after the Republican losses of the post-Watergate years. Under Brock, the RNC helped to provide salaries for the executive directors of all 50 state Republican Parties; offered expert assistance to the state parties in organizing, strategizing, and fund-raising; and contributed to more than 4,000 state legislative candidates. Bliss and Brock fashioned a new role for the RNC by making it into an exceptionally effective service organization for the state and local parties.[6]

There were two keys to success in performing this new service role: money and campaign technologies. Using a marketing innovation of that time, computer-generated mailing lists, the Republicans began a program of direct-mail appeals that brought in ever-higher levels of income. The RNC's fund-raising jumped from $29 million in 1975–1976 to $105.9 million in "hard money" (contributions regulated by federal law; the terms *hard money* and *soft money* are explained in Chapter 12) in 1983–1984—a record for national committee fund-raising that wasn't broken until 1995 (see Table A.1 in the online Appendix at www.pearson.com/hershey). The RNC used the money, as Bliss and Brock had, to offer a broad array of services to candidates and state and local party organizations, including candidate recruitment and training, research, public opinion polling, data processing, computer networking and software development, production of radio and television ads, direct mailing, and legal services. State party leaders were glad to accept the help; as the party more closely identified with the business community, Republicans felt comfortable with these marketing techniques.

The Democrats' Procedural-Reform Path

At about the same time, Democrats expanded the power of their national party organization for other reasons. Reformers supporting the civil rights movement and opposing American involvement in the Vietnam War pressed for change in the Democratic Party's positions on these issues. The reformers focused on the rules for selecting presidential candidates. Their aim was to make the nominating process more open and democratic and, in particular, more representative of the concerns of people like themselves: blacks, women, and young people.

The reforms started in the mid-1960s with efforts to keep southern Democratic Parties from sending all-white delegations to the national convention and excluding blacks from participation. After the 1968 election, the first of a series of reform commissions overhauled the party's presidential nominating process. (This story is told in more detail in Chapter 10.) The Democrats limited the autonomy of the state parties and the authority of state law in determining how convention delegates were to be selected, thus giving the national party the authority over the rules for nominating a presidential candidate.[7] Key court decisions upheld these actions, further solidifying the newfound power of the national party.

This change was limited to the Democrats, however. Republican leaders, consistent with their party's commitment to states' rights, did not want to centralize power in their own party organization.[8] Yet the GOP was still affected by the tide of Democratic Party reform because the bills passed by state legislatures to implement the reforms usually applied to both parties.

In the early 1980s, the Democrats took stock of the reforms and did not like what they saw. The newly centralized authority in nominating a presidential candidate and increased grassroots participation in the nominating process had done little to win elections. Further, it had divided the party and alienated much of the Democratic Party in government, many of whom stayed home from party conventions in the 1970s. Therefore, the national Democrats decided to soft-pedal procedural reforms and move toward the Republican service model. The party rushed to broaden the base of its fund-raising and to help recruit candidates and revitalize state and local party organizations. When the dust from all this effort settled, authority over party rules had become more nationalized, and what had been two models for strengthening the national party were rapidly converging into one.[9]

Both Parties Take the Service Path

The good news for the Democrats in the 1980s was that they were dramatically improving their fund-raising, reducing their long-standing debt, and increasing their activities in the states and localities. The bad news was that the Republicans were far ahead of them to begin with and were continuing to break new ground. The national Democrats made no secret of their effort to imitate the Republican success in raising money and using it to buy services. Slowly, they began to catch up; what began as a three-to-one and even five-to-one financial advantage for the Republicans was reduced over time (see Figure 4.1).

One reason was the Democratic Party's increasing reliance on "soft money" (see Chapter 12)—funds donated to party organizations in unlimited amounts, most often by labor unions, businesses, and wealthy individuals, and exempted from federal campaign finance rules. Big contributions from labor unions made it easier for the Democrats to compete with Republicans in soft money than they could in raising federally regulated donations. Both national parties' committees began major efforts to solicit soft money in the early 1990s. In 2000, the national Republicans established the "Republican Regents" program for individuals and corporations who gave at least $250,000 in soft money to the party during a two-year period, which helped produce record soft-money donations. The Democratic "Jefferson Trust" honored givers of at least $100,000. By that year, almost half of the national parties' fund-raising came in the form of soft money.

Some of the money went into building up the state and even the local parties. A much larger portion of the national parties' money went into races for the U.S. House and Senate. Since the mid-1980s, both parties provided increasing amounts of aid to selected candidates. The Republican committees opened an early lead; the stunning success of GOP candidates in the 1994 congressional elections, for example, was due in part to aggressive fund-raising as well as candidate recruitment by their Hill committees.

Campaign finance reform adopted in 2002 (the Bipartisan Campaign Reform Act, or BCRA, discussed in Chapter 12) barred the national committees from collecting soft money after the 2002 elections. The Democrats

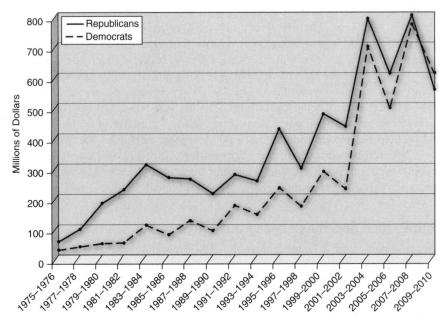

Ratio of Republican to Democratic Receipts:
2.9 3.2 4.6 5.5 3.0 3.9 2.1 2.4 1.5 1.8 1.9 1.8 1.7 2.0 1.1 1.2 1.0 –0.9

FIGURE 4.1
Democratic and Republican Fund-Raising, 1975–1976 to 2009–2010.

Note: The data points are total party receipts (including state/local, House, Senate, and national committees) in millions of dollars. Soft money is not included, nor is money (after 1987) transferred among committees. Table A.1 in the online Appendix (at www.pearson.com/hershey) provides a breakdown of these totals by type of party committee within each party.

Source: Federal Election Commission, at www.fec.gov/press/2010_Full_summary_Data.shtml (accessed July 6, 2011).

saw the coming ban on national party soft money as a particular threat because their soft-money collections had been flourishing—the Democratic Hill committees outraised their Republican counterparts in soft money by $151 million to $136 million in 2002—but their federally regulated contributions had expanded only gradually.

Rising to the Challenge of New Campaign Finance Rules

Once the BCRA rules came into effect in the 2004 campaigns, many observers felt that the loss of soft money would seriously weaken the national parties. In fact, the transfers of money from national party committees to state and local parties dropped markedly in most states, because BCRA allowed the transfer of federally regulated money only. But as they have so often in their history, the parties adapted successfully to the new rules.

Who Got the Most National Party Money in 2007–2008 and 2009–2010?

State parties

2007–2008	2009–2010
Ohio Democratic Party $10.3 million	Virginia Republican Party $4.9 million
Florida Democratic Party $10.1 million	Pennsylvania Democratic Party $4.3 million
Florida Republican Party $9.9 million	Florida Democratic Party $3.6 million
Pennsylvania Democratic Party $7.4 million	New Jersey Democratic Party $3.6 million

Senate candidates (including party direct contributions, coordinated spending, and party independent spending)

Jeff Merkley, Oregon Democrat (challenger—won) $12.5 million	Kenneth Buck, Colorado Republican (challenger—lost) $11.4 million
Kay Hagan, North Carolina Democrat (challenger—won) $11.7 million	Patrick Toomey, Pennsylvania Republican (challenger—won) $8.8 million
Jeanne Shaheen, New Hampshire Democrat (challenger—won) $9.6 million	Alexi Giannoulias, Illinois Democrat (open seat—lost) $7.7 million
Al Franken, Minnesota Democrat (challenger—won) $9.5 million	Michael Bennet, Colorado Democrat (incumbent—won) $7.4 million

House candidates (including party direct contributions, coordinated spending, and party independent spending)

Travis Childers, Mississippi Democrat (incumbent—won) $3.1 million	John A. Boccieri, Ohio Democrat (incumbent—lost) $3.1 million
Carol Shea Porter, New Hampshire Democrat (incumbent—won) $2.5 million	Mark Schauer, Michigan Democrat (incumbent—lost) $2.9 million

Note: National party money includes money spent or transferred by all six national party committees (DNC, RNC, NRSC, DSCC, NRCC, and DCCC).

Source: Federal Election Commission data, at www.fec.gov/press/2010_Full_summary_Data.shtml (accessed July 6, 2011).

Both national parties tried to make up for the lost soft money by working harder to attract hard-money donations from individuals. The DNC greatly expanded its direct mail fund-raising program, which had been minimal during the 1990s, and reaped millions of new donors. In all, the DNC collected almost five times as much federally regulated money in 2004 as it had in 2002—$312 million compared with $67 million, and raised more than 40 percent of its total fund-raising in contributions of less than $200. The DCCC and the RNC both doubled their hard-money fund-raising in 2004, and the DSCC came close. BCRA made it easier for the party committees to raise hard money by setting the cap on an individual's aggregate donations to party and political action committees (which reached $70,800 in 2012) higher than the aggregate cap on donations to candidates. Both parties encouraged big hard-money donors to solicit similar contributions from their friends and colleagues and to "bundle" these donations to reach totals of $100,000 or $200,000 or more, in return for recognition from the party.

With all these incentives, the national parties broke all fund-raising records in the 2000s. Even after the BCRA reforms, the two parties' national and Hill committees came up with an eye-popping $1.7 *billion* in 2004 and more in 2008. Remarkably, the Democrats almost matched the Republican Party's fund-raising during the 2008 election cycle for the first time in at least 30 years, and actually outraised the Republicans nationally in 2010.

Party Money and Activism in 2008, 2010, and 2012

Although the biggest portion of party fund-raising comes from individual citizens, an increasing proportion of the contributors to party committees and candidates were members of Congress. In the early 1990s, some Republican House leaders, fed up with their long-time minority status, pressed party colleagues to donate some of their campaign war chests to Republicans in more competitive races. The aim was to redirect campaign money from those who could most easily raise it to those who most needed it and therefore to increase the number of Republicans in the House. Winning a majority of seats would give all House Republicans the power to achieve their policy goals, given that the flow of legislation in the House is controlled by the majority party. Republicans did capture control of both the House and Senate in 1994, and soon after, the new Democratic minority also saw the value of spreading the wealth to help vulnerable incumbents and promising challengers.

Since then, both parties' Hill committees have urged, and even required, their members to channel money to the party committee, not just to particular candidates. This gives the party the opportunity to target the races it considers the most winnable, rather than leaving the decisions to individual incumbent donors. House members can donate funds from their personal campaign committees and their "leadership PACs" (see Chapter 12) and also ask their own contributors to give to the party's Hill committee. In 2010, for instance, the DCCC chair asked for contributions of $1 million from each of the powerful committee chairs, $250,000 or $150,000 from many others, and $30,000 from rank-and-file Democratic House members. The House Speaker at the time, Nancy Pelosi, raised more than $23 million for the DCCC. In the Senate, the leading donor was Senator Charles Schumer (D-N.Y.), who gave $4 million to his party and colleagues from his unused campaign funds. Each member's contributions were tracked by party leaders, just as party whips track legislative votes.[10]

Getting members of Congress to give to their parties can be a difficult sell, especially for incumbents of the weaker party, who are understandably worried about protecting their own seats. As a result, although Democratic senators and House members gave their Hill committees more than twice as much as Republicans did in 2008,[11] their donations were harder to get in 2010 when Democratic incumbents feared for their own reelection. But the parties' success in getting incumbents to hand over these impressive sums and to put their fund-raising skill in the service of other party candidates demonstrates the extent to which the congressional parties have become important instruments of collective power for their members.

The increased fund-raising from Congress members and other sources gave the Democratic committees the money to take a page or two from the Republicans' playbook. Starting in 2000, the national GOP had created a massive databank of voter information gleaned from party canvassers and commercial databases—individuals' past voting records and their opinions and consumer preferences—so that, just as corporate market researchers do, party strategists could make predictions as to how particular types of people were likely to behave. This "micro-targeting" helped the Republicans focus their persuasive efforts and GOTV activities on the individuals most likely to support Republican candidates. The resulting database, called Voter Vault, required funding and computer facilities on a scale that the national Republicans could afford. It was widely heralded as a major reason for the Republican victories in 2002 and 2004.

Democrats were slow to respond, but later created two separate national databases. One, maintained by the DNC, was made available to Democratic candidates at all levels. The other, a huge dataset managed by Catalist, an organization headed by Democratic political operative Harold Ickes, was used extensively by the Obama campaign and liberal groups supporting Obama. Voter contact programs ("field operations") based on these datasets were field-tested in some congressional special elections in 2008, all of which resulted in Democratic wins. The DCCC and DSCC then applied these programs nationally, beginning well in advance of the presidential election.

By early September 2008, the DCCC had four times more money than did the NRCC to spend on House races and embarked on a lavish independent spending drive. As you'll see in Chapter 12, court cases have allowed party organizations to run unlimited amounts of advertising in House and Senate campaigns as long as the party spends its money independently of the candidate it intends to help ("independent spending"). This produces the odd picture of two groups of partisans from the same party—those helping the candidate and those doing independent spending—working to elect the same candidate but officially ignorant of one another's activities. The great majority of party funds in recent House and Senate races have come in the form of independent spending (see Figures 4.2 and 4.3). Although the Republican

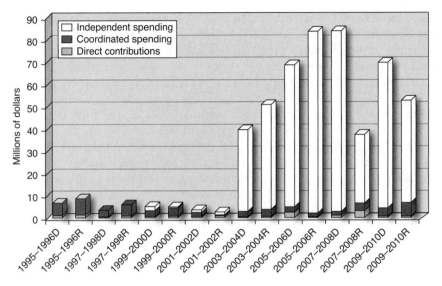

FIGURE 4.2
National Party Money in House Races, 1995–1996 to 2009–2010.

Source: Federal Election Commission, at www.fec.gov/press/2010_Full_summary_Data.shtml (accessed July 6, 2011).

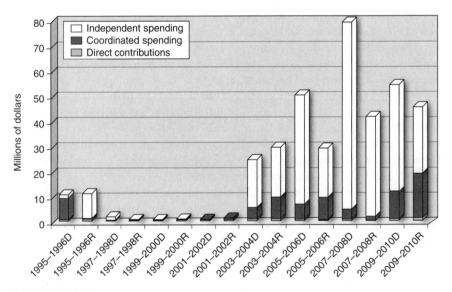

FIGURE 4.3
National Party Money in Senate Races, 1995–1996 to 2009–2010.

Source: Federal Election Commission, at www.fec.gov/press/2010_Full_summary_Data.shtml (accessed July 6, 2011).

committees' independent spending fell dramatically in 2008, in tandem with their election prospects, Democratic spending reached unprecedented levels. The DCCC put $1 million or more into each of 38 House races, largely open seats and challengers' campaigns, and won most of them.

Freshman legislators, especially those elected in districts that normally vote for the other party's candidates, tend to be most vulnerable in their first reelection race. To protect the freshman Democrats elected in 2006, Democratic House leaders had given them helpful committee assignments and followed up with careful targeting of funds and other services. With this help, only four of the freshman Democrats lost in 2008. Flush with money, the DCCC also aggressively went after Republican-held seats, recruiting experienced challengers and backing them with party funds. The NRCC was forced to use most of its independent spending to defend embattled incumbents.[12]

The parties' situations were reversed in 2010. The Democratic Party "brand" suffered mightily after 2008 due to the continuing economic downturn and President Obama's controversial health care and stimulus programs. Democratic committees pulled back in 2010 to support only those vulnerable incumbents with a chance of winning, whereas the NRCC had the opportunity to successfully target some powerful Democratic veterans as well as a number of freshmen who had been elected in 2008 in Republican-leaning districts. The result was a record-breaking Republican sweep.

But the NRCC then had 87 freshman incumbents to defend in 2012. It raised money to support the most promising candidates by offering these "Young Guns" funding, training, and other assistance. In its "Patriot Program," begun in 2009, the committee set a series of fund-raising, voter contact, and coalition-building benchmarks for the freshmen and some other vulnerable incumbents if they wanted to get NRCC money. Since the mid-1980s, then, both national parties have become institutionalized as active, well-staffed "service parties" working to support party candidates and state and local party organizations, not only through direct contributions and independent spending but also through investments in voter identification and database management.[13]

WHAT IS THE IMPACT OF THESE STRONGER NATIONAL PARTIES?

These dramatic changes in the national party organizations have helped to beef up the parties' roles in nominating and electing candidates, roles that had been seriously undercut a century ago with the advent of the direct primary. To an important degree, the national and state parties are now actively involved in the campaign support functions that private campaign consultants and other political groups had monopolized until recently. The money and services provided by the national parties have helped to raise their profiles in the eyes of candidates. The increasing strength of the national parties has also altered the relationships within the parties.

Effects on Candidates' Campaigns

The strengthened national parties perform a number of vital functions in presidential campaigns. As we have seen, both national committees research issues, study the opponent's record and background, and search for their own candidate's weak points and ways to thwart attacks. They train state party staff and field directors and maintain relationships with important groups in the party's network.

In Senate and House campaigns, however, there have been some marked recent changes in the national parties' decisions as to where to deploy their new-found strength. In the 1980s and 1990s, the national party committees had supported a wide range of viable candidates. The committees tended to protect their incumbents when they expected a lean election year and to invest in challengers and open seats when a big victory looked likely. But by the early 2000s, the House and Senate were so closely divided by party and the number of truly competitive seats had shrunk so much that both parties' congressional committees were pouring the great majority of their money and help into those competitive races.[14]

There was so much party money and field staff coming into these competitive campaigns that at least in those targeted races, party money at times outweighed candidate spending. The national party committees' money and other resources have given them real power over the targeted campaigns. For instance, early in the 2000s, the national parties spent more in a closely fought Colorado congressional race than the candidates' own campaigns did, and the national party committees specified exactly what the campaigns had to do with the party money. The Democratic candidate's campaign manager probably spoke for both candidates in his exasperation at the national party's micromanaging: "They crawl up our ass on a daily basis."[15] Although most candidates are grateful for the support, the party-funded advertising can sometimes backfire. Party-funded ads are much more likely to feature attacks on the opposition than are the candidates' own ads. Because most voters do not distinguish between candidate and party ads, a candidate can be tarred with a negative image that he or she has worked hard to avoid.

The "wave" elections in 2008 and 2010 greatly expanded the playing field for the dominant party. But most congressional races are not competitive. In the remaining elections, the national party committees have not put in enough money or other resources to attract even some attention from, much less power over, the candidates and their staffs. That can result in a great deal of frustration for the less-competitive candidates and, in some cases, missed opportunities. As Gary Jacobson points out, nine Democratic House challengers lost narrowly in 2008, each receiving more than 45 percent of the vote, but did not receive substantial help from the DCCC. Some of these candidates might have won if they had received party money.[16]

Effects on State and Local Parties

More generally, have the increasing visibility and resources of the national parties led to a transfer of power from the state and local to the national party organizations—to centralization rather than decentralization of the parties? Probably not. The forces that encourage a state and local party focus remain strong.

But it is clear that the national parties' new strength has lessened the *de*centralization of the party organizations. When the national parties have a lot of money and services to give, their power and influence grow. In a number of cases, as in the Colorado campaign mentioned above, national party committees have made their funding or other help contingent on the campaign's or state party's acceptance of certain requirements: that they hire particular staffers or consultants or use particular campaign techniques. The result can be more of a national imprint on the nature of state and even local campaigns, the kinds of candidates recruited, and the ways in which the parties are organized. Is this a good thing for American politics? "Which Would You Choose?" (on this page) provides arguments on both sides of this question.

▶ WHICH WOULD YOU CHOOSE?

Could a Stronger National Party Help You?

YES! Political parties offer you a valuable shortcut. Government decisions affect almost everything you do, but you may not have time to research dozens of complicated issues (health care, energy prices) and candidates in order to vote for those who will act in your interest. A party can do the research for you. If you generally agree with, say, the Republican Party, it can offer you a set of recommended candidates with no effort on your part. But if each state and local Republican organization can act independently, and if some of these organizations are moderate and others are conservative, then how can you be sure that your state and local Republican candidates will support the positions that drew you to the party? A strong national party could help recruit candidates whose views are consistent with the party's philosophy and help them get elected. Besides, who would you rather have raising campaign money: the national party or the individual candidates who will soon be voting on bills affecting the donors' interests?

NO! The United States is very diverse; the concerns of Democrats in Omaha may well be different from those in San Francisco, New Hampshire, and the Florida Panhandle. If a national party is strong enough to promote a clear set of ideas on what government should be doing, then whose ideas should it promote: those of the Omaha Democrats or the San Francisco Democrats? If a national party is strong enough to elect its candidates, wouldn't it be capable of telling them how to vote in Congress, whether or not their constituents agree? Even if a national party organization confines itself to raising money and giving it to candidates, doesn't that give the national organization a great deal of influence over state and even local candidates? In a nation with a tradition of hostility to "boss rule," couldn't a strong national party raise those fears again?

At times, state parties have welcomed this national involvement. One of the more successful examples of national and state party cooperation was former DNC Chair Howard Dean's *"50-state strategy"* in the 2006 and 2008 elections. As Chapter 3 mentioned, Dean used DNC money to pay field organizers to work with each of the state parties. Colorado, for instance, had been a Republican state for several decades but had experienced an influx of younger, more liberal voters in the early 2000s. So starting in 2005, the DNC provided money for the state party to fund field directors in rural areas and to purchase a new database of voter information. The DNC investment also invigorated several other state parties in areas that the national Democrats had previously written off as Republican-dominated. One study found that these DNC staffers improved the candidates' vote totals in these races, even beyond the other advantages that Democrats had in 2006.[17] Dean and his supporters argued that this was the foundation for the Obama campaign's successful national strategy in 2008.[18] The Obama campaign felt differently, noting that it had relied almost entirely on its own staff and money in these "red" states; it contended that the candidate's own strengths and the Bush administration's weaknesses were at least as important.[19]

Under other conditions, the increased national influence can strain the relationships among party organizations at different levels, just as it has produced strains between the parties and some candidates. One of the areas of greatest conflict between the national parties and their state and local brethren centers on national party involvement in primaries. It is always a temptation for national party officials to try to select and groom the candidate they think will have the best odds of winning in a district. The House and Senate campaign committees, whose chance for a majority in Congress depends on the effectiveness of candidates in competitive races, dread the possibility that a less-capable candidate will win their party's primary and go on to run a less-than-professional campaign for the seat. But the risk of becoming involved is that if the national party backs a candidate who later loses the primary, then the party could suffer; it might alienate the winning candidate, make itself look weak, and even split the state party and lose the election.

In 2010, Republican national leaders took that risk. After a wide range of candidates flooded into Republican primaries, anticipating a coming Republican wave, the national Republican campaign committees endorsed the candidates in a number of House and Senate primaries who they felt were most likely to win the general election. In several of these states, Tea Party supporters and other strongly conservative voters rejected the party establishment's advice. Perhaps the best example was the Delaware Senate race, where the national and state parties' preferred candidate for the nomination was defeated by a Tea Party-endorsed challenger, Christine O'Donnell. A campaigner with an all-too-colorful past, O'Donnell decided to deal with an earlier admission that she had dabbled in witchcraft by opening her first general election TV ad with the words, "I am not a witch." The ad quickly went viral, and O'Donnell lost the November election—a seat the national party had considered a likely pick-up if its preferred candidate had won the primary. Although the NRSC chair vowed to stay out of Republican primaries in 2012, the national Republicans did convince a number of "A list" candidates to run in the hopes of gaining a Senate majority in that year, far outstripping the DSCC's recruitment successes.

In short, when national party committees use their money to affect the choice of candidates or the direction of a campaign, it is likely that there will be ruffled feathers within the state party and the campaign, who feel that they are better judges of what works in the district (see box "Hoosier Candidate?" on this page). That was the case with the Democrats in 2006, when DCCC Chair Rahm Emanuel bulldozed more than a few local party chairs to get moderate candidates nominated in socially conservative areas and thus increase the party's likelihood of winning.[20] However, the temptation will always be present; Emanuel, after all, could claim that these moderate "majority makers" produced the Democratic victories that brought the party a House majority in that year.

Hoosier Candidate?

Moderate Democrat Evan Bayh's popularity in the Hoosier state was legend. But the National Republican Senatorial Committee (NRSC) thought it had found a candidate who could beat Bayh for reelection to the U.S. Senate from Indiana. The NRSC courted former Indiana Senator Dan Coats and convinced him to run. Some state Republican leaders and Tea Party groups did not appreciate the national party's efforts. They felt that Coats was too moderate, too weak on gun rights, and had few remaining ties to Indiana politics. They resented the interference of "Washington insiders" in a state contest. One Tea Party group e-mailed supporters with this subject line: "NO to RNC/Coats for force feeding us this crap sandwich." Although Coats did win the primary, the national party's efforts to endorse the most electable candidates prior to the primaries raised controversy in several other states as well, including New Hampshire, Florida, Kentucky, Nevada, and Delaware. And when Bayh announced suddenly that he would not seek reelection, and state and national Democratic leaders worked to clear the primary field for Democratic U.S. Rep. Brad Ellsworth, Republicans campaigned against Ellsworth as the candidate of party "bosses." In short, national party pressure to nominate an electable candidate can backfire, especially when local and state activists value ideological purity over electability (see Chapter 5). A reporter concluded, tongue in cheek, "The public, it turns out, prefers a say in the electoral process."

Sources: Alex Isenstadt, "Coats Comeback Hits GOP Pushback," *Politico*, February 13, 2010, at www.politico.com/news/stories/0210/32922.html (accessed March 23, 2011); and Carl Hulse, "Seeing Hand-Picked as a Bad Thing," *New York Times*, March 12, 2010, p. 1.

Effects on the Presidency

Is a stronger national party likely to compete with the president's power or to add to it? Clearly, the increasing resources of the national committees give them the opportunity for a more independent political role. Federal funding of presidential campaigns, with its strict limits on party spending for presidential races, freed the national committees from their traditional concentration on presidential elections and allowed them to dedicate at least some of their resources to party-building at the state and local level. At the same time, the party committees carved out new roles in raising money for use in federal campaigns.

On the other hand, these new capabilities make the national committee an even more attractive resource for presidents. Naturally, presidents want the new party power to be at their service, and every president in recent memory has kept his party's national committee on a short leash. RNC Chair Jim Gilmore was edged out in late 2001, for example, because he clashed with the White House over control of the committee. Presidents will certainly want the party committees to mobilize all those members of Congress whom they recruited, trained, financed, and helped elect to support the president's program. Presidents in their first term will want to draw on the assets of the national party for their reelection campaigns, as much as campaign finance rules permit. Thus, there is considerable pressure on these stronger national parties to put their capabilities at the service of presidential goals.

Effects on Congress

At around the time that the Hill committees have become much more active in recruiting and supporting party candidates, Congress members have been more likely to cast legislative votes with the majority of their party (as Chapter 13 shows). Did these new campaign resources help convince Congress members to vote for their party's positions on bills? To this point, the party committees have not given out campaign money and services on the basis of a candidate's support for the party's program. In 2010, for instance, the DCCC gave only last-second aid to Colorado incumbent Betsy Markey in her close (and ultimately losing) race in Colorado, though she supported the Democratic leadership on some tough votes in Congress, whereas it spent $1 million on ads in the campaign of Bobby Bright, an Alabama Democrat who had cast hundreds of votes against his party leaders. Party funds usually go to competitive races rather than to candidates who are ideologically "pure."[21]

Even though the party committees have not used their funding to influence the ideological complexion of Congress, some members of the party in Congress have tried to do so. In 2010, conservative Republican Senator Jim DeMint used his leadership PAC—groups whose contributions are normally used to gain a leadership position for the PAC's sponsor by helping other members—to funnel campaign money to strong conservative candidates such as Tea Party favorite Marco Rubio, running in the primary for a Florida Senate seat. DeMint's aim was to make the Senate Republican contingent more deeply conservative.

Yet the committees have not been bashful in reminding members, especially newly elected members, that the party played some role in their election success. Party campaign help is only one part of the story of party support in Congress, but the remarkable cohesion of the House Republicans since 1995 was surely bolstered by the party leadership's financial and other support for Republican candidates. Constituency pressures will always come first in Congress. However, the more that senators and representatives can count on campaign help from the congressional party, the more open they will be to party-based appeals.

Relationships Within the National Party

The three national committees of each party—the DNC or RNC and the party's Hill committees—have good reasons to cooperate with one another. When the party's presidential candidate does well, most of the voters he or she attracts will also vote for the Senate and House candidates of the president's party. Similarly, an effectively run Senate campaign can bring out voters for party colleagues running for president and House seats.

But the party's resources are not unlimited, and each of the party's national committees would prefer the biggest share. Democratic congressional candidates in 2010 worried that the DNC's activities in their districts might have more to do with laying the groundwork for the 2012 Obama reelection campaign than with supporting their own races. In the run-up to the 2012 election, DNC efforts to raise money from wealthy donors for Obama's campaign threatened the ability of the Democratic Hill committees to get substantial donations from the same sources, because individuals' total donations to committees, campaigns, and PACs are limited (see Chapter 12). The party committees have long competed with one another in raising as well as spending money. They seek financial support from the same contributors (and jealously guard their contributor lists) and recruit political talent from the same limited pool.

THE LIMITS OF PARTY ORGANIZATION

In sum, the national party organizations have recently generated remarkable amounts of new money and other resources. They have used these resources, expertise, and energy to become major players relative to the state and local parties and major influences on the lives of many federal and even state-level candidates. Organizations capable of raising and spending a billion dollars during a two-year period are not easily ignored. The rise of Super PACs (see Chapter 12) is likely to cut into the parties' fund-raising capability, but the national party organizations remain stronger than they have been through most of their history.

This impressive increase in strength has not come at the expense of the state and local parties; in fact, the national parties have used at least some of their resources to build the capabilities of these party organizations. Nor has the national parties' new strength made the local and state party organizations into branch offices of their national parties, following their orders in developing campaign strategy and taking stands on public policy. There are still too many forces in American politics encouraging independence, especially in the local parties, to permit the two major parties to centralize their organization and power. The federal system, in which most public officials are elected at the local level, the separation of powers, variations among states and local areas in public attitudes and regulation of the parties, and the BCRA rules that discourage cooperative campaigns between federal and nonfederal candidates all work against a centralized party system.

Thus, as resource rich as they have become, the American party organizations remain fairly decentralized by international standards. At a time when Americans can be assured of getting the same Big Mac in Cincinnati as they can in San Diego, the American parties lack the top–down control and efficiency, the unified setting of priorities, and the central responsibility that we often find in other nations' parties. Where the party organizations of many other Western democracies have had permanent, highly professional leadership and large party bureaucracies, most American party organizations, especially at the local level, are still in the hands of part-time activists.[22]

The parties have increased their emphasis on grassroots campaigning through canvassing and phone banks and have used the information to develop micro-targeting, aiming specific messages at individuals known to be receptive to those messages. Yet even this greater reach into the grassroots may not be enough to make the party organizations more prominent in the public's mind. The parties' messages focus on the candidates rather than on the party itself. More professional, service-oriented parties may be better at helping candidates run for office than in expanding the role of the party organization in citizens' political thinking.[23] American political values do not welcome stronger and more centralized party organizations with more power in American political life.

The American party organizations are fundamentally flexible and election oriented. Their purpose is to support candidates for office and to make the adjustments needed to do well in a pragmatic political system. As a result, they have long been led by candidates and officeholders, not by career party bureaucrats. As the political system grows more polarized, the party organizations have taken the opportunity to expand their roles and to add to the polarization. But at least to this point, even though the national party committees now have unprecedented levels of funding and activity, they remain candidate-centered organizations in a candidate-centered political world.

Party Activists

arty organizations can't survive without the volunteer help of millions of activists. But party leaders may sometimes wonder if they can survive *with* that volunteer help. In 2012, Democratic leaders were severely criticized by liberal Democratic activists who felt that President Obama and congressional Democrats had not pushed hard enough for progressive policies, and conservative Republican activists vowed to punish elected Republicans who had failed to cut the federal budget to the bone.

Yet without the efforts of all these volunteer activists, the party organizations would not be able to register voters, get out the vote, build support for their policies, or even maintain their Facebook page. To meet their own needs, then, party organizations must make sure that they satisfy the needs of their (sometimes quarrelsome, always demanding) activists as well. How party organizations achieve this difficult balance, and whether they do, is determined by the ways they attract volunteers and sustain their commitment.

WHAT DRAWS PEOPLE INTO PARTY ACTIVITY?

People become involved in organizations of all kinds, from party organizations to dance marathons, for three types of reasons. *Material incentives* are tangible rewards for activity—direct cash payments or other concrete rewards for one's work. *Solidary incentives* are the intangible, social benefits that people can gain from associating with others, networking, and being part of a group. *Purposive incentives* are intangible as well, referring to the sense of satisfaction people feel when promoting an issue or cause that matters to them.[1] Although the American parties once offered a lot of material incentives for party work, now individuals are attracted to party organizations and campaigns mainly for the purposive and solidary benefits they provide.

Material Incentives

For many years, the main material, or tangible, reason why people became involved in party activity was to share in the "spoils" gained when a party controlled the government. These "spoils" came in the form of patronage and preferments. *Patronage* is the appointment of an individual to a government job as a reward for party work. Although patronage is very limited today, the party can still provide loyal workers with a base of support if they seek elected office. *Preferments* are other favors a governing party can grant to party supporters, such as contracts or preferred treatment in enforcing laws. Patronage, access to elected office, and preferments have all played important roles in building and sustaining the American party organizations.

Patronage   Early in the life of the American republic and for more than a century afterward, people were attracted to party work by the prospect of being rewarded with government jobs if the party won. Patronage has been used in other nations as well, but no other party system relied on patronage as fully and for as long as the American system. When party "machines" controlled many cities, city governments were staffed almost entirely by loyalists of the party in power.[2] As the price to be paid for their jobs, patronage appointees traditionally "volunteered" their time, energy, and often even a part of their salary to the party organization. Campaign help was especially expected; American party politics is rich with tales of the entire staff of certain government departments being put to work in support of their boss's reelection. Even now, when such practices are usually frowned on and sometimes illegal, government employees can still face a lot of pressure to contribute time or money to their party.

As the number of government jobs grew, however, the number of patronage jobs available to the parties dropped dramatically. Most government employees are now hired under civil service and merit systems, in which applicants get jobs based on their scores on competitive exams. The number of full-time federal positions filled by political appointees has dwindled over the years to fewer than 10,000 today, many of them high-level policy-making positions. States and cities have followed the same path, though more slowly.

The Supreme Court has helped to dismantle patronage at the state and local levels. In 1976 and 1980, the Court ruled that some county political employees could not be fired simply because the party in power changed. The Court went further in a 1990 Illinois case, determining that politically based hiring and promotion violated the First Amendment freedoms of speech and association. In each case, the Court agreed that party affiliation might be a relevant qualification in filling policy-making positions but not in lower-level offices.[3] Even where patronage jobs remain, they are usually under the control of elected executives—mayors, governors, and others—who are more interested in using patronage to build their own political followings than in rewarding loyal service to the party itself.

Yet some patronage still survives. Mayors, governors, and presidents continue to reserve top policy-making positions for their trusted supporters. Legislatures often resist bringing their staff members under the protection of civil service systems. Civil service rules for governmental employees can be bypassed by hiring politically loyal, "temporary" workers outside of the civil service system or by channeling party loyalists into jobs in private firms that depend on government business. A few big campaign contributors will continue to be named ambassadors to small and peaceful nations.

Wherever political leaders have some discretion in hiring people, in short, they will find a way to award jobs to their supporters, who usually share their party affiliation, so these opportunities will attract at least some people to party activity.

Keep in mind that some observers are sorry to lose the practice of patronage. Its use was promoted by President Andrew Jackson as a means of encouraging a more democratic and less elitist government.[4] When government jobs are filled (and then protected) only by civil service procedures, it becomes almost impossible for reform-minded leaders to replace a sluggish or ineffective bureaucrat with a more efficient worker. Patronage was also thought to keep party organizations strong as instruments of democracy. Material incentives can be very effective in attracting workers. Those who participate for reasons other than material rewards may make other demands, for example, for the party to take an ideological stand that might alienate moderate voters. That could undermine the ability of a party organization to act pragmatically and inclusively.

Patronage jobs in government are not the only employment opportunities a party can offer. State and national party organizations now hire hundreds of professional campaign workers, as do consulting firms associated with the parties. To provide services to their candidates, party organizations need computer specialists, pollsters, field organizers, researchers, fund-raisers, strategists, Webmasters, direct mail specialists, and others. Some activists are drawn to party work by the chance of landing these jobs, but in general, patronage is no longer an important force in motivating activists.

Elected Office   Some women and men become party activists because they see party work as a first step toward running for office. This has been true for a long time; about 40 percent of the county chairs interviewed in a 1979–1980 national survey hoped to hold public office, and an earlier study found that one-third of all state party chairs became candidates for elective office after serving the party.[5] Because of primary elections, of course, very few party organizations can simply "give" nominations to public office to loyal party activists. It is far more common for candidates to see the party as one of the bases of support for winning votes and, in some areas, as the most important one. Candidates need money, advice, and people (staff and volunteers), and the party remains a likely source of all of these. So the lure of party support in a later campaign for elected office may bring some people into party work.

Preferments   Party activity can bring tangible rewards for some people, other than elective or appointive office. Because public officials can use at least some discretion in distributing government services and granting government contracts, there is the potential for political favoritism. Some people contribute money or time to their party in the hope of attracting these favors. The head of a construction company might give a big campaign contribution in order to win a government contract to build a new school or library. It is no accident that leaders of the construction industry are so active politically in states and cities that spend millions every year on roads and public buildings.

There are other forms of preference as well. People may hope that in return for activism on behalf of the party, they will get special treatment such as tolerant inspection of their restaurant by the health department, prompt snow removal in front of their place of business, or admission for their child to a crowded state university. It may also involve the granting of scarce opportunities, such as liquor licenses, in return for some form of political support.

Reformers have promoted a number of safeguards to limit government's discretion in giving out benefits and buying goods and services from private firms. Examples are competitive and sealed bidding, conflict of interest statutes, and even affirmative action. Yet, because the potential benefits are so great for both sides, there always seem to be ways of evading even the tightest controls. In addition, many reformers don't want to eliminate *all* government discretion in the awarding of contracts just in order to stamp out *partisan* discretion. The result is that preferments may have taken the place of patronage as the main material incentive for political activity. Unfortunately for party leaders, however, now it is elected officials who grant the preferments, not the party leaders themselves.

Solidary (Social) Incentives

Many more people are drawn to party work by the social contact that it provides. In an age when some people's closest relationship is with their computer or their cell phone, the face-to-face contact found at a party headquarters or in a campaign provides a chance to meet like-minded people and to be part of an active group. Family traditions may lead some young adults to go to party activities looking for social life, just as others may look to a softball league or a bar. Some find it exciting to meet local officials or others who appear on the news. Researchers find that a large number of party activists cite the social life of party politics as a valuable reward for their efforts.[6]

These social contacts may produce other rewards as well. Networking has become a standard means of looking for a job. Young lawyers may find potential clients among the activists and elected officials they meet in the party organization. More generally, party activity can help people feel a part of something larger than themselves—a charismatic leader, an important moment in history. The party can be a small island of excitement in a sea of routine.

Purposive (Issue-Based) Incentives

To an increasing extent, people are led to party activism by their commitment to particular issues. Someone dedicated to abortion rights, for example, might begin by working for a pro-choice Democratic candidate and then come to see the candidate's party as a vehicle for keeping abortion legal. A highly observant Christian who believes that life begins at conception might be drawn to the Republican Party as a means of stopping abortion. Since the parties have polarized on many issues in recent years, most of those who volunteer for party work seem to be motivated by a desire to use the party to achieve policy goals[7] (see box "A Day in the Life" on pages 95–96). Although we do not have comparable data on earlier periods, there is reason to believe that this was less true of party workers earlier in the nation's history.[8] The energy and passion in party organizations come increasingly from issue-driven activists—those on the right in the Republican Party and those on the left for the Democrats.

Issue-driven party activism has played a vital role in shaping politics at all levels. In many 2010 House races, the activism of Tea Party supporters helped elect dozens of new Republican Congress members, most of them highly conservative on taxes, government spending, and illegal immigration. Some issues and ideological movements have had enough power to lead activists to switch parties. The abortion and race issues, for example, induced many formerly Democratic pro-lifers and southern conservatives to join the Republican Party beginning in the 1970s, and they soon cemented a set of favored issue positions into the platform of their new party.[9]

▶ **A DAY IN THE LIFE**

From Campus to the Obama Campaign

Like most incoming college students, Megan Trusnik had never been involved in politics before. But when she arrived at Indiana University as a freshman, seeking her own "niche" on campus, she signed up on the Indiana Democratic Party Web site and offered to volunteer. That's all it took. Soon she was working in a governor's race, was offered an internship, and had the chance to make a number of political contacts on and off campus.

A dozen campaigns later, in what was supposed to be her last semester, she says, "I was browsing Facebook when I got a message from an old political acquaintance. There was a job opening in the Obama campaign in Ohio. It took a little persuasion by friends and family, because I would have to postpone graduating for a semester. But after thinking about the grand and historical opportunity this was, I e-mailed him my resume." Days later, Megan was hired as Obama Regional Volunteer Coordinator for nine counties in the Appalachian area of southeastern Ohio.

"I had only three days to get out to Appalachia, in which I had to pack, organize myself a car because I didn't have one, and get a root canal that was scheduled for a week later," Megan recalls. When she arrived in Ohio, she walked into the Obama office and found it almost empty. A field organizer was sitting at a desk in the back of the room. "No one was greeting people; people would walk in, look around, and go back out again!" This was not the way to attract the volunteers the campaign needed so badly.

Megan's job was to bring in those volunteers—in an area where she knew no one. Although the Obama campaign was well funded, the staff was expected to gather most of its own resources, from food to housing to supplies. "We organized many of our resources purely from connections we made in the communities," she said. She tried to humanize the office by adding couches from Goodwill, having food constantly available, and covering the walls with posters. To energize volunteers, she set up competitions to motivate them to meet their quotas of campaign phone calls. She encouraged them to work independently and coached them on

(continued)

(continued)

how to be persuasive. She became skilled in soothing personality clashes between local party leaders and East Coast volunteers with decidedly non-Appalachian lifestyles.

She also learned a lot about the rural communities that were her responsibility. "It made me more aware of the extent to which rural areas struggle with poverty—to a degree that we often think doesn't touch Americans," she said. One of "her" counties had a McDonald's and a diner but no hospital. In another, the only Internet availability in the entire county was a single Internet café with a dial-up connection. Even though many local voters were uneasy about voting for a man some termed "colored"—and in fact, an effigy of Obama was hung from a stoplight in one town—many were convinced by the candidate's plans to bring Internet access to rural areas and recruit more doctors.

And she was excited to be part of what she considered a state-of-the-art campaign. In her previous campaign experience, Megan said, she'd wonder: Why is this candidate not using Facebook? Why isn't that candidate's Web page interactive? The Obama campaign was different: Web-savvy, well organized, and rooted in local communities. "I always knew that this is how politics *should* work." ■

A large proportion of these issue-based activists are convinced that their activity has made a difference; in one survey, three-quarters of those who said that they had volunteered in a campaign believed that their involvement had affected at least some votes.[10] So even though it might seem irrational to spend a lot of time on party activity in support of an issue that could be termed a "collective good"—one that, if achieved, will benefit the whole society rather than only the activists who worked hard to achieve it—many people become active in a party to do just that. Others become party activists out of a more general sense that citizen participation is essential in a democracy.

Mixed Incentives

Most party organizations rely on a variety of incentives. Activists hoping to build support for a later run for office work together with those motivated by a particular issue and with those who come to party activities for social contact. That can produce strains among party volunteers who are motivated by different incentives. Someone who became a Democratic activist to work for abortion rights, for instance, is not likely to be satisfied with a party that supports a pro-lifer running on the Democratic label. Others who participate in the party for social reasons may feel that the party ought to be a "big tent," including people who differ in their attitudes toward abortion.

The incentive that attracts people to party work may not be the incentive that keeps them there. Several studies suggest that those who become active in the party to fight for certain issues are more likely to remain in the party if they come to value the social contact it gives them. The motive that sustains their party work, in short, often shifts to solidary incentives: friendships, identification with the party itself, and other social rewards.[11] It may be that committed issue activists simply burn out or that the pragmatic American parties, in their effort to remain flexible enough to win elections, do not always provide the level of ideological dedication needed to sustain party workers whose lives are devoted to a set of uncompromising ideals.

Professionals and Amateurs

Drawing on research on these incentives for party work, scholars have classified party activists into two types, based on their beliefs about the purpose of parties in political life. One type of party activist is the *professional* (sometimes known as "pragmatist")—the party worker whose first loyalty is to the party itself and whose operating style is pragmatic. These are the party "regulars" who support their party in good times and bad, when it nominates candidates they approve of and even when it doesn't. A different type is the *amateur* (or "purist")—the issue-oriented activist, motivated by purposive incentives, who sees party activity as only one means of achieving important political goals.[12] (On the differences between these two types, see Table 5.1.)

A party organization populated by amateurs may behave very differently from a party dominated by professionals. Above all, amateur activists are drawn into the party in order to further some issues or principles; for them, the issue is the goal and the party is the means of achieving it. If the party,

TABLE 5.1

Comparing Professionals and Amateurs

	Professionals	Amateurs
Political style	Pragmatic	Purist
What do they want?	Material rewards (patronage, preferments)	Purposive rewards (issues, policies)
Their loyalty is to	Party organization	Officeholders, other political groups
They want the party to focus on	Candidates, elections	Issues, ideology
The party should choose candidates on the basis of	Their electability	Their principles
The style of party governance should be	Hierarchical	Democratic
Their support of party candidates is	Automatic	Conditional on candidates' principles
They were recruited into politics through	Party work	Issue or candidate organizations
Their SES level is	Average to above average	Well above average

or its candidates, pulls back on its commitment to their issue, they may pull back on their commitment to the party. So they tend to be less willing to compromise their positions in order to win elections. (See box "Ben Affleck: 'Amateur' Party Activist" on this page.) Amateur activists are likely to insist on full participation within the party organization in order to put their issues at the top of the party's agenda. When they lead party organizations, they often bring a strong push for reform in both the party's internal business and the larger political system.

Ben Affleck: "Amateur" Party Activist

To actor Ben Affleck, policy change is the goal; the Democratic Party is one means to achieve it. That makes Affleck a good example of an "amateur" party activist.

Affleck's main concerns are health care reform and achieving peace and justice in international affairs. He has publicly supported same-sex marriage and criticized the growing gulf between corporate executives' salaries and those of their employees. "I would say I'm a moderately liberal guy," he told Fox News host Bill O'Reilly in 2008. As a result, he usually supports Democratic candidates. Affleck campaigned for Barack Obama in 2008, just as he had for Democratic presidential candidates John Kerry in 2004 and Al Gore in 2000. Together with Matt Damon, John Legend, the liberal group MoveOn.org, and others, he sponsored an "Obama in 30 Seconds" contest to choose and air the best 30-second Obama ad submitted by supporters on the Internet in the 2008 presidential race. In fact, some Democratic activists urged him to run for the U.S. Senate from Virginia, where he owns a home.

But his support for the Democratic Party and some of its candidates reflects his agreement with their policy preferences rather than his dedication to the party itself. "There are things that I agree with the Democratic Party. There are things I don't. For example, I'm not a big gun control guy. I believe in all the Bill of Rights, including the Second Amendment. I'm not a party guy one way or another ... it's about what your agenda is for the country.... I object to me getting a tax cut where we got soldiers who have to pay for their own body armor in Iraq. That's what; I don't deserve a tax cut. I believe that money ought to be spent on education."

Just as Affleck fits the definition of a political "amateur," Chris Van Hollen is a consummate party "professional." When he served as chair of the Democratic Congressional Campaign Committee in 2008, Van Hollen, a liberal, recruited moderate Democrats to run for House seats in moderate to conservative districts. For Van Hollen, the success of the party is more important than any specific candidate or issue.

Source: Excerpted from transcript from "The O'Reilly Factor," July 27, 2004, at www.foxnews.com/story/0,2933,127324,00.html (accessed April 4, 2011).

For professionals or pragmatists, on the other hand, the goal is the party's success in elections; issues and candidates are the means of achieving that goal. If they believe that their party is most likely to win by downplaying an issue, moderating a position, or nominating a candidate who is popular but not in lockstep with their views, then that is the course they are likely to favor. Party leaders, then, must find a balance between the demands of the growing numbers of issue-oriented, purist activists and those of their more pragmatic colleagues. It is a common dilemma: whether to remain loyal to the group (or the nation) in order to keep it strong and vibrant or to give priority to the principles for which the group was formed.

This conflict may not necessarily be as troublesome as it seems; differences in attitudes between amateurs and professionals do not always show up clearly in their behavior. Although policy-driven amateurs prefer to win with a candidate "they can trust to safeguard their most intense concerns,"[13] most realize that they can't achieve their policy goals unless their candidates win office. Among county party chairs in 1972, a time when amateurs were thought to hold the upper hand in the Democratic Party, the amateurs did not differ from professionals in their effort to communicate within the party, maintain party morale, or run effective campaigns.[14]

Yet the increase in amateur activists, and the accompanying increase in party polarization on issues, can cause rifts that damage a party's chances in particular races. In Minnesota, for instance, Republican primary voters in 2010 nominated a conservative state representative, Tom Emmer, as their candidate for governor over moderate Tom Horner. Horner then filed to run as a minor-party candidate instead and split the Republican vote in the general election, leading to a razor-thin Democratic victory. Infuriated, the Minnesota Republican Party State Central Committee decided to punish some of Horner's supporters; it voted to ban 18 moderate Republicans from participating in party activities for two years and barred them from attending the 2012 Republican national convention. The banned partisans included two former governors and a former U.S. Senator. Conservative "purist" activists argued that the party was better off without these moderates. Some of the moderates replied that the purists were engaging in a "purge" that would reduce the party's appeal and result in the defeat of Republican candidates. Pragmatists from both parties could well understand that fear.

WHERE DO ACTIVISTS COME FROM?

Like almost all other community groups, party organizations have a difficult time attracting volunteers. Except at the national level and in some states where there has been an increase in paid positions and exciting professional opportunities, parties often have few effective means of enlisting new activists. To add to the challenge, state laws often take at least part of the recruitment process out of the party's hands. Rules requiring open party caucuses and the election of party officials in primaries limit the party's control over its personnel. This can lead to the takeover of a local (or even a state) party organization by an intense group of issue activists. At the least, it leaves a party vulnerable to shifts in its direction as some leaders and activists move on and new, self-recruited leaders take their places.

Finding Volunteers: Is Anybody Home?

In a much discussed set of writings, political scientist Robert Putnam has shown that Americans' participation in community activities has declined in recent years. Not just party organizations but also groups ranging from churches to bowling leagues have been starved for participants. Fewer people are involving themselves in the face-to-face activities of politics—attending a political speech or a meeting—even as the lonely activities of Internet surfing and check writing are on the increase. Many culprits have been identified, from the number of hours Americans spend watching television and surfing the net to the increasing numbers of dual-career families. The consequences, Putnam argues, are profound: a reduction in "social capital"—the social connections, values, and trust that enable communities to solve their problems more easily.[15]

The lack of participation in party organizations has been carefully documented. One well-designed survey found that only 8 percent of its national sample reported working on a campaign and just 5 percent said they were involved in a party organization, among the smallest percentages reporting activity in any type of civic organization. Much larger percentages of people say that they take part in charitable, sports, and business and professional groups.[16] Similarly grim conclusions come from the American National Election Studies, in which, in each year since 1994, only about 5 percent have reported going to any political meetings and only about 3 percent said they worked for a party[17]—even in 2008, when the Obama campaign attracted an unusually large number of volunteers. Granted, that is still a lot of people; 3 percent of the adult population would be about 6 million party and campaign activists. But although some of these activists spend a lot of time on political work, mainly at the local level, others are "checkbook participants" who mail in their contributions but do not volunteer their time and energy.

Party organizations need a constant supply of activists of all kinds, so when volunteers are in short supply, the parties tend to accept whatever help is available. The nature of that help often varies from one political period to another, depending on events in the political world at that time. Thus, activists' political outlooks may differ considerably, depending on the time at which individuals became active and the reasons that prompted their activism.[18] The nature and direction of the Democratic Party were heavily influenced by the influx of liberals activated by the Vietnam War and the civil rights movement in the 1960s and 1970s. Tax revolts in the 1980s and efforts to limit the number of terms that incumbents could serve brought new blood into Republican Party organizations. In recent years, activists from the conservative Christian community, some energized by their enthusiasm for former Alaska Governor Sarah Palin, have brought their issues and styles of partisanship into state and local Republican Parties. Because this recruitment process often depends on the presence of magnetic personalities and powerful issues, it tends to take place in spurts rather than continuously.

The parties' recruitment system, then, is not very systematic, and it is closely linked to the movements and passions in the larger society at the time. Yet, although the parties have only limited control over their own recruitment, it clearly affects the parties' ability to achieve their goals. A local Democratic Party whose activists come mainly from labor unions will have different concerns from a local Democratic Party dominated by environmental activists, and a Republican organization run by local business leaders can differ from one controlled by evangelical Christians. Depending on the nature of the community that these parties are trying to persuade, these local parties may have different levels of electoral success as well.

WHAT KINDS OF PEOPLE BECOME PARTY ACTIVISTS?

People are most likely to become involved in party politics if they have the resources to take part, the attitudes that support involvement, and if somebody has encouraged them to do so.[19] The resources needed to become a party activist include time, money, and civic skills such as the ability to organize and communicate. It takes free time to help plan a party's activities, canvass or call people, and attend other party events. People need money if they plan to contribute to the party organization or its candidates or go to party conventions. Their educational levels help to determine how much money and time they have available to spend.

Their attitudes toward politics are also important. People are more likely to take part if they are interested in what happens in campaigns and concerned about the workings of government, if they feel attached to a party, and if they believe that their involvement could make a difference. Most of these attitudes are related to one's income and education levels and thus add to their impact.

The third important question is simply: Has anybody asked them? The parties now have a whole arsenal of tools to contact potential activists: e-mail, regular mail, Facebook, Web sites, text messaging, Twitter, telemarketing, and in-person canvassing. However, most appeals to take part in campaign work—and especially most *successful* appeals—come from friends or other people known to the potential activist. Over the years, most activists have reported that they first became involved with the party as a result of these informal, personal requests for help.[20] Being urged to participate is a powerful motivator; in a major study, almost half of those who were asked to do campaign work said yes. Most people are never asked, however; only about 12 percent of the respondents in that study reported that anyone had ever invited them to work on a campaign.[21] This helps to explain why the proportion of party activists is relatively small.

Who are these people who are active in party affairs? How representative are they of the rest of the American population?

People from "Political Families"

Although they differ in motivations, American party activists have several characteristics in common that set them apart from the general population. First,
they often come from families with a history of party activity. Studies indicate
that many party activists had an adult party activist in their immediate family
when they were growing up.[22] Consider the case of George W. Bush. His grand-
father was a long-time Republican Party official and U.S. senator from Connecticut. His dad, a former Republican National Committee chair, had served
his party in many other posts as well before being elected president. Some of
his siblings have been involved in Republican politics, including his brother
Jeb, who served in the cabinet of a Republican governor and then won the governorship of Florida. Even the father of his son-in-law was a state Republican
Party chair. With such a background, politics becomes the family business.

Better Educated and Wealthier Than Average

A second distinctive characteristic of party activists is that they tend to have
higher incomes, more years of formal education, and higher-status occupations
than does the average American. People with higher incomes are much more
likely to do campaign work than are people whose income is at or below the
poverty line. As would be expected, the gap between the wealthy and the poor
is greater among those who contribute money to the parties and among online
activists as well. Even protest activity is more frequent among the wealthy than
among the poor![23]

This tendency for party activists to be better educated and wealthier than the
average citizen may seem perfectly natural; people with more money and higher
education are more likely to have the means to participate in politics, the interest
in political affairs, and the expectation that they would be successful at it. As a
result, we might expect this pattern to hold in other democratic nations as well.
But that is not the case. Most other democracies have a viable socialist party that
recruits many of its activists from within labor unions. That tends to dampen the
relationship between party activism and higher education and wealth.

In fact, it was not always true of American politics either. The urban political machines of the 1800s and early 1900s tended to recruit party activists
who were more representative of the populations with which they worked.
The machines' jobs and favors were the main reasons for political activism
at this time. When patronage and other material incentives dwindled, the
social character of these parties changed. A comparison of county committee
members from both Pittsburgh parties in 1971, 1976, and 1983 shows that as
machine control declined, the education levels of party workers increased.[24]
As issue-based incentives become more common in the American parties, the
educational and income differences between party activists and the average
citizen tend to grow.

The social characteristics of Democratic activists differ from those of
Republicans, just as the social bases of the parties' voters do. Democratic activists
are more likely than their Republican counterparts to be black, unmarried,

female, and union members. But differences in education, income, and occupation between the two parties' activists have declined in recent years. Although they may come from different backgrounds and certainly hold different political views, the leaders of both parties are drawn especially from higher-status groups in American society, even more now than in decades past.[25] As a result, it is even more true in the United States than in many other nations that party activism and other forms of political participation amplify the voices of privileged groups.

Different Agendas

In addition to these differences in income, education, and family background, party activists also differ from other Americans in the types of issues that they regard as important. A large study of political activists found that the questions of education, abortion, the economy, and human needs (including Social Security and Medicare, jobs, health care, and housing) were the main reasons for their activism. Almost one in five mentioned abortion, a larger proportion than is usually found in polls of citizens as a whole, and one in four mentioned education. International issues were close to the bottom of the list,[26] though the wars in Iraq and Afghanistan may have prompted party activism in the early 2000s.

The activists' issue agendas varied according to their levels of income and education. Higher-income activists expressed greater concern about abortion and the environment, whereas lower-income activists' involvement was more likely to be motivated by a concern about basic human needs.[27] To the extent that higher-income activists are better represented in the parties, issues such as abortion may get more attention in party activities than such issues as housing and health care, at least in recent years.

The types of issues that most clearly divide Democratic from Republican activists have changed over time. In the early 1970s, one of the primary distinctions between the two major parties' activists was the question of social welfare—how big a role government should play in issues such as welfare and other social services. At that time, there was much greater similarity between the two parties' activists on the abortion issue. Today, by contrast, there are few issues that more clearly divide Democratic from Republican activists than their views on abortion, though the issue is more important to Republican activists than it has been to Democrats.[28]

More Extreme Views

Most significantly, party activists (and people who take active roles in other areas of politics as well) tend to hold more extreme views on issues than does the average American. Within the last 20 years, the tendency for liberals to become more active as Democrats and for conservatives to dominate activity within the Republican Party has become more pronounced.[29] This growing gap between the two parties' issue positions is found in Congress as well, as we will see in Chapter 13.

The main reason for this widening gap has been the increasing conservatism of Republican activists.[30] Especially since 1994, when Republicans won a majority in both houses of Congress, Republican activists have been motivated by issues and principles to an even greater extent than Democratic activists have, and their dedication to conservative principles has become more pronounced. So now, on most issues, those active in the Republican Party stand even further to the right of the average voter than Democratic activists are to the left of the average voter. Because party activists are so important a presence in candidates' campaigns—they constitute a noticeable proportion of primary voters, financial contributors, and volunteers and audiences at campaign events—they have been pushing party candidates and elected officials to take more extreme stands on issues as well, leading to the polarization that has become so painfully noticeable in Washington.[31]

PARTY ACTIVISTS AND DEMOCRACY

In short, research tells us that the major parties attract men and women with the time and financial resources to afford political activity, the attitudes that make politics a priority to them, and the connections with others who are similarly engaged. These activists also tend to be motivated by controversial issues, hold more extreme attitudes than other citizens do, and are more polarized by party than was the case in the mid-1900s. These findings raise some important questions: Does it matter if party activists are not very representative of other Americans? What has been the impact of the increase in issue-oriented, "amateur" activists? More generally, how do the characteristics of Republican and Democratic activists affect party organizational strength?

The Problem of Representation

As we have seen, American party activists differ a great deal from other citizens—the very people these activists aim to persuade—and the gulf has been growing. In particular, Democratic volunteers, party officials, and officeholders tend to be more liberal than the average Democrat, and Republican leaders and activists are often more conservative than other Republicans.

When party activists give the appearance of being "true believers" on contentious issues and don't seem to share the concerns of less involved voters, then it is not surprising that many Americans think of the party organizations as alien places. There is a delicate balance to be achieved in party politics. When the two parties sound too much alike on issues, citizens may not feel that they have clear choices in politics. Democracy can be well served when the major parties take clear and distinctive stands on major policy questions. However, when Republican and Democratic activists take polarized positions, especially on questions that are not central to most Americans' daily lives, and try to marginalize anyone who disagrees, then the parties expose themselves to public distrust, an old problem in American politics. The impact increases when these activists recruit and support extremists as party candidates for public office.

Amateurs and Pressure for Internal Party Democracy

The increase in issue-oriented, "amateur" activists often increases the demands on the party organization itself. In the past four decades, these activists have come to insist on a much louder voice in the party's organization, and their demands have been met. Because volunteer activists are so essential to the party's success, party leaders are often willing to tolerate greater levels of internal party democracy in order to retain their volunteers' loyalty.

An internally democratic party organization might, under some circumstances, result in a stronger party, better able to fulfill its responsibilities in a democracy. Rank-and-file activists who are contributing their time and effort in the service of a strongly held principle and who feel sure that their views are taken seriously by party leaders may be even more likely to work hard on the party's behalf. They might also press the party to remain consistent in its issue stands and strive to hold the party's leaders accountable, at least to the activists themselves.

On the other hand, pragmatic parties, dedicated to the party's success above all else, have a long tradition in American politics. Much of the discipline in the classic party machine resulted from the willingness and ability of party leaders to give or withhold material rewards. A disobedient or inefficient party worker sacrificed a patronage job or the hope of one. The newer incentives cannot be given or taken away so easily. A local Republican organization is not likely to punish an errant, ideologically motivated activist by ending the party's opposition to same-sex marriage. Even if it did, the activist could find many other organizations that may be more effective at pursuing that goal, such as religious lobbies or other organized interests.

Activists, Party Strength, and Democracy

Strong party organizations have often been considered a threat to American politics. Since the beginning, American political culture has been dominated by a fear that a few "bosses," responsible to no one but themselves, will control the selection of public officials and the choice of policies. The result has been a series of efforts to keep the parties from playing too powerful a role in the lives of candidates, elected officials, and voters.

Several characteristics of party activists help to keep the parties decentralized and limited in power. The shortage of volunteers means that party organizations have to pay attention to their activists' concerns; that prevents a centralization of party power (unless, of course, the party activists push for such a centralization, as they sometimes have). The demand by many activists for internally democratic parties restrains the authority of party leaders at the top. And, in turn, because power in the American parties is diffused through the various levels of party organization, precinct committee members, city leaders, county officials, and activists at all levels are free to define their own political roles and to nourish their separate bases of party power.

The traditional worry about the excesses of party power, then, is probably misplaced. There have been few occasions in American history when the parties have been able to corral the kinds of incentives and resources that they would need to develop a fully staffed, vibrant organization at all levels of government. Although the national, state, and local party organizations have all raised more money and mastered new campaign skills in the past two decades (as Chapters 3 and 4 show), the continuing challenge of putting "boots on the ground"—attracting volunteers—remains one of the biggest challenges faced by the American parties.

The Political Party in the Electorate

If there were a Pollsters' Hall of Fame, surely the first question in it would be: Generally speaking, do you usually think of yourself as a Republican, a Democrat, an independent, or what? The question is meant to classify *party identifiers*—people who feel a sense of psychological attachment to a particular party. If you respond that you do usually think of yourself as a Democrat or a Republican, then you are categorized as belonging to the *party in the electorate*—the third major sector of the American parties. Party identifiers (also called *partisans*) make up the core of the party's support: the people who normally vote for a party's candidates and who are inclined to see politics through a partisan's eyes. They are more apt to vote in their party's primary elections and to volunteer for party candidates than are other citizens. They are, in short, the party organization's, and its candidates', closest friends in the public.

Survey researchers have measured Americans' partisanship since the 1940s. The dominant measure, just cited, has been used in polls conducted by the University of Michigan, now under the auspices of the American National Election Studies (ANES). After asking whether you consider yourself a Republican or a Democrat, the question continues:

[If Republican or Democrat] Would you call yourself a strong [Republican or Democrat] or a not very strong [Republican or Democrat]? [If independent, no preference, or other party] Do you think of yourself as closer to the Republican Party or to the Democratic Party?

Using these answers, researchers classify people into seven categories of party identification: strong party identifiers (Democrats or Republicans), weak identifiers (Democrats or Republicans), independent "leaners" (toward the Democrats or Republicans), and pure independents.[1]

Note that this definition is based on people's attitudes, not on their actual voting behavior. Strong party identifiers usually vote for their party's candidates, but the essence of a party identification is an attachment to the idea of the party itself, distinct from feelings about particular candidates. Someone can remain a committed Republican, for example, even while choosing to vote for the Democratic candidate in a specific race. Given the large number of elective offices in the United States and the value American culture places on independence, we can often find party identifiers who vote for some candidates of the other party. In the same sense, we do not define the party electorate by the official act of registering with a party. Two-fifths of the states do not have party registration, and in states that do, some voters change their party attachments long before they change their official registration.[2]

The party electorate's relationship with the other two party sectors, the party organization and the party in government, is not necessarily close and cooperative. Party organizations and candidates ask their party identifiers for contributions and votes during campaigns but often don't keep in touch with partisans at other times. Party identifiers, in turn, seldom feel any obligation to the party organization other than to vote for its candidates, if they choose. Party identifiers are not party "members" in any real sense. In these ways, the American parties resemble cadre parties (see page 48): top heavy in leaders and activists without any real membership, in contrast to the mass-membership parties that have been such an important part of the European democratic experience.

Even so, party identifiers give the party organization and its candidates a continuing base of voter support; the parties, then, don't have to start from scratch in each campaign. The party in the electorate also determines most of the party's nominees for office by voting in primaries. It is a potential source of activists for the organization. Partisans help keep the party alive by transmitting party loyalties to their children. A party identification can be the most significant landmark in an individual's mental map of the political world.

A party in the electorate is not just a collection of individuals; it is a coalition of social groups. Our images of the two parties often spring from the types of people the parties have attracted as identifiers. When people speak of the Democrats as the party of minorities, or of the Republicans as the party of business, they are probably referring, at least in part, to the party in the electorate. The groups in a party's coalition help to shape its choice of nominees and its stands on issues, and in turn, those candidates and appeals help to structure elections and political debate.

The three chapters in Part III explore the nature and importance of these parties in the electorate. Chapter 6 looks at the development of party identification and its impact on individuals' political behavior. Chapter 7 examines the parties as coalitions of social groups and traces the meaning of changes in those coalitions over time. Chapter 8 focuses on the parties' efforts to affect voter turnout, not only by mobilizing their supporters but also by trying to change the rules that govern who can vote.

Party Identification

Before you had even left elementary school, if you are like millions of other Americans, you had already begun to identify yourself as a Democrat, a Republican, or an independent. This sense of psychological attachment that most Americans develop toward a political party is called a *party identification,* or *party ID.*[1] The great majority of Americans are partisans. About one-third call themselves "strong" partisans, and almost as many express some party attachment, though not a strong one. Even among those who at first claim to be independents, most admit to feeling "closer to" one party or the other and favor that party in their voting.

Researchers characterize party identification in several ways. The dominant approach is to look at a party attachment as a form of social identity, similar to a religious or ethnic identity. Party ID, then, is viewed as a form of "team loyalty" that helps people find their place in the group conflicts that characterize the political world. It often grows out of other deeply rooted loyalties; a college student, for instance, might have a long-standing sense of herself as a Republican because her parents and relatives are Republicans or because she is an evangelical Christian. Many of these researchers see party ID as a perceptual screen—a lasting picture of the political world that can filter out any conflicting information the individual may receive.

For another group of researchers, party identification is more changeable. It is like a running tally of an individual's positive or negative experiences with the party's stands or its performance in office. This assessment, constantly being updated, can be a decision-making shortcut. Politics is complicated, even for political junkies. Americans cope with more elections and longer ballots than do citizens of any other democracy. A party ID offers a useful means of cutting through the complexity. It can help him or her make efficient voting decisions without taking time to learn much about specific candidates.[2] These differing perspectives on the nature of party identification can lead to different conclusions about its stability.

No matter how we characterize or measure partisanship, however,[3] people's party ID tells us more about their political attitudes and behavior than does any other single piece of information. A party ID will probably be the individual's most enduring political attachment. Where do these party identifications come from?

HOW PEOPLE DEVELOP PARTY IDENTIFICATIONS

Families are the most common source of our first party ID, as they are of so much else in our early lives. As children become aware of politics, they absorb their family's judgments about political parties and usually come to think of themselves as sharing their family's partisanship.

Childhood Influences

Although they do not usually consciously indoctrinate their children into partisanship, parents are the main teachers of political orientations in the American culture. Their casual conversations about political events are enough to convey their party loyalties to their children, just as children learn where their family "belongs" in relation to other social groups. In fact, in these polarized times, you can even find children's books titled *Why Mommy Is a Democrat* (in which the narrator points out, "Democrats make sure we all share our toys") and *The Liberal Claus* (Christmas is threatened when elves unionize and make the North Pole into a socialist disaster).[4] Family and other early influences can be powerful enough to last into adulthood, even when young adults are pulled toward independence in other aspects of their lives.

This early party ID usually takes hold before children have much information as to what the parties stand for. It is not until the middle-school and high-school years that students begin to associate the parties with general economic interests—with business or labor, the rich or the poor—and thus to have some reasoning to support the party ID that they have already developed. Note the importance of the sequence here. Party loyalty comes first, so it can have a long-lasting impact on attitudes toward politics. Only later do people learn about political issues and events, which may then be filtered, at least to a degree, through a partisan lens.[5]

Once developed, people's party loyalties are often sustained because they tend to gravitate toward people like themselves; thus, their friends, relatives, and coworkers typically share the same partisanship.[6] Some people do leave the party of their parents. Those whose early party loyalty is weak are more likely to change. So are people whose mother and father identified with different parties or who live in a community or work in a setting where the dominant party ID differs from their own. But when parents share the same party ID, they are more likely to produce strong party identifiers among their children.

Other sources of political learning tend to support a person's inherited party loyalty or at least do not challenge the family's influence. Schools typically avoid partisan politics; they are probably more inclined to teach political independence than partisanship. During the early and mid-1900s, most American churches steered clear of partisan conflict even at a time when church-connected political parties existed in Europe. Many churches and other religious groups have become very engaged in politics recently, but they are not likely to lead young people away from their parents' partisan influence. And the American parties themselves do much less outreach than do some European parties, which maintain party youth groups, social, and recreational activities.

Influences in Adulthood

These influences on children's and teenagers' political learning are more likely to be challenged in young adulthood, when an individual moves into new environments: college, work, marriage, a new community, and the unexpected honor of paying taxes. At this time, young adults can test their childhood party loyalties against their own personal experience with politics. They can get to know others with different party preferences. Their adult experiences may reinforce their early-learned loyalties or may undermine those loyalties.[7] Or the old loyalties may exist peacefully alongside contradictory new information; people can learn more about candidates and issues, and even change their attitudes toward those political objects, without necessarily changing their party ID.[8]

The longer an individual holds a particular party ID, the more stable it normally becomes.[9] Older adults are least likely to change their party attachments. After decades of watching and taking part in politics, party ID tends to become a habit. Partisanship may grow stronger across the life cycle because it is so useful a shortcut for simplifying the political decision making of older voters,[10] or because they surround themselves increasingly with others who share their party loyalties.

There are times, however, when even committed Democrats and Republicans are driven to change their partisanship. During periods of major party change, when the issue bases of partisanship and the party coalitions themselves are being transformed, some voters switch party loyalties. (We look more fully at the idea of party coalitional change or realignment in the next chapter.) This happened in the South in the late 1900s as conservative whites moved from Democratic partisanship to independence and then to Republican Party ID. Economic calamities and debates about strongly felt issues such as abortion, especially when party leaders' stands attract a lot of media coverage,[11] can make someone rethink her partisanship. Older adults may be caught up in the excitement of the moment as well, but their partisanship, often reinforced by years of consistent partisan behavior, resists change more effectively. Thus, when partisan turmoil begins, young adults are more likely than older adults to embrace the change.[12]

PATTERNS OF PARTISANSHIP OVER TIME

Large-scale change in party identifications is the exception, however, and not the rule. Most Americans, once they have developed party loyalties, tend to keep them. People who do change their party ID often change only its intensity (e.g., from strong to weak identification) rather than convert to the other party.

At the national level, we can see this stability in Americans' responses to the poll question measuring party ID that has been asked in every presidential election year since 1952 by researchers for the American National Election Studies. The data are summarized by decade in Figure 6.1; the full data set can be found in Table A.2 in the online Appendix.[13] The figure shows some change in the overall partisanship of Americans: Although Democrats

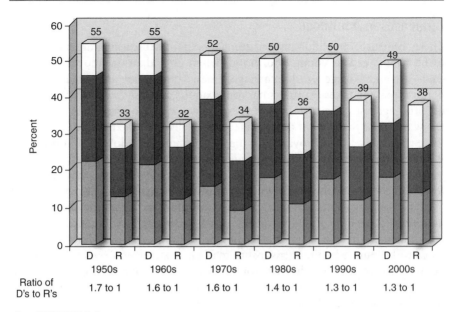

FIGURE 6.1

Party Identification by Decade, 1950s–2000s.

Note: Based on surveys of the national electorate conducted immediately before each presidential and most congressional elections as part of the American National Election Studies program. For each party grouping in each decade, the gray segment at the base of the bar is the percentage of respondents calling themselves strong Democrats or Republicans; in the middle are weak Democrats or Republicans, and at the top is the percentage calling themselves independents who lean toward the Democratic or the Republican Party. For the full presentation of data for presidential election years, including the "pure" independents, see Table A.2 in the online Appendix at www.pearson.com/hershey.

Source: American National Election Studies, University of Michigan; data made available by the Inter-University Consortium for Political and Social Research.

have been in the majority throughout these years, the gap narrowed in each decade, and especially beginning in the 1980s, until the two groups of partisans had become more equal in size by the early 2000s. This increase in Republican support, as we will see in Chapter 7, was propelled largely by the gradual movement of white southerners from Democratic to Republican identification.

Changes in overall partisanship usually happen slowly. In Figure 6.1, look, for example, at the percentage who call themselves strong Republicans (represented by the gray portion at the bottom of each Republican column). When summarized by decade, this proportion never rises above 14 percent nor drops below 9 percent. The full dataset in the Appendix shows that during 60 years of history, from years when the Republican Party was triumphant to years when it seemed almost dead, the proportion of strong Republicans has stayed within a 7-percentage–point range, between 9 and 16 percent of those surveyed. Overall, the percentage of respondents in each category of partisanship tends to change very little from one election year to the next;

the usual difference is just 2 percent. Election campaigns and other events can produce "bumps" in the short term, but these are often short lived.[14]

There are a few exceptions to this story of fairly stable partisanship. During an especially turbulent period—1972 through 1976, spanning President Richard Nixon's landslide reelection, the Watergate scandals that caused Nixon to resign, his subsequent pardon by President Gerald Ford, and Ford's own 1976 defeat—researchers interviewed the same set of individuals in three successive surveys. Almost two-thirds of the respondents remained in the same broad category of party identification (44 percent were stable strong/weak Democrats or Republicans, 20 percent stable independents) throughout all three surveys. Only 3 percent changed parties.[15] The stability of party identification during these agitated times is impressive.[16]

Yet a third of the respondents did change from a party ID to independence during these three waves of surveys. And at the national level (see Figure 6.2), there was a drop in the proportion of respondents calling themselves *strong* partisans (Democrats or Republicans) during the 1960s, and an increase in the percentage of independent "leaners," especially among younger voters first entering the electorate. Combined with other major changes at that time—the civil rights movement, protests against American involvement in the Vietnam War, the women's movement, environmental activism—the growing number of independents suggested to many observers that partisanship was fading in the United States.

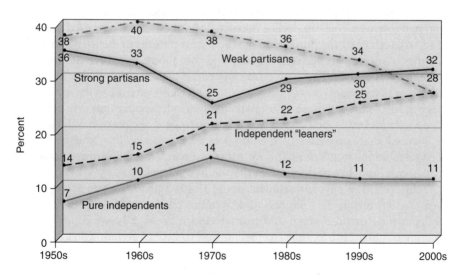

FIGURE 6.2
Change in Strength of Party ID, 1950s–2000s.

Note: This is a "folded" party ID scale in which Democrats and Republicans in each category are combined (i.e., the category "strong partisans" includes strong Democrats and strong Republicans).

Source: Calculated from American National Election Studies, University of Michigan; data made available through the Inter-University Consortium for Political and Social Research.

Has There Been a Decline in Partisanship?

Research in other democracies bolstered the argument that partisanship was in decline in the 1960s and 1970s. Across the western industrialized world, analysts found a rise in the proportion of independents, a drop in confidence expressed in political parties, and an increase in *split-ticket voting* (supporting candidates of more than one party).[17] The effects of this "party decline" would have been profound.[18] What could have caused it? Education levels were rising in democracies; perhaps the better-educated voters had so much other information available that they didn't need parties as a decision shortcut any more. Maybe candidates were becoming independent of party ties and influencing other citizens. Perhaps media coverage of politics stressed nonpartisanship or ignored parties.

These explanations provoked even more questions, however. If Americans have more information available than ever before, wouldn't they need a device, like a party ID, to help them sift through it? Even though education levels are rising, we know that most Americans are not very interested in politics, do not know very much about it, and therefore depend on shortcuts to make sense of their voting decisions.[19] Party ID, then, would probably remain a helpful tool. And among people for whom partisanship is a strong group attachment, more information would probably not lead to a decline in partisan feelings.

In fact, indicators of partisanship *have* rebounded since the 1970s. In particular, there has been a resurgence of strong partisanship (see Figure 6.2). The proportion of strong party identifiers in 2008 was only four percentage points lower than it had been in the 1950s, which was considered a very partisan time. Among those who vote, the decline in party ID has been largely reversed.[20] In fact, in some recent polls, the proportion of voters who considered themselves partisan, and the consistency between partisanship and vote choice, have been the highest in more than 20 years.[21] The main changes between the 1950s and today have been a decrease in the proportion of weak partisans and a big increase in the numbers of independent "leaners," those who call themselves independents but then acknowledge, when probed by poll takers, that they lean toward one party. It is the increase in "leaners" that is typically used to support the contention that Americans have become more independent politically. Most of these "leaners," however, vote and think much more like partisans than they do like independents.[22]

The revival of party attachment in the 1980s and 1990s was prompted by greater partisanship in Congress and by more partisan political leaders such as President Ronald Reagan and former House Speaker Newt Gingrich. The increase in partisanship, then, seemed at first to benefit Republicans.

Recent Changes in the Direction of Party ID

Another unusually quick change in the direction of partisanship has taken place more recently. Both congressional parties' approval ratings had risen until after the September 11, 2001, terrorist attacks and then declined steadily (see Figure 6.3). But beginning in 2005, the bottom fell out for the Republicans. Approval ratings for the Republicans in Congress continued to slip. During the same period, the proportion of Republican identifiers fell sharply, as did the number of voters

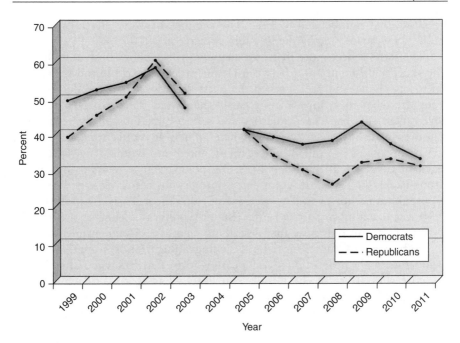

FIGURE 6.3

Public Approval Ratings of the Parties in Congress, 1999–2011.

Note: Data points are the percentages who say that they "approve of the way the (Democrats/Republicans) in Congress are handling their job?"

Source: Calculated from Gallup Polls accessible via www.gallup.com/poll/148568/Amid-Debt-Clash-Approval-Parties-Congress-Low-Steady.aspx (accessed November 9, 2011).

registering as Republicans. One apparent cause was the big decline in public approval of Republican President George W. Bush. Democrats' approval ratings, by contrast, leveled off after 2005, and the numbers of people registering to vote as Democrats or independents rose, especially among younger voters.

Just when Republicans had reached the point of desperation in the 2008 elections, however, their prospects improved. A few months into the new Obama administration in 2009, as the economy continued to languish and controversy arose about the Obama stimulus program and health care reform, Republican partisanship and the approval ratings of congressional Republicans rebounded. Now it was the Democrats who found themselves in free-fall, especially among younger and lower-income whites.

The Democratic Party's favorability rating dropped about 10 percentage points from early 2009 to early 2011, and Democratic candidates lost in almost unprecedented numbers in the 2010 midterm elections. Even more dramatic change could be seen in state-by-state measures of party ID. Democratic identification had risen to a recent peak in 2008, during the Obama wave, when 30 states could be classified as solidly Democratic (those with at least 10 percentage points more Democratic identifiers than Republicans).

By 2010, that number fell to 14.[23] The Democratic wave elections in 2006 and 2008 were undone by the Republican wave in 2010.

The shifts reflect more than just changing views about Bush and Obama. The sharper differentiation between Democratic and Republican stands has led to big changes in policy when the party in power changes. Voters often recognize what they oppose more easily than what they favor. Thus, when government cuts back its regulatory and service functions, many voters find that they miss the lost services; and when big new government regulatory and service programs are put in place, many voters are irritated by the greater reach of government into their lives. Big policy change tends to produce a strong backlash. The most recent party shift has not been a clear endorsement of Republicans, however. The increase in Republican Party ID in 2009 and 2010 was due almost entirely to the rise in Republican "leaners," who admit to being partisans only after first describing themselves as independents.[24]

Some suggest that longer-term demographic trends should help the Democrats.[25] The proportion of Americans who are married, white Christians— the core supporters of the Republican Party—has seriously declined. The fastest-growing groups in the adult population are Latinos and young people who came of age politically during the declining popularity of the Bush years. Both groups leaned heavily Democratic in 2004 and 2008. But their continued enthusiasm for politics depends heavily on the Obama administration's ability to keep its young and minority supporters engaged. To an even greater extent than is usual in midterm elections, voter turnout by younger people and people of color dropped in 2010. Democrats must hope that major Republican figures continue to take stands on abortion, gay rights, and immigration that are unpalatable to many in these groups, so that their motivation to vote as well as their Democratic leanings are maintained. No matter which party is favored at the time, however, party remains an influential political attachment, and the earlier discussion of party decline is at an end.

PARTY IDENTIFICATION AND POLITICAL VIEWS

Because of their early development, stability, and power, individuals' party loyalties can affect their views on a variety of political topics, from issues to candidates.[26] Figure 6.4 shows that feelings about the federal government can change markedly, consistent with party ID, when partisan control of the government changes. In 2006, during the big slide in Republican President Bush's approval ratings, fully 57 percent of Democratic identifiers agreed that the federal government "poses an immediate threat to the rights and freedoms of ordinary citizens," as did only 21 percent of Republicans. In sharp contrast, just before the 2010 elections, with Democrat Obama in the White House and Democrats in control of Congress, the number of Republicans feeling threatened by the federal government had tripled, whereas the number of worried Democrats dropped by more than half. During that time, "pure" independents' sense of threat had hardly changed at all.[27]

For an even more dramatic example, consider the controversial 2000 election, when the Supreme Court stopped the recount of votes in some

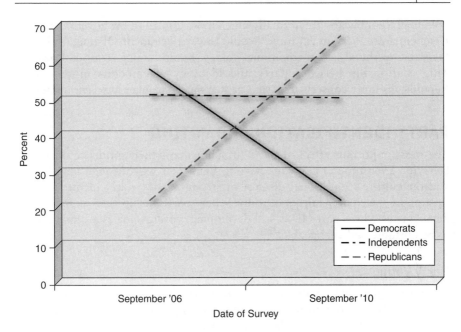

FIGURE 6.4

Does the Federal Government Pose an Immediate Threat? by Party ID, 2006 and 2010.

Note: Data points are the percentages of each group who say "yes" to the question, "Do you think the federal government poses an immediate threat to the rights and freedoms of ordinary citizens, or not?"

Source: Gallup Poll at www.gallup.com/poll/143717/Republicans-Democrats-Shift-Whether-Gov-Threat.aspx (accessed November 9, 2011).

Florida counties and decided the presidential election in favor of Bush. In a poll taken two months before the election, 70 percent of Democratic identifiers had said that they approved of the Supreme Court's job performance, and only 18 percent disapproved. A month after the Court's verdict on the presidential race, just 42 percent of Democrats now said they approved of the way the Court was handling its job, and 50 percent said they disapproved. Conversely, approval of the Court among Republicans rose from 60 percent in August 2000 to 80 percent in January 2001.[28]

Party loyalty can affect people's attitudes even when it has to compete with other valued loyalties. Democrat John Kerry was the third Catholic presidential nominee in American history. Catholics were more likely to vote for Kerry in 2004 than Protestants were. Catholic Republicans, however, were not as positive toward Kerry as were Catholic Democrats. Party ID still made a difference, even among those with the same religious affiliation. Party identification is not the only cause of political attitudes, but it helps to condition the way people feel about issues, candidates, and public officials.[29]

The result is that we see clear differences between Democrats' and Republicans' views. The biggest difference has to do with attitudes toward government spending; Republicans are normally much more critical of big government than Democrats are, very much more hostile toward President Obama, and more favorable to the idea that traditional values should be universally followed.[30] This relationship between party and ideology—Democrats more liberal, Republicans more conservative—has grown much stronger in recent decades.[31]

PARTY IDENTIFICATION AND VOTING

The most important effect of party attachments is their influence on voting behavior. Even though partisans have to fight their way through long ballots and the culture's traditional distrust of strong parties, party identifiers tend to support their party fairly faithfully. Where partisanship is weak, as in new democracies where party ID is still developing, voting choices are more likely to be unstable and changeable.[32]

Party Voting

During the past half-century, party identifiers have voted for their party's candidates most of the time. As you can see in Figures 6.5 and 6.6, a majority in each category of partisanship has voted for their party's presidential candidate in every year, except for weak Democrats in 1972 and independent Democrats in 1980 (both GOP landslide years). As with party ID, party voting declined

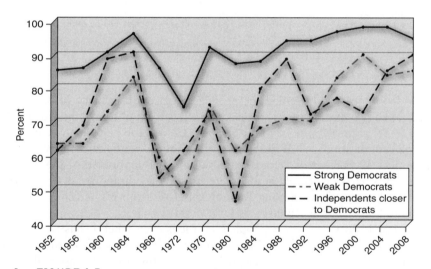

FIGURE 6.5

Percent of Democrats Voting for Their Party's Presidential Candidates, 1952–2008.

Note: The numbers for each election year can be found in Table A.3 in the online Appendix at www.pearson.com/hershey. Comparable data on voting for the respondent's party's congressional candidates can be found in Table A.4.

Source: American National Election Studies, University of Michigan; data made available by the Inter-University Consortium for Political and Social Research.

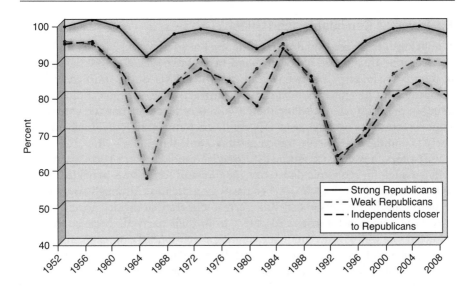

FIGURE 6.6

Percent of Republicans Voting for Their Party's Presidential Candidates, 1952–2008.

Note: The numbers for each election year can be found in Table A.3 in the online Appendix at www.pearson.com/hershey. Comparable data on voting for the respondent's party's congressional candidates can be found in Table A.4.

Source: American National Election Studies, University of Michigan; data made available by the Inter-University Consortium for Political and Social Research.

somewhat during the late 1960s and early 1970s. But recent studies show that the overall impact of party ID on voting behavior has been on the upswing since the mid-1970s[33] and continued to increase in the 2000s. The polarization of the major parties in recent years has probably helped some voters to clarify their political attachments and to heighten their sense of loyalty to a party and its candidates. The most faithful are the strong partisans. In the last four presidential elections, at least 94 percent of strong Democrats supported their party's candidate. Strong Republicans have been even more loyal; only once in 50 years has their support for the GOP presidential candidate dipped below 90 percent.

These patterns appear in congressional elections as well. (The data can be found in Table A.4 in the online Appendix.) A majority within each group of partisans has voted for their party's congressional candidates in each election, and strong partisans have been the most consistent party voters. We find similar results in voting at the state and local levels. *Straight-ticket voting*—voting for one party's candidates only—declined among all partisan groups during the 1960s and 1970s, but the stronger an individual's party ID, the more likely he or she was to vote a straight ticket.[34] And as with other indicators of party influence, the decline has reversed. In 1984, 190 congressional districts out of 435 (44 percent) voted for a House member of one party and a presidential candidate of the other. By 2004, there were only 59 such districts—a 50-year low, and the number increased only to 83 in 2008 (19 percent).

Party versus Candidates and Issues

What causes these ups and downs in the level of party voting? Individuals' voting decisions are affected by the give-and-take of two sets of forces: the strength of their party loyalty (if they have one) and the power of the *short-term forces* operating in a given election, such as the attractiveness of the candidates and issues in that campaign. Usually these two sets of forces incline the voter in the same direction; as we have seen, a party ID encourages an individual to see the party's candidates and issue stands in a favorable light.

At times, however, an especially attractive candidate or a particularly compelling issue—an economic disaster or the threat of terrorism—may lead a voter to desert one or more of his or her party's candidates. Although some voters seem to split their tickets in order to create a moderate or divided government,[35] it is more common for voters to defect from their party ID because they are attracted to a well-known candidate running a well-funded campaign, most often an incumbent of the other party.[36] Typically, those with the weakest party ID or the most ambivalent attitudes about the parties—for example, those who have at least some positive feelings about both parties[37]—are the most likely to defect.

Partisanship as a Two-Way Street

Which is more important in influencing people's votes: party ID, candidate characteristics, or current issues? One challenge for political scientists in answering this question is that these three forces are strongly interrelated. The early studies of party ID in the 1950s assumed that party "came first" in the causal ordering—that it affected people's feelings about candidates and issues but was not in turn influenced by them. These early studies did not have good measures of how close the voter felt to the candidates on issues.

Since then, with the use of better measures, researchers have shown that there are reciprocal relationships among these three influences. Just as an individual's party loyalty influences the way he or she views politics, feelings about candidates and issues can affect the individual's party ID. In particular, reactions to a president's management of the economy (so-called *retrospective evaluations*, in that they refer to past actions rather than hopes for the future) can feed back on party loyalties and weaken or change them. In this way, it is possible to see partisanship as a kind of running tally of party-related evaluations.[38] Even if party ID is usually stable enough to withstand an individual's disappointment in a particular party candidate or in the party's position on an issue or two, an accumulation of these negative experiences, especially on an issue important to him or her, can weaken or change an individual's partisanship.[39] That is what happened over several decades to the long-standing Democratic loyalties of many conservative white southerners, in response to Democratic administrations' handling of racial and other issues.

In the short run, then, issues and the candidates in a particular election can have a major impact on the outcome. But party ID has continuing power to influence voters' choices and to affect their feelings about issues and candidates as well.[40] So whether we want to explain the general trends of American voting behavior or the choices of voters in a particular election, party ID plays a prominent role.

PARTY IDENTIFICATION AND POLITICAL ACTIVITY

Another important effect of party ID is that individuals who consider them-selves Democrats and Republicans are more involved in political life than are those who call themselves independents. Partisanship is emotionally engaging; it gives partisans a stake in the outcome of political events. Therefore, it is the strongest partisans who are the most likely to vote, to pay attention to politics, and to become politically active. In 2008, as in previous years, strong Democrats and Republicans were more likely than weak identifiers or independents to be interested in politics and to follow media reports about the campaign (Table 6.1).

Strong partisans are also the most active in other ways. A total of 90 and 95 percent, respectively, of the strong Democrats and Republicans reported having voted in 2008—higher than the turnout levels among weaker partisans or independents.[41] Strong identifiers were much more likely than other citizens to try to persuade others to vote a certain way, to display bumper stickers or yard signs, and to contribute to a party or candidate. The only anomaly here is that strong partisans were less likely to seek campaign information on the Internet,

TABLE 6.1

Political Involvement of Partisans and Independents, 2008

	Democrats		Independents			Republicans	
	Strong	Weak	Closer to Dem.	Closer to Neither	Closer to Rep.	Weak	Strong
Follow public affairs most of the time	33	25	26	19	34	32	32
Watched programs about campaign on TV	96	91	88	87	85	98	97
Read about campaign in newspapers	66	53	55	39	54	54	62
Used Internet to gather information about campaign	40	42	52	20	52	58	38
Voted	90	78	66	50	75	86	95
Tried to influence the vote of others	57	33	37	25	47	49	67
Displayed button, bumper sticker, sign	34	15	13	11	9	10	24
Attended rally or meeting	18	7	6	5	7	4	7
Contributed money to:							
Candidate	20	7	10	4	6	8	20
Party	14	6	7	1	5	8	15

Source: 2008 American National Election Study, University of Michigan; data made available by the Inter-University Consortium for Political and Social Research.

mainly because Internet use tends to be concentrated among people under the age of 50, whereas strong partisanship is much more likely among people over 50.

PARTY IDENTIFICATION AND ATTITUDES TOWARD THE PARTIES

Strong party identifiers see a greater contrast between the Republican and Democratic Parties than do weak identifiers and independents, both in general and on specific policy issues (see Figure 6.7). They are more polarized in their evaluations of the two parties' candidates as well as of the parties' ability to govern for the benefit of the nation. In the mind of the strong partisan, in short, the parties are clearly defined and very different from one another on the important dimensions of politics.

A stronger party ID, by itself, is not enough to account for greater political activism and sharper party images. Other factors, such as higher socioeconomic status (SES), can also promote political activity. The relatively greater involvement of partisans (and, in most years, of Republicans) comes in part from their generally higher SES as well as from their more ideological commitment to politics.[42] Even so, party ID has a major impact on people's political activity.

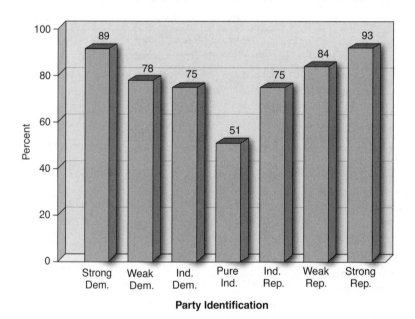

FIGURE 6.7

Percent Seeing Important Differences Between the Parties, 2008.

Note: The question was, "Do you think there are any important differences in what the Republicans and Democrats stand for?"

Source: 2008 American National Election Study, University of Michigan; data made available by the Inter-University Consortium for Political and Social Research.

THE MYTH OF THE INDEPENDENT

It is intriguing that party loyalties govern so much political behavior in a culture that so warmly celebrates the independent voter. There is clearly a disconnect between the American myth of the high-minded independent—the well-informed citizen who is moved by issues and candidates, not parties—and the reality of widespread partisanship. The problem is with the myth.

Attitudinal Independents

The definition of "independent" used so far in this chapter is someone who tells a poll taker that he or she does not identify with a political party. Studies show that these independents tend to split their tickets more often than other voters do and wait longer in the campaign to decide how to vote. In those ways, they would seem to fit the myth of the thoughtful, deliberative citizen. But they fall short of the mythical picture of the independent in most other ways. In 2008, as you saw in Table 6.1, independents stayed home from the polls at a higher rate than did party identifiers and scored lower than partisans on several other indicators of political involvement.

Within this group, it is important to distinguish between independents who say they feel closer to one of the two parties (independent leaners) and those who do not ("pure" independents). The independent leaners often turn out to be more politically involved (see Table 6.1) and sometimes even more partisan in voting than weak partisans are (see Figures 6.5 and 6.6). It is only in comparison with strong partisans that these leaners fall short. By contrast, the pure independents typically have the most dismal record; they are less involved and less informed, on average, than are other Americans.[43]

Behavioral Independents

We can also define independents in terms of their behavior. In his final work, the unparalleled researcher, V. O. Key, Jr., explored various definitions of political independence.[44] Concerned about the picture of the American voter that was emerging from research in the 1950s and 1960s, showing an electorate much more driven by deeply ingrained party loyalties than by an understanding of major political issues, Key looked for evidence of rational behavior among voters. He focused in particular on "party switchers"— those who supported different parties in two consecutive presidential elections—rather than on the self-described independents. In practice, party switchers came much closer to the flattering myth of the independent than did the self-styled independents. These party switchers, Key found, expressed at least as much political interest as did the "stand-patters" (those who voted for the same party in both elections). Above all, the switchers showed an issue-related rationality that fit the mythical picture of the independent. They agreed on policy issues with the stand-patters toward whose party they had shifted, and they disagreed with the policies of the party from which they had defected.

It is the attitudinal independents, however—those who call themselves independents, rather than those who switch parties—who are the subject of the most study. They have always been a diverse group containing not only some who resemble the image of the sophisticated independent but also many of the least involved and informed voters in American politics.[45] The myth that they are a carefully informed and active group of voters who operate above the party fray has withered under the glare of survey research.

Are Independents a Likely Source of Support for Third-Party Candidates?

Even if the attitudinal independents don't know or do much about politics, they still could play an important role in elections. Because they have the weakest ties to the two major parties, they could be more open to the charms of minor-party and independent candidates than other citizens are.[46] That has happened on occasion. One of the biggest stories of the 1992 presidential election was the unprecedented showing of independent candidate Ross Perot. A very rich man, Perot spent millions on a campaign criticizing the two major parties as irresponsible and corrupt. Unlike most independents, Perot flourished rather than faded as the campaign came to an end. He finished with almost 20 million votes, 19 percent of those cast.

On Election Day, Perot did draw many of his votes from pure independents and to a lesser extent from independent leaners.[47] Fully 37 percent of pure independents said they voted for Perot, compared with only 4 percent of strong Democrats and 11 percent of strong Republicans. The same was true of Perot's third-party candidacy in 1996, although the percentages decreased by more than half. In the end, however, there were not enough independents and disgruntled partisans to make a majority for Perot. It would be difficult for any independent or third-party candidate to construct a winning coalition from a group as diverse as independent voters, who have little in common other than their dislike of the major parties. Such a candidate can serve as a "spoiler," however. Ralph Nader got enough votes as the Green Parties candidate in 2000, most of them from independents, to give the election to Bush.

In the close party competition that has characterized recent elections, even a small percentage of voters has the power to determine the winner. One big difference between the election results in 2008 and 2010, for instance, was that pure independents, who favored Democratic U.S. House candidates in 2008, switched to Republican candidates by a substantial margin in 2010. It is a sobering thought that when an election is close, independent voters with the least interest and information about the candidates may be the ones who tip the balance.

CHANGE IN THE IMPACT OF PARTY ID

Party ID, then, is a psychological commitment that is often strong enough to guide other political beliefs and behavior. Strong partisans tend to see issues and candidates through "party-tinted" glasses. They are more likely to vote for their party's candidates and to be politically active than other citizens are. Yet partisanship functions in a very different context now than it did a century ago.

A More Candidate Centered Politics

Although the great majority of Americans still hold a party ID or "lean toward" the Democrats or the Republicans, the parties have faced major challenges to their influence on citizens. Early in the 1900s, states began adopting the direct primary, in which voters had to choose candidates without the useful guidance of a party label. Partisanship remains a helpful shortcut in general elections but does not distinguish one candidate from another in a party's primary. New campaign and fund-raising technologies developed that were harder for party organizations to monopolize. Candidates with enough money could use television, direct mail, and now the Internet to reach voters directly, over the parties' heads.

During the turbulent years of the 1960s and 1970s, as we have seen, the number of self-identified independents grew, and the impact of party ID on people's voting choices declined. Candidates found it helpful to downplay their party label, running instead as individual entrepreneurs. Now, even though party loyalties have regained much of their influence, candidates still tend to downplay their partisanship as a means of attracting voter support. In addition, other elements of American politics—new and traditional media, organized interests, campaign consultants, candidates' characteristics, issues, and current events—have important effects on campaigns. The consequence is that elections have become less party centered and more candidate centered (see Chapter 11).[48]

The weakness of candidate centered elections is that they make it more difficult for voters to hold government responsible. Voters may be able to hold a single candidate accountable for his or her campaign promises, but given that a typical election may include dozens of candidates, it is very difficult for most busy citizens to gather the information necessary to evaluate each candidate as an individual. When elections focus on individual candidates, rather than on teams of candidates in which each team stands for an identifiable, if broad, policy orientation, elections may ask more of voters than they are willing to give.

The Continuing Significance of Party

Yet party ID remains a powerful force in American politics. Voters continue to perceive candidates, issues, and elections in partisan terms and often vote accordingly. The elections of the 2000s have mobilized strong partisans to an exceptional degree. Party-dominated contests are still very possible, even in a candidate centered political world. Will this continue, or will the instability of modern politics eat away at the parties' bases of support? The story continues in the next chapter, where we look more closely at the two major parties' supporting coalitions and their changes over time.

Party Coalitions and Party Change

Former California Governor Arnold Schwarzenegger had a mixed marriage, politically speaking. Schwarzenegger, a wealthy white man, has owned several businesses. His father was a military officer. The governor's ex-wife, Maria Shriver, is a journalist and comes from a large Catholic family of lawyers and activists for nonprofit groups. Using just the information in this description, would you be able to tell which member of this couple is a Democrat and which is a Republican?

Party identifications are not distributed randomly among Americans. Some social groups lean heavily toward a Republican identification—small business owners, Mormons, and evangelical white Protestants, for example—and other groups, such as single mothers, African Americans, and many highly educated professionals, are more likely to consider themselves Democrats. Without any knowledge of their voting history, then, and purely on the basis of their links with certain social groups, we could predict (accurately) that Schwarzenegger is the Republican and Shriver is the Democrat.

The types of people who support a party make up what is called the party's *coalition*—the social, economic, or other groups most inclined to favor that party's candidates through good times and bad. Groups may align with a party for many reasons, but once a group has become linked with a party's coalition, its interests are very likely to affect the stands the party takes on at least some issues and the strategies it follows in campaigns.

The differences between the two parties' coalitions are a helpful clue as to which issues dominate the nation's politics at that time. The facts that African Americans have identified overwhelmingly as Democrats in recent decades and that southern whites are now dominantly Republican remind us that racial issues continue to be powerful in American elections.[1] At various points in U.S. history, regional conflicts, ethnic and religious divisions, disputes between agriculture and industry, and differences in social class have also helped form the basis for differences between the two parties' coalitions, as they have in other Western democracies.

Although there are other important sources of change in the party system—for instance, switches in party control of the federal government[2] and organizational changes producing "service parties"[3] (see Chapters 3 and 4) and more candidate-centered campaigns (see Chapter 11)—party researchers have lavished the most attention on coalitional changes. In much of this literature, great and enduring changes in the parties' coalitions have been called *party realignments*.[4] The concept of realignment is a controversial one, as you'll see later in the chapter. But no matter how we conceptualize them, changes in patterns of group support for the Democrats and the Republicans make a fascinating story and have made a major difference in American politics and policies over time.

In this chapter, then, we will look at party change with special attention to the parties' supporting coalitions. We'll examine the development of the parties' current coalitions: from what races, religions, regions, educational backgrounds, and other social groups do these supporters come and what attracts them to one party rather than the other. Finally, we will consider how best to characterize the changes in the parties' coalitions since the New Deal.

THE AMERICAN PARTY SYSTEMS

Many analysts agree that the United States has experienced at least six different electoral eras or *party systems*. (See Table 7.1 for a summary of each party system.) Although some common themes run through all of these eras, each has had a distinctive pattern of group support for the parties. Each party system can also be distinguished by the kinds of issue concerns that dominated it and the types of public policies that the government put into effect. In Chapter 1, we looked at party history to learn about the interrelationships among the three parts of the party. Now let us get a different take on these events, from the perspective of changes in social group support for the parties.

TABLE 7.1

Years of Partisan Control of Congress and the Presidency, 1801–2012

	House		Senate		President	
First party system	*D-R*	*Opp.*	*D-R*	*Opp.*	*D-R*	*Opp.*
(1801–1828)	26	2	26	2	28	0
Second party system	*Dem.*	*Opp.*	*Dem.*	*Opp.*	*Dem.*	*Opp.*
(1829–1860)	24	8	28	4	24	8
Third party system	*Dem.*	*Rep.*	*Dem.*	*Rep.*	*Dem.*	*Rep.*
(1861–1876)	2	14	0	16	0	16
(1877–1896)	14	6	4	16	8	12
Fourth party system						
(1897–1932)	10	26	6	30	8	28

(*continued*)

◤ TABLE 7.1 (CONTINUED)						
	House		Senate		President	
Fifth party system	Dem.	Rep.	Dem.	Rep.	Dem.	Rep.
(1933–1968)	32	4	32	4	28	8
Sixth party system						
(1969–1980)	12	0	12	0	4	8
(1981–2012)	18	14	15	17	12	20
(1969–2012)	30	14	27	17	16	28

Note: Entries for the first party system are Democratic-Republicans and their opponents; for the second party system, Democrats and their opponents (first Whigs and then Republicans); and for subsequent party systems, Democrats and Republicans. In 2001, Republicans were in the majority in the Senate for the first five months and Democrats for the last seven, so the Senate is counted as being under Democratic control.

The First Party System

The initial American party system (from about 1801 to 1828)[5] emerged out of a serious conflict between opposing groups in George Washington's administration: How much power should the national government exercise relative to that of the states? As Chapter 1 noted, the Federalists, led by Alexander Hamilton, wanted a strong national government that would work closely with business and industry to build the nation's economy. A national bank would centralize the states' banking systems. This plan would benefit business owners and wealthier citizens, who were concentrated in New England; these groups became the core support for the Federalists.

Farmers and the less well-off, living in the southern and mid-Atlantic states, could see that the Federalists' proposals would hurt them financially; farmers would pay taxes, but businesses and speculators would reap more of the benefits. So they supported Thomas Jefferson and James Madison's demand for states' rights, limits on the national government's power, and a more egalitarian vision of the new democracy. The Jeffersonians won the debate; in the hotly contested 1800 election, these Democratic-Republicans, as they came to be called, gained the presidency. The Federalists slowly slipped into a fatal decline, and the supporters of Jefferson and Madison then dominated politics for more than two decades.

The Second Party System

The next party system (from approximately 1829 to 1860) developed when the one-party rule of the Democratic-Republicans could not contain all the conflicts generated by a rapidly changing nation. The party split into two factions on the major issues of the period: not just the national government's economic powers but also how the Union should expand and, increasingly, how to handle the explosive question of slavery. One faction continued the

Jeffersonian tradition of opposition to a strong national government; it included the farmers of the South and the western frontier, as well as the addition of many urban workers and their political bosses. Led by Andrew Jackson, it would later call itself the Democratic Party or, at times, "the Democracy." The other, a more elitist and eastern faction represented by John Quincy Adams, referred to itself as the National Republicans and was eventually absorbed into the Whig Party.[6]

This second party system was just as class based as the first; wealthier voters supported the Whigs and the less privileged identified as Democrats. The Democrats dominated, growing as the franchise was extended to more and more Americans and the party system became much more mass based. Democratic rule was interrupted only twice, both times by the election of Whig war heroes to the presidency. As the issues of this period grew more disruptive, however, several minor parties developed and the Whigs began to fracture, especially over the issue of slavery.

The Third Party System

One of these new parties, an antislavery party called the Republicans, quickly gained support. Founded in 1854, it replaced the seriously divided Whigs within two years as the main opposition to the Democrats. Its rapid rise signaled the end of the second party system. The bitter conflict of the Civil War ensured that the new third party system (1861 to 1896) would have the most clearly defined coalitions of any party system before or since. War and Reconstruction divided the nation roughly along geographic lines: The South became a Democratic bastion after all white southern males were permitted to return to the polls in 1876, and the Northeast and Midwest remained a fairly reliable base for Republicans.[7]

The sectional division was so clear that the Democratic Party's main strongholds in the North were in the cities controlled by Democratic machines (e.g., New York City's Tammany Hall) and areas settled by southerners (such as Kentucky, Missouri, and the southern portions of Ohio, Indiana, and Illinois). In the South, GOP support came only from blacks (in response to Republican President Abraham Lincoln's freeing of the slaves) and people from mountain areas originally opposed to the southern states' secession. By 1876, there was close party competition in presidential voting and in the House of Representatives as these sectional forces offset one another. Competition was so intense that this period contained two of the four elections in American history in which the winner of the popular vote for president lost the vote in the Electoral College.

American industries were growing rapidly during this time, especially in the Northeast and then in the Midwest. The Republicans dominated the areas where these new businesses were expanding, and the GOP leadership, which had long been identified with "moral Puritanism and emerging industrial capitalism,"[8] worked to support the new industries with protective tariffs (taxes) on imported goods, a railroad system that could haul products from coast to coast, efforts to develop the frontier, and high taxes to pay for these programs. By contrast, the Democrats represented groups that had been passed over by economic expansion and who were deeply suspicious of capitalism, such as farmers and the working class, as well as the white South. Economic issues, and especially attitudes toward the growth of huge industrial monopolies, were thus closely linked with the regional divisions between the parties.

The Fourth Party System

The imprint of the Civil War continued to shape southern politics for the next century. However, the Civil War party system soon began to fade elsewhere, under the weight of farm and rural protest and the economic panic of 1893. Tensions within the Democratic Party between poor whites and the more conservative party leaders erupted into a fight over the party's leadership in the 1890s. The less wealthy, more egalitarian wing won, nominated populist William Jennings Bryan as the Democratic presidential candidate in 1896, and reformed the party's issue stances. Bryan lost, however, and Republicans began a long domination of American national politics, disrupted only by their own internal split in 1912.

This period (from approximately 1897 to 1932) reflected both regional and economic conflicts. It pitted the eastern business community, which was heavily Republican, against the southern rural "periphery," with the South even more Democratic than before, and the Midwest in contention. Southern Democrats, out from under the heavy hand of Reconstruction, were able to reinstitute racially discriminatory laws and to keep blacks from voting in the southern states. The waves of immigrants into an increasingly urban America swelled the ranks of both parties, although Catholic immigrants, especially from Europe, tended to be mobilized by the Democratic Party.

The Fifth Party System

The shock of the Great Depression of 1929 and the subsequent election of Democrat Franklin Roosevelt produced the fifth, or New Deal, party system. During the 1930s, as a means of pulling the nation out of economic ruin, Roosevelt pushed Congress to enact several large-scale welfare state programs. These Roosevelt "New Deal" programs—Social Security, wages and hours laws, and protection for labor unions—again strengthened the Democrats' image as the party of the disadvantaged. Even groups such as blacks, long allied with the Republicans, were lured to the Democratic banner; socioeconomic needs were powerful enough to keep both blacks and southern whites as wary allies in the Roosevelt coalition. So by 1936, the new Democratic majority party had become a grand *New Deal coalition* of the less privileged and minorities—lower-income people, industrial workers (especially union members), poor farmers, Catholics, Jews, blacks—plus the South, where the Democratic loyalty imprinted by the Civil War had become all but genetic.

The costs of the New Deal and the impact of its programs heightened the stakes of the conflict between higher- and lower-income groups and between business and labor.

It is clear from this brief tour of much of party history that the effects of socioeconomic, racial, and regional divisions have waxed and waned, but all have played a major role in shaping the parties' coalitions over time. What is the nature of the two parties' coalitions today?

THE SOCIAL BASES OF PARTY COALITIONS

Socioeconomic Status Divisions

Most democratic party systems reflect divisions along social class lines, even if those divisions may have softened over the years.[9] James Madison, one of the most perceptive observers of human nature among the nation's founders, wrote in the *Federalist Papers* that economic differences are the most common source of factions.[10] The footprints of socioeconomic status (SES) conflict are scattered throughout American history. Social and economic status differences underlay the battle between the wealthy, aristocratic Federalists and the less privileged Democratic-Republicans. These differences were even sharper between the Jacksonian Democrats and the Whigs a few decades later, and again during the fourth and fifth party systems. The connection between SES and partisanship weakened during the 1960s and 1970s but strengthened again beginning with the Reagan years in the 1980s.

SES is still clearly related to people's partisanship, as you can see in Table 7.2. Read across the top row of Section A, for instance. You will find that among survey respondents whose incomes are in the lower third, in 2008, 19 percent called themselves "strong Democrats," 18 percent could be termed "weak Democrats," and 18 percent leaned toward the Democratic Party; but, toward the right side of the row, only 10, 10, and 10 percent, respectively, called themselves leaning, weak, or strong Republicans. The next column, titled "Dem. minus Rep.," shows that Democrats (counting strong and weak identifiers and Democratic "leaners") outnumbered Republicans by 25 percentage points among these lower-income people.

Those with very limited education are even more likely to call themselves Democrats than lower-income people are (Table 7.2, Section B). Here, 24 percent of those who didn't finish high school identified as strong Democrats, 17 percent as weak Democrats, and 22 percent as Democratic leaners. On the Republican side of the table, there are only 7 percent Republican leaners, 7 percent weak Republicans, and 9 percent strong Republicans among those who didn't finish high school, for an overall Democratic edge ("Dem. minus Rep.") of 40 percentage points.

Lower-income voters have become more consistently Democratic in the past two decades as income inequality has increased.[11] Several forces help sustain the relationship between lower SES and Democratic partisanship, including differences between the parties' stands on issues of special concern

TABLE 7.2

Social Characteristics and Party Identification, 2008

	Democrats		Independents			Republicans		Dem. Minus Rep.	Cases
	Strong	Weak	Closer to Dem.	Closer to Neither	Closer to Rep.	Weak	Strong		
A. Income									
Lower third	19%	18	18	14	10	10	10	25	701
Middle third	22%	15	19	10	12	10	12	22	632
Upper third	17%	14	15	10	12	17	16	1	933
B. Education									
No high school diploma	24%	17	22	14	7	7	9	40	261
High school grad	18%	16	17	14	12	10	11	18	704
College	22%	14	14	5	10	18	17	5	581
C. Region									
South	19%	12	15	13	12	12	18	4	974
Nonsouth	19%	18	19	10	11	13	10	22	1292
D. Religion									
Jews	32%	34	15	0	0	11	8	62	30
Catholics	18%	17	16	10	13	13	12	13	437

(continued)

Protestants	20%	15	13	10	11	15	17	5	1233
White Protestants*	12%	12	12	11	13	19	21	-17	937
E. Race									
Blacks	48%	23	15	8	3	1	1	81	270
Whites	14%	14	16	11	13	15	16	0	1797
F. Gender									
Female	20%	17	18	10	11	12	13	19	1251
Male	18%	13	16	13	12	14	14	7	1016

* The survey did not ask how many of these white Protestants consider themselves to be fundamentalist or "born again."

Note: Totals add up to approximately 100 percent reading across (with slight variations due to rounding). Dem. minus Rep. is the party difference calculated by subtracting the percentage of strong, weak, and leaning Republicans from the percentage of strong, weak, and leaning Democrats. Negative numbers indicate a Republican advantage in the group. The number of cases is weighted to account for the oversample of blacks and Latinos in the survey.

Source: 2008 American National Election Study, University of Michigan; data made available by the Inter-University Consortium for Political and Social Research.

to lower-income people (such as government-insured health care and social services) and the very high Democratic identification among blacks, who are predominantly lower income.[12] The result is that, especially in congressional elections, Democrats are even more likely to win in lower-income districts now than they were 20 years ago,[13] and in 2008, Barack Obama won a greater percentage of low- and lower-middle-income voters (with incomes up to $50,000) than had other recent Democratic presidential candidates.

Table 7.2 also shows that the current relationship between *higher* SES and party differs in some interesting ways from that of the New Deal coalition. As a larger proportion of Americans from a wider variety of backgrounds has attended college, voters with a college degree have become somewhat less Republican. In 2008, exit polls showed that a slight majority of college-educated voters supported Obama, as did an even larger majority of those with advanced degrees. Similarly, upper-income people are no longer as distinctively Republican as they used to be—perhaps because this group now contains a larger proportion of professionals, such as teachers and health care specialists, many of whom are concerned with quality-of-life issues such as the environment and women's rights. The identification of many professionals with the Democratic Party is reflected in the support Democratic candidates receive from teachers' unions and trial lawyers.[14] Consistent with this, in 2008, voters with incomes over $100,000 split their votes between Obama and McCain.

The impact of SES should not be overstated. Although American voting behavior is more strongly associated with income than is voting in Canada and Australia, several other democracies, including Britain, are even more polarized by SES.[15] And even at the height of the New Deal, the SES differences between the parties were less clear than the parties' rhetoric would suggest. Some groups locate themselves in the "wrong" party from an SES point of view; for example, white fundamentalist Protestants have voted Republican in recent years even though their average income is closer to that of the typical Democrat than to the average Republican.[16] Because SES divisions between the Republicans and Democrats can be fuzzy, the parties do not usually promote explicitly class-based appeals; they try to attract votes from a variety of socioeconomic groups.

Regional Divisions

Historically, geographical location has divided Americans almost as much as SES. Different sections of the country have often had differing political interests. When a political party has championed these distinct interests, it has sometimes united large numbers of voters who may disagree about other issues.

The most enduring sectionalism in American party history was the one-party Democratic control of the South. Well before the Civil War, white southerners shared an interest in slavery and an agricultural system geared to export markets. The searing experience of that war and the Reconstruction that followed made the South into the "Solid South" and delivered it to the Democrats for most of the next century. The 11 states of the former Confederacy cast all their electoral votes for Democratic presidential candidates in every election from 1880 through 1924, except for Tennessee's defection in 1920. Al Smith's Catholicism frightened five of these largely Protestant states into the Republican column in 1928, but the New Deal economic programs and the South's relative poverty brought it back to the Democratic Party from 1932 through 1944.

As we will see later in the chapter, however, the civil rights movement was the opening wedge in the slow process that separated the South from its Democratic loyalties. Even now (Table 7.2, Section C), southerners on average are still slightly more Democratic than Republican in their basic partisan leanings, thanks largely to the overwhelming Democratic partisanship of southern blacks. But this Democratic edge is much less pronounced than it had been until the 1960s, and in voting behavior, southern states are now predominantly Republican.

At times, the party system has also reflected the competition between the East, which used to dominate the nation's economy, and the South and West. In the first years of the American republic, the Federalists held on to an ever-narrowing base of eastern financial interests, while the Democratic-Republicans expanded westward with the new settlers. Northeasterners remained largely Republican—though moderate Republican—until recent decades, when the party's platform began to shift away from their policy stands.

The Mountain West has sometimes acted as a unified bloc in national politics on concerns that these states share, such as protecting western coal deposits and ranchers against federal environmental laws. But as these states become more urban and suburban, there has been some movement back toward the Democrats. Colorado in particular has experienced a swing from Republican control to close party competition.

Age

Democrats typically have more support among young adults than Republicans do, especially in recent years. Although the Democratic advantage in party ID appears in all age groups, the party now has its greatest advantage among those who are in their 20s and among "baby boomers" aged 49–60. Those in between, especially those ages 34–46, trend Democratic by a smaller margin. These age-related trends in party ID reflect both the greater enthusiasm for Democratic candidates and policies among younger people and also the special circumstances of the era in which each age cohort first experienced politics. For those currently in their 40s, that was roughly the time of the Ronald Reagan presidency, when Republican identification was on the rise.[17]

Race

A century ago, the Republican Party, which was founded to oppose slavery, was associated with racial equality in the minds of both black and white Americans. When the New Deal's social welfare programs began to help lift blacks and other disadvantaged groups out of poverty, however, the partisan direction of racial politics changed. Especially since the civil rights revolution in the 1960s, it is now the Democratic Party that is viewed as standing for racial equality. As a result, blacks identify as Democrats in overwhelming numbers today, as they have since 1964, regardless of their SES, region, or other social characteristics. Look at the stark contrast in Section E of Table 7.2: Democrats outnumber Republicans by 81 percentage points among blacks, but there is no Democratic advantage among whites. No Democratic presidential candidate has won a majority of whites' votes in almost 50 years. Interestingly, this is true even though blacks tend to be much more conservative than other Democrats on issues such as same-sex marriage and abortion.[18] The vital importance of civil rights to black Americans has outweighed the impact of these other issues. There is no closer tie between a social group and a party than that between blacks and the Democrats.

Religion and Religiosity

There have always been religious differences between the American party coalitions, as there are in many other democracies. The relationship between religion and party loyalty can be traced in part to SES differences among religious groups but also to religious conviction and group identification. In the early days of the New Deal, Catholics and Jews were among the most loyal supporters of the Democratic Party, although Catholic support for Democrats has declined in recent years (Table 7.2, Section D).

Currently, the most notable such relationship is the close tie between white evangelical Protestants and the GOP. Although white evangelicals split evenly between the two parties as recently as the late 1980s, they have since become a substantial part of the Republican base. In 2010, for instance, 77 percent of white evangelicals, comprising about a quarter of the electorate, reported in CNN's exit poll that they voted for Republican candidates. This tie is now so strong that most Americans see evangelical Christians as a largely Republican constituency.[19] More generally, almost half of Republican identifiers can be classified as "highly religious," in that they say they attend religious services weekly or almost weekly and that religion is important in their daily lives. That is true of only 19 percent of Democrats.[20] These changes reflect (and have encouraged) the Republican Party's movement since 1980 to a stand against abortion and same-sex marriage and to the emphasis of many Republican leaders on traditional values and social conservatism.[21]

Ethnicity

Latinos, who are now about one in every six U.S. residents, have surpassed non-Hispanic blacks as the nation's largest minority group. Although Latinos have long exercised voting strength in states such as California, New Mexico, and Texas, they cast only 8 percent of the votes nationwide in the 2010 election. But because they are the fastest-growing segment of the population, both parties have made serious efforts to attract Latino voter support.

Most Latino voters identify as Democrats, but their diverse ethnic roots produce a more varied voting pattern than that of blacks. The wealthy Cuban émigrés who settled in Miami after Fidel Castro took power in the 1950s tend to be conservative, strongly anti-Communist, and inclined to vote Republican, whereas the much larger Mexican American population in California leans Democratic. In 2004, President Bush's proposal to give temporary legal status to undocumented (largely Mexican and Central American) workers met with some success among Latinos, as did the party's advertising in Spanish-language media. However, in elections since then, the economic downturn and the hard-line stand taken by many conservative Republicans against illegal immigrants undermined these Republican gains.[22] In 2010, for instance, Republicans won only 38 percent of the Latino vote.

Gender

For more than three decades, women have supported Democrats to a greater extent than men have (see Table 7.2, Section F). Similar findings were seen in 2008 exit polls, where 56 percent of women said they voted for Barack Obama for president and 43 percent voted for Republican John McCain—a 13-percent Democratic margin—compared with a 1-percent Democratic edge among men.[23] Although there has been a leftward shift in women's political preferences in many Western democracies,[24] the gender gap in American politics has shown a somewhat different pattern. During the 1980s and 1990s, both men and women became more Republican, but men did so at a faster pace and to a greater degree.[25] After 2000, women returned to the Democratic Party more quickly than men did.

Why should gender be related to partisanship? Men's and women's attitudes differ on some major issues. On average, women express greater support for social programs and less support for defense spending than men do. These differences correspond with the two parties' issue agendas; the Democratic Party emphasizes health care, education, and other social programs, whereas the Republicans put a priority on tax cuts and military strength. People's attitudes toward gender equality and abortion, in particular, have become more closely correlated with their party identification during the past three decades, and when these and other "women's issues" are stressed by candidates, a gender gap is more likely to appear.[26] The national parties also project some lifestyle differences that may affect men's and women's partisanship. Among members of the U.S. House and Senate first elected in 2010, for instance, all but 4 of the 93 married Republicans list their spouse as sharing their last name, but 4 of the 7 married Democrats had a spouse with a different or a hyphenated last name.[27]

Black women and single women have become particularly distinctive Democratic constituencies. According to CNN's exit poll in 2008, 70 percent of single women (comprising more than one in five voters) supported Obama, compared with only 47 percent of married women.[28] Single women, especially single mothers, are more economically insecure on average than married women are, and thus could be more likely to see government social programs as an ally.

THE CENTRAL ROLE OF ISSUES
IN THE GROUP–PARTY LINKAGE

As this discussion of the gender gap suggests, there is a close relationship between the alignment of social groups with parties and the parties' stands on issues. A group's presence in a party coalition indicates that many of the group's members—white evangelical Christians, for instance—have some shared reactions to major issues and candidates, which have drawn them to one party rather than the other. To keep their support, the party is likely to express solidarity with the group's concerns, to speak its language, and to feature some of the group's leaders in its conventions and campaigns.

This relationship between social groups and parties' stands is dynamic; it can change over time, as a party adapts its stands on issues to pick up new sources of support, or as a group senses that another party is becoming more sensitive to its concerns.[29] Consider, for example, the fact that as recently as 1988, there was no relationship between the abortion issue and party ID; attitudes toward abortion cut across party lines, dividing Democrats from Democrats and Republicans from Republicans.[30] By that time, however, pro-choice activists had gained strength in Democratic ranks and had committed the party to policy stands that left many conservative Democrats, including white evangelical Christians and southerners, feeling alienated from their national party.

Some of these conservatives, many of them pro-life on abortion, saw an opportunity to be heard within the Republican Party and were welcomed as a new source of Republican support. As they became a larger proportion of the voters in Republican primaries, they encouraged their new party's candidates to take stronger and clearer pro-life stands. Over time, Republican Party leaders and activists responded to these new Republican enthusiasts by incorporating stands against abortion, same-sex marriage, and embryonic stem cell research into their platform and faith-based initiatives into their rhetoric.

As a result, abortion has become a partisan issue. As Table 7.3 shows (see Section A), more than 60 percent of those who feel that abortion should be the woman's own choice now consider themselves Democrats (strong and weak Democrats plus Democratic "leaners"). On the right side of the table, you can see in the "Dem. minus Rep." column that Democrats greatly outnumber Republicans among those who favor abortion rights, and among those who feel abortion should be illegal, there are 12 percent more Republicans than Democrats. This issue shows a clear evolution in the relationship between the parties' issue stands and their coalitional bases. On other issues, such as attitudes toward labor unions, both parties' stands and coalitions have been very stable for many decades.

Clearer Differences Between the Two Parties' Coalitions on Issues

The data in Table 7.3 show that the two parties in the electorate differ clearly from one another in their attitudes toward some major issues. These party differences in attitudes closely track the issue preferences of key groups in the

TABLE 7.3

Issue Attitudes and Party Identification, 2008

	Democrats		Independents			Republicans		Dem. Minus Rep.	Cases
	Strong	Weak	Closer to Dem.	Closer to Neither	Closer to Rep.	Weak	Strong		
A. Abortion									
Own choice	28%	14	21	9	11	11	6	35	410
In between	14%	15	15	12	14	17	14	−1	463
Illegal	12%	14	9	19	12	9	26	−12	145
B. Government spending on services									
More	28%	17	22	11	8	8	5	46	473
Same	16%	14	20	13	14	12	13	11	226
Less	6%	7	7	5	19	26	30	−55	263
C. Government role in providing jobs and a good standard of living									
Gov. help	36%	17	19	10	9	4	5	54	312
In between	23%	15	18	16	12	10	6	28	200
Help self	6%	11	16	10	16	20	21	−24	497
D. Government role in improving position of blacks									
Gov. help	39%	17	22	7	5	6	4	63	409
In between	21%	19	19	11	11	9	9	30	438
Help self	11%	11	14	11	15	18	20	−17	1076

(continued)

TABLE 7.3 (CONTINUED)

	Democrats		Independents			Republicans		Dem. Minus Rep.	Cases
	Strong	Weak	Closer to Dem.	Closer to Neither	Closer to Rep.	Weak	Strong		
E. Government spending on defense									
Decrease	30%	18	22	9	8	10	4	48	327
Same	14%	16	16	12	11	15	16	4	544
Increase	14%	15	10	10	15	12	25	-13	226
F. Ideological self-identification									
Liberal	40%	24	22	5	3	4	1	78	444
Moderate	16%	18	25	17	12	9	4	34	486
Conservative	7%	6	5	5	17	26	34	-59	716

Note: Totals add up to approximately 100 percent reading across (with slight variations due to rounding). Dem. minus Rep. is the party difference calculated by subtracting the percentage of strong, weak, and leaning Republicans from the percentage of strong, weak, and leaning Democrats. Negative numbers indicate a Republican advantage in the group. The number of cases is weighted to account for the oversample of blacks and Latinos in the survey.

Source: 2008 American National Election Study, University of Michigan; data made available by the Inter-University Consortium for Political and Social Research.

parties' coalitions. Democrats, for instance, are much more favorable than are Republicans (see Table 7.3, Sections B and C) to welfare state programs: maintaining government spending on services and a government role in providing jobs for the unemployed. Blacks, lower-income people, those with only a high school education, and those in blue-collar or unskilled jobs—all important groups in the Democratic coalition—are especially likely to favor government provision of these services. The recipients of these services and jobs tend to be lower SES people, whose Democratic leanings can be seen in Table 7.2.

People also differ markedly by party on issues such as civil rights and defense spending (see Table 7.3, Sections D and E). On racial policy, since the 1960s, Democrats have been much more likely to favor a government role in helping minorities than are Republicans. Recall from Table 7.2 the strong tendency for blacks, who are much more likely than whites to support government efforts to integrate schools and fair treatment in jobs, to identify as Democrats. And there is a truly striking party difference between those who call themselves liberals and those who identify themselves as conservatives (Table 7.3, Section F). As one pollster puts it, "We have two massive, colliding forces... One [the Republican coalition] is rural, Christian, religiously conservative, with guns at home.... And we have a second America [the Democratic coalition] that is socially tolerant, pro-choice, secular, living in New England and the Pacific coast, and in affluent suburbs."[31] Party divisions increasingly reflect differences that have been termed "the culture wars."[32]

In short, there is a close but evolving relationship between the stands a party takes and the groups that form the party's core support. Parties take positions on issues to maintain the support of the groups in their existing coalition. Sometimes party leaders use issue positions to draw members of other social groups to the party, as Republicans did with white southerners since the 1960s. At times, it is the group that tries to put its concerns on the party's agenda, as we have seen in the case of the abortion issue. As these newer groups become a larger force within the party coalition, the party's leadership will try to firm up their support with additional commitments on their issues. In recent years, this process has led to a growing division on issues between the two parties' coalitions. The result is that even if most voters have not become more ideologically extreme, political debate has become more clearly divided by party, as voters have sorted themselves into the party that is closer to their views on issues.[33]

THE DEVELOPMENT OF THE SIXTH PARTY SYSTEM

The current alignment of social groups with the parties differs in some significant ways from that of the New Deal coalition. That should not be surprising; the political environment has changed a lot during the past 70 years. Once World War II brought an end to the Depression in the United States, some groups that had benefited from government assistance under Roosevelt moved up into the growing middle class. In return for this economic gain, however, they found themselves paying higher taxes to support those who still needed the assistance. That led many people to reevaluate the costs and benefits of the welfare state in their own lives. At the same time, the issue of race, which had been held in check by Roosevelt's deft maneuvering, was pushed to the top of both parties' agendas by activists hoping to change their parties' stands.

The party system has changed in other important ways since the New Deal as well. Democratic dominance gave way to closer competition between the parties. The party organizations do not expect to anoint candidates now, run their campaigns, or hand out patronage jobs. Rather, the party organizations work primarily to help fund and support campaigns that are run by candidates and their paid consultants. And the relationship between party ID and election results has changed. Until 1952, the elections of the New Deal party system had usually been *maintaining elections*, in which the presidential candidate of the majority party—the party with the most identifiers—normally won. Since 1952, most national elections have been *deviating elections*—those in which short-term forces such as candidate characteristics or issues are powerful enough to cause the defeat of the majority party's candidate. Racial issues have figured prominently in this change.

Major Changes in the Parties' Supporting Coalitions

Liberal northern Democrats in the late 1940s pressed their party to deliver on the long-delayed promise of civil rights for blacks. When Democratic administrations responded and used federal power to end the racial segregation of schools and public accommodations such as restaurants and hotels, some conservative white southerners felt betrayed by their national party. They found an alternative in 1964 when Republican presidential candidate Barry Goldwater opposed the Civil Rights Act. Goldwater, the candidate of the party's newly triumphant conservative wing, argued that no matter how much Republicans supported civil rights, the party's commitment to smaller government and states' rights prevented the federal government from forcing integration on reluctant state governments.

Southern whites responded by moving slowly in the direction of Republican partisanship. The same forces caused blacks to shift rapidly toward the Democrats. When the Voting Rights Act restored southern blacks' right to vote, their overwhelmingly Democratic voting patterns led the national Democratic Party to become even more liberal on race and related issues. A further push came from legislative redistricting in 1992, in which legislatures were asked to draw majority–minority districts (see Chapter 8), and which led to the defeat of a number of longtime conservative southern Democrats.[34] Both national parties, then, had markedly changed their positions. The Democrats moved from an acceptance of segregation in the South to a commitment to use government as the means to secure rights for black Americans. The Republicans reacted against the big government programs of the New Deal with a stand in favor of states' rights and small government, even at the cost of the party's traditional pro–civil rights stand.[35]

These changes in the parties' positions led to a steady reformation of their constituencies.[36] Table 7.4 shows shifts between the 1950s and 2008 in the representation of various groups within the Democratic and Republican Parties in the electorate. Look first at the dramatic changes with regard to race. Blacks were only 6 percent of the Democratic Party in the electorate, on average, between 1952 and 1960; at this time, of course, very few southern blacks were permitted to vote. During 2000–2008, on average, blacks constituted 22 percent of all Democrats, and Latinos, Asian Americans, and Native Americans added another 11 percent, for a total of one-third of Democratic voters. The change was especially profound in the South; by 2000, blacks made up a majority (52 percent) of the Democratic voters in the Deep South states of Alabama, Georgia, Louisiana, Mississippi, and South Carolina.[37]

At the same time, southern whites, who were a quarter of all Democratic partisans in the 1950s, dropped to just 16 percent in the 2000s (and this is probably an exaggeration of Democratic strength in the South, because change in people's party ID often lags behind change in their voting behavior). Surveys show that in 1956, 87 percent of white southerners called themselves Democrats, but in 2000 only 24 percent did so.[38] In the 2010 election, only

TABLE 7.4

Change in the Parties' Coalitions, 1952–1960 to 2000–2008

	Democratic Voters (%)		Republican Voters (%)	
	1952–1960	2000–2008	1952–1960	2000–2008
Blacks	6	22	3	2
Latinos, Asian Americans, and Native Americans	1	11	0	9
Southern whites	24	16	8	32
Northern whites	69	51	89	58
Upper income	40	35	46	45
Middle income	30	30	26	30
Lower income	31	35	28	25
Protestant	61	56	83	62
Catholic	31	26	14	27
Jewish	6	4	2	1
Other, no religion	2	14	2	11
Married	82	56	79	71
Unmarried	18	44	21	29

Note: Entries are the proportion of all Democratic or Republican Party identifiers, among those who say they voted, who belong to the group named in the first column.

Source: American National Election Studies data for 1952–1960, calculated by Alan Abramowitz and excerpted with kind permission from Abramowitz, *Voice of the People* (New York: McGraw-Hill, 2004), p. 87, and for 2000–2008, calculated by Nathaniel Birkhead.

one white Democrat was elected to Congress from the Deep South region, and an Associated Press story's lead was, "The white Southern Democrat—endangered since the 1960s civil rights era—is sliding nearer to extinction."[39] The Democratic Party's loss was the Republican Party's gain; southern whites had increased from a mere 8 percent in the 1950s to almost a third of the Republican Party in the electorate in the 2000s. Consistent with the change in the national parties' stands, it was the conservatives among these southern whites who were more likely to move to a Republican identification.

This change was part of a larger shift in the parties' regional bases. In the mid-1950s, as you can see in the upper part of Figure 7.1, almost half

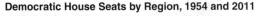

Democratic House Seats by Region, 1954 and 2011

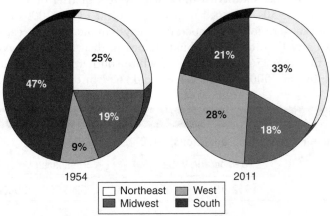

1954   2011

Northeast   West
Midwest   South

Republican House Seats by Region, 1954 and 2011

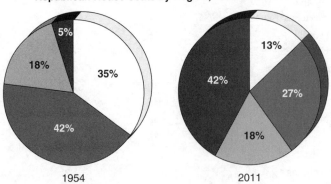

1954   2011

FIGURE 7.1
Democratic and Republican House Seats by Region, 1954 and 2011.

Source: CQ Weekly, April 20, 2009, for 1954 data; 2011 data calculated by the author (as of May 28, 2011).

of all Democrats in the U.S. House were southerners. By 2011, the drop in Democratic support among white southerners left the party's House contingent much more regionally balanced. Republicans in the House, on the other hand, have moved from one regional base to another. In 1954, the great majority of Republican House members were from the Midwest and Northeast, and a substantial number of northeastern Republicans were liberals and moderates. But the Republican platform changes that drew conservative southern support made it harder for the party to appeal to liberals and moderates in New England and the Midwest. So the Northeast is predominantly Democratic now; in fact, in the 2008 elections not a single Republican U.S. House member was elected from New England, for the first time ever.

Another shift has been the interesting income difference between the two parties. As noted earlier and as Table 7.4 shows, lower-income people are becoming a larger part of the Democratic coalition, whereas middle-income people (but not those with higher incomes) are more prominent among Republicans. And people's income relates differently now to the new issues—those involving religiosity, gender, and sexual identity—that divide the parties. Although SES predicts individuals' positions on economic policies pretty well, that is not the case with people's attitudes toward "values" issues such as stem cell research.[40]

The Democratic Coalition in 2010

Group (Percentage of the Voting Population)	Percentage Reporting a Democratic Vote for U.S. House
Liberal (20%)	90
African American (11%)	89
Gay, lesbian, or bisexual (3%)	69
Labor union household (17%)	61
Disapprove of U.S. war in Afghanistan (54%)	61
Latino (8%)	60
Didn't complete high school (3%)	57
Live in an urban area (31%)	56
Age 18–29 (12%)	55
Moderate (38%)	55
Income under $50,000 (36%)	54
Live in Northeast (21%)	54
Postgraduate education (21%)	53
Don't attend church weekly (52%)	53

Source: CNN exit poll, at www.cnn.com/ELECTION/2010/results/polls/#val=USH00p1 (accessed April 4, 2011).

In sum, the current Democratic Party in the electorate differs from the New Deal coalition in several important ways. Although it continues to include blacks and Latinos, lower-income and less-educated whites, and young people, the Democrats have lost a portion of white union members and Catholics and most white southerners. On the other hand, the party has gained support among liberals, Northeast and West Coast residents, unmarried people, gays, and those who don't consider themselves religious (see box "The Democratic Coalition in 2010" on page 145). Although the Republican coalition is still heavily white, married, and Christian, its Protestant base has shifted from mainline denominations to evangelical churches. Religiously observant whites have become the largest single group of Republican supporters,[41] and the party now has a southern base. Republicans have also gained more support from Catholics, men, rural or exurban people, and those who define themselves as conservatives.

From Democratic Majority to Close Competition

The second major change has been the gradual wearing away of Democratic dominance in party identification. In the 1950s and early 1960s, many more Americans called themselves Democrats than Republicans or independents. The Democratic edge began to erode after 1964, but Republicans were not immediately able to capitalize on the Democrats' losses. The proportion of "pure independent" identifiers increased, and there was a steady stream of independent and third party candidates.[42] These changes in partisanship struck many scholars as resembling a *dealignment*, or a decline in party loyalties.

Yet as we have seen, even as both parties were losing adherents nationally, signs of the coming change were apparent in the South. The movement toward Republican partisanship in southern states began to speed up in the late 1960s, and Republican candidates reaped the fruits. In 1960, there had been no Republican candidate on the general election ballot in almost two-thirds of southern U.S. House districts. The only real competition was in the Democratic primary. By 1968, the number of these one-party House races had been cut by half.[43]

The speed of partisan change increased again during the 1980s. Across the nation, for the first time in 50 years, young voters were more likely to call themselves Republicans than Democrats.[44] Two powerful reasons were President Reagan's popularity and the increased efforts of evangelical Christian groups to promote Republican affiliation. Republicans gained a majority in the U.S. Senate in 1980 that lasted 6 years, and in 1994, the GOP won control of both houses of Congress for the first time in 40 years. Republicans were now competing effectively with the Democrats in statewide races in the South. In 1994, there was a Republican majority among the region's Congress members and governors for the first time since Reconstruction, and the Republican congressional leadership is weighted toward southerners. Republicans ran candidates in 430 of the 435 U.S. House districts in 2010—an all-time high for the party.

How Can We Characterize These Changes: Realignment, Dealignment, or What?

A number of researchers have argued that these changes can best be called a *party realignment*—a significant and enduring change in the patterns of group support for the parties, usually (but not always) leading to a new majority party. We have certainly seen the big changes in group support for the parties; the Republican coalition has become more southern, more evangelical, and more conservative, and a Democratic Party that used to draw much of its strength from the white South now depends to a much greater extent on the votes of blacks, liberals, and secularists.

These changes in the parties' coalitions affect their policy stands. A Democratic Party that draws a substantial minority of its followers from among blacks is likely to take different stands from a Democratic Party that depended heavily on conservative white southerners. Southern whites have provided the critical mass for their new party, the Republicans, to adopt more socially conservative positions, not only on civil rights, affirmative action, and racial profiling but also on health care, abortion, women's rights, aid for big cities, and support for private schools. Chapter 15 shows these changes in the two parties' platforms. Further, as the policy preferences of blacks, southern whites, and evangelical Christians have become more consistent with their partisanship, each party has become more homogeneous internally, and more distinct from the other party on issues, than had been the case in decades; the Democratic Party's identifiers in 2012 are much more consistently liberal than was the Democratic Party in the electorate in the 1970s, and Republican identifiers are even more homogeneously conservative.

As added support for the realignment perspective, the successes of Republican presidential candidates since 1968, the growth of the GOP in the once-Democratic South, and Republican gains in Congress are often cited as evidence that the Democrats are no longer the real majority party.[45] The Bush administration tried diligently to create a Republican majority by attracting a larger proportion of Latino, Catholic, and black votes and by working with evangelical preachers to promote voter turnout among conservative Christians,[46] presumably aware that the groups that have become the backbone of the Republican Party—in particular, white, married Christians—are declining as a share of the voting population.[47]

Problems with the Idea of Realignment

There are both practical and theoretical reasons why other scholars are reluctant to use the *R* word (realignment) to describe these changes. In practical terms, although Republican strength has increased, Democrats still hold the edge among party identifiers. And in a theoretical sense, the idea of realignment is difficult to apply with any precision. How much change has to occur in the parties' coalitions in order to call it a realignment? As political scientist David Mayhew points out, there are no clear standards for sorting elections into periods of realignment as opposed to nonrealigning periods.[48] Many prefer to use the concept of "issue evolutions" to discuss the variety of ways in which issues have affected partisanship over time.[49]

Changes in the partisanship of southern whites and blacks are highly significant. Yet in several ways the parties retain their New Deal character. The Democrats remain the party of the disadvantaged and of minority racial and religious groups, but the minorities have changed; as Catholics have entered the mainstream of economic and political life, they have divided more evenly between the two parties, but the Democrats still represent the majority of lower-income, black, Latino, gay, and nonreligious people. And even if the movement of blacks and white southerners has been dramatic enough to propel the United States into a new party system, when did that system begin? Was it during the 1960s, when southern blacks regained the right to vote and the civil rights movement shook the South? Was it in the 1980s, when southern partisan change accelerated and Ronald Reagan attracted many new voters to the Republicans? Was it in the early 1990s, when Congress finally came under Republican control? Or does it encompass all of these periods in a constantly evolving (so-called secular) change?

The debate will continue as to whether the concept of realignment is a valuable tool in understanding change in the party system. Perhaps a more useful approach is to recognize that there are many different kinds of party changes and that we have seen all of them to at least some degree in the past 50 years. The evidence for party organizational change, as presented in Chapters 3 and 4, is convincing. There is little doubt that the Democratic dominance of the New Deal party system gave way to more of a balance in national party strength. And whether we call it a realignment or not, there has been enough change in the two parties' coalitions to produce a palpable shift in campaign and congressional debate. When Democrats call for federally funded embryonic stem cell research and Republicans are opposed, and when Democrats support civil unions for same-sex couples, whereas Republicans agree with the pope on abortion, we know that there is a broader agenda in national politics than simply the economic conflicts of the 1930s and 1940s.

At the beginning of the second decade of the 2000s, then, the American electorate is composed of two groups of partisans of roughly comparable size. There is a group of Democrats, including liberals, lower-income people, and minorities, whose size has shrunk a bit in recent decades but shows the potential for recovery. There is a group of Republicans dominated by conservatives, southerners, and churchgoers. And there is a third group that could truly be termed "dealigned," in that it feels no lasting party loyalties and usually stays out of political activity.[50] Because of the demonstrated ability of both major parties to bounce back from defeat, it is also an electorate capable of producing mercurial election results. The trajectory of American politics, then, has the potential for rapid change.

Parties and
Voter Turnout

L ike a fierce game of tennis, national election results in recent years have bounced back and forth between the parties. Republicans did well in 2004. Then there were major Democratic wins in 2006 and 2008. Republicans rebounded in 2010, big-time. These dramatic shifts were caused not only by changes in voter preferences but also by changes in voter turnout. Some types of voters who went to the polls to support Barack Obama in 2008—many young voters, for instance—chose to sit out the 2010 election, and the candidates of Obama's party lost.

The Democrats and Republicans must not only win supporters but also bring them to the polls on Election Day and, if possible, discourage those who oppose the party's candidates from turning out to vote. Parties can do so in three ways. First, each party has worked hard over time to get its likely supporters the *right* to vote. The early Jeffersonians and then the Democrats fought to expand voting rights to include renters and other non–property owners—groups that would naturally favor their candidates and stances rather than Federalist or Whig ideas.

Second, once its supporters have the right to vote, the party can promote policies that make voting *easier and more accessible* to them (and less accessible to its opponents). Laws governing the ease of voting may seem nonpartisan, but they often have partisan effects in practice. State laws requiring a prospective voter to show a photo ID, for instance, cause controversy because they may increase the burden on some types of people more than on others. (Drivers' licenses are the most common form of photo ID, but people who can't afford a car or who are unable to drive because of physical disabilities—groups that are more likely to support Democratic candidates—will need to make more effort to get the required photo ID.) Other such laws include requirements that a prospective voter bring proof of citizenship to the polls and decisions by local governments to provide satellite voting centers in some parts of the community rather than others.

Finally, party organizations and their candidates can work actively to bring more of their supporters to the polls in a particular election. This *voter mobilization* has become a key focus in competitive elections. Democrats benefited greatly in 2008 from the rise in blacks' voter turnout relative to

2004, but blacks' turnout dipped again in 2010; these turnout shifts were due in part to differences in effectiveness between the two parties' get-out-the-vote (GOTV) efforts.

As we examine these party efforts, we need to consider their impact on American democracy. Voter turnout in the United States is relatively low. Even in the well-publicized 2008 election, less than 64 percent of eligible voters went to the polls—essentially unchanged from 2004 and well below the turnouts of most other industrialized democracies. Granted, the drop in turnout from the 1970s through the 1990s has ended, at least for the present. But we need to ask why voter turnout in American elections is comparatively low and what responsibility the parties bear for these low turnouts.

ELECTIONS: THE RULES AFFECT THE RESULTS

The rules in politics, as in everything else, are never neutral. Each rule of the electoral process—such as who is eligible to vote or when elections must be held—affects different parties and candidates differently.[1] For example, if polling places close at 6:00 P.M. (as they do in Indiana and Kentucky), making it hard for office and factory workers to get to the polls on time, then the Democratic Party may lose a disproportionate number of votes. If the state makes it easy to vote by mail, then any local party organized enough to distribute mail-in ballots to its supporters will benefit.

Reformers have struggled with the parties to influence the rules governing voting. These battles have generally taken place at the state level, because the Constitution allows the states to decide who is eligible to vote. The national government has acted occasionally, however, most often through constitutional amendments, to keep states from imposing especially offensive restrictions on voting. The story begins with parties' efforts to expand or limit voting rights.

EXPANSION OF THE RIGHT TO VOTE

White male citizens were given the right to vote earlier in the United States than in any other democracy. In the early 1800s, prompted by the Jeffersonians (who expected to benefit from the change), the states gradually repealed the property, income, and taxpaying qualifications for voting by which they had so severely limited male suffrage.[2] By 1860, no states required property holding, and only four required substantial taxpaying as a condition for voting.

Women did not win the right to vote in all states until much later. The Nineteenth Amendment, forbidding states to deny the right to vote based on gender, was finally ratified in 1920 after a decades-long struggle. The most recent change, the constitutional amendment lowering the voting age to 18 for all elections, was ratified by the states in 1971.

The history of black Americans' voting rights is more complex—a story not only of human rights but also of partisanship. Some New England states granted suffrage to blacks before the Civil War. The Fifteenth Amendment, adopted after that war with support from the Republican administration, declared that no state could abridge the right to vote on account of race. (Most blacks supported Republicans, who had championed the emancipation of slaves.) But the federal government soon turned its attention to other matters, and Democratic-run southern states worked effectively to keep blacks from voting, as we will see. By the early 1900s, black turnout in the South had dropped to negligible levels. It remained that way in most southern states until the 1960s, when the Democratic Party, then the majority in Congress, changed its stance on civil rights, and federal authorities began to enforce the Fifteenth Amendment and new voting rights laws in the states.

RULES AFFECTING ACCESS TO VOTING RIGHTS

Even after the right to vote was greatly expanded, states have continued to pass laws governing access to the vote. Many of these regulations were promoted by the Progressive movement in the late 1800s and early 1900s in an effort to weaken the political parties.

The Secret Ballot

American elections did not always use secret ballots. In the early 1800s, in many areas, voters simply told the election officials which candidates they preferred. Gradually, this "oral vote" was replaced by ballots printed by the parties or candidates. The voter brought the ballot of a particular party to the polling place and put it in the ballot box. The ballots of different parties differed in color and appearance, so observers could tell how an individual had voted. That was how the party "machine" wanted it; if party leaders had done a favor for someone in exchange for a vote, they wanted to be sure they had gotten their money's worth.

To discourage vote buying and to weaken the party machines, Progressives pushed for a new ballot system, which came into widespread use in the 1890s. Called the Australian ballot after the country where it originated, these ballots were printed by the government and marked by the voter in private. Because the ballot is administered and paid for by the government, this reform involved the government in running elections, which opened the door to government regulation of the parties. It also made it easier for voters to split their tickets— to vote for the candidates of more than one party on the same ballot.[3]

The Progressives did not succeed in doing away with the *long ballot*, however, in which each state's voters are asked to elect large numbers of state and local officials who would be appointed in other democracies. To cast a meaningful vote on each of 60 or 70 state and local offices, citizens would need to spend a lot of time gathering information, a task most citizens do not find fascinating. That drives down voter turnout. People who do vote may cast ballots for some offices but not others. This "roll-off" can reduce the vote for minor offices and referenda by 20 or 30 percent compared with offices at the top of the ballot.[4] The voter fatigue caused by the long ballot leads people to use various shortcuts to make their choices. Party identification is the most common shortcut—an outcome the Progressives would certainly have wanted to avoid.

Citizenship

Prior to 1894 at least 12 states permitted noncitizens to vote,[5] although some required the individual to have applied for American citizenship. Since the 1920s, all states have required that voters be U.S. citizens. This is the biggest legal barrier to voting; millions of adults, most of them in California, Florida, Texas, and New York, work and may even pay taxes but cannot vote until they are "naturalized" as citizens, a process that can take years to complete. Given their average income levels and ethnicity, these noncitizen residents would be more likely to vote Democratic than Republican.

Residence

For most of American history, states could require citizens to live in a state and locality for a certain period before being allowed to vote there. Southern states had the longest residence requirements (which kept migrant farm workers from voting). In 1970, Congress limited states' residence requirements to a maximum of 30 days for voting in presidential elections. Since then, almost half of the states have dropped these requirements altogether. Even so, many Americans move frequently, and those who have moved recently are much less likely to vote, in part because they must take the time and initiative to find out where and when they need to register.[6]

Registration

Another major obstacle to voting is the registration requirement—the rule in most states that citizens must register in advance in order to vote in an election. During much of the 1800s, voters needed only to show up on Election Day to cast a ballot, or to be listed on the government's voting roll—the same rules that most European democracies use today. Progressive reformers in the late 1800s urged states to require advance registration in order to limit voter fraud by party bosses. That increased the motivation needed to vote because it doubled the effort involved: one trip to register and a second trip to vote. These registration requirements helped to reduce the high turnout levels of that time.[7]

THE SPECIAL CASE OF VOTING RIGHTS FOR BLACK AMERICANS

Legal barriers to voting were especially effective in denying the vote to southern blacks. The electoral system was manipulated in the South by a variety of laws, capricious election administration, and intimidation and violence when these subtler methods were not effective. The result was that although blacks had been granted the right to vote in the 1860s, they were denied access to the polls in the former Confederacy and some neighboring states for almost a century afterward.

The Long Struggle for Voting Rights

For years after the end of Reconstruction, southern states and the Supreme Court played a game of constitutional "hide and seek." States would devise a way to disenfranchise blacks, the Court would strike it down as unconstitutional, and the states would find another. One example was the "white primary." The Republican Party barely existed in the South at this time, so the candidate who won the Democratic primary was assured of winning the general election. Faced with the threat of blacks voting in the Democratic primary, some states declared the party to be a private club open only to whites, so blacks could not cast a primary ballot. It took 21 years of lawsuits and five Supreme Court cases to end this practice.[8]

In addition, most southern states required payment of a poll tax in order to vote—just one or two dollars, but often demanded well before an election, with the stipulation that the taxpayer keep a receipt and present it weeks later at the voting booth. And local election officials in some states used tests to decide who was "literate" enough to vote. These laws were intentionally directed at the poor and uneducated black population.

Southern lawmakers also designed endless delays and other technicalities to prevent blacks from registering to vote (see box "Barriers to Black Registration in the South" on pp. 153–154). Those who kept trying were often faced with economic reprisal (the loss of a job or a home) and physical violence. It is not surprising, in this relentlessly hostile environment, that only 5 percent of voting-age blacks were registered in the 11 southern states as late as 1940.[9]

Barriers to Black Registration in the South

In their account of the civil rights movement in the South, Pat Watters and Reese Cleghorn describe how blacks were prevented from registering by simple but effective administrative practices:

> Slowdowns were common. Separate tables would be assigned to whites and Negroes [the customary term for African Americans before the mid-1960s]. If a line of Negroes were waiting for the Negro table, a white might go ahead of them, use the empty white table, and leave. In Anniston, Alabama, a report said the white table was larger, and Negroes were not allowed in the room when a white was using it. Another variation was to seat four Negroes at a table, and

(continued)

(*continued*)

make three wait until the slowest had finished, while others waited outside in line. These methods were particularly effective when coupled with the one or two day a month registration periods.... In one north Florida county, the registrar didn't bother with any of these refinements, and didn't close his office when Negro applicants appeared. He simply sat with his legs stretched out across the doorway. Negroes didn't break through them.

Source: Pat Watters and Reese Cleghorn, *Climbing Jacob's Ladder* (New York: Harcourt Brace Jovanovich, 1967), pp. 122–123.

Because courts found it difficult to counter these extra-legal hurdles, reformers turned to Congress and the executive branch. The federal Voting Rights Act of 1965, extended in 1982 and 2006, authorized the U.S. Justice Department to seek injunctions against anyone who prevented blacks from voting. When the Justice Department could convince a federal court that a "pattern or practice" of discrimination existed in a district, the court could send federal registrars there to register voters. It could also supervise voting procedures in states and counties where less than 50 percent of potential voters had gone to the polls in the most recent presidential election.[10]

This unprecedented federal intervention in state elections, combined with the civil rights movement's efforts to mobilize black voters, enabled the black electorate to grow enormously in the South. By the 1990s, black registration finally reached a level close to that of white southerners (for current figures, see Figure 8.1.) In the process, the conflicts between these new black voters and southern whites ate away at the Democratic Party from within and caused dramatic changes in the two parties' supporting coalitions (see Chapter 7).

From Voting Rights to Representation

Even after blacks gained voting rights, some states continued trying to dilute the impact of black votes. The federal government responded with a new twist on an old practice. Every 10 years, after the U.S. Census, state legislatures must redraw the boundaries of congressional and state legislative districts so that these districts remain equal in population size. This *legislative redistricting*, ordered by the Supreme Court in the 1960s to stop state legislatures from overrepresenting rural areas and underrepresenting bigger cities,[11] has often been used by resourceful politicians for at least short-term political gain. *Gerrymandering*—drawing district lines to maximize one's own party's strength and disadvantage the other party—is prevalent and is usually permitted by the courts.[12] For years, in the case of black Americans, it was common for legislators to draw legislative district lines that divided black voters among several districts, so as to weaken their voting strength, or to pack black voters into a few districts so that pro-civil rights candidates won these districts by large, wasteful majorities.

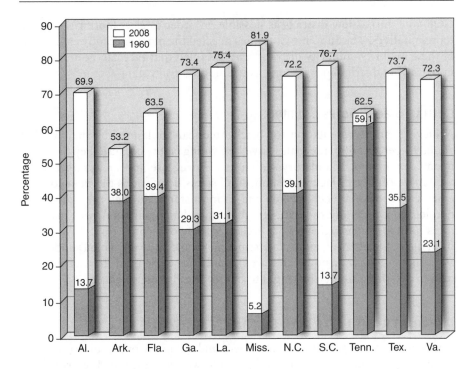

FIGURE 8.1

Black Voter Registration in the South, 1960 and 2008.

Note: Bars show the number of blacks in the two years who were registered to vote, as a percentage of the voting-age citizen population.

Source: U.S. Census Bureau data, at www.census.gov/hhes/www/socdemo/voting/publications/p20/2008/tables. html, Table 4B (accessed November 12, 2011).

After the 1990 census, the first Bush administration pressed southern states to redraw congressional district lines so as to create some districts with a majority of black or Latino voters, called *"majority-minority" districts.* The argument was that these districts would usually elect minority legislators to Congress and thus improve the representation of minority citizens. Many of these districts were created by an interesting alliance of black and Latino Democrats with white Republicans, and they did increase the number of congressional seats held by black Americans.

Another effect of these majority–minority districts, however, was to elect more Republicans to Congress from the South—one reason why Republicans supported their creation. Because the districts are fashioned by packing as many (heavily Democratic) black voters into a district as possible, the neighboring districts are left with a higher proportion of whites and Republicans. According to one estimate, "for every overwhelmingly black Democratic district created, there is a good chance of creating two or more districts that are overwhelmingly white and Republican."[13] In turn, Democratic state legislatures try to pack the

GOP vote into as few districts as possible, in order to elect more Democratic representatives. The Supreme Court has rejected the most flagrantly engineered of these majority–minority districts, but has ruled that race can be an element in redrawing district lines, as long as it is not the controlling factor.[14]

Getting Blacks' Votes Counted

Achieving fair representation for black Americans is limited by the fact that about 13 percent of black males have lost voting rights because they have had felony convictions. Mandatory sentences for drug use appear to target drugs used more often by blacks, and almost all states deny felons the right to vote, at least while they are behind bars and, in most states, through the individual's parole. More generally, estimates are that more than 4 million Americans of all races have lost their right to vote because of a felony conviction.[15] Predicting from their SES and race, most of these people would probably vote Democratic. So, although black turnout rates are much higher now than they were in the mid-1900s, more subtle challenges to blacks' voting rights remain.

EFFORTS TO LIBERALIZE VOTING RULES

Concern that the registration requirement and the many other rules governing voting were holding down turnout has led to waves of proposed reforms.[16]

Election Day Registration

North Dakota does not require its citizens to register at all, and nine other states have passed laws to allow citizens to register and vote on the same day, known as *Election Day Registration (EDR)*. These states tend to have higher turnout rates,[17] because citizens can cast a ballot even if they do not get interested enough to take part until the last, most engaging days of the campaign.[18] However, in the great majority of states, prospective voters must still take the initiative to find out where and when to register, make the effort to do so, and then register again whenever they move or fail to vote for a number of years. One expert estimated that about 9 million eligible people, many of whom are less educated, lower income, or residentially mobile, tried but were unable to register in time for the 2008 election.[19]

"Motor Voter" Laws

Another effort to ease restrictive registration rules was the so-called *Motor Voter law*, passed in 1993, which required the states to let citizens register to vote at driver's license bureaus, by mail, and through agencies that give out federal benefits. Voter registration surged in many areas as a result. Some opponents of "motor voter" feared that it would result in increased numbers of low-income, Democratic votes on Election Day. Most studies have shown, however, that although stricter registration rules are linked with lower voter turnout, reforms to ease these rules, including "motor voter," do not necessarily increase turnout substantially. Those who register at these alternate sites are less likely to vote than are other registrants.[20]

Early and No-Excuse Absentee Voting

To increase the convenience of voting, two-thirds of the states allowed some form of early voting in person in 2010 or no-excuse absentee voting, in which an individual can request an absentee ballot without having to explain why. In Oregon, Washington State, and most counties in California and Colorado, all voting is now conducted by mail. As a result, almost a third of American voters cast their ballots prior to Election Day. Early and no-excuse absentee voting did not usually lead to higher turnout. Rather, it redistributed the votes over a six-week period; voting in some states began as early as late September.

Spreading voting out over a longer period proved to be a boon for local election officials, because it helped identify problems with voting systems, which could then be fixed by Election Day. But it posed challenges for parties and candidates; the traditional plan of building a campaign toward a big finish on Election Day doesn't work very well if large numbers of voters cast their ballots in October. To take advantage of early and no-excuse absentee voting, party organizations must be prepared to explain these new options to their likely supporters and to mobilize early voters. In 2008, many Republican campaigns had difficulty adapting to this rules change. The national party had held very effective GOTV drives on the weekend before several recent elections, but this program did not function as well when so many people voted early. The Obama campaign took account of the change, incorporating a mobilization of early voters into its voter registration activities.

THE VOTER ID CONTROVERSY

Very recently, these efforts to liberalize the requirements for voter participation have provoked a backlash in a number of state legislatures. For instance, in 2011, four states reduced the length of their early voting periods. More significantly, some states have tightened the voting rules by requiring people to present certain documents at the polls.

Voter ID Laws

In a remarkably short time, many states have passed and most others are considering laws requiring voters to show a state or federal government-issued photo ID card at the polls. Proponents, usually Republicans, contend that the laws are needed to limit vote fraud. Democratic opponents argue that vote fraud at the polls is extremely rare and that much larger numbers of poor, minority, and disabled people—groups that tend to support Democrats—might lose their chance to vote simply because they are less likely to have driver's licenses and passports. In 2008, the U.S. Supreme Court upheld an Indiana law requiring a government-issued photo ID in order to cast a ballot.[21] Studies show, however, that these rules have often been applied in an arbitrary way; blacks are more likely to have been asked by election officials to show identification than whites are, regardless of the state's voter ID laws.[22] In several states whose legislatures gained Republican majorities in 2010, bills were introduced to prevent college students from using university IDs to satisfy voter ID requirements or to make it harder for students to be able to vote in their college towns at all.[23]

Proof of Citizenship

Arizona requires all voters to bring documents to the polls (usually, an original birth certificate, naturalization papers, or a passport) proving that they are American citizens. Three other states added this requirement in 2011. Supporters of these laws say they are needed to curb voting by noncitizens. Others claim that, as with voter ID laws, poor and disabled people and minorities have a harder time obtaining the required documents, which require a fee and travel to the relevant government office, and could therefore have their access to the ballot taken away improperly.

State legislatures and counties frequently vote on other bills that would expand or contract the ease with which individuals can vote. These include legislation allowing people to vote at malls and grocery stores, creating more or fewer precinct polling places,[24] and sending absentee ballot requests and sample ballots to all registered voters. In general, Democrats have been more likely to favor these changes than Republicans have; it is often assumed (though not often proved) that less educated and lower-income people, who tend to identify as Democrats, would be more likely to cast a ballot if voting were made less costly in time and effort.

Voter Intimidation

In addition to affecting the rules for voter turnout, in some instances parties, candidates, and other groups have relied on the more straightforward techniques of voter intimidation that have stained American political history. One time-honored technique has been to station police cars near some polling places and warn prospective voters (falsely) that they could be arrested for unpaid parking tickets or child support if they cast a ballot. In 2010, voters in a largely black neighborhood in Houston were mailed fliers signed by a fictitious group called "Black Democratic Trust of Texas" telling them that voting a straight Democratic ticket would cancel their votes.[25] An uptick in these incidents has led both parties to recruit large numbers of lawyers as poll watchers in recent elections.

VOTING SYSTEMS: ARE VOTES COUNTED FAIRLY?

Once people have gotten to the polls, most of us assume that their choice of candidates will be registered accurately. At least, we *would* have made that assumption until the aftermath of the 2000 presidential race.

Recounts prompted by the closeness of the vote showed that on 1.5–2 million ballots (about 2 percent of all those cast), the counting machines found no presidential vote or votes for more than one candidate; these voters' ballots, then, were not counted. Some of these "undervotes" or "overvotes" could have been intentional, but studies showing that these problems occurred much more frequently in some types of voting machines (such as punch card systems) suggest that the voting system itself may have been the culprit.[26]

In other cases, analysts charged that confusing ballot layout, such as the so-called butterfly ballot used in Palm Beach County, Florida, in 2000, led many voters to cast their ballot for a different candidate than they had intended (see Figure 8.2). This was an especially worrisome issue in Florida, which decided the election for President Bush by a margin of only 537 votes. Other problems included malfunctioning voting machines and lines so long that would-be voters gave up and went home.

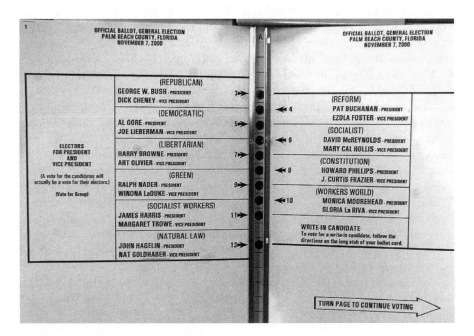

FIGURE 8.2
The Famous Palm Beach, Florida, "Butterfly Ballot," 2000.

This ballot format was designed by a Democratic official in Palm Beach County to make it easier for visually challenged older voters to read. As illustrated in this graphic by Daniel Niblock of the South Florida *Sun-Sentinel* (showing the angle at which most voters would have seen the ballot), the problem was that the punch card holes did not always line up with the candidates' names, so in order to vote for Al Gore, whose name was second on the list of candidates, voters had to punch the *third* hole.

Source: Robert Duyos/South Florida Sun-Sentinel. Reprinted by permission of the *South Florida Sun-Sentinel*. Photograph by Susan Stocker.

Why does this happen? Voters cast ballots at almost 700,000 voting machines in 200,000 voting precincts across the nation. The precincts are tended by about 2 million poll workers who are typically poorly paid, lightly trained partisan volunteers, supervised by local election officials who are often elected on partisan ballots.[27] Simple human error is as likely to occur in running elections and counting votes as it is in any other large-scale activity. Because elections are decentralized, voters in one state, even in one county, may be treated differently from voters in another.

In particular, counties differ in their ability to pay for the most reliable (and costly) voting systems. The result is that error-prone systems are more likely to be found in poorer and minority-dominated counties, which tend to vote Democratic. The U.S. Commission on Civil Rights reported in 2001 that although it found no evidence of a systematic effort to disenfranchise blacks, they were ten times more likely than whites to have their ballots undercounted or rejected in the 2000 Florida vote because they lived in districts with less reliable voting systems.[28]

In the wake of these revelations, Congress passed the 2002 Help America Vote Act (HAVA) devoting more than $3 billion to help states upgrade their voting systems, set minimum federal standards, and create computerized statewide voter registration rolls. Many counties used the money to buy electronic—touch-screen or direct-recording electronic (DRE)—voting machines. In 2006, over 80 percent of all voters used some form of e-voting, more than a third of them for the first time.

That produced new problems. The e-voting systems raised issues familiar to anyone who has used a college computer lab: computer crashes, programming errors, and the possibility of hacking and rigged machines. One Florida newspaper found that voters in counties using touch-screen machines were six times more likely to have their vote go unrecorded as were voters in counties using optical-scan devices, like those often used to grade multiple-choice exams.[29] Another issue was that HAVA granted the right to cast a "provisional" ballot to anyone whose eligibility to vote was challenged by an election official. But Congress set no uniform national standards as to which of these provisional ballots should be counted, which produced concerns about partisan and unequal treatment.

Many counties later abandoned these touch-screen machines. Yet problems persisted (see box "Democracy on the Cheap: Is Every Vote Counted?" on page 161). According to one study in 2008, 3 million registered voters were prevented from voting in that election due to a variety of administrative failures: their names were accidentally purged from or not recorded properly on the registration rolls or they didn't bring the proper identification to the polls.[30] These are challenging problems to solve; even though accurate and reliable voting systems are vital to a democracy, cash-starved counties and state governments may find it difficult to devote the necessary resources to elections, which take place at most only once or twice a year, when they face daily demands to fund other crucial services, such as law enforcement, garbage collection, and road repair.

Democracy on the Cheap: Is Every Vote Counted?

After more than a decade of concern about voting machines, problems remain:

- In 2010, about 25 percent of all voters had to use voting machines that provided no paper record of each vote. That means there's no possibility of an independent recount. Even machines with paper records, which can be verified by the voter before leaving the machine, can have printer jams.
- Wisconsin used a new statewide database to verify voter registrations in 2008. When names were moved into the database, any voter whose date of birth was not recorded was automatically given the birth date January 1, 1900. According to the database, then, 95,000 of Wisconsin's voters were 108 years old. Six members of the state elections board—all retired judges—ran their registrations through the system; four were incorrectly rejected because of data discrepancies between their registration information and other official records, such as a wrongly-listed age (though retired, none of the judges was 108).
- In at least one precinct in Washington, DC, people waited for hours to vote—not because of the record turnout but because poll workers didn't like the precinct's electronic touch-screen voting machines and had hidden them.
- There has been a big increase in mail-in ballots in recent elections. Anticorruption laws prevent party workers from "helping" voters mark their ballots at the polls, but there is no guarantee that mailed-in ballots will be free from such influence.

As one expert put it, "We'd never tolerate this level of errors with an ATM. The problem is that we continue to do democracy on the cheap."

Sources: Ian Urbina, "High Turnout May Add to Problems at Polling Places," *New York Times,* November 2, 2008, p. 1; Mary Pat Flaherty, "Thousands Face Mix-Ups in Voter Registrations," *Washington Post,* October 18, 2008, p. A1; and "America's Voting Systems in 2010," October 20, 2010, at www.verifiedvoting.org. (December 3, 2011).

THE LOW TURNOUT IN AMERICAN ELECTIONS

These problems with voting systems, as well as efforts by parties to change the rules for casting a vote, take on special importance in light of the relatively low turnout rates in American elections. From the 1970s to 2000, turnout dropped to a degree that generated widespread concern. Only between 51 and 57 percent of voting-age Americans made it to the polls in the presidential elections between 1992 and 2000—low turnouts even by American standards.[31]

In 2004, feelings were still raw from the contested 2000 presidential election; this led to a closely fought 2004 campaign in which a variety of groups mounted feverish GOTV drives. The 2008 presidential election, the first in which a black and a woman candidate were front-runners for a major party nomination, generated at least as much excitement. Many observers expected voter participation to rise dramatically as a result.

There was some good news in both 2004 and 2008 for proponents of high turnouts. In 2004, about 64 percent of eligible voters went to the polls—the highest voting rate in the United States since 1968 (see Figure 8.3).[32] After an all-time-low turnout of 15 percent in the 2006 congressional primaries, the 2008 presidential nomination race produced record-breaking participation in many states' primaries and caucuses. Yet turnout in the 2008 general election was about the same as in 2004, and 2010 turnout matched that of 2006.

Some groups' turnout rates did increase substantially in 2008. Turnout was up by almost five percentage points among blacks and about three percentage points among Latinos and Asians. Young people's voting rate rose. The turnout increases were selective, however. Among first-time voters, who made up 11 percent of the electorate, 69 percent voted for Obama.[33] And although Democratic turnout went up by 2.6 percentage points, turnout declined by 1.3 percentage points among Republicans and by about one point among whites. In 2010, all these increases were inverted; turnout declined among blacks, younger people, and Democrats and increased among older people and Republicans. The composition of the voters in a given election clearly makes a difference in who wins and who loses.

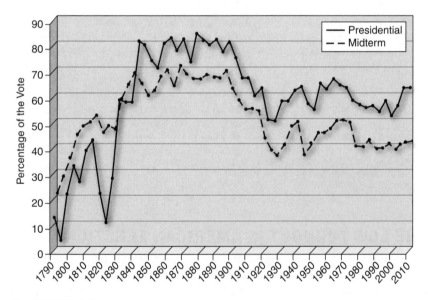

FIGURE 8.3
Turnout in American Elections, 1790–2010.

Note: These are the percentages voting for president and for the office with the highest vote in midterm elections, calculated as described in Note 31 to this chapter. Data are from Walter Dean Burnham, "The Turnout Problem," in A. James Reichley, ed., *Elections American Style* (Washington, DC: Brookings Institution, 1987), pp. 113–114, updated for presidential elections since 1984. Midterm data since 1986 come from Curtis Gans, Director of the Center for the Study of the American Electorate.

Turnout rates in American elections have been higher at other times, particularly toward the end of the 1800s.[34] In more recent times, presidential turnout reached 65 percent in 1960, and turnout in off-year elections peaked at 49 percent in 1966. But even these percentages are low compared with most other industrialized democracies. Voters in Sweden and Denmark regularly turn out at rates of 80 percent or more, and voter turnout in the 2007 French presidential election reached 85 percent.

WHY DON'T MORE AMERICANS VOTE?

Even taking account of higher turnouts in 2004 and 2008, many observers wonder why voter participation in the United States is not much greater. For several reasons, voting turnout should have risen dramatically since the mid-1900s.[35] Educational levels have increased substantially, and higher education is linked with higher voter turnout. Liberalized registration, residence, and early voting rules have made it easier to cast a ballot. Yet the increase in actual voter turnout has simply returned the nation to the voting levels of the 1960s.

INDIVIDUAL DIFFERENCES IN TURNOUT

We can think about the decision to vote in terms of its costs and benefits to the individual. Each of us pays some costs for voting, not in cash but in time, energy, and attention. What we get in return may seem minimal; the influence of a single vote in most elections is likely to be small. From that perspective, it may be remarkable that anyone votes at all.[36] A variety of economic and social forces, from citizens' levels of education to their social connections, affect the ways in which individuals weigh the costs and benefits of voting. That in turn affects the parties' ability to increase the turnout of different types of voters.

Education

The biggest difference between voters and nonvoters is their level of education; less educated Americans, who tend to identify as Democrats, are much less likely to vote[37] (see Figure 8.4, Section A). Because of the close relationships between education, income, and job status, poorer people also vote in lower proportions. More education helps people understand the political system and locate the information they need to make political choices. People with more education are more likely to feel that they ought to vote, to gain satisfaction from voting, and to have the experience with meeting deadlines and filling out forms that will be necessary to register and vote.[38]

This relationship between education and voting sounds so obvious that we would expect to see it everywhere. Yet the relationship is weaker in many other democracies, where labor parties and other groups work to bring less-educated and lower-income people to the polls; this can compensate for the dampening effect of lower educational levels on voter turnout.[39]

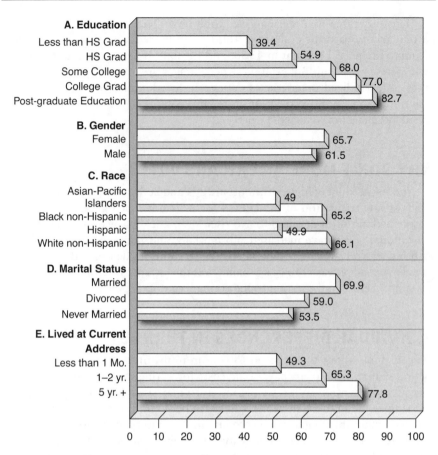

FIGURE 8.4
Group Differences in Voter Turnout, 2008.

Note: Bars show the percentage of each group who reported having voted in the 2008 presidential election, based on the voting-age citizen population.

Source: U.S. Census Bureau data at www.census.gov/hhes/www/socdemo/voting/publications/p20/2008/tables.html, Tables 6, 10, 11, 15a, and 15b (accessed November 12, 2011).

Youth

Although the gap has been shrinking, younger Americans, disproportionately Democratic in their party ID, are much less likely to go to the polls than are older people (see Figure 8.5). Younger people are no less likely than their elders to take part in other community activities, such as volunteer work.[40] But their political knowledge and interest have lagged behind; their interest in service has not extended to include political service. In a recent survey, the only occupation young people (age 26 and under) rated less attractive than being an elected official was farming.[41]

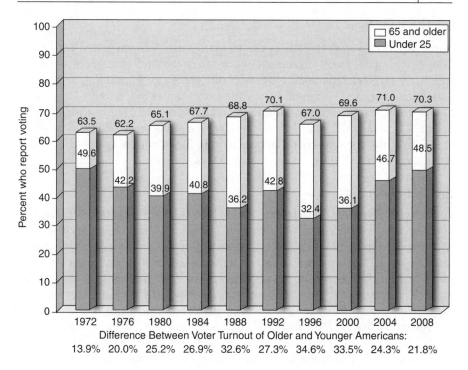

FIGURE 8.5
Voter Turnout of Younger and Older Americans, 1972–2008.

Source: U.S. Census Bureau data at www.census.gov/hhes/www/socdemo/voting/publications/p20/2008/tables.html, Table 5 (accessed November 12, 2011).

There was a massive increase in the youth vote during the early 2008 primaries, but only a slight increase in the general election relative to 2004. This increase was notable primarily because the youth vote was much more one-sidedly Democratic in 2008 (a 34-percentage point margin for Barack Obama) than it had been in 2004 (an 8-percentage point margin for Democrat John Kerry). In 2010, however, people aged 18–29 dropped from about 18 percent of all voters to 11 percent.

Why does the lower turnout of young adults matter? There are some interesting differences in attitudes between younger and older generations. Current young adults, on average, are more likely to favor privatizing public services (for instance, letting people invest some of their Social Security taxes in the stock market) than older people are, and also more tolerant of interracial dating and same-sex marriage.[42] When large numbers of young people don't vote, candidates pay greater attention to the issues that concern those who do vote. Social Security and Medicare rank high on the campaign agenda because older people, for whom these issues are important, have higher turnout rates than younger adults do.

Gender and Race

For many decades after getting the right to vote, women voted less often than men, but women's increasing education levels and changes in women's roles have largely eliminated this gender difference (see Figure 8.4, Section B). Any remaining racial differences in voting (see Figure 8.4, Section C) are due almost entirely to the average differences in education and occupational status between whites and blacks,[43] and these were overcome in 2008 by the great enthusiasm for the Obama candidacy among black voters. Latino and Asian Americans have the lowest voter turnout rates.

Social Connectedness

People who have a lot of social ties—those who belong to several organizations and are closely connected with friends and family—are much more likely to vote than others are. Contact with politically knowledgeable people increases that likelihood.[44] These organizations and knowledgeable people help to mobilize voters. Voting is also more common among those who are well integrated into the community through home ownership, long-time residence, church attendance, or a job outside the home. Even being married affects the likelihood that an individual will vote (see Figure 8.4, Sections D and E).[45]

Some forms of social connectedness have declined in recent decades. Americans are less inclined to attend religious services now and less likely to be married. These declines may counteract the effects of rising educational levels and liberalized registration rules, by weakening the social networks that stimulate voter participation.

Political Attitudes

Some "civic attitudes" predispose individuals to vote: feelings that government is responsive to citizens (***external political efficacy***) and can be trusted to do what is right (***trust in government***), and a sense of responsibility to take part in elections (***citizen duty***).[46] These civic attitudes have faded in recent decades. Many relatively well-informed, well-educated young people have become cynical about government and politics. More education and easier access to the vote, then, do not tempt them to become politically involved.[47] And variations in the strength of people's partisanship are also connected with voting; when party ID weakened in the 1970s, turnout declined.[48]

Why Didn't You Vote?

Here's why people registered to vote said they didn't cast a ballot in 2008:

Too busy	18%
Sick or disabled	15

Not interested	13
Didn't like the candidates	13
Out of town	9
Registration problems (among registered citizens)	6
I forgot	3
Inconvenient polling place	3
Transportation problems	3
Other	18

And here's why others didn't register to vote:

Not interested	39%
Missed the deadline to register	14
Permanent illness or disability	5
Did not know where or how to register	4
Did not meet residency requirement	4
My vote won't make a difference	4
Other	31

Source: U.S. Census Bureau data at www.census.gov/hhes/www/socdemo/voting/publications/p20/2008/tables.html, Table 12 (accessed November 12, 2011).

THE IMPACT OF THE CURRENT CAMPAIGN

Declines in civic attitudes and social connectedness help to explain why voter participation has not increased more substantially in the United States. Yet turnout does rise in some elections, and party activity has been responsible for some of these increases.

The Excitement of the Election

Voter participation is usually highest in presidential elections and lowest in local races.[49] A main reason is that presidential races are highly publicized and usually exciting. Because of the publicity, people will not have to put much effort into locating information about the candidates, and because of the excitement of the race, they will probably pay more attention to the information they encounter. Both of these conditions reduce the costs of voting and increase its appeal.

Close Competition

Hotly contested races bring voters to the polls; in addition to their excitement, competitive elections give voters more assurance that their vote will matter.[50] The presidential elections of 1992, 2004, and 2008 had the highest turnouts in recent decades. Both 1992 and 2004 were highly competitive. Although the 2008 election was not as close, it was a hard contest for pollsters to predict; throughout the race, analysts wondered whether some voters might be lying to polltakers about their willingness to vote for the first black presidential nominee in American history, and thus, whether the outcome would be closer than the polls were forecasting. Turnout rose especially in states that were newly competitive in 2008, such as Virginia, Indiana, and North Carolina, and dropped in some noncompetitive states.[51]

PARTY EFFORTS TO MOBILIZE VOTERS

One of the most important determinants of voter turnout levels is the degree to which the party organizations, as well as campaigns and organized interests, mobilize to get out the vote on Election Day. People go to the polls when somebody encourages them to do so. Person-to-person contact tends to be more effective in increasing turnout than are mail or phone appeals.[52] Personal canvassing is especially useful in mobilizing first-time voters; in 2004, three-fifths of new voters said they came to the polls because "my family or friends encouraged me to vote," compared with only one-fifth of repeat voters.[53]

Face-to-face voter mobilization had become less common in the late 1900s. But during the past decade, a number of groups have developed programs to increase turnout among their supporters. Civil rights groups worked closely with the Democratic Party in the early 2000s to bring more blacks to the polls. Organized labor mounted a major GOTV drive in 2000 and again in 2006 and 2008, built on union members' contacts with other members and their friends and neighbors. One analyst writes, "Voter mobilization is…among the plausible explanations for increasing voter participation levels over the past three presidential elections."[54]

Conventional wisdom says that because nonvoters tend to come from groups usually inclined to vote Democratic, such as lower-income and less-educated people, voter mobilization drives should help Democratic candidates. That is why proposals to make registering and voting easier are often assumed to benefit the Democrats. It explains why organized labor spends so much money and effort on registration and GOTV campaigns. It even explains politicians' belief that rainy weather is Republican weather, in that Republicans will come to the polls anyway.[55]

Conventional wisdom is not always correct, however. As we have seen, close contests, dramatic conflicts, and exciting candidates can bring more people to the polls, and these conditions are not always generated by Democratic candidates. In fact, Republican presidential candidates have won most of the large-turnout elections in the past five decades.[56]

Do Party Efforts Diversify the Electorate?

Have these party mobilization drives helped to create an American electorate that more closely reflects the diversity of the American people? Or have they simply increased the representation of those already inclined to vote?

Researchers find that both parties tend to contact higher-income and older people more than they contact less wealthy and younger people, a tendency that has increased in most recent elections.[57] This reflects the fact that wealthier and older people are more likely to have stable addresses and phone numbers than are, for instance, highly mobile college students, so party activists can find them more easily. It also stems from the experience of both parties that it is easier to activate those already predisposed to vote than it is to entice previous nonvoters to the polls.

As a result, most voter mobilization drives do relatively little to increase the turnout of groups that have had low voting rates over time. The most recent exception was the 2008 Obama campaign. Its organizers set out to expand the playing field with respect to voter turnout, because many of Obama's most likely supporters were a part of groups with traditionally low turnout. In addition to minority racial and ethnic groups, the campaign especially targeted young people who had recently become eligible to vote. Their efforts paid off. One pollster estimated that Obama won the vote of people under age 30 by about 8.3 million votes; Obama's overall margin in the popular vote was about 8 million.[58] The Obama campaign is trying to maintain these mobilization efforts in 2012. "Obama for America" was transformed into "Organizing for America" and, together with its extensive e-mail list and contact database, moved into the Democratic National Committee in 2009. The group began with a grassroots campaign mobilizing support for President Obama's proposed budget and policy initiatives.

THE CHALLENGE TO THE PARTIES

One argument in favor of democracy is the notion that the best decisions are made when the responsibility for decision making is most widely shared. This would seem to be an argument for the widest possible participation in elections (see "Which Would You Choose?" on page 170).[59] Yet we have seen that in current American politics, turnout is lower than in most other democracies, and the nonvoters are more likely to come from disadvantaged groups: young people, Asian and Latino Americans, and those with fewer economic resources and greater need for government help. Groups that have more resources—education, higher incomes, majority status—are those already in the habit of voting.

What responsibility do the parties bear for these low turnouts? Party organizations are among the main sponsors of voter mobilization drives. They have the capacity to recruit large and diverse groups of people into politics. But parties, like individuals and other groups, are self-interested; they want to stimulate turnout only among their likely supporters and to limit turnout by those unlikely to vote for their candidates. And they find it easier to locate and contact people who have already joined the voting population. In practice, then, the parties usually adjust their mobilization strategies to the electorate as it currently exists; they don't often work hard to attract new voting groups, especially the disadvantaged.

We Need Every Vote...

Democracy is most vibrant when all views are heard. When as many people as possible take part in elections, government is more likely to come up with the creative solutions needed to solve problems.

Politicians pay more attention to the needs of those who vote than to those who don't. So the views and interests of the nonvoters, though real, may go unrepresented.

The most committed voters tend to be older, more educated, and more affluent than other citizens are. These people will get more than their fair share of government benefits and attention from elected officials anxious to get their votes.

It is the alienated and dissatisfied people who stay away from the polls. They can become ripe for extremist appeals. It's better to bring them into the political system where they can voice their concerns in more productive ways.

Let Sleeping Dogs Lie ...

Those who are least likely to vote are also the least well informed and the least interested in government. Why should we encourage them to take part in elections? If they don't care enough or know enough to vote, shouldn't we be grateful that they stay home?

If people have the right to vote and choose not to, maybe this means they are satisfied with things as they are. If they really wanted change, they could use their votes to obtain it.

If we relax registration and residence requirements to encourage more people to vote, we're opening the floodgates to vote fraud: people voting more than once or voting under other people's direction.

American democracy has been strong enough to survive impeachments, scandals, and candidates who lose the presidency even though they won the popular vote. If it ain't broke, why fix it? ∎

The fact that the active electorate in the United States is not as diverse as the nation's population probably reduces the amount of conflict in American politics and the range of political interests to which the parties must respond. Understandably, candidates and elected officials think more about the needs of those who take part in elections than those who don't. For example, studies show that members of Congress direct more federal spending to counties in their district with higher voter turnout than to those with lower turnout.[60] The cost, however, is that in the area of voter participation, the American parties have fallen short of fulfilling their democratic capabilities.

Parties, Nominations, and Elections

As elections draw near, the distance between the party in government and the other two sectors of the parties—their organizations and their identifiers—shrinks. During campaigns, party activists work to energize party identifiers and bring them to the polls to vote for the party's candidates. The importance of winning elections encourages all three parts of the parties to work together and reconcile their differences—at least until the votes are counted. Elections also link the parties at different levels of government. The process of nominating and electing a presidential candidate binds the state and local parties to the national party, at least for a while, just as a statewide election focuses the energies of local party organizations and leaders within the state.

There is good reason why elections ought to encourage cooperation within the party. When candidates run more capable campaigns, they improve not only their own ability to attract money and other resources but also that of their party organization. When candidates are elected, their party's activists are more likely to see action on their issue agendas. When a party's candidate wins the governorship or the local executive office in some areas, then party leaders may gain access to patronage jobs and contracts, which in turn can bring more contributors to the party organization. In the effort to win, candidates and party activists have to mobilize as many of the party's identifiers as possible. Because victory holds so many attractions for all three parts of the party, it is a powerful lure for them to work together.

All this cooperation does not come easily. Almost every aspect of the electoral process, and especially the nominating process, can also pit the needs of one part of the party against those of another. When primaries are used to select a party's candidates, there will be times when party voters choose a nominee regarded as a disaster by party leaders. Efforts by the party organization to raise money will compete with candidates' own fund-raising. Candidates choose which issues they will emphasize, which advisers they will hire, and which strategies they will adopt, and these choices affect the image of the party as a whole, even when the party's leaders and activists do not share these preferences. Once in office, the party's candidates may have reason to ignore or downplay some questions that are "hot button" issues to party activists.

In addition to the competition within each party, the parties also compete on the larger electoral stage with other political organizations. Groups such as single-issue organizations, labor unions, religious lobbies, insurance companies, and other corporations involve themselves in campaigns in order to achieve their political goals. Some of these groups work very aggressively to help candidates get nominated, raise money, influence public opinion, and win elections. Democratic state party leaders, for example, will probably have to compete with environmental groups, women's rights groups, civil rights organizations, pro-choice activists, and unions representing trial lawyers and government employees to get the attention of a Democratic candidate for statewide office.

This competition and cooperation is guided by a set of rules, just as the cooperation and competition in a basketball game are. These rules range from laws to standard practices, and, as in basketball, they have a big impact on the results. One of these "rules" is the widespread use of primary elections, which takes control over candidates' nominations out of the hands of party leaders. Other influential "rules" include the laws and practices that govern campaign fund-raising.

The first two chapters in this section focus on parties' involvement in nominating candidates. Chapter 9 explores the nomination process in general, and Chapter 10 considers the fascinating and peculiar practices through which the American major parties select their presidential candidates. In Chapter 11, we turn to the role of parties in general elections, and Chapter 12 discusses money in politics. The constant search for dollars to run campaigns gave rise to extensive reform efforts in the 1970s, the passage of a new campaign finance reform law in 2002, and numerous court decisions. This chapter traces the flow of money into campaigns and considers how it can both expand and contract the influence of parties on their candidates.

How Parties Choose Candidates

In addition to public opinion polls, drive-through restaurants, and other means of democratizing life, Americans invented primary elections. In a primary (more formally known as a *direct primary*), the party electorate chooses which candidates will run for office under the party's label. Then, in a later *general election,* all voters can make the final choice among the parties' nominees for each office. To American voters neck-deep in primaries during an election season, this may seem like the "normal" way for parties to nominate candidates. But, in reality, it isn't. Although the idea of a primary election has spread recently, candidates in most of the rest of the democratic world are still selected by party leaders, activists, or elected officials, not by voters.[1]

These differences in nomination procedures help us understand how American party politics differs from those of other democracies. The shift to primaries forced the American parties to develop a different set of strategies in supporting candidates, contesting elections, and trying to hold elected officials accountable than we would find in nations that do not hold primaries.

The direct primary permeates every level of American politics. The great majority of states use it in all nominations. The other states use it for most elective offices. It dominates the presidential nominating process (see Chapter 10). Even though it is just the first of two steps in electing public officials, it reduces voters' choices to a manageable number. The selection of nominees in the primary can affect the party's chance of winning the general election. In areas where one party dominates, the voters' only real choice is made in the primary. What led to the use of this two-step election process? How does it work and how well does it serve the needs of voters, candidates, and parties?

HOW THE NOMINATION PROCESS EVOLVED

For the first 110 years of the American republic, candidates for office were nominated by party caucuses and, later, by party conventions. In both cases, it was the leaders and activists of the party organizations who chose the party's nominees, not the rest of the voting public.

Nominations by Caucus

In the early years, as the parties began to establish local and state organizations, they held local party caucuses to choose candidates for county offices. Caucuses of like-minded partisans in Congress continued to nominate presidential and vice-presidential candidates. Similar party caucuses in state legislatures chose candidates for governor and other statewide offices. These caucuses were generally informal, and there were no procedures for ensuring that all the major figures of the party would take part.[2]

Nominations by Convention

As the push for popular democracy spread, these caucuses came to be seen as an aristocratic elite—"King Caucus"—that ignored public opinion. In 1831, a minor party called the Anti-Masons held a national convention to nominate its presidential candidate, hoping to get enough press attention to gain major party status. The Jacksonian Democrats held their own convention in time for the 1832 election. From then on, through the rest of that century, conventions were the main means of nominating presidential candidates. These conventions were composed of delegates chosen by state and local party leaders, often at their own lower level nominating conventions.

These large and chaotic conventions looked more broadly representative than the caucuses but often were not. Delegates were chosen and the conventions managed by the party leaders. Reformers denounced the convention system as yet another form of boss rule. By the end of the 1800s, the Progressive movement led the drive for a new way of nominating candidates.[3]

Nominations by Direct Primaries

The Progressives suggested that instead of giving party leaders the power to choose, voters should be able to select their party's candidates for each office directly. This direct, primary (or first) election reflected the Progressives' core belief: The best way to cure a democracy's ills was to prescribe larger doses of democracy. Robert M. La Follette, a Progressive leader, argued that in a primary, "The nomination of the party will not be the result of 'compromise' or impulse, or evil design [as he felt it was in a party-run caucus/convention system] ... but the candidates of the majority, honestly and fairly nominated."[4]

Some southern states had already used primaries at the local level in the years after the Civil War, to legitimize the nominees and settle internal disputes in their one-party Democratic systems. In the first two decades of the twentieth century, all but four other states adopted primaries for at least some of their statewide nominations. This was a time when one party or the other dominated the politics of many states—the most pervasive one-party rule in American history. It might be possible to tolerate the poor choices made by conventions when voters have a real choice in the general election, but when the nominees of the dominant party have no serious competition, those shortcomings were harder to accept. So the Progressives, who fought economic monopoly with antitrust legislation, used the direct primary as their major weapon in battling political monopoly.

Although the primary was designed to democratize the nominating process, many of its supporters hoped that it would have the further effect of crippling the political parties. Primaries would take away the party organization's most important power—the nomination of candidates—and give it instead to party voters. In fact, some states, such as Wisconsin, adopted a definition of the party electorate so broad that it included any voters who chose to vote in the party's primary on Election Day.

Primaries were not the first cause of party weakness in the United States. If party leaders had been strong enough throughout the country when primaries were proposed, then they would have been able to stop the spread of this reform and keep control of the nominations themselves. But primaries did undermine the party organizations' power even further. Elected officials who were nominated by the voters in primaries were unlikely to feel as loyal to the party organization as were officials who owed their nominations to party leaders. Because of the existence of primaries, party leaders in the United States have less control over who will receive the party nomination than in most other democracies. In some states, the reforms required that even the party organization's own leaders be chosen in primaries; the result was that the parties risked losing control over their own internal affairs.

THE CURRENT MIX OF PRIMARIES AND CONVENTIONS

Although conventions are no longer common, they are still used to nominate candidates in a few states and, most visibly, in the contest for the presidency. Because states have the legal right to design their own nominating systems, the result is a mixture of primaries and conventions for choosing candidates for state offices.

Every state now uses primaries to nominate at least some statewide officials, and most states use this method exclusively.[5] In four southern states, the party may choose to hold a convention instead of a primary, but only in Virginia has the convention option been used in recent years, as a means of unifying the party behind a particular candidate. Other states use conventions for some purposes. Iowa requires a convention when no candidate wins at least 35 percent of the primary vote. Three states (Indiana, Michigan, and South Dakota) use primaries for the top statewide offices but choose other nominees in conventions. Some (Colorado, Connecticut, Delaware, New Mexico, New York, North Dakota, Rhode Island, and Utah) hold conventions to screen candidates for the primary ballot, though in some cases, candidates can bypass the convention by filing a petition signed by party members.[6] This variety of choices reminds us again that, in spite of the national parties' growing strength, the state and local parties still hold a great deal of independent decision-making power.

TYPES OF PRIMARIES

States also differ in the criteria they use to determine who can vote in their primaries. There are three basic forms, although each has a lot of variations.[7] In states with so-called closed primaries, only voters who have formally declared their affiliation with a party can participate. This makes it easier for party activists and identifiers to keep their party's choice of nominees in their own hands. Voters in states with "open" primaries have more freedom to choose which party's primary they want to vote in. And in a few states, Democratic and Republican candidates for state and local offices all run on the same primary ballot, so a voter can select some candidates of each party.

Closed Primaries

About a dozen states hold a fully *closed primary*, in which voters have to register as a Democrat or a Republican prior to the election.[8] Then they receive the primary ballot of only their own party when they come to vote. If they want to vote in the other party's primary, they must formally change their party affiliation on the registration rolls before the primary. States with traditionally strong party organizations, such as New York and Pennsylvania, are among those that have been able to keep their primaries fully closed.

In most other states, whose primaries are often called *semiclosed* or *semiopen*, voters can change their party registration at the polls, or they can simply declare their party preference at the polling place. They are then given their declared party's ballot and, in a few of these states, are considered to be enrolled in that party. This allows independents and even the other party's identifiers to become "partisans for a day" and vote in a party's primary. From the point of view of the voter, these primaries are not very different from an open primary. The difference is important from the party's perspective, however, because in many of these semiclosed primaries there is a written record of party registration that can then be used by party organizations to target appeals to the people who claim to support them.

Open Primaries

Citizens of the remaining states can vote in the primary of their choice without having to state publicly which party they favor.[9] In these *open primaries*, voters receive either a consolidated ballot or ballots for every party, and they select the party of their choice in the privacy of the voting booth. They can vote in only one party's primary in a given election. Many of these states have histories of Progressive strength.

Blanket Primaries

The state of Washington adopted the *blanket primary* in 1935. It gives voters even greater freedom. The names of candidates from all parties appear on a single ballot in the primary, just as they do in the general election, so that in contrast to an open primary, a voter can choose a Democrat for one office and a Republican for another. Alaska later adopted the blanket primary as well.

California voters approved an initiative in 1996 to hold a blanket primary. Proponents said it would bring more voters to the polls and encourage the choice of more moderate candidates.[10] Party leaders saw it differently. They claimed that the plan prevented the party's loyal supporters from choosing the candidates who best represented their views. That, they said, violated their First Amendment right to freedom of association and kept the party from offering a clear and consistent message to the voters. In 2000, the U.S. Supreme Court sided with the parties and gave the right to decide who votes in a primary, at least in California, back to the party organizations.[11]

"Top Two" Primaries In 2008, Washington moved to a type of blanket primary called a *top two (or nonpartisan)* system: Not only do all candidates' names appear on the same ballot, but the top two vote getters for each office, regardless of party, advance to the general election. The party organization can still endorse a candidate, but if voters prefer (and they often do), they can select two Democrats, or two Republicans, to run against one another in the general election. California voters adopted a similar system two years later.

Louisiana uses a version of this system for state and local elections: If one candidate for an office wins more than 50 percent of the votes in the nonpartisan primary, he or she is elected to that office immediately. If no candidate for the office wins an outright majority in the primary, then a runoff between the two top candidates (again, regardless of party) is held at the time scheduled for the general election. Not surprisingly, major and minor parties oppose the use of a nonpartisan or top two system and prohibit states from adopting it in their presidential primaries.

When states shift from one type of primary to another, it is usually because state party leaders are trying to protect their party's interests in the nominating process under changing political conditions. In some cases, a state party has attempted to attract independent voters by switching to an open primary. In others, party leaders have urged the legislature to adopt new primary rules that would advantage candidates the party leaders favor in a particular election year. However, change has also been prompted by nonparty or antiparty groups, as was the case in California's moves to a blanket and then a top two primary.

WHY DOES THE TYPE OF PRIMARY MATTER?

These varieties of primaries represent different answers to a long-standing debate: Is democracy better served by competition between strong and disciplined parties or by a system in which parties have relatively little power? The closed primary reflects the belief that citizens benefit from having clear choices in elections, which can best be provided by strong, internally unified parties; therefore, it makes sense for a party's candidates to be selected by that party's loyal followers. By contrast, open and blanket primaries are closer to the view that rigid party loyalties can harm a democracy, so candidates should be chosen by all voters, regardless of party.

Most party organizations prefer the closed primary in which voters must register by party before the primary. It pays greater respect to the party's right to select its candidates. Prior party registration also gives the parties a bonus—published lists of their partisans. Further, the closed primary limits the greatest dangers of open and blanket primaries, at least from the perspective of party leaders: crossing over and raiding. Both terms refer to people who vote in the primary of a party that they do not generally support. They differ in the voter's intent. Voters *cross over* in order to take part in a more exciting race or to vote for a more appealing candidate in the other party. *Raiding* is a conscious effort to weaken the other party by voting for its least attractive candidates.

Studies of primary contests in Wisconsin and other states show that crossing over is common in open primaries. Partisans rarely cross over in off-year gubernatorial primaries because that would keep them from having a voice in other state and local-level party contests. But independents and partisans are more likely to cross over in a presidential primary or when only a few offices are on the ballot. In a 2006 Rhode Island Senate race, for example, more Democrats and independents voted in the open Republican primary than Republicans did. These crossover voters often support a different candidate than the party's partisans do. In the Rhode Island race, crossover voting led to a victory for the more moderate Republican candidate, who was closer to the views of the Democrats and independents voting in the Republican contest.

Candidates, then, take the type of primary into account in building their campaign strategies. More moderate candidates for president, and those with a nontraditional appeal or a more independent image, often campaign especially in states with open primaries, where they can benefit from the support of crossover voters. They encourage crossovers in these primaries by discussing issues that appeal to the other party's voters.[12] In 2008, Barack Obama beat Hillary Clinton by a larger margin among crossover Republicans and independents than among self-identified Democrats. Thus, he did better in open primaries such as Wisconsin's, where a larger proportion of the votes came from independents and crossovers, than he did in closed primaries (see Figure 9.1). Even in New York, the state Clinton represented in the Senate, Obama was able to hold down her margin of victory because of his support among the small percentage of primary voters who told pollsters that although they were registered Democrats, they actually considered themselves independents.

Organized raiding would be a bigger problem. It is a party leader's nightmare that opponents will make mischief by voting in the party's primary for the least appealing candidate. People with intense views sometimes encourage raiding. In Utah, for instance, a Republican state legislator encouraged Republican voters switch to the Democratic U.S. House primary in 2010 and vote for a lesbian candidate who favored abortion rights—not a candidate they would otherwise have supported—because she would have been easier for a Republican to beat. (He later renounced the idea.) Studies of open primaries have found little evidence of raiding, however. Voters usually

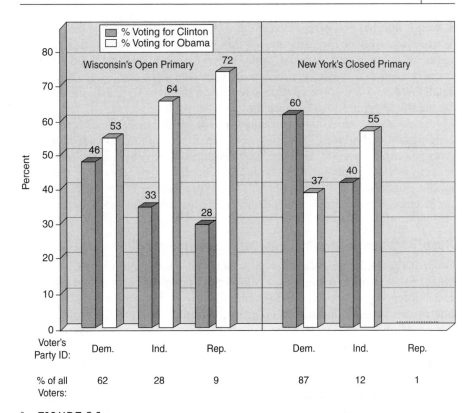

FIGURE 9.1

The Impact of Crossover Voters in Closed and Open Primaries: Obama Vs. Clinton, 2008.

Note: Bars show the percentage of voters in Wisconsin's open primary and New York's closed primary casting a ballot for Hillary Clinton and Barack Obama, by party identification. The much larger proportion of independent and Republican voters in Wisconsin's open primary gave Obama a big advantage in that state.

Source: Entrance and exit polls conducted by Edison/Mitofsky for the National Election Pool, at http://projects. washingtonpost.com/2008-presidential-candidates/primaries/exit-polls/topics/party-identification/d/ (accessed November 13, 2011).

cross over to vote their real preferences rather than to weaken the party in whose primary they are participating.[13]

HOW CANDIDATES QUALIFY

States also vary in the ease with which candidates can get their names on the primary ballot and in the support required to win the nomination.

How Do Candidates Get on the Ballot?

In most states, candidates get on the primary ballot by filing a petition. State election laws specify how many signatures the petition has to contain—either a specific number or a percentage of the vote for the office in the past election.[14] States vary a lot in the difficulty of this step. Some have complicated rules requiring a lot of signatures, designed to favor party insiders. In some other states, a candidate needs only to appear before the clerk of elections and pay a small fee. A few states even put presidential candidates on the ballot if they are "generally recognized" to be running.

These simple rules have consequences for the parties. The easier it is for candidates to get on the ballot, the more likely it becomes that dissident, or even crackpot, candidates will enter a race and engage the party's preferred candidates in costly primary battles. In states with easy ballot access, citizens can be treated to grudge campaigns, in which people file to oppose the sheriff who arrested them, for instance, or who simply enjoy the thought of wreaking havoc in a primary.

Runoffs: When Too Many Candidates Get on the Ballot

What if the leading candidate in a primary gets less than a majority of the votes? In most states' primaries, a plurality is enough. Almost all the southern and border states, however, hold a runoff between the top two candidates if one candidate does not win at least 50 percent of the vote. During the long period of one-party Democratic rule of the South, Democratic factionalism often produced three, four, or five serious candidates for a single office in a primary. The runoff was used to ensure a majority winner in order to present a unified face to the electorate and to ward off any challenges in the general election from blacks and other Republicans.

The southern runoff primary has long been controversial. Citing instances in which black candidates who received a plurality in the first primary lost to whites in the runoff, recent studies show that runoffs disadvantage minority groups.[15]

WHAT PARTIES DON'T LIKE ABOUT PRIMARIES

The Progressives designed the direct primary to break the party organization's monopoly control of nominations, and, in important respects, it did. In the process, it challenged parties' effectiveness in elections more generally.

Difficulties in Recruiting Candidates

Candidate recruitment has never been an easy job, especially for the minority party. The direct primary makes the challenge even more difficult. If an ambitious candidate can challenge the party favorite in the dominant party's primary, he or she is less likely to consider running for office under the minority party's label. So, some argue, the minority party will find it even harder to recruit good candidates for races that it is not likely to win. Little by little, the majority party becomes the only viable means of exerting political influence, and the minority party atrophies.[16]

This argument should not be taken too far. One-party politics declined after primaries became more common. And even in areas dominated by one party, the internal competition promoted by primaries can keep officeholders responsive to their constituents.[17] Nevertheless, the fact that party organizations cannot guarantee the outcome of their own primaries means that they have less to offer the candidates they are trying to recruit.

The Risk of Unappealing Nominees

Normally, only about half as many voters turn out for a primary as for a general election.[18] If this smaller group of primary voters is not representative of those who will vote later, then it may select a candidate who, because of his or her issue stands or background, may not appeal to the broader turnout in the general election. Imagine the discomfort of Democratic Party leaders in southern California, for instance, when a former official of the Ku Klux Klan captured the Democratic congressional nomination in a multicandidate primary race. In particular, some primary voters might be tempted to choose a candidate who is more extreme than the party's supporters as a whole.

Another reason why primary voters might choose a weak candidate is that in a race in which all the candidates are of the same party, voters cannot use their party identification to select candidates, and many voters will not have any other relevant information available. They may choose a candidate because his or her name is familiar or may simply vote for the first name listed on the ballot (see box "The Senate Nominee Who Thinks Out of the Box," on page XXX). If the nominations were made by a party convention, it is often argued, convention delegates would know the prospective candidates better, so they would not be prone to these misjudgments.

The Senate Nominee Who Thinks Out of the Box

To national Democratic leaders, Vic Rawl was a credible candidate for the Democratic nomination for a U.S. Senate seat in 2010. Rawl, a South Carolina local elected official and former judge, spent about a quarter of a million dollars on his primary campaign and felt confident that he'd win the nomination. Yet Rawl won only 41 percent of the primary vote. The candidate who won 59 percent was a 32-year-old political newcomer named Alvin Greene. After having paid the $10,400 filing fee required for his candidacy—an impressive sum for someone who had been unemployed for months—Greene raised no more funds and did no campaigning. (He later insisted that he had campaigned "across the state," though he couldn't remember where.) Greene was not an ideal candidate; he had been "involuntarily" discharged from the military and faced a felony charge of obscenity. But he had ideas; one way to create jobs in South Carolina, he suggested, would be to mass produce action figures of Greene himself in his army uniform—a proposal he said would assure voters that "I think out of the box." (He later said he was joking.)

(continued)

(continued)

How could Greene have won the Democratic nomination? He was listed first on the ballot, and very few voters had ever heard of either candidate. After losing the general election to incumbent Republican Senator Jim DeMint, Greene shifted focus, announcing that he was "born to be president."

Sources: Rachel Weiner, "Alvin Greene Suggests Making Dolls of Himself," *Washington Post,* July 7, 2010, at http://voices.washingtonpost.com/44/2010/07/alvin-greene-suggests-making-d.html; and Manuel Roig-Franzia, "In South Carolina, Greene Is Mystery Man Despite Winning Democratic Senate Nod," *Washington Post,* June 11, 2010, at www.washingtonpost.com/wp-dyn/content/article/2010/06/10/AR2010061002499.html (both accessed November 13, 2011).

Divisive Primaries

Primaries can create conflict that may reopen old party wounds or produce new ones. Activists who had campaigned for the candidate who lost the primary may sit out the general election rather than work for their party's nominee. Supporters of Hillary Clinton during the Democratic presidential primaries in 2008, indignant when she lost the nomination to Barack Obama, were less likely to vote for Obama in the general election than were those who had supported Obama in the primaries.[19] If Obama's general election race had been close, the loss of these Clinton supporters could have been decisive. Several Republican leaders had similar fears in 2010 when some GOP incumbents came under attack from primary candidates favored by the Tea Party. The charges raised by a candidate's primary opponent are often reused by the opposition in the general election, a source of free campaign help to the other party. If a divisive primary is expensive, it may eat up much of the money the primary winner will need to run an effective campaign in the general election.

A divisive primary could be especially damaging if the losing candidate refuses to take "no" for an answer and runs in the general election anyway, as an independent or minor party candidate. The sore loser could draw enough support to destroy the chances of his or her primary rival. In the great majority of states, however, "sore loser" laws and simultaneous filing deadlines prevent primary losers from using this kind of end run to get on the general election ballot.

Despite these concerns, divisive primaries don't always weaken a party. Running in a competitive primary contest might make the winner an even stronger candidate in the general election. In 2008, the experience Obama gained in his long nomination contest with Clinton gave him the opportunity to build and test his campaign organization prior to the general election race (see Chapter 11). And at times, when an incumbent candidate has shown signs of diminishing support due to scandal or change in the district, the national party has encouraged viable challengers. Although that might provoke a divisive primary, it could also produce a party nominee who is better able to hold the seat for the party in the fall.

The large numbers of safe House seats can increase the incidence of divisive primaries. After the redistricting that followed the 2000 U.S. Census created so many safe congressional seats, several ambitious candidates saw primary elections as their best and least expensive way to win a House seat. That attracted the attention, and the lavish spending, of dozens of national interest groups that wanted to change the ideological orientation of Congress by supporting a challenger who shared their views. The Democrats are famous for their internal disputes, but we can see just as many divisive primaries in the Republican Party: for instance, when candidates linked to the Christian Right challenge Republicans who are more moderate on social issues.[20] Other groups, including the antitax Club for Growth, have financed primary campaigns as a way to warn other Republicans that they will face a primary opponent if they don't take the strictest possible antitax position.[21]

Problems in Holding Candidates Accountable

When candidates are chosen in primaries rather than by party leaders, the party loses a powerful means of holding its candidates and officeholders accountable for their actions. In England, for example, if an elected official breaks with the party on an important issue, party leaders can usually keep him or her from being renominated. If the party cannot prevent the renomination of a maverick officeholder, then it has no way of enforcing loyalty. That, of course, is just what the Progressives had hoped. Thus, primaries have the following drawbacks:

- Primaries permit the nomination of candidates hostile to the party organization and leadership, opposed to the party's platform, or out of step with the public image that party leaders want to project.
- Primaries greatly increase campaign spending. The cost of a contested primary is almost always higher than that of a convention.
- Primaries extend political campaigns, already longer in the United States than in other democracies, to a length that can try many voters' patience.

THE PARTY ORGANIZATION FIGHTS BACK

Parties are clearly aware of the threats posed by primary elections, but they are just as aware that a direct attempt to abolish primaries would fail. So party organizations have developed a range of strategies for trying to limit the damage primaries can cause. The success of these strategies varies. As we will see in Chapter 10, the presidential nomination process has often been dominated by party leaders, and some local parties have been able to influence primaries effectively. Other party organizations have neither the strength nor the will to try.

Persuading Candidates to Run (or Not to Run)

The surest way to control a primary is to make sure that the candidate the party favors has no opponent. Some party organizations try to mediate among prospective candidates or coax an attractive but unwilling candidate to run. If they have a strong organization, they may be able to convince less desirable candidates to stay out of the race, perhaps by threatening to block a candidate's access to campaign money. Even if they have little to offer or withhold, many party leaders have the opportunity to influence prospective candidates' decisions; researchers have found that almost 70 percent of nonincumbent state legislative candidates discussed their plans to run with local party leaders before announcing their candidacy.[22]

Endorsing Candidates

Some of the stronger state parties, such as those in Massachusetts and Minnesota, go beyond this informal influence and offer some form of preprimary endorsement to the candidates they prefer. Recall that in several states, at least one of the parties holds a convention to formally endorse candidates for state office. Usually, a candidate who gets a certain percentage of the convention's vote automatically gets his or her name on the primary ballot. Endorsements are sometimes accompanied by campaign money and organizational help. In some other states, including Illinois, Ohio, and Michigan, party leaders may meet informally to endorse some candidates.

Do these endorsements influence voters? The record is mixed. Formal endorsements can often discourage other candidates from challenging the party's choice in the primary and can keep some interest groups from flooding a race with outside money in support of nonendorsed candidates. Besides, the process of winning a formal endorsement usually involves the candidate in so many face-to-face meetings with party activists that the resulting visibility, and the resources that the endorsing party can provide, can give the endorsed candidate some vote-getting benefits.[23]

On the other hand, since 1980, endorsed candidates have won only about half the primaries in which they faced competition—a big drop compared with the success rate of endorsed candidates in the 1960s and 1970s.[24] Some states have passed laws preventing parties from endorsing candidates in advance of the primary. When the parties are restricted to offering informal endorsements before the primary, which are not listed on the ballot, their effectiveness is even more limited. Only the most politically attentive voters are likely to know that the party is supporting a particular candidate, and they are the ones least in need of the guidance provided by a party endorsement.[25]

Providing Tangible Support

If the party is not able to prevent a challenge to its preferred candidates, then it must fall back on more conventional approaches. It may urge party activists to help the favored candidates circulate their nominating petitions or offer party money and expertise to these candidates. It may publish ads announcing the party's endorsements or print reminder cards that voters can take into the polling booth. On the day of the primary, the party organization may help to get party voters to the polls.

Although state and local parties vary in their efforts to influence primaries, recruiting candidates is probably the most frequent form of activity. Trying to clear the field for a favored candidate is less common. In most parts of the country, parties are only one of a number of groups encouraging men and women to run for office. Local business, professional, and labor groups; civic associations; ethnic, racial, and religious organizations; and other interest groups and officeholders may also be working to recruit candidates. The party organizations that seem best able to control candidate recruitment are generally those that endorse and support candidates in the primary itself.

CANDIDATES AND VOTERS IN THE PRIMARIES

Two facts help make the primaries more manageable for the parties: Often only one candidate runs for each office in a primary, and the majority of voters do not vote in them. The party may be responsible for one or both of these situations. There may be no competition in a primary, for example, because of the party's skill in persuading and dissuading potential candidates. The result is that nomination politics can be more easily controlled by aggressive party organizations.

Many Candidates Run Without Competition

All over the United States, large numbers of primary candidates win nominations without a contest. Probably the most important determinant of the competitiveness of a primary is the party's prospects for victory in the general election; candidates rarely fight for the right to face almost certain defeat. Primaries also tend to be less competitive when an incumbent is running (unless the incumbent is already thought to be vulnerable), when parties have made preprimary endorsements, and when the state's rules make it harder to get on the ballot.[26]

The power of incumbency to discourage competition is one of the many ironies of the primary. In an election in which voters cannot rely on the party label to guide their choices, name recognition and media coverage are important influences. Incumbents, of course, are more likely to have these resources than are challengers. To dislodge an incumbent, a challenger will often need large amounts of campaign money, but few challengers can raise large campaign budgets. By weakening party control of nominations through the direct primary, then, Progressive reformers may have unintentionally made it harder to defeat incumbents.

... And Voters Are in Short Supply

If competition is scarce in primaries, so are voters. Turnout tends to be especially low in the minority party's primary, in primaries held separately from the state's presidential primary, and in elections in which independents and the other party's identifiers are not allowed to vote.[27] In addition to the lack of competition in many primary contests, the fact that no one is elected in a primary probably depresses turnout; a race for the nomination lacks the drama inherent in a general election that is followed by victorious candidates taking office.

Southern primaries in earlier years were the one great exception to the rule that few people vote in primaries. Because winning the Democratic nomination in a one-party area was tantamount to winning the office itself, competition and turnout in Democratic primaries were relatively high. When the Republican Party became more competitive in the South, however, the Democratic primaries lost their special standing. The result is that participation has declined in southern primaries. Republican primaries are attracting many more voters now because their candidates' prospects in the general election have greatly improved, but the GOP increase has not been large enough to offset the drop in Democratic turnout.[28]

The primary electorate is distinctive in several ways. Many primary voters are strong party identifiers and activists, which makes them more responsive to party endorsements of certain candidates. As would be expected, people who vote in primaries have higher levels of education and political interest than nonvoters do. There is not much recent evidence that primary voters hold more extreme ideological positions than those of other party voters or are more intense in their ideological commitments.[29] But because primaries usually attract such a small sample of the eligible voters, they can be more easily dominated by well-financed organized interests, such as antitax or pro-gun groups, than can general elections.

Primary voters often make unexpected choices. Because primary campaigns don't get much media coverage, the candidates are often not well known. Thus, the voter's choice in a primary is not as well structured or predictable as that in a general election. Many voting decisions are made right in the polling booth. It is small wonder that parties are rarely confident about primary results and pollsters find it hard to predict them accurately.

THE IMPACT OF THE DIRECT PRIMARY

Americans have had a century of experience with the direct primary. On balance, how has it affected us? Has the primary democratized nominations by taking them out of the hands of party leaders and giving them to voters? Has it weakened the party organizations overall? In short, have the Progressives' hopes been realized?

Has It Made Elections More Democratic?

Many more people vote in primaries than take part in conventions or caucuses; in that sense, the process has been made more democratic. But the democratic promise of primaries is reduced by the number of unopposed candidates and the low levels of voter turnout. If voters are to have meaningful alternatives, then there must be more than one candidate for an office. If the results are to be meaningful, then people must go to the polls.

By its very nature, however, the primary tends to discourage participation. Would-be candidates are put off by the cost of an additional race, the difficulty of getting on the primary ballot, and the need to differentiate themselves from other candidates of their party. The lack of party cues reduces the quantity and quality of voter participation. If widespread competition for office and extensive public participation in the nominating process were goals of the primary's architects, then they would be seriously disappointed.

The direct primary has not fully replaced party leaders in making nominations. Caucuses and conventions are still used, most visibly in presidential nominations, although they are more open than they used to be. And as we have seen, parties can influence the competition in primaries. If only 25 percent of registered voters go to the polls, then 13 percent will be enough to nominate a candidate. Parties count on the fact that a large part of that group will be party loyalists who care about the party leaders' recommendations. Thus, strong party organizations—those able to muster the needed voters, money, activists, and organization—can still make a difference in the results.

Even so, trying to influence primary elections is very costly and time consuming, even for strong parties. The large number of elected offices in the United States, from senator to surveyor, forces party organizations to be selective in trying to affect primaries. Parties sometimes stand aside because picking a favorite in the primary might produce resentment. Of course, the greatest fear of party leaders is that if they support one candidate in a primary and the other candidate wins, they could lose all influence over the winning officeholder.

In some ways, then, the primary has been a democratizing force. In competitive districts, especially when no incumbent is running, voters have the opportunity for choice envisioned by the reformers. In all districts, the primaries place real limits on the power of party leaders. Parties, even strong ones, can no longer award a nomination to anyone they choose. Research in some other nations shows that in comparison with systems where party leaders select the candidates, primaries can help the weaker party choose a candidate with greater voter appeal.[30] And the primary gives dissenters a chance to take their case to the party's voters, so it offers them a potential veto over the party leaders' preferences.

How Badly Has It Harmed the Parties?

On the other hand, is it possible to say that the direct primary has strengthened democracy in the United States if it weakens the political parties? From the risk of divisive primary races to the added campaign funding and voter mobilization that they require, primaries strain party resources and create headaches for party leaders and activists. Even though some state party organizations have been able to maintain some control over their primaries by making preprimary endorsements or holding conventions to nominate some candidates, the bottom line is this: When a party organization cannot choose who will carry the party label into the general election, the party has been deprived of one of its key resources.

The direct primary has redistributed power within the parties. The Progressives' goal was to shift the power to nominate candidates from the party organization to the party in the electorate, but a funny thing happened along the way. Because candidates (especially incumbents) can win the party's nomination even when they defy the party organization, the idea of party "discipline" loses credibility. Just as the direct primary undercuts the ability of the party organization to recruit candidates who share its goals and accept its discipline, it prevents the organization from disciplining partisans who already are in office. The primary, then, empowers the party's candidates and the party in government at the expense of the party organization. This sets the United States apart from many other democracies, in which the party organization has real power over the party in government.

Primaries also contribute to the decentralization of power in the American parties. As long as the candidates can appeal successfully to a majority of local primary voters, they are free from the control of state or national party leaders. In all these ways, the direct primary has gone beyond changing the nominating process; it has helped to reshape the American parties.

Is the Primary Worth the Cost?

How to nominate party candidates has been a controversial question since political parties first appeared in the United States. It raises the fundamental question of what a political party is. Are parties only alliances of officeholders—the party in government? That seemed to be the prevailing definition in the early years when public officials nominated their prospective colleagues in party caucuses. Should the definition be expanded to include the party's activists and organizational leaders? The change from a caucus to a convention system of nominations, in which the party organization played its greatest role, reflects this change in the definition of party.

Should we extend the idea of party well beyond the limits accepted by most other democracies and include the party's supporters in the electorate? If so, which supporters should be included—only those willing to register formally as party loyalists or anyone who wants to vote for a party candidate in a primary election? The answer has evolved over the years toward a more inclusive definition of party. Even though the Supreme Court insists that the parties' freedom of association is vital, the "party," especially in states with an open or blanket primary and, in practice, in semiclosed primary states, has become so permeable that its boundaries are hard to define.

The methods we use to nominate candidates have a far-reaching impact. The Jacksonians promoted the convention system in order to gain control of the party from congressional party leaders. Progressives used their preference for the direct primary as a weapon with which to wrest control of the party and, ultimately, the government from the party organization. Because of the importance of nominations in the political process, those who control the nominations have great influence on the political agenda and, in turn, over who gets what in the political system. The stakes in this debate, as a result, are extremely high.

Choosing the Presidential Nominees

The countdown had begun. In just a few months, the first states would cast votes to nominate the major parties' presidential candidates. There was not much suspense on the Democratic side. Like the great majority of presidents, Barack Obama would not face a serious challenge for renomination in 2012. But the Republican race was wide open. A dozen candidates—ranging from former governors and senators to a pizza company executive—took turns in leading the preprimary polls. The winner of a party's presidential nomination is never an overnight success. The nominee will have traveled a long road, both literally and figuratively, to reach that coveted spot. Who would he or she have to convince, and what would it take, to gain a party's nomination?

THE "INVISIBLE PRIMARY"

Most serious presidential candidates begin several years before the election to take polls, raise money, identify active supporters in the states with early contests, and compete for the services of respected consultants (see box "How a Presidential Candidate Is Chosen" on page 182). The competition heats up during the months before the first primaries and caucuses. Journalists are competing at this time as well; they each want to be the first to predict who will win the nomination. The indicators they use are the candidates' standing in polls and their fund-raising success. This process of early fund-raising and jockeying for media attention and public support has become so important to the eventual result that it has come to be called the *invisible primary* or the "money primary."[1]

Party leaders and activists and interest groups closely linked with the party are watching carefully as well. They want to determine which candidates would best serve the party's and groups' interests. Although party leaders have no formal power over the nominating process, they can communicate their

How a Presidential Candidate Is Chosen

Step 1: *Assessing Their Chances.* Many people who think they might have public support—governors, senators, House members, people well known in another
field—consider running for president. They take private polls to see how
they are viewed by prospective voters. To assess their chances of getting
the resources they'd need, they contact fund-raisers and potential donors
and try to get well-respected consultants to commit to their candidacy.
They visit states with early primaries and caucuses to gain support from
local officials. *Timing: Typically, several years before the presidential election.*

Step 2: *Entering the Race.* Those who feel they have a good chance—and some who
don't—set up exploratory committees to raise money for advertising
and to fund their increasingly frequent trips to Iowa, New Hampshire,
and other states with early delegate selection events. Then they formally
declare their candidacy and work to get on every state ballot. *Timing:
Typically, at least a year before the presidential election.*

Step 3: *Primaries and Caucuses.* Voters cast a ballot in their states for the candidate
they want their party to nominate for president. Most states hold primary
elections for this purpose; the rest use participatory caucuses and state
conventions. Delegates are chosen to represent each state and to vote
in the party's national convention for the candidate(s) selected by their
state's voters. *Timing: Between January and June of each presidential election year.*

Step 4: *National Nominating Conventions.* The delegates vote in their party's convention for the presidential candidate(s) chosen by the voters in their state's
primary or caucuses (Step 3). Then they vote for the winning candidate's
choice of a vice presidential nominee and to adopt a party platform. *Timing:
By tradition, the party that does not currently hold the presidency schedules its convention
first, normally in August; the other party's convention is held soon after.*

Step 5: *General Election.* The two major parties' candidates run against one
another. *Timing: From the conventions until the first Tuesday after the first Monday in
November.*

choices to party activists by publicly endorsing particular candidates. In fact,
in most recent presidential races, voters in the primaries and caucuses have
nominated the consensus choice of the party's leaders and activists.[2] Especially
in this early phase of the process, many partisans don't yet know much about
the prospective candidates and welcome these informal suggestions.

Candidates who fall behind in the money and endorsement chase are
likely to be winnowed out of the race even before most Americans have had
the chance to assess their capabilities. Early in 2011, for instance, some candidates pulled out of the crowded Republican field, including South Dakota

Senator John Thune and former Mississippi Governor Haley Barbour, because they didn't attract enough money and activist support. On the other hand, those who raise more than expected can greatly improve their chances. Congresswoman Michele Bachmann (R-MN), formerly known largely for her controversial statements against same-sex marriage and evolution, made herself into a contender by outraising better-known Republican rivals in the early months of the "invisible primary."

The candidates who survive the "invisible primary" must then face a gauntlet of state party primaries and caucuses to win delegates who will support them at the party's national convention. This process, which has evolved during two centuries and keeps changing, challenges the strategic capabilities of every presidential candidate.

THE ADOPTION OF PRESIDENTIAL PRIMARIES

In the early years of presidential nominations, prospective candidates needed to impress their colleagues in Congress, because it was congressional party caucuses that made these nominations. When the parties started nominating their presidential candidates in national conventions in the 1830s, as Chapter 1 showed, the real power in the process moved to the local and state party leaders. They were the ones who chose their state's delegates to the national convention and told those delegates which presidential candidate to support. The selection was usually done in a series of party-controlled meetings, called caucuses, held first at the local level and then in statewide conventions.

At the urging of Progressives, who aimed to weaken party leaders' power, Florida passed the first presidential primary law in 1901; it let the voters pick the party's candidate. Many other states followed. The parties later struck back; by 1936, only 14 states were still holding primaries to choose their delegates to the national conventions. That number had hardly changed by 1968.[3] Even in many of the states that held primaries, voters could take part in only a "beauty contest" to express their preferences about presidential candidates; the delegates who went to the national convention and actually chose the candidates were selected elsewhere. A fascinating story began to unfold in 1968, however, in which the national Democratic Party took control of the delegate selection process away from the state parties and gave new life to the use of presidential primaries.

Turbulence in the Democratic Party

The 1968 Democratic convention was a riotous event. Struggling with the painful issues of civil rights and American involvement in the Vietnam War, the convention nominated the party leaders' choice, Vice President Hubert Humphrey, as the Democratic presidential candidate, even though he hadn't run in a single state primary. Antiwar activists within the party protested that Humphrey's nomination did not fairly reflect the views of most Democrats. To try to make peace with their critics, the national party leaders agreed that the next convention's delegates would be selected in a more open and democratic manner.

A party commission chaired by liberal Senator George McGovern (and later by U.S. Representative Donald Fraser and known as the *McGovern-Fraser Commission*) recommended, and the Democratic National Committee and the next Democratic convention approved, major changes to increase the influence of insurgent Democrats in the 1972 presidential nominating process. One of the striking elements of this story is the remarkable ease with which state Democratic Party leaders accepted rule changes that greatly reduced their power over the awarding of the party's greatest prize, the presidential nomination.[4]

In trying to comply with the complicated new McGovern-Fraser rules, many states stopped using caucus-convention systems and reinstituted primaries. The remaining caucuses were guided by strict party requirements that delegates be selected in open and well-publicized meetings. Techniques formerly used by state party organizations to control the caucuses were outlawed. In the process, not only were the delegate selection procedures radically changed but also the principle was established that the national party, not the states or the state parties, makes the rules for nominating presidential candidates.

Once the reform genie was let out of the bottle, it was hard to contain. The Democrats tinkered with their nomination rules prior to almost every election for the next 20 years. First, they used national party leverage to make the process more open and more representative of women, blacks, and young people. Then, the Democrats required the use of proportional representation, so that voter support for candidates was more faithfully represented in delegate counts. Starting in 1980, in order to bring party leaders (and their "peer review" of candidates) back into the process, many elected and party officials were guaranteed a vote at the convention as uncommitted "superdelegates" (to be discussed later in the chapter).

The result has been a stunning transformation of the process by which the Democrats select their presidential nominees. Many state legislatures responded to the new Democratic rules by changing state election laws to require primary elections in both parties. Thus, the Republicans became the unwilling beneficiaries of the Democratic reforms. Republicans have preserved their tradition of giving state parties wide latitude in developing their own rules, however, which has kept the national party out of much of the rules debate.

Presidential Primaries and Caucuses Today

Each state decides whether to choose its delegates to the parties' national conventions in a primary election or a series of caucuses. Although primaries are more common, states can change their method of selection from one presidential election to the next (see Figure 10.1).

A state holding a primary selects a date on which its eligible voters can go to a polling place (or cast a mail or absentee ballot) and choose who they'd like to be their party's presidential nominee. The popular vote for each candidate

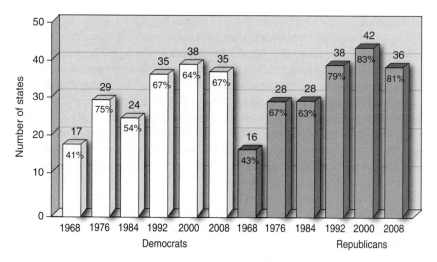

FIGURE 10.1

Change in the Number of Presidential Primaries, 1968–2008.

Note: The number above each bar is the number of states that held primaries to select delegates (not purely advisory primaries) in that year; inside the bar is the percentage of convention delegates elected in those primaries. All 50 states plus Washington, DC, are included, but not the territories (American Samoa, Guam, Puerto Rico, Virgin Islands) or Democrats Abroad. Delegate percentages include Democratic superdelegates.

Sources: For 1968–1992, Michael G. Hagen and William G. Mayer, "The Modern Politics of Presidential Selection," in William G. Mayer, ed., *In Pursuit of the White House 2000* (New York: Chatham House, 2000), pp. 11 and 43–44. Figures for 2000 and 2004 were kindly provided by Mayer and were calculated by the author for 2008 from data provided by the National Association of Secretaries of State. (As of this writing, not all states' plans for 2012 were firm.)

determines how many of the state's delegates will go to the party's national convention supporting that candidate. The list of delegates who will represent each candidate is usually approved by the candidate or his or her agent. This all but guarantees that the delegates sent to the national convention will vote for the contender they have been instructed by voters to support, even though no laws require delegates to do so.[5]

Other states use a longer delegate selection process that begins with precinct caucuses. In these meetings, party identifiers are invited to gather, often for an hour or more, to debate which candidates for president will best represent their party and the issues they believe in. Then they choose delegates to communicate their presidential preference to caucuses at higher levels, typically at the county, congressional district, and then the state level. The state's final delegate slate for the national convention is determined at the higher-level conventions. The first-in-the-nation Iowa caucuses, for example, began with precinct meetings in January 2012, but Iowa's national convention delegates would not be chosen until the district and state conventions in April and June.

The selection of delegates in the caucus states was all but ignored by the media until 1976, when a little-known Democratic governor, Jimmy Carter, made himself a serious presidential candidate by campaigning intensively in Iowa and winning an unexpectedly large number of delegates. After that time, the Iowa caucuses joined the New Hampshire primary as the first and most significant delegate selection events. Most of the media coverage of the nomination race focuses on these two states' events.[6] To dilute their impact in 2008 and 2012, the two national parties allowed Nevada and South Carolina, states with large minority populations, to move up their delegate selection dates as well.

Candidates campaign differently in a caucus state than they do in a primary. Because the turnout at caucuses is much smaller and consists mainly of party activists, winning caucuses requires extensive organizing to appeal to these likely caucus goers. (In contrast, media ads are better suited to reach the larger turnout of voters in a primary.) A major reason for Obama's success in winning the Democratic presidential nomination in 2008 was that his campaign understood this to a greater extent than did the campaign of his main rival, Hillary Clinton. Obama deployed large field organizations and won big victories in several caucus states early in the nominating season.[7]

THE RACE FOR DELEGATES: TIMING AND MOMENTUM

Candidates who survive the "invisible primary" know that winning states whose contests are held early in the nominating process creates momentum. These early wins attract more media coverage for the candidate and, in turn, more name recognition among voters. The candidate looks more and more unstoppable, so it is easier to raise money, which makes later victories more likely. This happens especially in contests when winner-take-all rules are used: Because the other candidates aren't winning any delegates, they fall further and further behind.

State legislatures also realize that holding an early primary or caucus can benefit their state. The media interest generated by an early contest brings a lot of journalists (who spend money on food, lodging, and other needs) and campaign money into the state, so the state's concerns gain national attention. Iowa's first-in-the-nation status, for example, means that ethanol use, favored by Iowa's corn farmers, gets more notice from presidential candidates than it would receive otherwise. Thus, the nomination process has become highly *front-loaded* in recent elections, as states have moved their primaries and caucuses closer to the beginning of the nominating season (see box "Front-loading the Nomination Process" on page 187). In 2008 and 2012, front-loading nearly pushed the first delegate selection events into the "invisible primary"; Iowa and New Hampshire held their caucuses and primary in the first ten days of January, and several states advanced the dates of their primaries.

Candidates' Strategic Choices

As they approach these front-loaded primaries and caucuses, the surviving candidates continue to face crucial strategic decisions. How much effort and money should they put into each state? Which of their issue stands and personal

Front-Loading the Nomination Process

In the first presidential election after the Democratic nomination reforms, the New Hampshire primary—the leadoff event of the 1972 nominating season—was held during the first week in March. By that week in 2008, the race for the Republican nomination was already over. The first presidential selection event in 2008, the Iowa caucuses, took place less than two weeks after Christmas 2007. Holiday decorations vied for space with campaign yard signs.

The nomination race has become "front-loaded." States have increasingly pushed their delegate selection events closer to the beginning of the election year, when they would get more media coverage, bring in more money from campaign ads, and, they thought, give the state's voters more of a chance to influence the choice of the parties' nominees. By tradition, the first events are the Iowa caucuses and the New Hampshire primary. Because the prime positioning of these states—neither one very typical of either party's national constituency—had often been criticized, the DNC agreed to let Nevada and South Carolina add their delegate selection events to the early days of the 2008 primary season, and thus increase the voice of Latinos and African Americans in the nominating process. That opened the floodgates, and soon, Michigan and Florida also decided to hold their events before the DNC-authorized "window" opened on February 5. The DNC warned both states that they would lose all their convention delegates if they went ahead. Both went ahead anyway.

But the joke turned out to be on the states that rushed ahead. Although the winner-take-all Republican events produced a nominee in less than two months, Hillary Clinton staged a comeback in New Hampshire after losing the Iowa caucuses, and from that point on, neither Democratic candidate was able to open up a commanding lead in delegate votes. The proportional representation required by DNC rules, just as the party's reformers had hoped, gave the second-ranking candidate chance after chance to remain a contender. Obama did not wrap up the nomination until early June. So in fact, in the Democratic race, the states at the end of the calendar, particularly Ohio, Pennsylvania, Indiana, and North Carolina, had enormous influence on the outcome. Even so, states held early primaries or caucuses again in 2012, though they risked penalties from the national parties for doing so.

Front-loading has several important effects on the nominating process. It forces presidential candidates to raise money very early. It gives an extra boost to the candidates who were front-runners in the "invisible primary." The cost of a strategic mistake in these early events could be very high. This "rush to judgment," as two political scientists call it, makes the nominating system "less deliberative, less rational, less flexible and more chaotic."

Source: Quote from Andrew E. Busch and William G. Mayer, "The Front-Loading Problem," in William G. Mayer, ed., *The Making of the Presidential Candidates 2004* (Lanham, MD: Rowman & Littlefield, 2004), pp. 1–43; and David P. Redlawsk, Caroline J. Tolbert, and Todd Donovan, *Why Iowa?* (Chicago: University of Chicago Press, 2011), Chapter 8.

qualities will be most persuasive to which voters? Different types of candidates face different challenges. An early front-runner, for example, normally has to demonstrate overwhelming support in the first delegate selection events, or his or her supporters' and contributors' confidence may be so badly shaken that the candidate's chances fade. The Democrats' early front-runner in 2008, Hillary Clinton, based her strategy for winning the nomination on creating a sense of inevitability about her candidacy, but that strategy was undermined by her loss in the Iowa caucuses. Many other formal and informal "rules" structure the nominating process and affect campaigns' strategies.

The Democrats' rules differ from those of the Republicans. Recall that the Democrats' nomination reforms require the use of proportional representation (PR), so that a candidate with significant support will not be shut out in any state. Since 1988, candidates who win at least 15 percent of the vote in primaries and caucuses get approximately the same share of the delegates as they received of the popular vote. For instance, when 36 percent of voters in the 2008 New Hampshire Democratic primary chose Barack Obama, approximately the same percentage of New Hampshire's delegation was directed to vote for Obama in the Democratic National Convention to be the party's nominee.

Until 2012, the Republicans had no national rules as to how to count these votes, and most states' Republican parties used some form of a winner-take-all system: The candidate who gets the most votes in a state primary or caucus wins all or most of the state's delegates. A winner-take-all rule makes a big difference in the results.[8] For example, John McCain won 33 percent of the vote in the 2008 Missouri Republican primary, and Mike Huckabee and Mitt Romney were close behind with 32 and 29 percent, respectively. Although the three candidates were separated by fewer than 22,000 votes, all 58 of the state's convention delegates were assigned to McCain, the narrow winner. Huckabee and Romney got none. In contrast, when Obama lost a primary narrowly to Clinton, under the Democrats' PR rules he got almost as many delegates as she did. As one reporter put it, "the Republican who kills the buffalo gets all the meat; the Democrat has to crouch around the campfire and share it with his brethren and sistren."[9] The Republicans' winner-take-all rules allowed McCain to build a big delegate lead quickly and to clinch his party's nomination much earlier than Obama did.[10]

Comparing the Clinton and Obama Strategies

Taking account of these rules, presidential candidates have chosen many different types of approaches to the nomination race. Consider the contrast between the Clinton and Obama campaigns in 2008. At first, the race was seen by many as the story of an old pro, backed by her party's most experienced advisers, who would quickly demolish an inexperienced young upstart. Except that the old pros fought among themselves rather than doing their homework, and the young upstart had advisers who studied the rules, formed a tightly disciplined team, and understood cutting-edge technologies.

Clinton ran a relatively traditional race as the "establishment" candidate for the nomination.[11] Her strategy, as we have seen, was based on the assumption that if she started early and established the belief that she was the presumptive nominee, then the contest would be over within a month of the Iowa caucuses. She expected that her experience, contacts, and support from party regulars and women's and labor groups would smooth her way.

Obama's organization didn't gear up in earnest until much later: a year before the Iowa caucuses. Obama and his advisers knew that he couldn't challenge Clinton's great strengths—her almost-universal name recognition and her (and her husband's, former president Bill Clinton) extensive relationships with state Democratic officials and activists. Obama's staff had to design a different route to the nomination. Under the Democratic Party's PR rules, a candidate could gain a big lead in delegates only by winning landslide victories. That wasn't likely to happen in most of the large, Democratic-leaning states, where both Clinton and Obama had substantial support.

Therefore, Obama's staff put enormous organizational effort into states where Democratic candidates didn't usually campaign, and thus where Clinton had fewer advantages. Many of these dominantly Republican states, including Idaho, Alaska, and Kansas, held caucuses early in the nominating season. Because caucuses attract much smaller turnouts than primaries do, "mobilizing a few thousand people in a caucus state can have as much impact as getting several hundred thousand voters to the polls in a primary state."[12] Obama's staffers recruited a lot of enthusiastic volunteers in these states, including college students and other young people, blacks, and affluent professionals.

In Idaho, for instance, the Democratic Party chair said of the Obama campaign, "It was the most impressive political organization I've seen in my thirty-one years here."[13] The Obama organization used ground war strategies (see Chapter 11) very successfully to increase turnout among prospective supporters. Clinton's campaign, following the traditional plan of focusing on states with the most delegates, made no organized effort at all in the state. Obama beat Clinton in Idaho by 62 percentage points and won the great majority of its delegates.

With similar efforts, Obama won a series of landslides, and big delegate leads, in other caucus states. But Obama's narrow win in the Iowa caucuses was his biggest prize. Not only was Iowa's the first delegate selection event of 2008, but by winning Iowa, Obama showed that he could do well in a state with only a tiny black population and few major cities.

In the more traditional Democratic states, with their larger trove of delegates, the Obama campaign's aim was to hold down the size of Clinton's victories. Under the PR rules, a narrow loss would give Obama almost as many delegates as Clinton in these states. The Obama efforts were effective; slim Clinton victories in the later primary states did not yield enough delegates to surmount the small lead that Obama had built with his landslide wins in several early caucuses.

Because Obama's delegate lead was narrow, however, the nomination fight didn't end until early June, when the last of the states held their primaries.

Democratic activists feared that the drawn-out nomination race would weaken Obama's chances against McCain in the fall. Instead, the lengthy nomination contest proved to be a blessing in disguise. The Democrats were forced to organize in almost every state and thus to "field-test" local and state organizers. Large numbers of new voters registered as Democrats. The close race brought out big Democratic turnouts, which gave the Democrats expanded voter lists to use in the general election campaign.

Obama did not run a perfect campaign; in the second half of the nominating season, his prospects suffered from the kinds of verbal slips, embarrassing associations, and simple fatigue that bedevil most candidates. Nevertheless, his superior game plan—his ability to stimulate enthusiasm among volunteers, his staff's extensive organizational work, their detailed knowledge of the Democratic Party's nomination rules and their ability to use the rules to their advantage—made the difference. Interestingly, although Obama's campaign was widely regarded as innovative, in fact it simply applied new technology to a time-honored approach to winning elections: contacting voters individually and bringing them to the polls.

Changes in the Schedule for 2012   After Obama beat McCain in the 2008 general election, Republican leaders began to question whether it had been wise to reach an early decision on their own nominee. To slow down the party's next nomination race, the Republican National Committee broke with its usual states' rights policy and mandated that state Republican Parties holding primaries and caucuses before April 1, 2012, must use some form of PR in allocating delegates to presidential candidates. Only states holding later nominating events could use winner-take-all rules. The use of PR in the earlier contests would help candidates other than the front-runner to stay in the race longer, and the new rule would give states a reason not to front-load their caucuses and primaries. But the result was to combine front-loading with a longer nominating season.

What Is the Party's Role?

The party organizations' interests in the nominating process are not necessarily the same as those of the presidential candidates. State and local parties want a nominee who will bring voters to the polls to support the party's candidates for state and local offices; a weak presidential candidate may hurt their chances. Party leaders also worry that a hotly contested nomination race could stimulate conflict within local and state parties, which might weaken them in the general election.

Historically, some state parties protected their interests by selecting delegates uncommitted to any candidate and then casting the state's delegate votes as a bloc for a particular nominee. The ability to swing a bloc of delegates to a candidate could increase the state party's influence at the convention. But the current nominating system prevents the state parties from sending an uncommitted delegation. In most primary states, the candidates set up their own delegate slates, so the delegates' first loyalty is to the candidate. In caucus states, delegates committed to a candidate simply have greater appeal to caucus participants than do uncommitted delegates. Party leaders, then, have a harder time protecting the party's interests in a nominating process that is dominated by the candidates and their supporters.

The Democrats tried to enhance the party's role in 1984 by setting aside delegate seats at the national convention for elected and party officials. These *superdelegates*—all Democratic governors and members of Congress, current and former presidents and vice presidents, and all members of the Democratic National Committee—were meant to be a large, uncommitted bloc now totaling almost 20 percent of all delegates, with the party's interests in mind. But because the nomination race concluded so quickly in most election years, superdelegates did not play an independent role in the nominating process.[14]

The closeness of the delegate count during the 2008 nominating season raised concerns that the superdelegates' votes might actually decide the race. Some observers hinted darkly that this could raise suspicions about "boss rule." The suspicions were probably unfounded. All the superdelegates are either elected officials, who have a natural interest in maintaining constituent support, or party leaders, who want to choose the nominee who is most attractive to voters. And in fact, although Clinton seemed to have greater superdelegate support early in the nominating season, Obama's superdelegate support grew in tandem with his lead in elected delegates. In practice, then, superdelegates did not act as an independent voice for the party's interests. The presidential candidates in 2008, as in past nominations, owed their selection largely to their own core supporters rather than to the party organization. This limits the party organization's influence over the president once he or she has been elected.

VOTERS' CHOICES IN PRESIDENTIAL NOMINATIONS

The move to primaries and participatory caucuses has increased citizen involvement in nominating a president. What determines the level of voter turnout and guides the voters' choices in these contests?

Who Votes?

Turnout varies a great deal from state to state and across different years in any one state. The Iowa caucuses and the New Hampshire primary usually bring out a large number of voters because of the media attention to those early contests. Turnout is greater in states with a better-educated citizenry and a tradition of two-party competition—the same states where there is higher turnout in the general election. The nature of the contest matters, too. Voters are most likely to participate in early races that are closely fought and in which the candidates spend more money and the excitement is high, all of which increase interest in the election.[15]

Are Primary Voters Typical?

However, turnout is lower in primary than in general elections, especially after the parties' nominations have been largely wrapped up. Are the people who turn out to vote in presidential primaries, and who therefore choose the nominees for the rest of the public, typical of other citizens? Critics of the reforms have charged that they are not and, thus, that candidates are now being selected by an unrepresentative group of citizens.

We can explore this question in several ways. When we compare presidential primary voters with nonvoters, we find that those who vote in primaries are, in fact, better educated, wealthier, and older, but then, so are general election voters. A more appropriate comparison is with party identifiers because primaries are the means by which the party electorate chooses its nominees. Using this comparison, just as is the case with primary voters more generally, voters in presidential primaries tend to be slightly older, better educated, more affluent, better integrated into their communities, somewhat more partisan and interested in politics, and less likely to be black or Hispanic, but the differences are not substantial.[16]

Do Voters Make Informed Choices?

Another criticism of the primaries is that voters do not make very well-informed decisions. Compared with voters in the general election, primary voters seem to pay less attention to the campaign and to have less knowledge about the candidates. Especially in the early contests, voters are influenced by candidate momentum, as bandwagons form for candidates who have won unexpectedly or by a large margin. Candidates' personal characteristics influence voters in the primaries,[17] but issues often have only a minor impact. The result, so the argument goes, is a series of contests decided mainly on the basis of short-run, superficial considerations.[18]

Many analysts think that this is too strong an indictment, however. They feel that voters respond with some rationality to the challenge of having to choose among several candidates in a short campaign without the powerful guidance provided by party labels.[19] Although it may seem unproductive to support a candidate simply because he or she has momentum, primary voters often find only minor issue differences among their party's candidates and just want to pick the candidate with the best chance of winning the presidency. Momentum seems to matter especially when voters are being asked to sort through a pack of candidates about whom they know little[20] and when there is no well-known front-runner.[21] Even then, the candidates who move to the head of the pack are usually subjected to more searching evaluations, which give voters more reasons to support or oppose them. In short, even though primary voters often have less information about the candidates than do general election voters, the quality of their decisions may not differ very much from those in general elections.[22]

Do Primaries Produce Good Candidates?

Both the current primary-dominated system and the earlier nominating system have attractive and unattractive qualities. Talented candidates have been nominated by both and so have less distinguished candidates. The older nominating system tended to favor mainstream politicians who were acceptable to the party's leaders, including some candidates who had earned their nomination through party loyalty rather than through their personal appeal or their skills at governing. Primaries are more likely to give an advantage to candidates whose names are well known to the public and those who have the support of issue activists and people with intensely held views.[23]

Compared with the earlier nominating process, the current system gives presidential candidates a better chance to demonstrate their public support, raise more campaign money, and test their stamina and ability to cope with pressure. On the other hand, candidates' performance in the primaries may not be a good indicator of their likely competence in the White House. The front-loading of the current system also increases the risk that party voters will choose a nominee too hastily and later experience buyer's remorse.

ON TO THE NATIONAL CONVENTIONS

Once the states have chosen their delegates in primaries and caucuses, the delegates go to their party's national convention and vote for a presidential nominee. By that time, of course, the nation already knows which candidate in each party won the most delegates in the primaries and caucuses, and every convention since 1968 has nominated that winner on the first ballot. Is the national convention then just a statement of the obvious, or is there anything left for the delegates to do?

Roots of the Conventions

The national party convention is an old and respected institution, but it began, at least in part, as a power grab. In 1832, the nomination of Andrew Jackson as the Democratic-Republican candidate for president was a foregone conclusion, but state political leaders wanted to keep Henry Clay, the favorite of the congressional caucus, from being nominated as vice president; they preferred Martin Van Buren. So these leaders pushed for a national convention to make the nominations. In doing so, they wrested control of the presidential selection process from congressional leaders. By the time the Republican Party emerged in 1854, the convention had become the accepted means through which major parties chose their presidential candidates. Since 1856, both major parties have held national conventions every four years.

What Conventions Do

The convention normally warms up with a keynote address by a party "star," showcases as many of its popular older leaders and attractive new faces as possible, and reaches a dramatic peak in the nomination of the presidential and vice presidential candidates. This general format has remained basically the same for decades.

Formalizing the Presidential Nomination Before the nomination reforms of the 1970s, delegates chosen by state and local party leaders would select the party's nominee during the national convention. When the first round of balloting did not produce a majority for one candidate, intense bargaining would follow among the remaining candidates and state party leaders. The leading candidates would work to keep their own supporters while negotiating for the votes of state delegations that had come committed to other candidates. In recent years, however, one candidate has won a majority of delegate votes well before the convention starts, so only a single round of balloting has been necessary at the convention.

Approving the Vice Presidential Nominee The day after the presidential nominee is chosen, delegates vote again to select the vice presidential candidate. This, too, is ceremonial; presidential nominees choose their own running mates and conventions ratify their choice.[24] In years past, the vice presidential nominee was selected by the (usually exhausted) presidential candidate at the time of the convention. Now, presidential nominees announce their "veep" choice before the convention begins, often as a means to increase their support among some group of voters.

Approving the Platform In addition to nominating candidates, the convention's main job is to approve the party's *platform*—its statement of party positions on a wide range of issues. The platform committee often asks for public comments, online as well as in hearings, long before the convention opens. The finished platform is then presented to the convention for its approval.

Because they are approved in nominating conventions whose main purpose is to choose a presidential candidate, platforms usually reflect the candidate's views or the bargains that the candidate has been willing to make to win support or preserve party harmony.[25] So a platform usually lists the policy preferences of various groups in the party's (and the candidate's) supporting coalition. Platforms are also campaign documents, intended to help the party's candidates win their races.

Yet platforms are much more than just a laundry list of promises. They often define the major differences between the parties, as the leading scholar of party platforms shows.[26] As a result, they can provoke spirited debates at the convention because many delegates care deeply about this statement of the party's beliefs on such issues as abortion, taxes, pollution, and American involvement in the world (see Chapter 15).

Launching the General Election Campaign   The final business of the convention is to present the party's presidential candidate to the American public. The candidates hope that the glowing portrayal presented by the convention will produce a boost in public support, known as a "convention bounce."

Many other events take place at the conventions as well. Lobbyists host lavish dinners and receptions to curry favor with elected officials. Even though conventions are partly funded by tax dollars, most of their costs are paid by big donors with an interest in federal policies—corporations (especially for the Republicans), unions (for the Democrats), and wealthy individuals.

WHO ARE THE DELEGATES?

Convention delegates help to shape the public's image of the two parties. Who are these delegates?

Apportioning Delegates Among the States

The national parties determine how many delegates each state can send to the convention. The two parties make these choices differently. The Republicans allocate delegates more equally among the states; the Democrats weigh more heavily the size of the state's population and its record of support for Democratic candidates.

These formulas affect the voting strength of various groups within the party coalitions, as they do in the two national committees (see Chapter 4). The GOP's decision to represent the small states more equally with the large states has advantaged its conservative wing. In contrast, by giving relatively more weight to the larger states with stronger Democratic voting traditions, the Democrats have favored the more liberal interests in their party, and in particular, urban areas with large minority populations.

How Representative Are the Delegates?

The delegates to the Democratic and Republican conventions have never been a cross section of American citizens or even of their party's voters. White males, the well educated, and the affluent have traditionally been overrepresented in conventions. Reflecting their different coalitional bases, since the 1930s, Democratic delegations have had more labor union members and black Americans, and Republican conventions have drawn more Protestants and small business owners.

Demographics   Since the nomination reforms, the delegates of both parties have become more representative of other citizens in some ways and less representative in others. The Democrats used affirmative action plans after 1968 to increase the presence of women, blacks, and, for a brief time, young people. At the 2008 Democratic convention, more than a third of the delegates were people of color (compared with only 6 percent of Republican delegates), and since 1980, the DNC has required that half of the delegates be women. The percentage of female delegates at Republican conventions has increased during this period as well, without party mandates. The DNC has urged state parties to recruit more low- and moderate-income delegates, but their lesser political involvement and the high price of attending a convention stand in the way. So conventions remain meetings of the wealthy and well educated (see Table 10.1). In 2008, for instance, 34 percent of Republican delegates and 22 percent of Democrats said they were millionaires, the largest proportion in over a dozen years, and most had postgraduate education.[27]

TABLE 10.1

How Representative Were the 2008 Democratic and Republican Convention Delegates?

	Dem. Delegates (%)	Dem. Voters (%)	All Voters (%)	Rep. Voters (%)	Rep. Delegates (%)
Gender					
Female	49	58	54	56	32
Race					
Black	23	23	12	2	2
White	65	72	83	93	93
Latino	11	9	8	10	5
Education					
HS graduate or less	5	42	37	32	4
Some college	12	28	30	29	15
College grad	26	17	21	28	31
Postgraduate	55	13	12	11	50
Total family income					
Under $50,000	10	43	39	31	5
Over $75,000	70	26	31	39	66
Religion					
Protestant	43	52	55	61	57
Evangelical or born again*	14	23	27	39	33
Catholic	26	23	24	25	30
Jewish	9	5	3	1	3
Other or none	18	19	17	12	8

*Asked in a separate question, so percentages for "religion" do not add up to 100 percent.

Source: Data on convention delegates are from *New York Times*/CBS News polls taken during July 16–August 17, 2008 of Democratic National Convention delegates (*n*=970) and July 23–August 26 for Republican delegates (*n*=854). "Voters" are all registered voters in nationwide polls (*n*=1014) taken by the same polling organization during August 15–20, 2008.

Political Experience We might assume that delegates would be recidivists, making return appearances at convention after convention. That has not been the case. After the reforms, the percentage of convention first timers jumped to about 80 percent. Even after the Democrats began granting convention seats to politically experienced superdelegates, most of the delegates were newcomers. However, the great majority are long-time party activists. In 2008, most of a random sample of delegates reported that they had been active in their party for at least 20 years, and a majority said they currently hold party office.

Issues Convention delegates are more extreme in their views and more aware of issues than most other voters are. In 2008, Democratic delegates were slightly more likely to call themselves very liberal (19 percent) than were Democratic voters (15 percent) and about twice as likely to consider themselves liberal or very liberal as was the average voter. Forty percent of Republican delegates called themselves very conservative, compared with 30 percent of GOP voters and only 15 percent of all voters. Delegates' views, then, are very polarized by party.

The distance between delegates and their party's voters varies from issue to issue. As Table 10.2 shows, although Democratic delegates in 2008 were more

---

TABLE 10.2

Views on Issues: Comparing Delegates and Voters in 2008

	Dem. Delegates (%)	Dem. Voters (%)	All Voters (%)	Rep. Voters (%)	Rep. Delegates (%)
Providing health care coverage for all Americans is more important than holding down taxes	94	90	67	40	7
Abortion should be permitted in all cases	58	33	26	13	5
Illegal immigration is a very serious problem for the country now	15	36	49	64	58
Many of the tax cuts Congress passed in 2001 should be made permanent	7	34	47	62	91
United States did the right thing in taking military action against Iraq	2	14	37	70	80

(continued)

TABLE 10.2 (CONTINUED)

	Dem. Delegates (%)	Dem. Voters (%)	All Voters (%)	Rep. Voters (%)	Rep. Delegates (%)
Environmental protection should be a higher priority for government than finding new energy sources	25	30	21	9	3
Gay couples should be allowed to legally marry	55	49	34	11	6
Gun control laws should be more strict	62	70	52	32	8

Note: Figures are the percentage of each group who agreed with the statement.

Source: Data on convention delegates are from *New York Times*/CBS News polls taken during July 16–August 17, 2008 of Democratic National Convention delegates (*n*=970) and July 23–August 26 for Republican delegates (*n*=854). "Voters" are all registered voters in nationwide polls (*n*=1014) taken by the same polling organization during August 15–20, 2008.

liberal than most voters on several key issues, they came closest to the views of Democratic voters (and all voters) in favoring health care coverage for all Americans, environmental protection, and gun control. Republican delegates most closely resembled other Republicans, as well as the average voter, in their views on the importance of illegal immigration, but scored well to the right on other questions. Democratic and Republican delegates differed most from one another on health care coverage and the Bush tax cuts. So, although supporters of the McGovern-Fraser reforms had hoped that the new system would better represent the views of most party identifiers than the old system did, the reforms have not made much difference in that regard.[28] The real effect of the reforms has been to link the selection of delegates more closely to candidate preferences. As a result, when an issue-oriented candidate does well in the primaries and caucuses, more issue-oriented activists become convention delegates. That may not make the conventions more representative of the party in the electorate, but it usually offers clearer choices to voters.

Amateurs or Professionals? The reforms were also expected to result in delegates with a different approach to politics. Using the terms described in Chapter 5, some convention delegates can be described as amateurs, others as professionals. Amateurs are more attracted by issues, more insistent on internal party democracy, and less willing to compromise. Professionals, in contrast, are more likely to have a long-term commitment to the party and to be more willing to compromise on issues in order to win the general election.

There is some evidence that the Democratic Party's reforms had, as intended, reduced the presence of party professionals between the 1968 and the 1972 conventions.[29] As we have seen, however, the party later moved to reverse this trend by adding superdelegates. Research shows that both before and after the reforms, delegates have remained strongly committed to the parties and their goals.[30] It may be that for both professionals and amateurs, involvement in this very public party pageant strengthens delegates' commitment to the party's aims.

Who Controls the Delegates?   It would not matter how representative delegates are if they act as pawns of powerful party leaders. In fact, for most of the history of party conventions, that is exactly how the state delegations behaved. But state party leaders no longer control their state delegations. When the Democrats eliminated their long-standing unit rule in 1968, through which a majority of a state delegation could throw all the delegation's votes to one candidate, they removed a powerful instrument of leadership control. Perhaps the most powerful force preventing state party leaders from controlling the conventions is the fact that the delegates in both parties now come to the conventions already committed to a candidate. That makes them unavailable for "delivery" by party leaders. If anyone controls the modern conventions, then, it is the party's prospective nominee for president, not leaders of the state parties.

HOW MEDIA COVER CONVENTIONS

In addition to all these changes in the convention's delegates and power centers, media coverage of conventions has changed significantly. On one hand, conventions have been reshaped and rescheduled to meet the media's needs.[31] On the other hand, ironically, media attention to the conventions has declined sharply in recent years.

Beginning with the first televised national party conventions in 1948, TV journalists and politicians found ways to serve one another's interests. In the early days of television before the convenience of videotape, networks were desperate for content with which to fill broadcast time, so they covered the party conventions live, from beginning to end. The convention became a major story, like the Olympics, through which TV news could demonstrate its skill and provide a public service. Reporters swarmed through the convention halls, covering the strategic moves of major candidates, the actions of powerful party leaders, and the reactions of individual delegates.

For party leaders, television coverage offered a priceless opportunity to reach voters and to launch the presidential campaign with maximum impact. So they reshaped the convention into a performance intended as much for the national television audience as for the delegates. Party officials gave key speaking roles to telegenic candidates, speeded up the proceedings, and moved the most dramatic convention business into prime-time hours. More and more, the aim of the convention shifted from the conduct of party business to the wooing of voters.

These two sets of goals, however—the networks' interest in a good story and the parties' interest in attracting supporters—increasingly began to conflict. Once the nomination reforms took effect, and the choice of the parties' presidential candidates was settled before the convention started, conventions lost most of their suspense. To hold viewers, media searched the conventions for new sources of excitement, such as potential conflicts. But party leaders had no interest in making their disputes public; that would interfere with the positive message they were trying to convey. As the conventions' audience appeal continued to decline, the major networks reduced their coverage markedly. Although convention junkies still can turn to cable TV to watch the entire convention, coverage on ABC, CBS, and NBC decreased from about 60 hours per convention in 1952 to a grand total of 4 hours in 2008.

DO CONVENTIONS STILL HAVE A PURPOSE?

Since the nomination reforms, then, conventions have greatly changed. They are no longer the occasions when the major parties actually select their presidential nominees. That happens in the primaries and caucuses; the conventions simply ratify the results. The national conventions have lost much of their deliberative character and independence.

In another way, however, the conventions have become more significant. Because candidates must mobilize groups of activists and voters in order to win primaries and caucuses and because many of these groups are concerned with particular policies, the nomination reforms have made issues all the more important in convention politics. Many delegates arrive at the convention committed not only to a candidate but also to a cause. The pressures exerted by Christian conservatives at recent Republican conventions to preserve the party's stated opposition to same-sex marriage and abortion are a good illustration.

In spite of all these changes—or perhaps because of them—the national conventions are living symbols of the national parties. They provide an occasion for rediscovering common interests and for celebrating the party's heroes. They motivate state and local party candidates, energize party workers, and launch presidential campaigns. They may not compete with *American Idol* for ratings, but they do remind party activists and identifiers why the party matters to them.

SHOULD WE REFORM THE REFORMS?

The increasing use of primaries in the presidential nominating system was part of a time-honored pattern in American politics: efforts by reformers to break up concentrations of party power. As we have seen, however, the reforms have had many unintended effects as well. Primaries can create internal divisions in party organizations that may not heal in time for the general election. The low turnouts in many primaries and caucuses may increase the influence of well-organized groups on the ideological extremes: the right wing of the Republican Party and the left wing of the Democrats. The results of a few early contests in states not very representative of the nation have a disproportionate effect on the national outcome.[32] In most years, by the time most voters know enough about the candidates to make an informed choice, the nominees have already been chosen. And candidates must invest such an enormous amount of time, energy, and money in the nomination process that the ultimate winner can arrive at the party convention personally and financially exhausted.

There is no going back to the old system, however. As the reformers charged, it was controlled by state and local party leaders who were often out of touch with the electorate. It kept many party voters and even party activists out of the crucial first step in picking a president. It violated the desire for a more open, democratic politics, and it did not help presidential candidates learn how to prepare for the most powerful leadership job in the world.[33]

What Could Be Done?

Could the reforms' drawbacks be fixed by more reforms?[34] Both parties feel some pressure to do just that. Among Democratic delegates in 2008, only 21 percent claimed to be "very satisfied" with the party's nominating system as a whole.

One possible reform would be to create regional nominating events, in which the states in a given region would all schedule their primaries on the same day. That might bring more coherence to the welter of state contests by limiting the number of dates on which they could be held and reducing the enormous strain on the candidates. For a time in the late 1980s and 1990s, most southern states chose to hold their primaries early in March on a single day, referred to as Super Tuesday. Their aim was to draw greater attention to southern concerns and to encourage the nomination of moderate candidates acceptable to the South.

A system of regional primaries has drawbacks, however. Which region would go first? Even if the order were rotated from one election to the next, the first region to vote, with its peculiarities and specific concerns, would disproportionately influence the nominations. Regional primaries could still produce all the complaints listed above, from internal party divisions to low turnouts.

Another option is to hold a national primary in which all the states' primaries and caucuses take place on a single day. The United States is almost halfway there; in 2008, about half of the states chose to hold their delegate selection events on Super Tuesday, February 5. But a mega-primary has mega-drawbacks; it advantages the candidates with the most money and the greatest name recognition, those capable of campaigning in dozens of states at the same time, and reduces the roles of the party organizations and the states in the process. As is so often the case in politics, there is no "right" answer here—just a series of options, each of which favors some kinds of candidates and interests and disadvantages others.

The General Election

If Abraham Lincoln had run for president in 2012, his campaign manager would have said, "Cancel the torchlight parades and the wall posters, Abe. You need a Twitter feed. You need bloggers. You need Webmasters, database managers, bundlers, and pollsters. No offense, but image consultants will tell you to ditch the top hat! And don't forget lawyers: lots of lawyers." Campaigning, which is always evolving, has been changing at warp speed in recent years.

Until the mid-1900s, most campaigns were *party centered*; party leaders planned and managed candidates' campaigns with the party's interests in mind, just as they do today in most other democracies. The state and local party organizations provided most of the money and volunteers used by candidates.

But a series of changes had occurred that would undermine parties' control over campaigns. Reformers pushed for greater use of primary elections. Because it is risky for a party to take sides in a primary, candidates had to create their own campaign organizations to compete for the party's nomination, which they tended to keep and expand after winning the primary. State and local parties were weakened by other reforms, ranging from civil service laws to nonpartisan elections, and their flow of volunteers dried up (see Chapter 3). New and effective technologies emerged that could be purchased by wealthy candidates as easily as by parties. Some public relations experts began to specialize in political consulting and provided the services—for a fee, of course—that the parties had provided for free (or at least for no monetary payment) in earlier years.

These changes freed candidates from having to depend on their parties for money, volunteers, and advice. Campaigns became more *candidate centered,* directed by the candidates and their staffs and consultants rather than the party organizations and focusing on the candidate's own needs, not the parties'. But just as they have throughout their long lives, the parties are adjusting to these changes. This chapter will look at the technologies, information sources, and means of persuasion that candidates now have available for their use and that contribute to the candidate centered nature of most campaigns. We will also explore the conditions in which party organizations have been able to reclaim an important role in at least some campaigns.

CAMPAIGN STRATEGY

The key factors in designing strategy for a general election campaign[1] differ in several respects from those in a primary. Campaigning in a primary election focuses mainly on the party electorate, especially in states with closed primaries (see Chapter 9). In contrast, the general election audience is much larger, more diverse, and has a longer time in which to observe the candidates. The general election campaign is also powerfully affected by whether the candidate's party is in the majority or the minority in that district (see box "Party Campaign Strategies in 2012 and 2016" on this page).

Party Campaign Strategies in 2012 and 2016

As the manager of a general election campaign, one of your first critical decisions will involve how much of your resources to devote to mobilizing your base—your core supporters—and how much to spend on appealing to independents and supporters of the other party. If you are running the campaign of the majority party's candidate in a district, you'll win if you can turn out enough of your majority, so you'll probably try to rally your base by stressing the party's core values. With more U.S. House districts "safe" for one party, the use of this "base strategy" has increased. If your party is in the minority or the race is competitive, then you need to promote aspects of your candidate's record or personality that attract independents and to raise issues that cross party lines.

In recent presidential campaigns, neither party has started with an assured majority. But it is still common that one party—typically, the party advantaged by national conditions at the time—is more likely to follow a "base" strategy and for the other party to focus more on independents and the other party's identifiers. In 2000, George W. Bush stressed that he was a "compassionate" conservative and emphasized bipartisanship and an end to "partisan bickering" in order to appeal to independents and Democrats. Democrat Al Gore, in contrast, stressed the traditional Democratic core issues of Social Security and Medicare to consolidate Democratic support.

When Bush ran for reelection in 2004, he chose a different approach. Although he continued to appeal to independents and weak Democrats by stressing his leadership in the war on terror, Bush's campaign put major effort into energizing its base. Believing that millions of conservative Christians had sat out the 2000 election, presidential adviser Karl Rove used issues such as same-sex marriage and abortion to mobilize these core Bush supporters. Democrat John Kerry's campaign, in contrast, worked to attract independents and weak Republicans by stressing Kerry's record as a Vietnam War hero.

Why did the two parties' campaigns switch strategies? In 2004, the Republicans put major effort into mobilizing their base because the party's sophisticated

(continued)

(continued)

campaign apparatus had become better able to locate and turn out its core supporters. The polarization of the electorate and the decline in split ticket voting influenced strategists as well; if the center is shrinking, a centrist appeal makes less sense. The Republican strategy worked in 2004.

By 2008, however, Bush's approval ratings had dropped sharply. The drag of Bush's unpopularity and the economic recession meant that the Republican base was smaller and harder to mobilize. So the Republicans worked hard to appeal to independents, nominating a war hero and party maverick, Sen. John McCain. And the Democrats' ability to follow a "base strategy" was put at risk by their uncertainty about white, working-class Democrats' response to the first black presidential nominee in American history. Therefore, the Democrats not only used economic appeals to hold the base but also relied on Barack Obama's charismatic appeal to attract moderate suburbanites and independents.

If you were managing a presidential campaign in 2012, which approach would you take? If you're a Democrat, the state of the economy will affect your ability to rely on your base. If you are a Republican strategist, you must decide whether to broaden your appeal well beyond your conservative Christian base—and, if you do, whether you'll infuriate the base and weaken yourself further. If your strategy works, you'll be hailed as a genius, and your party's candidates for president in 2016 will seek your counsel. If it doesn't, expect frequent mentions by Jon Stewart and Stephen Colbert.

In both primary and general election campaigns, however, one of the best ways to win many offices is to already hold the office you seek.[2] Incumbents normally have greater name recognition and more success in attracting (usually favorable) media coverage than do their potential opponents. The constituent service provided by their government-paid staff members and their paid travel to and from the district give them a substantial edge over their challengers, unless they throw it away due to scandal. Their access to power makes it easier for incumbents to raise as much campaign money as they think they need, and their experience helps them use it effectively. Also, incumbents are usually part of the majority party in the district, which helps them win. Because of these advantages, in both types of elections, incumbents often need to do little more than to stress their experience, their trustworthiness, and the benefits they bring to the district, including the "earmarks" in the federal budget that help the district's economy.

Challengers face a much harsher campaign environment. Especially if they have not won any other political office before, challengers do not start with an experienced organization, proven fund-raising skills, or the other incumbent advantages.[3] In the days when party organizations ran campaigns, this might not have been a problem. At a time of candidate centered campaigns, it is. One obvious answer might be to purchase an experienced campaign organization by hiring political consultants, but most challengers do not have the money.

Thus, the predictable cycle begins: The challenger lacks an existing organization and enough money to attract the interest of well-known consultants and buy media time, so he or she cannot reach many voters, and without these vital resources, a challenger will not rise in the polls or raise enough money to be able to afford either one.

No matter how resource poor they are, however, challengers can raise issues. Thus, policy issues such as abortion, health care, and taxes are more important tools for challengers than they are for incumbents.[4] Researchers find that challengers usually do better when they campaign on issues "owned" by their party, such as health care and Social Security for Democrats and national defense and taxes for Republicans.[5] But even the most powerful issues won't do a challenger much good if he or she can't attract media coverage to publicize them.

Candidates for open seats (those where no incumbent is running) are more likely to run competitive races. Those who choose to run for the most visible offices—the presidency, governorships, the U.S. Senate—typically start with considerable name recognition, which increases because of the attention given to an open seat race. They can attract enough funds to pay for extensive media campaigns. Their major challenge will be to spend their money effectively and to define themselves to the voters before their opponent gets the chance to define them. John McCain's media consultants were trying to define their opponent in the summer of 2008 when they put up an ad calling Barack Obama "the biggest celebrity in the world" and comparing him to Paris Hilton, to suggest that he was a presumptuous empty suit rather than an experienced president-to-be. (Hilton responded with an ad referring to McCain as "the wrinkly, white-haired guy," another attempt at defining an opponent.)

HOW CAMPAIGNING HAS CHANGED

Candidates now have campaign tools available that would have been the envy of their counterparts decades ago. With the help of an expanding industry of professional consultants, campaigns have found effective ways to apply advances in polling, media use, and computer technology.

Professional Consultants

Political consultants deliver a variety of campaign services.[6] Some are general consultants, similar to the general contractors who oversee the construction of a home. Others focus on specialized tasks, such as the development of media messages, Web page design, or fund-raising. Many firms concentrate on polling; some provide the organizational skills needed to stage rallies, coffee parties, canvassing, and phone banks.

Professional consultants typically work for several different campaigns at a time, but they almost always work with clients from only one party. Some consultants restrict themselves even further to one wing, or ideological grouping, within the party. Although they function independently of the party organization, they normally try to keep a cooperative relationship with that party's leaders, because national party committees often play a matchmaking role in bringing together consultants and candidates.

Sources of Information

Polls No campaign technology has been employed more fully than the public opinion poll.[7] Candidates poll before deciding to run for an office in order to assess voters' views and to probe for weaknesses in the opposition. When the campaign begins, polls are used to determine what issues are uppermost in voters' minds and how the candidate's first steps are affecting his or her "negatives" and "positives." Poll data can help the campaign decide whether its ads should emphasize party loyalties or ties with other party candidates. *Tracking polls* can follow the reactions of small samples of voters each day and measure immediate responses to a campaign event or a new ad.

Computers Experienced candidates develop a picture of their constituency in their minds. After years of contact with constituents, they sense what kinds of people support them and how they believe they can trigger that support again. In past years, this "theory" of the campaign would have guided the candidate's strategy, even if the beliefs were inaccurate or the constituency had changed.

Computer technology now provides a sophisticated check on the candidate's beliefs. By combining pollsters' and canvassers' findings in databases, it is possible to determine which types of people are most likely to be swayed by which types of appeals. Fund-raisers can merge mailing lists from groups and publications whose members may be predisposed to favor their candidate and then produce targeted mailings within hours. Using computerized records, "oppo" researchers can locate statements made by the opponent on any conceivable issue.

METHODS OF PERSUASION: THE AIR WAR

Because of the large size of most state and federal election districts, candidates (and national parties as well) make extensive use of the mass media, especially television, radio, and the Internet.

Television

Television consumes most of a typical campaign's budget. In the early and inexpensive days of TV, candidates bought large chunks of time to air entire speeches to a national or statewide audience. Now, because of TV's increased cost and voters' shorter attention spans, campaign messages are compressed into 30-second spot ads that can be run frequently.[8] In several close House races in 2010, for example, virtually every minute of advertising time in the weeks before Election Day was filled with campaign ads. Placement of these spot ads is a major concern of media specialists. If a candidate wants to appeal to middle-aged men, for instance, then the specialist would run ads on programs such as *CSI* and *Monday Night Football*. The value of broadcast advertising has been reduced, however, by technology that viewers can use to screen out campaign ads, from the "mute" button to TiVo.

Cable TV is a cost-effective alternative to the traditional networks and works well in local campaigns, whose constituencies are too small to warrant buying time in major media markets. Most cable stations, such as TLC and CBN (Christian Broadcasting Network), have more specialized "niche" audiences than do the bigger networks. This permits campaigns to target their messages (called *narrowcasting*).

Campaigns also try to get as much *free media* coverage as possible on TV and radio news and in newspapers. (Campaigners prefer to call it *earned media*.) When newscasts and print reporters cover a candidate, the information may seem more credible and "objective" than if it is conveyed through the campaign's own ads.

To get free media coverage, campaigns need to provide material that meets the media's definition of "news."[9] If "news" is that which is dramatic, controversial, and immediate, then a candidate is not likely to earn media coverage with yet another reading of a standard stump speech. Dave Barry offers this illustration: "Let's consider two headlines. FIRST HEADLINE: 'Federal Reserve Board Ponders Reversal of Postponement of Deferral of Policy Reconsideration.' SECOND HEADLINE: 'Federal Reserve Board Caught in Motel with Underage Sheep.' Be honest, now. Which of these two stories would you read?"[10] Candidates who depend on free media need to stage campaign events that use the tamer, political equivalent of the underage sheep: dramatic confrontations, exciting settings, or meetings with well-known or telegenic people.

But the media's campaign coverage is all too brief. A study of seven major Midwestern cities during the 2006 campaign found that viewers were exposed to less than two minutes of election news during a typical 30-minute local newscast, most of it discussing strategy and polls, compared with four and a half minutes of paid political ads.[11] And for those Americans who have little or no interest in news, there are now enough other media choices to be able to avoid it altogether—a big change from the 1970s, when most Americans watched the same three network newscasts. The political information these news avoiders receive, then, comes entirely from campaign ads and entertainment programming.[12]

The Internet

First used by candidates in 1996, Web sites are now a part of every major campaign and many local races as well. Campaigns can reach their supporters directly on the Internet, thus bypassing the needs and biases of the broadcast media. Many Web sites ask visitors to register, which allows the campaign to contact them later via e-mail. By loading spots or longer ads online—on the free video-sharing site YouTube, for instance—campaigners can get their messages distributed nationally without paying for costly TV time. During the

2008 primary season alone, more than 1,000 videos about Barack Obama were posted on YouTube and viewed more than 53 million times.[13]

Ads on other Internet sites are another effective way to reach potential supporters. In 2010, both parties bought ads on Google, so that when someone entered a search term indicating his or her political sympathies (for instance, "Obama socialist"), a pop-up ad would appear featuring the party closest to those views. People clicking on the party's ad were directed to a page where they could donate to the party. By examining the "take," a party could measure which search terms brought the best results.

Not all voters have ready access to the Internet, but its use has expanded rapidly. More than twice as many people went online for campaign news (55 percent) in the 2008 election than in 2000. People under the age of 30 are most likely to be Internet users, not surprisingly, but older adults who use the Internet are almost as likely to watch political videos and share election news online as younger people are.[14]

In short, the broadcast media are an efficient way to reach large numbers of prospective voters. Their greatest strength, however—the breadth of their reach—is also one of their greatest weaknesses. (The other is their high cost.) If you were running for office, you would want to target different messages to different kinds of people so that you could speak to each individual about the issue that most concerns him or her.

Direct Contact by Mail, Text, and Twitter

Direct Mail   By merging postal mail lists of people who are of special interest to a campaign, consultants can direct personalized letters to millions of people who might be inclined to respond to a particular appeal. A candidate who wants to appeal to pro-gun voters, for example, could send computer-generated letters to people on mailing lists of the National Rifle Association, donors to other pro-gun candidates, and subscribers to hunting magazines. Because these messages are designed to be read by like-minded individuals in the privacy of their homes, direct mail appeals can be highly emotional and inflammatory, appeals that would not work as well in the "cool" medium of television.

E-mail   E-mail has the great advantage that it is cheaper than regular mail; fund-raising using e-mail and Web sites costs about one penny for each dollar raised, compared with about 40 cents per dollar raised by direct (postal) mail.[15] Online fund-raising, first used effectively by John McCain in 2000 and then Howard Dean in 2004, played a vital role in elevating Obama and Republican Mitt Romney to the status of serious presidential candidates in 2008.

Several groups and campaigns amassed huge e-mail lists in the 2008 campaign. The King Kong of these lists was the Obama campaign's, with more than 13 million e-mail addresses. Online contributions accounted for an estimated two-thirds of the candidate's record-breaking $750 million in contributions. The campaign sent more than 7,000 discrete messages to its e-mail list, for a total of over a billion e-mails. Many of the messages were targeted specifically to certain groups—for instance, people who had already donated small sums to the campaign. The Republican National Committee and the liberal organization MoveOn.org also maintain extensive e-mail lists.

Text Messaging   Because postal mail misses large numbers of young people whose addresses change from year to year, text messages have become an increasingly common method of turning out the vote.[16] In addition to Obama's mammoth e-mail list, his campaign collected a million cell phone numbers from people who had agreed to receive text messages from the campaign. Supporters received 5–20 texts a month, targeted to the individual's interests and locations. In battleground states on Election Day, every voter who had signed up for Obama texts got at least three such messages reminding him or her to vote and to bring others to the polls too.

Social Networking Sites ("Socnets")   As of the 2010 election, 6 out of 10 American adults used social networking sites such as Facebook and 21 percent of online adults used these socnets to connect with a campaign or to follow or post about the election.[17] Many candidates maintain profiles on these sites to communicate with their supporters and others. By sending a campaign message on Facebook (or through e-mail, texting, or blogs) and urging each recipient to forward it to his or her already-existing network of contacts, the campaign can increase its reach exponentially at little or no cost. This *viral marketing* was used more often by Democrats in 2008, but Republicans caught up in 2010.

Twitter   The 2008 election was the first in which Twitter, a free social networking site, received campaign use. Campaigners can send "tweets," messages of up to 140 characters, to update supporters. Tweets can be used to respond quickly to an opponent's attacks—or to distribute those attacks more widely.

THE GROUND WAR: "UNDER THE RADAR"

Campaigners have traditionally used more personalized appeals as well. These are known as the *ground war*: house-to-house canvassing and phone calls that permit communication with selected groups of people. These ground-war techniques were used with great sophistication by Republican campaigns in 2004, and the 2008 Obama campaign organization surpassed even that standard for personal as well as online contact (see box "What Made Obama's 2008 Campaign So Effective?" on page 210).

Canvassing and Phone Banks

In the days of machine politics, party organizations sent their patronage workers and other volunteers to the homes of people who might vote for party candidates, to tell them about the party ticket. Although candidates' staffs now can tweet, call, and e-mail just as easily as party leaders can, canvassing does not lend itself

What Made Obama's 2008 Campaign So Effective?

The Obama campaign's strategy in 2008 was unusual for a presidential race. Most presidential campaigns have spent 70–75 percent of their funds on broadcast media advertising. The Obama campaign's media expenditure was less than 50 percent. Instead, the campaign's first priority was the ground war—the block-by-block, phone-by-phone effort to contact as many individuals as possible. "We knew that we had to get really good turnout," said Campaign Manager David Plouffe, "and we thought that a human being talking to a human being... is the most effective in communication." The Obama field operation was the most extensive in modern political history, far outmatching that of his Republican opponent, John McCain.

Another reason for Obama's success, according to Plouffe, was that the lengthy nomination race against the "formidable" and aggressive candidacy of Hillary Clinton toughened up the young Obama organization for its run against McCain. The long march of primaries and caucuses "made us a stronger general election candidate. A lot of our dirty laundry was aired, and we had practice in testing a campaign... we went into the general election in very much fighting shape." McCain's campaign, Plouffe said, "careened from message to message, strategy to strategy. We had one message, one strategy."

And, of course, the economic meltdown and Obama's calm response to it, the unpopularity of President Bush, and the excitement generated by the first African American major party nominee for president didn't hurt either.

Sources: Lloyd Grove, "World According to ... David Plouffe," at www.portfolio.com/views/columns/ the-world-according-to/2008/12/11/David-Plouffe-Interview (accessed November 13, 2011); and Alan I. Abramowitz, *The Disappearing Center* (New Haven: Yale University Press, 2010), p. 107.

as readily to candidate centered campaigns. It takes a lot of volunteers to go door to door, and for most of American history, party organizations were more likely than individual candidates to have the requisite numbers of canvassers.

Canvassing became less common from the early 1970s to the early 1990s, when party organizations had more difficulty finding volunteers. But since then, the parties have developed more sophisticated forms of canvassing to turn out their base voters and other targeted groups. Voter contacting by the parties has increased dramatically, especially in competitive contests.

Microtargeting   If you knock on every door in a big city, you'll reach a lot of Democrats. Republican voters are not as concentrated geographically as Democrats tend to be. Thus, Republican strategists determined in the early 2000s that they would have to use more high-tech means to locate likely Republican voters. Using commercial databases, the Republicans collected data on millions of people's viewing habits, magazine subscriptions, buying preferences, and voting patterns. They entered these data into the national

Republican database called **Voter Vault**. Analysis of the data showed that people who watch Fox News, country or religions stations or the Golf Channel, drive BMWs rather than Chevys, go to exercise clubs after work, drink bourbon or Coors beer, and watch college rather than pro football are more inclined to support Republicans.

With these data in hand, the Bush–Cheney campaign and the Republican National Committee, in coordination with Republican state and local parties, worked to cherry-pick likely Republican voters in the 2004 election. This is known as **microtargeting** or "niche marketing." They focused especially on 7 million likely Republicans and 10 million conservative-leaning independents who had not voted regularly in the past. Then they classified these targets into a series of types and determined which issues were the most likely to anger voters in each type. One voter type could be approached with a personal contact or a phone call dealing with same-sex marriage; another might receive an appeal about terrorism.

The success of the Republican effort led the national Democrats to ramp up their own program. In 2008 exit polls, a larger proportion (26 percent) of respondents said they were contacted personally by the Obama campaign than those reporting contact by McCain (18 percent).[18] The A.F.L.-C.I.O., the giant labor federation, contributed extensively to the Democrats' canvassing efforts in 2006, 2008, and again in 2010.

Contacting voters by phone is even quicker, though not as persuasive, as is "door-knocking." Many campaigns, then, bring supporters to a central location (a **phone bank**) with telephones—often a business, union, or party or campaign headquarters, or even an empty building where volunteers can use their cell phones—to dial lists of numbers identified by the campaign's microtargeting. Even cheaper are virtual phone banks, where supporters anywhere in the nation go online to get a list of phone numbers and a script to read, and **robocalls**, in which volunteers or computers can direct automated phone calls to large numbers of people on a campaign's target list. Robocalls are often used to send a negative message or to do **push polling**—attack messages disguised as public opinion polls. In high-profile races, households may receive several of these calls a night as the election approaches. But these techniques have limits, too: Caller ID lets people screen their calls, and the growing number of cell phone–only individuals makes calling more costly.

Negative Campaigning

It has become a staple of political consulting that, when a candidate is falling behind in the polls, one of the quickest ways to recover is to "go negative." Attacking an opponent is not new; politicians since the earliest days of the republic have been hit with vicious attacks. Concern about negative campaigns has increased recently, however, because they can be spread so much faster and farther by new technologies.

Harsh negative ads often attract news coverage, which carries their message to even more people. Information about the savage ads of the "Swift Boat

Veterans for Truth" in the 2004 campaign, making the unsubstantiated claim that John Kerry had not deserved the medals he was awarded in the Vietnam War, reached between half and three-quarters of respondents in national surveys even though the ads were broadcast in only seven small media markets. The proportion of negative ads in the 2010 election was the highest in recent history.[19]

Does negative campaigning work? Much of the recent evidence suggests that it does. Negative ads can be particularly memorable and emotionally engaging. In some circumstances, that can increase voter information and turnout.[20] The timing of the ads matters; before an individual chooses a candidate, negative ads can be informative and useful, but after the individual has made his or her choice, attack ads are more likely to depress turnout, especially among people who are not strong partisans.[21] No matter what their real impact was, the Swift Boat ads were widely assumed to have seriously hurt Kerry's campaign in 2004, so presidential candidates in 2008 drew the lesson that they needed to respond immediately and strongly to negative ads, rather than to ignore them.

These campaign tools have been used in a variety of ways in recent elections.

The 2004 Campaign

Attention focused heavily on a few highly competitive campaigns in 2004. Because the two parties were so evenly matched in the U.S. House and Senate, and because the overwhelming majority of House incumbents were expected to coast to easy wins, the parties and many interest groups ignored most congressional races and focused their resources on two or three dozen competitive seats as well as the presidential race. In the presidential contest, the air wars were limited to between 12 and 20 "battleground" states at any given time. Residents in these targeted states were hit by a virtual hurricane of campaign ads. In contrast, voters in 8 of the 10 biggest media markets— New York, Los Angeles, Chicago, Washington, San Francisco, Boston, Dallas, and Houston—saw no sustained advertising for either presidential candidate because their states were regarded as locked up for one candidate.

Although most campaigns continued to be candidate centered, there were signs of more party centered activity in these very competitive races. In particular, the national Republican Party geared up for an unprecedented ground war campaign. To counteract the expected canvassing drives by labor unions and the Democrats, the national Republicans had been conducting a series of experiments on how best to reach voters. They field-tested a program in 2002 in which the GOP flooded precincts in competitive states with Republican volunteers and paid staffers, especially during the last 72 hours of the campaign. This *72-hour project* was expensive, costing $200 million, but observers felt that it increased Republican turnout by about 3 percent in 2002 over that of the last midterm election, and Republicans won most of the close contests, maintained control of the House, and narrowly regained control of the Senate.[22] As a result, the Republicans expanded the model in 2004. A full year before the election, the RNC and the Bush campaign were already training thousands of volunteers to recruit canvassers for a massive "72-hour project." Because the president was unopposed for the Republican nomination, the full force of his huge campaign budget could be focused on the general election.

The Kerry campaign and the national Democrats put effort into the ground war as well. But much of Kerry's canvassing and almost 40 percent of his TV advertising was done by independent groups, who raised money to help the Democratic ticket compete under the constraints of the 2002 campaign finance reforms (see Chapter 12). By law, these independent groups were not allowed to consult with the Kerry campaign in planning or conducting their activities, nor could they ask people directly to vote for Kerry; so their messages and efforts were not always closely integrated with those of the campaign.

In the end, the Bush volunteers had an easier sell. A large majority of Bush voters were enthusiastic about their candidate, whereas many Kerry voters were motivated mainly by their dislike of Bush. The Republican eked out a narrow victory, and his party kept control of the House and slightly increased its Senate majority.

Democrats Regain the Advantage in 2006

Republican candidates anticipated a much tougher race in 2006. The climate of public opinion had changed. Bush's approval rating was dropping markedly, in part because of growing public discontent with the war in Iraq. As anti-Republican feeling grew, more and more previously "safe" Republican incumbents started looking over their shoulders. Democrats soon gained other targets, including several Republican congressmen who were linked to a corrupt lobbyist and one who resigned after having sent sexually explicit e-mails to underage House pages. The number of competitive House races, estimated to be about 35–45 at the beginning of the 2006 campaign, soon expanded to more than twice that number.

Anti-immigration stands taken by some Republican conservatives further hurt Republican chances by undercutting the party's recent efforts to appeal to Latino voters. To compensate, Republican strategists decided to start the party's microtargeting and canvassing campaign sooner and to expand it to include a larger portion of independents. As its chances worsened, the national party spent more than 90 percent of its funds on negative ads attacking the Democrats. Democratic candidates responded by linking their Republican opponents to Bush.

On Election Day, Democrats rode a wave just as the Republicans had in 1994. With a net gain of 31 seats in the House and 6 in the Senate, Democrats took control of both houses of Congress for the first time in 12 years. The Democratic trend, which was especially strong in the Northeast, was built on substantial support from moderates and independents as well as Democratic identifiers.

The Old and the New in 2008

Democratic strength continued to grow in 2008 as Bush's popularity hit new lows. By this time, as Chapter 4 showed, the DNC and several other Democratic-leaning groups had matched and perhaps even surpassed the Republicans' microtargeting skills. Using the DNC's upgraded Vote Builder databank as well as data from the privately owned Catalist, the Obama campaign designed an extensive ground game. In addition to this door-to-door canvassing, Obama's organization successfully used the Internet, text messaging, cell phones, and other electronic tools to contact voters.

Perhaps the most notable accomplishment of Obama's campaign was its ability to expand the playing field. Democratic presidential campaigns in the recent past had targeted a group of reliably Democratic East and West Coast states and then aimed to pick up just enough "battleground" states (typically, Ohio, Pennsylvania, and Florida) to reach an Electoral College majority. Obama's staffers tried to create more alternative ways to win. They put particular effort into some previously Republican states, such as Colorado and Virginia, whose demographic profile was becoming more favorable to Democratic candidates.

Even so, it wasn't an easy race for the Democrat. In many ways, Republican John McCain was the Obama campaign's worst nightmare. As a self-proclaimed "maverick" and reformer, McCain was able to draw distinctions between himself and President Bush. McCain was a war hero, a longtime political presence in comparison with Obama's relative inexperience in national politics, and a personality attractive to independents. McCain's campaign sought to overcome Democratic trends by portraying Obama as an elitist who did not "share our values," similar to Bush's successful characterizations of Kerry in 2004 and Al Gore in 2000. Obama fought to keep the focus on the Bush administration's failures. Although the polls showed Obama with a slight lead during the summer of 2008, McCain pulled ahead after the Republican convention. But the financial disaster of mid-September, and McCain's unsteady response to it, broke McCain's new momentum and foreshadowed Obama's victory in November.

In the end, the Obama efforts paid off. Blacks and Latinos, women, city dwellers, upscale suburbanites, and liberals formed the core of Obama's victory. Obama won not only every state that Kerry had carried in 2004 but also nine former Bush states. Several states, including Virginia and Indiana, gave their electoral votes to a Democratic presidential candidate for the first time in 44 years. Republicans held their own in Appalachia and other areas with large white, evangelical populations and even improved their performance among whites in the Deep South. But Obama's victory and Democratic gains of 8 Senate seats and 21 in the House made 2008 another Democratic wave.

Backlash in 2010

After two back-to-back victories for the Democrats—an unusual occurrence for either party—the tide turned again. The main predictors of midterm losses by the president's party—low presidential approval ratings and a bad economy—both pointed to major Democratic losses in 2010. President Obama's job approval ratings had slipped below 50 percent. And although a unified Democratic government had passed landmark legislation in 2009 and 2010, including health care reform and a major economic stimulus package to stem the runaway economic decline, these accomplishments did not produce a boost in the party's approval ratings. Instead, Republicans and many independents charged that Obama and the Democratic Congress were trying to engineer a government takeover of health care and other parts of the economy. Extensive coverage of bargaining on the health care bill made the process seem distasteful to many voters and triggered an energetic anti-Democratic protest by Tea Party activists.[23]

Democratic candidates were on the defensive for much of the 2010 campaign. Many of the Democrats elected in their party's wave elections of 2006 and 2008 had won districts and states that were normally Republican; these "exposed" incumbents were in danger when the partisan tide shifted. The national party was forced to use its resources to protect these vulnerable incumbents, whereas the national Republican committees were able to target powerful Democratic House members and senators as well as junior members.

The only real surprise was the magnitude of the Democratic losses. Even though Democratic campaign spending outpaced the GOP, Republicans gained a House majority by winning 66 seats while losing only three—the biggest gain by either party since 1948. The GOP also gained 6 Senate seats (but not majority control) and 6 governorships, plus more than 700 state legislative seats. That gave Republicans greater control over the redistricting of state legislative and congressional seats that took place in 2011. Democratic losses were especially heavy among moderates and those who supported the health care reform bill and the extension of President Bush's bank bailout.[24] The pattern of defeats left the Democratic congressional contingent more liberal, and the Republicans more conservative, than before. As always, however, the results were interpreted in different ways, depending in part on the agenda of the observer (see box "Why Did the Republicans Win in 2010?" on this page).

Within weeks of Election Day, the 2012 campaign had begun. Democrats attacked Republican candidates as extremists linked to the Tea Party. Republicans responded that the Democrats were a party "made in Washington." But although the charges were familiar, both sides knew that they would face a different electorate in 2012 than they had in 2010. Midterm voters are more likely to be white, older, and wealthier than are those in presidential elections. That was markedly true in 2010, when the midterm turnout was more conservative than usual, and independents, who had voted predominantly Democratic in 2008, swung heavily toward Republican candidates. If past patterns held, the 2012 electorate would be younger, more diverse, more weighted toward blacks and Latinos, and thus friendlier to Democrats. Every 2012 campaign's strategic choices would have to take these shifts into account.

Why Did the Republicans Win in 2010?

Many Republicans argued that voters had asked for change in 2008 but instead had gotten big government and big federal deficits. The voters, in this view, were protesting the Obama Administration's liberalism.

Many liberal Democrats contended that there hadn't been *enough* change. Democrats lost, they said, because the Obama administration and the congressional Democrats had been too moderate; therefore, disappointed liberals stayed home on Election Day. Democrats, they said, should have moved quickly to end the Bush tax cuts, push climate change legislation through Congress, and pull American troops out of Iraq and Afghanistan.

Many moderate Democrats differed. It was the moderates who deserted the Democrats, they insisted, because the party had promised progress on economic issues but had instead spent too much time on policies important to liberals, such as health care reform.

It is common for different groups to interpret (or "spin") the meaning of an election differently, to support their own preferred views. Journalists, who are the targets of the spin, often become cynical about it. Jon Margolis, former national political reporter for the *Chicago Tribune,* claims that he switched to the sports beat because he said he'd never seen a sports story that read, "The Chicago Cubs defeated the St. Louis Cardinals today by a score of 2-1. The Cardinals denied it."

Sources: Margolis quoted in Ronald D. Elving, "Campaign Data Can Be Calculated Nonsense," *CQ Weekly,* August 19, 1995, p. 2602.

DO CAMPAIGNS MAKE A DIFFERENCE?

Because campaigns attract so much media attention, money, and effort, many people naturally assume that campaign events are responsible for the election's outcome. Yet careful statistical analysis shows that election results can often be predicted fairly well from conditions that existed before the campaign began, such as the incumbent's previous poll ratings, economic conditions, and the distribution of party loyalties in the district. That doesn't leave much room for campaigns to determine the outcome. Instead, it suggests that campaigns simply remind voters of these longer-lasting conditions and, in this way, help them move toward a largely preordained outcome.[25] Does this mean that the candidates' strategies are not important?

The Argument That Campaigns Matter

Some campaigns have clearly made or broken a candidate. In 2010, U.S. Senate Majority Leader Harry Reid (D-NV) looked very likely to lose reelection. He ran behind his Republican opponent, Sharron Angle, for months in the polls. Yet Reid eked out a victory after Angle's campaign made a series of bad decisions. Her campaign manager never got around to hiring a political director and paid little attention to the campaign's budget and advertising. A national Republican operative referred to the "sheer, utter incompetence" of the manager: "If they were filming a sequel to the movie 'Dumb and Dumber,' [Angle's manager] would have a feature role."[26] Angle herself contributed a string of gaffes, including threatening to sue Reid for publicizing Angle's (controversial) stands on issues.

Other than sheer incompetence, what makes a difference in campaigns? A long line of evidence suggests that canvassing has a small but meaningful effect on both turnout and voters' choices.[27] Researchers find that door-to-door canvassing is more effective in activating voters than phone contact is, and both kinds of contact are more effective than mailings.[28] The quality of the contact can matter at least as much as the medium, however.[29] Canvassing probably makes more of a difference in local elections than in presidential races because there are fewer alternative sources of information in local contests. Where a party is active, its vote share can increase by at least a few percentage points, which could be the critical margin in a close race.[30]

As would be expected, television news and advertising—and the money that pays for the ads—can also influence voters' decisions.[31] The impact of TV ads is often short lived, however.[32] Campaign debates and other events make a difference in the election result under some circumstances.[33] All these sources of campaign information, taken together, can improve citizens' knowledge, influence their choices, and increase voter turnout.[34]

Various elements of campaigns affect some voters differently from others, depending on the voter's party identification and level of interest in politics. For instance, those with limited political interest may pick up only a little information about campaigns, but the few bits of information that break through—often, perceptions of a candidate's likeability—could have a big impact on their attitudes.[35] People who hold a weak party ID and who have had doubts about their party's candidate can be especially affected by the campaign communications they receive.[36] And the emphasis placed by media[37] and campaigns[38] on different aspects of the race or the candidate, such as the candidate's views on the economy or his or her age or ethnicity, can influence what the voters regard as important.

The Argument That They Don't

There are several reasons why campaigning may have only a limited effect. Television news, ads, and ground war activities offer viewers a wide range of conflicting messages about candidates—positive, negative, and neutral information and opinions, all mixed together. The inconsistency of these messages makes it harder for a campaign to have a single, consistent impact on viewers' minds.[39]

We know that voters pay selective attention to media and other campaign communications. They tend to surround themselves with friends, information, and even personal experiences that support their beliefs and loyalties,[40] and they often ignore information that conflicts with their opinions. The media environment has become highly diversified in recent years, with blogs, newsletters, talk media, and cable channels presenting a dizzying array of perspectives.[41] As a result, it is not hard for people to find media outlets that reinforce their views: Think of Fox News for conservatives and *Daily Kos* for liberals. Most campaign messages, then, probably have the effect of activating and reinforcing the voter's existing political inclinations, as they always have.[42] That can explain why so much campaign effort is directed at getting people out to vote—to act on whatever opinions they already hold—rather than at trying to change their voting decision.

Some Tentative Answers

There is much left to learn about the effects of campaigns. In the information-rich environment of current politics and among the large numbers of weak partisans and independent "leaners," the potential for campaigns to shape voters' perceptions may be at least as great as it has ever been. The impact of campaigns, however, will continue to be limited by the same forces that have always constrained it: voters' tendency to pay attention to the messages with which they already agree and their ability to tune out most political messages altogether.

CANDIDATE CENTERED OR PARTY CENTERED CAMPAIGNS?

The campaign techniques that we have explored in this chapter have affected the balance of power in campaigns between parties and candidates. Broadcast media, which need a large audience, tend to focus on individual personalities rather than institutions such as parties. Tools such as Internet ads and TV advertising are available to any candidate who can pay for them; they let candidates communicate with voters without the party's help. The technologies that have developed since the mid-1900s, in short, have helped candidates run their campaigns independently of the party organizations. If the American parties had been as strong organizationally as those in many other nations when these technologies developed, then they might have been able to monopolize the use of TV and other media for campaign purposes. But in fact, as we have seen, the American parties have always struggled to maintain their power in a political culture hostile to their functioning.

Many of the nation's electoral rules also make it easier for campaigns to be candidate centered, though the other necessary conditions for such campaigns didn't come together until the 1960s.[43] The American electoral process has few institutions, such as parliamentary-cabinet government or proportional representation, which would encourage voters to see elections as contests between parties for control of government. Instead, rules ranging from campaign finance regulations to the separation of powers encourage candidates to run as individuals, not as members of a party ticket, and make it hard for parties to coordinate the campaigns of several candidates. Progressive reforms strengthened this tendency. The direct primary, as we have seen, allows candidates to run without the party organization's approval.

Consequently, it is the candidates and their advisers, not the parties, who make the strategic decisions in most campaigns. Candidates have their own headquarters and staffers rather than using the party's facilities. Candidates maintain their own relationships with voters rather than relying on the party organization as an intermediary. Party organizations, rather than running campaigns, often work instead to enhance the appeal of individual candidates, and they compete with consultants, interest groups, and others for the chance to do so.

Party Influence in Competitive Campaigns

The parties, however, are fighting back. The large sums of money that have flowed into the national parties in the past three decades have helped them to assist individual campaigns with money and other services.[44] As Chapter 4 noted, soft money enabled party organizations to pour millions of dollars into campaign ads in a few battleground states until 2003. Since then, massive party fund-raising and voter contact drives have expanded the party presence in more races.

The national parties' visibility has grown especially in the most highly competitive Senate and House elections. That is where party organizations have used independent spending to make the biggest financial impact, in some cases spending even more than the candidates themselves do. But because independent spending does not allow the parties to coordinate their efforts with their candidates, much less to run their campaigns, party-funded ads have sometimes stressed different themes from those the campaign preferred to emphasize and, frequently, more negative messages than the campaign's own advertising.[45] Because voters rarely pay attention to the source of any particular message, candidates have gotten blamed for negativity and claims that they have not made. In most races, however, the party's role is not nearly as noticeable.

The Continuing Struggle Between Candidates and Party Organizations

An expanded party role in campaigns makes economic sense. Party organizations can distribute appeals for a number of candidates at the same time and register voters to help the entire ticket. Parties can buy media advertising and consultants' services for use by many candidates at cost-effective prices. Party organizations can coordinate Election Day activities for all the party's candidates, provide poll watchers to guard against voting irregularities, send cars to bring people to the polls, and check voter lists to mobilize nonvoters late in the day.

This efficiency is bought at the cost of limiting each candidate's independence, however. Party organizations and candidates do not always have the same goals. The party, aiming to maximize the number of races it wins, puts its scarce resources into the most competitive campaigns and spends as little as possible on the races it considers hopeless. Each candidate, in contrast, is committed above all to his or her own victory and to gaining the resources needed to achieve it, no matter how unlikely that victory may be. The party, in its drive to win every competitive race, is likely to do whatever it takes, whether through negative or positive campaigning. The candidate, in contrast, has to face the voters; a constant barrage of attack ads may make a candidate less appealing.

The result is a continuing struggle between the party organizations and the candidates—the party in government—for control of campaigns. In most elections, the candidates have won the fight. Although the parties have more to offer candidates than they did just a few years ago, party organizations still contribute only a fairly small percentage of candidates' overall spending in all but a few races. In contrast, European parties often provide more than half the funding used by most candidates.

Candidate centered campaigning has an important effect on governing. When they control their own campaigns, winning candidates can develop personal relationships with their constituents, unconstrained by party ties. Candidates are free to form close alliances with interest groups, which enhance the ability of these groups to influence public policy. In short, candidate centered campaigning strengthens the power of the party in government relative to that of the party organization. It also poses an important question: If strong party organizations can help to hold elected officials accountable for their actions, then how much accountability do voters get from a candidate centered politics?

Financing the Campaigns

U.S. senators running for reelection in 2010 spent an average of $9 million each on their campaigns.[1] If you had to raise that much money, then during *each week* of your six-year term you would need to collect about $29,000—maybe more than you've had to raise to spend a year in college. If you went a week without asking for money, then you'd need to raise $58,000 the following week. That is, of course, in addition to the time you'd need to spend communicating with your constituents, learning about proposed legislation, working with other senators, and voting on bills.

Why does it cost so much to keep a job whose salary is $174,000 a year? The development of expensive new campaign techniques, paid professional consultants, improved fund-raising methods, the growing polarization of the major parties, and the Supreme Court's evisceration of campaign finance laws have all helped to increase campaign spending. Money is the key to mobilizing the resources needed for a viable campaign. Thus, candidates, especially for statewide and national office, are not likely to be taken seriously unless they start with a big campaign budget or a proven talent for fund-raising.

Until the campaign finance reforms of the 1970s, much of the money used in campaigns was collected and spent in secret. Candidates were not required to disclose how they raised funds, and contributors were often unwilling to make their names public. Citizens had no way to be sure who was paying for a candidate's campaign or what the givers might be getting in return. As a result of the 1970s regulations, we now have a flood of data about campaign spending and contributions. In the wake of court decisions in 2010 and 2011, however, much of the money spent on campaigns in 2012 will be just as hard to trace as in the days before the reforms.

HOW MUCH MONEY IS SPENT ON CAMPAIGNS?

Campaigns for all levels of office in the United States cost well over $5 *billion* collectively in 2008 and $2 billion in the congressional races of 2010—enormous increases over the amounts spent in earlier decades. Inflation has reduced the purchasing power of the dollar during this period, so the real, inflation-adjusted increase is not nearly as dramatic. But the growth in real spending since 1996 is impressive by any standard.

Presidential Campaigns

The 2008 presidential race was, hands down, the most expensive political campaign in American history (see Figure 12.1). It began as a wide-open contest: the first presidential election in almost 80 years in which no sitting president or vice president was running for reelection. Democrats sensed the chance of a big victory due in large part to President Bush's unpopularity. But perhaps the biggest reason for the unprecedented spending was the uncommon fund-raising skill of some of the candidates, Barack Obama in particular.

Obama's fund-raising talent first became apparent during the invisible primary in 2007. By the end of December, he had already raised more than $100 million. Rather than just repeatedly asking supporters for money, as most other candidates have, his staff worked to build relationships with likely donors online, informed them about new developments, and encouraged them to volunteer as canvassers and at campaign events. This approach, combined with Obama's singular appeal, enticed more than 3 million people to give money to his campaign.

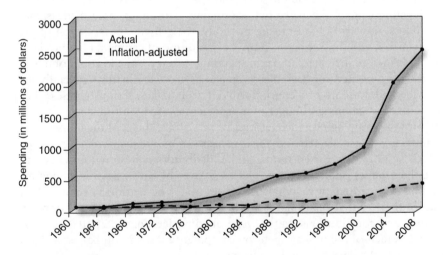

FIGURE 12.1

Total Spending by Candidates, Parties, and Groups in Presidential Elections, 1960–2008.

Note: Estimates are for two-year cycles ending in the presidential election years. Inflation-adjusted figures are computed by deflating the actual expenditures using the Consumer Price Index yearly averages (with 1960 as the base year).

Sources: John C. Green, ed., *Financing the 1996 Election* (Armonk, NY: M. E. Sharpe, 1999), p. 19; FEC data for 2000–2008 at www.fec.gov. Consumer Price Index deflator is based on Table 723 in the U.S. Census Bureau, *The 2011 Statistical Abstract,* "Purchasing Power of the Dollar," at www.census.gov/compendia/statab/2011/tables/11s0723.pdf (accessed May 24, 2011).

Obama raised almost $750 million in 2007–2008—more than all Democratic and Republican presidential candidates combined had collected in the previous election cycle. That made him the most successful candidate in the history of campaign fund-raising. He and his Republican opponent, John McCain, pulled in and spent a total of almost $1.1 billion in the primaries and the general election campaign (see Table 12.1). But perhaps the most striking figure is that Obama, the Democrat, greatly outraised and outspent his Republican rival. Until Democrat John Kerry came close to matching George W. Bush's overall fund-raising in 2004, the Republican advantage in raising money had been one of the certainties of presidential campaigning. In 2012, Obama's fund-raising far outpaced the early efforts of his Republican rivals as well.

TABLE 12.1

What It Cost to Nominate and Elect a President, 2008

I. Prenomination Receipts and Spending	Amount (in millions of dollars)	
	Raised	Spent
Republicans	472.4	450.2
McCain	219.6	202.1
Romney	105.2	105.1
Huckabee	16.1	16.0
All others	131.5	127.0
Democrats	752.4	539.4
Obama	424.2	224.8
Clinton	223.9	215.8
All others	104.3	98.8
II. Conventions		
Public funding for party conventions		33.6
Private funding:		
Republican		62.4
Democratic		61.9
III. General Election		
Candidate Funds		
Public funding for major party candidates (McCain only)		84.1
General election receipts and spending (Obama only)	321.5	504.5
Third party receipts and spending (Nader)	4.0	3.8
Compliance costs		46.4

(*continued*)

TABLE 12.1 (CONTINUED)

III. General Election (continued)	Amount (in millions of dollars) Spent
Party Funds (nomination and general)	
Parties' coordinated expenditures	25.3
Parties' independent expenditures	54.6
Parties' contributions to "hybrid" ads financed jointly with candidates	106.0*
Group Funds (nomination and general)	
PAC and individual independent spending	114.2
Spending by 527 groups	202.1**
Spending by 501(c) groups	195.9**
Internal communication costs	18.1
Electioneering communications by groups	27.8

*Estimates from party officials; no official figures are available at this writing, nor are there data for parties' voter mobilization (field operation) efforts.

** Although most of this spending went into the presidential race, an unspecified portion was spent on House and Senate campaigns. The figures represent groups that raised $200,000 or more by the end of November 2008.

Source: Based on FEC data as of September 12, 2009. Data on 527 and 501(c) groups from the Campaign Finance Institute.

As Sections II and III in Table 12.1 show, other groups also spent a great deal on the 2008 presidential general election race, though not as much as the candidates themselves. Taxpayers pick up part of the tab for the two parties' national conventions, though contributions from corporations and other interests cover the bulk of their cost. And the candidate nominated by each major party can choose to receive public funds for the general election. The catch is that he or she is then limited to spending no more than the public funds provide (except money the candidate raises to pay lawyers and accountants to deal with federal campaign finance laws, called "compliance costs").

Only McCain accepted the public funding; thus, he could spend no more than the $84.1 million he received from the government for his general election campaign. Obama, riding the wave of his fund-raising success in the primaries, guessed that he could raise much more than $84 million between his nomination and Election Day, so it would make sense for him to turn down the federal funds and avoid the spending limit that accompanied them. He guessed right; in September alone, the Obama fund-raising machine took in a record-shattering $150 million—almost twice what he would have received in total federal funding, and quadruple the largest sum any candidate had raised in one month in any previous presidential race.

Party organizations spent millions as well in the presidential campaign. The parties can put money into presidential races in four different ways.

They can use *coordinated spending*: money spent by party organizations *in coordination with* a candidate's campaign to purchase services such as media advertising or polling for the campaign. Parties, as well as individuals and other political groups, can also spend as much as they choose independently, known as *independent spending*, to expressly support or oppose a candidate, as long as they do so *without consulting with their candidate*. Almost all the party independent spending in the 2008 presidential race came from the Republican Party. When McCain fell far behind Obama in the money chase, and then agreed to accept public funds for his general election campaign, he was vastly outspent by Obama and needed his party's help to remain competitive.

Parties are also allowed to split the cost with a candidate's campaign on *"hybrid" ads*, which mention both the presidential candidate and other party candidates, and to *mobilize voters through grassroots efforts*. Party spending has become increasingly important, though the parties' role in American campaigns pales in comparison with most other democracies, where the party organizations, not the candidates, do most of the campaign spending.

A variety of other groups and individuals also pay for advertising and voter mobilization. "Internal communication costs" in Table 12.1 are the funds spent by labor unions and corporations to urge their members to vote for a particular candidate. Unions, corporations, and membership associations also spent millions on "nonpartisan" voter mobilization, to register voters and get them to the polls on Election Day. (Spending by political action committees and 527 groups will be discussed later in the chapter.)

Congressional Campaigns

The 2010 congressional elections also set a new record in campaign spending (see Figures 12.2 and 12.3). In each of four Senate races—Florida, which had a lively three-way contest; Connecticut and Nevada, where controversial Tea Party–backed candidates were well publicized; and California, where big spending is the norm—the winner and loser(s) spent a collective total of more than $50 million on their races.

Incumbents greatly outraise and outspend their challengers in every election year. In 2010, the average House incumbent raised about $1.6 million for his or her campaign, compared with about $627,000 for the average major-party challenger.[2] In Senate races, incumbents collected an average of $9 million compared with just under $5 million for challengers. Of the total dollars raised collectively by House incumbents and their major-party challengers, challengers accounted for only about 28 percent of the funds, and in Senate races, 39 percent. In House races, candidates for open seats—those where no incumbent is running—raised more money than challengers did (an average of $1.2 million) but not as much as incumbents. Open-seat candidates in Senate races did as well as Senate incumbents, raising an average of $9.1 million, led by a group of very well-funded Republican campaigns.

Republican candidates and organizations usually hold a fund-raising edge over Democrats in congressional campaigns. The size of that advantage

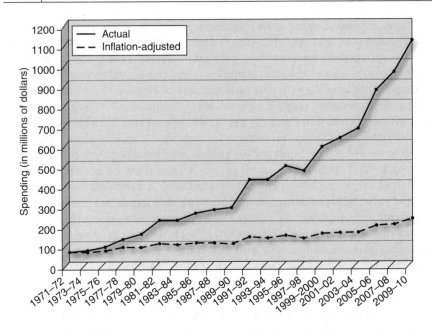

FIGURE 12.2

Total Spending by All Candidates in House Campaigns, 1971–1972 to 2009–2010.

Note: Inflation-adjusted figures are computed by deflating the actual expenditures by changes in the price level as measured by the Consumer Price Index (yearly averages) using 1972 as the base year.

Source: FEC data at www.fec.gov/press/bkgnd/cf_summary_info/2010can_fullsum/1all2010afinal.pdf (accessed November 20, 2011). CPI deflator is the same as that listed for Figure 12.1.

in a given election depends on which party has the most incumbents and, therefore, controls each House of Congress. Control of a legislative body is worth a great deal to a party, quite literally. Even though Republicans seemed very likely to do well in 2010, the Democrats' control of both the Senate and House leading up to that election kept them competitive. Democratic general election House candidates slightly outraised and outspent their Republican rivals, thanks to the money they received from incumbent-friendly PACs. But in the Senate, and especially in open-seat races, the expectation of Republican gains produced a clear Republican advantage in contributions from PACs and other outside groups.

State and Local Campaigns

Much less is known about spending practices in the thousands of campaigns for state and local offices, mainly because there is no central reporting agency comparable to the national Federal Election Commission (FEC). The range in these races is enormous. Many local candidates win after spending a few hundred dollars. On the other end of the scale are some top-dollar mayoral

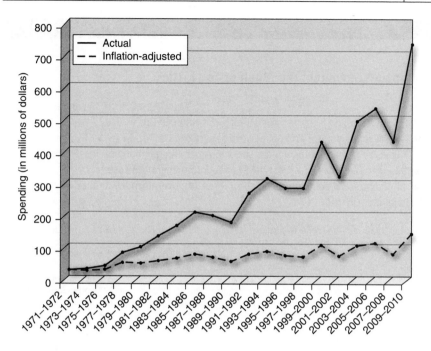

FIGURE 12.3

Total Spending by All Candidates in Senate Campaigns, 1971–1972 to 2009–2010.

Note: Inflation-adjusted figures are computed as in Figure 12.1.

Source: FEC data at www.fec.gov/press/bkgnd/cf_summary_info/2010can_fullsum/2allhistory2010.pdf (accessed November 20, 2011). CPI deflator is the same as that listed for Figure 12.1.

races. In 2009, Michael Bloomberg spent more than $100 million of his own money to win a third term as mayor of New York—about $91 for each voter in that election.

Campaigns for governor in large states often cost at least as much as races for the U.S. Senate. California typically sets the records, as in 2010 when Republican Meg Whitman, former head of eBay, spent more than $140 million of her personal funds in a losing race for the state's governorship. Winning a state legislative race in a large state is an increasingly expensive proposition as well. In 2007, for example, some legislative campaigns in New Jersey cost more than $1 million each, largely because their "local" media originate in the expensive markets of New York and Philadelphia.[3] Even state Supreme Court elections have become big-spending contests. Interest groups spent a total of $26.6 million in state Supreme Court campaigns during 2007–2008, and most of the money came from business interests and trial lawyers who have a big stake in the judges' rulings.[4]

These figures must be kept in perspective. As substantial as the spending has been, the total cost of all American campaigns still doesn't match the amounts some big corporations spend on advertising (see box "Campaign

Campaign Spending: Too Much or Too Little?

What will $5 billion buy in the United States?

- One-fourth the advertising budget of McDonald's in 2010
- All the spending on Facebook advertising in 2011
- About 14 percent of the dollars spent in American gambling casinos in 2010
- One Nimitz-class aircraft carrier (not counting operating costs)
- All the political campaigns run at all levels of government by and for all candidates in 2008

Sources: "McDonald's Looks for New Global Marketing Chief," Dow Jones Newswires, at http://archive.chicagobreakingbusiness.com/2010/05/mcdonalds-looks-for-new-global-marketing-chief.html; Alison Diana, "Facebook Ad Spending to Hit $4.05 Billion in 2011," *Information Week*, January 20, 2011, at www.informationweek.com/news/software/bi/229000995; Amanda Finnegan, "Casino Industry Notches Small Gain in 2010 After Declines, Report Says," *VegasInc.*, May 4, 2011, at www.vegasinc.com/news/2011/may/04/casino-industry-notches-small-gain-2010-after-decl/; and http://en.wikipedia.org/wiki/Aircraft_carrier (all accessed November 20, 2011).

Spending: Too Much or Too Little?" on this page). To the extent that campaigns give us the chance to learn about the strengths and weaknesses of the people who would govern us, the amounts spent on campaign advertising could be considered a real bargain.[5] There are important questions to be asked, however, about the motivations of contributors and the fund-raising disparities among candidates.

WHAT IS THE IMPACT OF CAMPAIGN SPENDING?

Money doesn't always buy victory, but it rarely hurts. In the general election for president, both sides usually have enough money to reach voters with their messages, so the candidate with the largest war chest does not gain an overwhelming advantage. Money matters more in the early months of the nomination race for president, especially in buying the early visibility that is so vital to an underdog. In later primaries and caucuses, when the candidates are better known, a monetary edge does not necessarily lead to a win.

In congressional elections, where we have even more evidence on the impact of campaign spending, most researchers find that money does make a real difference. The more challengers can spend when they run against incumbents, the better are their chances of victory. The same is not true for incumbents. Gary Jacobson found that the more incumbents spend, the worse they do in the race.[6] It is not that incumbent spending turns voters off, but rather that incumbents tend to spend a lot when they face serious competition. A big budget for an incumbent, then, typically means that he or she has (or worries about) an unusually strong challenger. That was true of many Democratic House members and senators who lost their seats in 2010 after outspending their opponents.

Other researchers disagree and report that when incumbents spend more, they do get a return in terms of votes. The dispute turns on thorny questions about the proper way to estimate the impact of spending,[7] but there is general agreement on three points. First, House incumbents do not often face a serious challenge for reelection. Second, challengers need a lot of money to have a chance of beating an incumbent. Third, when they do have a strong opponent, or when national tides run strongly against them (as happened to Democrats in 2010), incumbents may not be able to survive the challenge by pouring more money into their campaigns. For political scientists, measuring the effects of campaign spending is a difficult task. For candidates, the answer is simple: More is better.

WHERE DOES THE MONEY COME FROM?

Candidates can raise money *directly* from only five main sources: individuals, political action committees (PACs), political parties (including the party in government), the candidates' own resources, and public (taxpayers') funds. (Later in this chapter, we will discuss the increasing amounts of money spent on campaign advertising independently of the candidates' campaigns.)

Individual Contributors

It may surprise you to know that most of the money contributed *directly* to candidates comes from individuals, not parties or PACs (see Table 12.2). In the 2010 elections, individuals accounted for 58 percent of the contributions to general election House candidates and 64 percent of the money given to Senate candidates.

The nature of the individual contributor has changed, however. Before the campaign finance reforms of the 1970s, congressional and presidential candidates were allowed to take unlimited sums of money from individuals. For example, insurance magnate W. Clement Stone and multimillionaire Richard Mellon Scaife donated a total of $3 million to President Nixon's reelection campaign in 1972. Well-supported fears that these "fat cats" were getting something in return for their money—preferential treatment ranging from tax breaks to ambassadorships—led Congress to pass the *Federal Election Campaign Act (FECA)* amendments of 1974, which limited an individual's donation to any federal candidate to $1,000, as we will see.

For the next two decades, these limits seemed to work. Because of the reforms, congressional campaigns were financed not by a handful of big givers but by many people making relatively small (under $1,000) donations. That was also true of the nomination phase of presidential campaigns. Even so, this expanded group of small donors remains a very small percentage of the population. These givers tend to be older, wealthier, more conservative and

TABLE 12.2

Sources of Campaign Funds for Presidential and Congressional Candidates

Presidential, 2007–2008 (in millions of dollars)

	Democrats		Republicans		Total	
	Nomination	General	Nomination	General	Nomination	General
Individuals	699.7	320.0	389.9	0	1089.6	320.0
Candidates	13.2	0	45.7	0	58.9	0
PAC and party direct	2.7	1.0	2.4	0	5.1	1.0
Party coordinated*	0	6.4	0	18.9	0	25.3
Party independent*	0	1.1	0	53.5	0	54.6
Public funds	17.5	0	2.6	84.1	21.0	84.1
Legal, accounting	0.2	0	1.2	46.4	1.4	46.4
Other	5.6	0.5	6.2	0	11.8	0.6
Total	738.9	321.5	448.0	130.5	1187.8	452.1

Congressional, 2009–2010 (in millions of dollars)

	Democrats		Republicans		Total		Grand
	House	Senate	House	Senate	House	Senate	Total
Individuals	262.6	166.1	289.7	190.0	553.9	369.0	922.8
Candidate contributions	3.5	0.2	7.3	2.2	11.6	2.7	14.3
Candidate loans	7.9	6.3	34.8	71.5	44.0	78.1	122.1
PACs	191.2	36.9	128.1	41.3	319.3	78.8	398.0
National party contributions	0.6	0.7	0.6	1.1	1.2	1.8	3.0
National party coordinated*	3.7	10.8	6.1	17.3	9.8	28.1	37.9
Party independent*	65.7	41.5	46.2	25.9	111.9	67.4	179.3
Other	10.3	16.0	13.2	26.7	23.5	43.4	66.8
Total	476.1	226.2	473.7	332.8	953.5	573.8	1527

*Party-coordinated and party-independent expenditures are spent on behalf of the candidate rather than given to the campaign, so they are not included in the totals at the bottom of the table. In some cases, the figures for Democrats and Republicans do not add up to the sums in the "total" columns because the latter also include funds for minor party candidates. "Other" includes interest, dividends, and vendor and individual refunds.

Sources: FEC data: for the presidential nomination race, as of September 11, 2009; for party funding and general election congressional races, as of July 19, 2011.

Republican than the average American voter and more likely to be male than female.[8] But they resemble the typical American more closely than the Stones and the Scaifes did.

The $1,000 limit meant that campaigns had to learn new ways to get a lot of small donors to contribute. When wealthy "fat cats" were the preferred funding source, they were wooed by star-studded dinners and personal visits and phone calls with the candidate. The small contributors are usually solicited by mail and e-mail. Overall, about a third of the money Obama raised from individual donations in the 2008 general election came from small donors (of a total contribution of $200 or less), much of it online—a pattern repeated in his reelection campaign. Of course, this means that two-thirds of Obama's funds came from donors of more than $200, and that was even more true of congressional campaigns in 2010.[9]

Political Action Committees

PACs are political groups, other than party organizations, whose purpose is to raise and spend money to influence elections. Most PACs have been created by corporations, labor unions, or trade associations; the heavy hitters are in the fields of finance, real estate, health care, communications, and energy. Corporations and unions are currently allowed to give money to federal candidates only through a PAC. The corporation, trade association, or union then becomes the PAC's "parent" group and can support the PAC as it begins its work of raising money. Other PACs have no sponsoring organizations; these so-called *nonconnected PACs* are usually ideological groups of the right or the left. This category also includes *leadership PACs*—those set up by incumbents to distribute money to other incumbents or challengers in their party. Members of Congress contribute to other candidates to gain their support in elections for party leadership positions in Congress or because their Hill committee insists that they "share the wealth."

PACs grew in part because the campaign finance reforms of the 1970s allowed PACs to donate up to $5,000 per candidate, whereas individuals could give only a maximum of $1,000. The reforms also explicitly permitted corporations doing business with government to have PACs. Federal court decisions and the FEC confirmed the legality of PACs and the right of sponsoring organizations to pay their overhead expenses (as long as the PAC's political funds are collected and kept in a fund separate from the sponsoring organization's regular assets and revenues). Once their legality was clarified and their fund-raising advantages became obvious, their numbers exploded in the 1970s and 1980s.

The biggest expansion has been among corporate and nonconnected PACs. Corporate PACs increased from 15 percent of the 1974 total to 33 percent by 2011, and nonconnected PACs grew from 0 to 40 percent (but not all of these were active in 2010). The corporate committees are the biggest PAC givers overall; together with trade association PACs (most of which are business related), they provided almost two-thirds of the PAC contributions to federal candidates in 2010. Labor union PACs gave less than a quarter as much. But because labor unions give almost all their PAC money to Democrats, they help to compensate for the usual Republican edge in business contributions (see Table 12.3).

PACs put most of their money into congressional races, even in presidential election years. In 2008, for instance, PACs spent a total of $1.2 billion, but only $4.4 million on presidential candidates. In 2010, they gave a total of $398 million directly to House and Senate candidates. Because House candidates are less well funded overall than Senate candidates, PAC

TABLE 12.3

The Biggest PAC Spenders (in Contributions to Federal Candidates, 2009–2010)

		Contributions to Federal Candidates		
Rank	PAC	Total (in millions of dollars)	To Democrats (%)	To Republicans (%)
1	National Association of Realtors	3.8	55	44
2	Honeywell International	3.7	54	45
3	National Beer Wholesalers	3.3	53	47
4	AT&T	3.3	45	55
5	International Brotherhood of Electrical Workers*	3.0	98	2
6	American Bankers Association	2.9	32	68
7	American Association for Justice (Trial Lawyers)	2.8	97	3
8	Operating Engineers Union*	2.8	88	11
9	National Auto Dealers Association	2.5	44	55
10	International Association of Fire Fighters*	2.4	82	18
11	Credit Union National Association	2.4	57	43
12	American Federation of Teachers*	2.4	99	0
13	Teamsters Union*	2.3	97	2
14	AFSCME*,**	2.3	99	0
15	Carpenters & Joiners Union*	2.3	88	12

*Labor union PACs. Percentages do not always add up to 100 percent due to rounding error.

**American Federation of State, County, and Municipal Employees (government workers).

Source: FEC data from the Center for Responsive Politics at www.opensecrets.org/pacs/toppacs. php?Type=C&cycle=2010 (accessed November 20, 2011).

money accounts for a higher proportion (about a third) of House campaign budgets. In addition to their direct contributions, PACs put a lot of money into independent expenditures: in 2008, $98.8 million for and against presidential candidates and $36.4 million in congressional races. Their independent spending in 2010 congressional races rose to $65.1 million. Some PACs and corporate interests also donate funds to charities favored by powerful Congress members.

Candidates and parties work hard to get PAC money. Both parties' Hill committees connect their candidates with PACs likely to be sympathetic to their causes. Campaigners also seek PAC help directly, assisted by directories that list PACs by their issue positions, the size of their resources, and their previous contributions. Incumbent Congress members invite PACs or the lobbyists of their parent organizations to fund-raising parties in Washington. PACs take the initiative as well. Unlike most individual donors, they are in the business of making political contributions, and they don't necessarily wait to be asked.[10]

What do PACs buy with their donations to congressional campaigns? Most PAC money is intended to gain access for the giver: the assurance that the legislator's door will be open when the group hopes to plead its case on legislation. (Some groups expanded their access in 2011, when almost half of the newly elected senators hired lobbyists as their chiefs of staff.) The result is that most PAC contributions go to incumbents—in 2010, almost $8 for every $1 donated to a challenger. There is little advantage, after all, in getting access to a likely loser. PAC money, like individual donations, therefore flows to the party with the most incumbents. So even though corporate PACs generally prefer to give to Republican candidates, they gave most of their House donations to the majority Democrats in 2008, before switching sides in 2010 in expectation of a Republican sweep.

It seems likely that PAC contributions do help them get access to lawmakers. What elected officials will ignore groups that donated money to their campaigns? But it is harder to determine how intently they listen and whether the PAC's concerns will influence their legislative behavior. There is not much evidence that PAC contributions affect the recipients' roll call votes,[11] although legislators who receive PAC money do seem to be more active in congressional committees on behalf of issues that concern their PAC donors.[12]

There are many reasons why PAC money rarely "buys" votes. PACs generally support legislators who have already shown that they favor the PAC's interests, so it is difficult to claim that PAC money *caused* a legislator's behavior. PACs give most of their money to incumbents and must compete for incumbents' attention with many other sources of influence: party leaders, constituents, and other PACs. Because most PACs give much less than the $5,000 maximum per candidate, many PACs could be considered small donors. Their influence tends to be greatest when they represent powerful interests in the legislator's district, when they are not in conflict with his or her party's position, and when the benefit they seek is of little direct concern to anyone else (such as a small change in the tax laws giving a big break to a particular corporation).

Parties

At the time of the 1970s reforms, party organizations didn't have enough money to be big players in congressional or presidential races. Now that the parties are raising much more money from individuals, elected officials, PACs, and other interests, their role in campaigns has grown, especially in the most competitive races. Even after Congress prevented party committees from collecting unlimited "soft money" (see page 239), the two parties raised $1.5 billion in 2004, $1.6 billion in 2008, and $1.1 billion in 2010.

Parties are allowed to make small contributions (up to $5,000) directly to House campaigns and $43,100 to Senate candidates. More substantial are the two parties' coordinated spending—the funds they spend on behalf of their candidates and in coordination with the candidate's campaign, typically for services such as television and radio ads and polling. Coordinated spending is useful to the party because party committees have more control over how the money is spent than they do in making direct contributions to candidates.

Federal law limits the parties' coordinated expenditures in each race. As of 2012, each party was permitted to spend $44,200 per House race, except in states with only one House district, where the limit was $88,400. The state party can spend the same amount or authorize another party committee to do so. In Senate campaigns, the limit varies with the size of the state's voting-age population: from $88,400 in Delaware to $2.5 million in California.[13] Nationwide, the two parties put $53 million into coordinated spending in 2010. Each party could put a total of about $100,000 in direct and coordinated spending into a House race and much more into a Senate race. But in most races, this party money still amounted to only a small fraction of the candidate's total spending.

Since 2004, however, the national parties have greatly expanded their role in a smaller number of targeted congressional campaigns by using TV ads funded with independent spending. In 2006 and again in 2008, the two parties spent a remarkable $225 million on independent expenditures in House and Senate races. The greater party role depends on continued party fund-raising success. In 2009 and 2010, the declining economy made it more challenging to raise funds, and the Republican National Committee (RNC) suffered a series of administrative and public relations missteps that crippled its fund-raising, so party independent spending in congressional races dropped to $183 million. But in both 2008 and 2010, party independent spending in the most highly competitive House races matched the total amount spent by the candidates themselves.

As Chapter 4 showed, members of the party in government have become important campaign contributors in recent congressional elections. Party leaders and other members of the House and Senate are now expected to make major contributions to their party's congressional campaign committee from their personal campaign accounts and leadership PACs and by raising money for the party and its endangered candidates. These contributions indicate the value that incumbents place on their congressional parties in the effort to reach their policy and political goals.

The Candidates Themselves

Candidates, as they always have, continue to spend their personal wealth in trying to win political office. In 2010, about 6 percent of House general election candidates' campaign funds came from their own pockets in the form of contributions and loans. Senate candidates gave and loaned themselves 14 percent of their total campaign funds (see Table 12.2). These self-funders often lose, however, as did the great majority of the 2010 congressional candidates who spent at least $500,000 of their own money on their races.

Public Funding

Congress voted in the early 1970s to let taxpayers designate a dollar (now $3) of their tax payments to match small contributions to candidates for their party's presidential nomination and, as noted above, to foot most of the bill for the major-party presidential nominees in the general election. The intent was to reduce corruption by limiting the role of private funds. But acceptance of the public funds requires a candidate to abide by low spending limits in each state's primary or caucuses and for the nomination and general election races as a whole. Thus, a candidate who expects to be able to raise much more than the public funding will provide would logically decline the public money in order to escape those spending limits. In the 2008 nomination race, none of the major presidential candidates accepted matching funds, and Obama, as noted above, became the first to decline federal funding in the general election. The Republican-led House tried to end public financing of presidential campaigns in 2011.

Money in State and Local Campaigns

State campaigns generally follow a pattern similar to those at the national level.[14] Individual donors are the most important source of candidates' campaign funds in all but a handful of states, followed by PAC contributions, and then, at greater distance, by funds from state parties and legislative leaders and caucuses. A large portion of the individual donations are of large sums ($1,000 or greater). Individual donors are even more important in local campaigns because parties and PACs play a lesser (although expanding) role at this level.

REFORM OF THE CAMPAIGN FINANCE RULES

For years, American campaign finance laws were a flimsy structure of halfhearted and not very well-integrated federal and state statutes. Reformers tried periodically to strengthen legal controls over the raising and spending of campaign money. A new episode of reform was under way in the early 1970s when the Watergate scandals broke. The revulsion caused by these fund-raising scandals produced the most extensive federal law on the subject in U.S. history: the Federal Election Campaign Act amendments. The Supreme Court invalidated some of these reforms in 1976. Congress then revised the law and did so again in the late 1970s. The resulting legislation put limits on federal campaign contributions and spending and set up a system of public funding for presidential campaigns.

Contribution Limits

In order to end big contributions from wealthy "fat cat" donors, FECA limited the amounts of money an individual, a PAC, and a party organization could give directly to a candidate in each election (primary or general) per year. These limits apply only to federal campaigns—those for the president and Congress. The money contributed under these regulations was called *hard* (or *federal*) *money*—funds raised and spent in accordance with the FECA's rules. A new reform in 2002 called BCRA (which will be discussed later in the chapter) raised the limits for the first time in almost 30 years (see Table 12.4).

◤ TABLE 12.4

Limits on Campaign Contributions Under Federal Law, 2012

	Limit on Contributions		
	Individual	Political Action Committee	State or National Party Committee
To each candidate or candidate committee per election	$2,500	$5,000*	$5,000**
To all candidates combined, per two-year cycle	$46,200	No limit	No limit
To national party committees per year (An individual's total contribution to all PACs and party committees per two-year election cycle is limited to $70,800, with no more than $46,200 of this amount to go to PACs and state and local parties.)	$30,800	$15,000	No limit
To a state or local party committee per year	$10,000	$5,000	No limit
Total per two-year election cycle	$117,000	No limit	No limit

*If the political action committee qualifies as a "multicandidate committee" under federal law by making contributions to five or more federal candidates, the limit is $5,000. Otherwise, the committee is treated as an individual with a limit of $2,500.

**The limit is $5,000 for contributions to presidential and House candidates. National and Senate (campaign) party committees can contribute a joint total of $43,100 to each U.S. Senate candidate per election.

Note: These are the limits on so-called hard-money contributions for the 2012 elections. Individual limits are indexed for inflation; PAC limits (and individual limits to PACs and state parties) are not.

Source: Federal Election Commission *Record,* May, 2011, p. 12, at www.fec.gov/pdf/party_guide_supp.pdf (accessed November 20, 2011).

Public Disclosure

Another main aim of the reformers was to make the sources of campaign money public. They felt that voters could make a more informed choice if they knew who had contributed to each candidate. So FECA required that congressional and presidential candidates publicly disclose their spending and the names, addresses, and occupations of all contributors of $200 or more. All donations to a federal candidate must go through and be accounted for by a single campaign committee; before the reforms, candidates could avoid full public disclosure by using a complex array of committees. Each candidate must file monthly or quarterly reports on his or her finances during the campaign, through December 31 after the election. The FEC was established to receive these reports and make the data available. The FEC's power is limited by inadequate funding, but its public files, available online (www.fec.gov), provide a wealth of campaign finance information.

Public Funding of Presidential Campaigns

As another way to remove "interested money" from elections, Congress passed laws in 1971 and 1976 to provide public (tax) funding for presidential candidates. To get the money, a candidate for a party's presidential nomination must first raise $5,000 in contributions of $250 or less in each of 20 states, as a way of demonstrating broad public support. After that, public funds match every individual contribution up to $250. (This was intended to encourage candidates to focus on small contributions.) And as noted earlier in this chapter, each major party's candidate can choose to take public money to pay for his or her general election campaign. In addition, the two major parties each received $16.8 million in public funds to help pay for their 2008 national conventions.

The public funding treats minor party candidates differently. They receive only a fraction of that total and then only after the election if they have received at least 5 percent of the vote. Once they have reached that milestone, they qualify to receive their payment before the next presidential election. Because of the need to pay cash for many campaign expenses, this provision of FECA adds to the difficulty of financing even a modest third party campaign. Ross Perot, the Reform Party candidate in 1996, is the only minor party candidate ever to qualify for public funding.

Spending Limits

Candidates for president who accept this public funding in the race for their party's nomination must also accept spending limits in each of the 50 states and in the nomination race as a whole. Candidates who accepted these matching funds in 2008 were allowed to spend no more than about $50 million in the nomination race. These spending limits have not kept up with the fast-rising cost of presidential campaigns. As a result, although the availability of public money has helped lesser-known candidates stay in the race and therefore provide voters more choices, no viable presidential candidate would accept public funding in 2012 unless Congress votes to raise the amounts of matching funds and raise the spending limits dramatically.[15]

Congress tried to limit spending in House and Senate campaigns as well. However, the Supreme Court ruled in *Buckley v. Valeo*[16] that restrictions on a candidate's spending infringed on the candidate's right to free speech; those restrictions could be justified only in the case of a candidate who accepts public funding. Congress could apply spending limits to its own campaigns, then, only as part of a plan for subsidizing them with public money. That would mean subsidizing their challengers' campaigns as well. For congressional incumbents, who are normally quite capable of outspending their challengers, this was not an appealing idea.

THE LOOPHOLES THAT ATE THE REFORMS

Not long after Congress passed these reforms, those interested in funding campaigns began to find and exploit loopholes in the law's provisions. The FECA amendments of 1979 and action by the FEC and the Supreme Court steadily chipped away at the framework of the FECA reforms.

Independent Spending

If you run an ad supporting a candidate, and if you work with the candidate's campaign in doing so, then the law treats the ad as a campaign contribution, which is limited by FECA (see above). But the Supreme Court wrote in *Buckley* that if you run your ad independently of the campaign—if you don't consult with the campaign or tell it about the ad in advance—then your right to free speech allows you to spend unlimited sums on your advertising. The Court majority's reasoning was that free speech is fundamental in a democracy— more important than is limiting political corruption—and that because "free" speech costs money to disseminate through TV and other media, Congress can't limit the amount that groups and individuals spend on *ads that are run independently of a candidate's campaign*. The Court said in 1996 that political parties could also spend independently on campaign ads, and in 2003 the Court applied this ruling to publicly financed presidential campaigns.[17]

Since then, the national parties have put most of their campaign money into independent spending. The opportunity to spend unlimited amounts in a race is much more attractive to party leaders than giving money directly to a candidate, which is limited by FECA. Ads funded by independent spending can expressly call for the election or defeat of a candidate. How can a party run ads independent of the candidate for whom it is campaigning? The party is required to segregate the staffers doing the independent spending from the party staffers who are working with the candidate. However, there's nothing to stop the "independent" staffers from telling reporters or bloggers about their ad buys and hoping that media reports will convey the content and the timing of this "independent" advertising.

Independent spending poses many challenges for a democracy. Independent spenders tend to run negative, attack ads. That was true of the great majority of the parties' independent spending in 2010 as well as the larger sums spent independently by labor, business, and other outside groups. One especially memorable ad in a 2011 congressional race portrayed the female Democratic candidate as a pole dancer giving tax money to gang members to buy guns. If a *candidate* launches an outrageous attack, citizens can protest by voting for his or her opponent. If a party, interest group, or individual runs an outrageous ad as an independent spender, who can be held responsible? The independent spender can't be punished at the polls; he or she isn't running for anything. And because independent spenders are not supposed to be coordinating their efforts with a candidate, is it fair to punish the candidate for the offensive ad? Thus, independent spenders are free to say whatever they wish, and neither they nor the candidate they favor can be held accountable.

Soft Money

Congress amended FECA in 1979 to help strengthen state and local party organizations by letting them raise and spend unlimited amounts of money on party building and voter mobilization activities. This unlimited fund-raising, and other funds that the FEC permitted parties to raise outside the FECA limits, as long as it was used for nonfederal (in other words, state or local) party activity, came to be called *soft money*.

The law was interpreted to allow unlimited contributions not only to state and local parties but also to pass through national party committees on their way to state parties. So, although FECA permitted an individual to give no more than $1,000 to a federal candidate per election, citizens—and corporations and unions as well—could also give unlimited amounts of money to party organizations as soft money. These funds could not be spent directly on federal campaigns, but they could pay for any nonfederal portion of a campaign effort, and they had a tendency to migrate wherever they were needed.

In effect, then, soft money became a way for individuals and groups to launder large campaign contributions through a party organization. The parties pushed hard to get the money. In a letter made famous by a Supreme Court case, for example, then-Republican National Chair Jim Nicholson sent a draft of the party's health care proposals to the drug company Bristol-Myers Squibb and asked for any suggested changes—and a $250,000 contribution to the RNC.[18] Fat cats, in short, had reentered the building. It was not the law's stated intention for soft money to become an end run around the FECA contribution limits, but the difficulty of monitoring the uses of these funds made it so. In most states, soft money could be raised not only from individuals and PACs but also from corporations' profits and labor union dues—funds that could not be donated directly to federal candidates under FECA.[19]

Tremendous sums flowed through the soft-money conduit from the early 1990s until 2002, when it was banned at the federal level. In the 2002 election cycle, the national parties' last-ditch drive to beat the deadline for soft money resulted in an impressive intake of $496 million. Soft money had become so attractive a source of funding, especially for the Democrats, who did not have as many hard-money donors, that in 2002 it comprised more than half of the Democratic Party's receipts and more than one-third of the Republicans'.[20]

Issue Advocacy Ads

Issue advocacy ads (issue ads, for short) were originally defined as any political advertising that did not include the terms "elect," "vote for," "support," "oppose," or similar terms. As long as a political ad did not say these "magic words," courts held that the ad was not a campaign ad, because it did not *expressly advocate* electing a candidate. The courts again cited the vital importance of free speech in ruling that these issue ads could be aired by individuals or groups using unlimited funding, even while a campaign was in progress.

In 1996, the Democratic National Committee (DNC) argued that issue ads could be seen as a form of party building and voter mobilization, so soft money could be used to pay for them. The DNC spent a lot of soft money that year on issue ads supporting President Clinton's reelection.[21] This gave the parties another legal way to use big donations from corporations, unions, and individuals in federal elections, despite the spending limits imposed by FECA. These issue ads sounded very much like campaign ads. For example, an issue ad in Hillary Clinton's first race for the U.S. Senate from New York in 2000 featured several photogenic babies wearing New York Yankees caps, while a voice intoned, "Every one of these babies has lived in New York longer than Hillary Rodham Clinton." The ad's intent was clear. But because it did not explicitly say "vote against" Clinton or "vote for" her opponent, it was considered to be issue advocacy and thus could be funded with unlimited soft money.

From the candidate's perspective, issue ads were a mixed blessing. As with independent spenders, the issue ads run by outside groups often conveyed different messages than the campaign would prefer. The ads were usually negative, intended to hold down voter turnout for the opposing candidate rather than to support the candidate they favored. They frequently straddled the line between "hard truths" and outright lies. Some candidates' poll numbers declined after being "helped" by a group running issue ads.[22] And many of the groups funding issue ads use generic-sounding names in order to disguise their source of funding; the United Seniors Association, for instance, would appear to be a group of senior citizens but was actually funded mainly by big pharmaceutical companies trying to influence laws that would affect their profits.[23]

WHAT DID THE 1970S REFORMS ACCOMPLISH?

In short, by 2002, money raised under the FECA limits had been swamped by massive quantities of issue ads, paid for largely by unregulated soft money, and by independent spending. What, then, was the impact of FECA?

Intended and Unintended Effects

At first, the FECA reforms seemed to achieve *most* of their goals. They slowed the growth of campaign spending in presidential races, at least in spending by the candidates' own campaigns, for about three decades. Prior to the reforms, presidential campaign expenditures had tripled between 1960 and 1972. Real spending increased more slowly from 1972 to 2000 and actually declined in three of these eight elections. The contribution limits made small donations more valuable than ever to candidates, which broadened the base of campaign funding. The reforms also opened much of the campaign finance process to public scrutiny.

Like all reforms, however, the campaign finance laws of the 1970s had some worrisome, unintended effects. One of the largest was the imbalance between contributions to candidates, which are limited, and the unlimited spending that soft money, issue advocacy ads, and independent expenditures made possible. The cap of $1,000 on hard-money contributions held until 2002, although inflation had greatly eroded its value during that time. These relatively low ceilings on individual contributions made soft money and independent spending all the more attractive to parties and interest groups. Both these forms of spending raise real questions of accountability and bring back the types of money—big money from individuals and corporate and union treasuries—that the sponsors of FECA had hoped to clean out of federal campaigns.

In the long run, then, the reformers' efforts failed to meet one of their major goals: reducing the influence of "interested money." Currently, probably no more than 1 percent of Americans give money to any federal candidate,[24] and few give $200 or more. The other givers are groups—corporations, labor unions, and other organized interests—that want something specific from lawmakers. Whether they get what they want is not always clear, but we can assume they wouldn't be spending so much if they thought they were getting nothing in return.

Effects on the Parties

For the first two decades after FECA was passed, the prevailing view was that the reforms had harmed the party organizations. By limiting their direct contributions to presidential and congressional candidates, FECA treated the parties as no more privileged in the campaign process than were PACs or other groups. In addition, public funding of presidential campaigns went to the candidates themselves, not to the parties, as it does in most other democracies. That created more distance between the party organization and the presidential campaign.

Since 1996, however, the loopholes in the reforms, including independent spending, soft money, and issue advocacy, gave the national parties the means to raise and spend much more money than ever before. Large amounts of party money went into TV and radio advertising and beefed-up voter mobilization programs. State and local parties, energized by money received from the national parties and by their own fund-raising success, became more involved in campaigns. Some put major effort into the labor-intensive grassroots work that was the staple of party organizations in an earlier era. Soft money allowed the parties to play more of a role in the most competitive races than had been the case in more than half a century. Party organizations invested some of their new riches in long-term state and local party building.[25] However, very few of the party-funded issue ads even mentioned the party labels, so they probably did not help to strengthen the parties' ties with voters.[26]

ANOTHER TRY: THE BIPARTISAN CAMPAIGN REFORM ACT (BCRA)

The unintended effects of the 1970s reforms—and some of the intended effects as well—created pressures for new reforms. In 2002, thanks to the dogged determination of Senators John McCain and Russ Feingold and another set of fund-raising scandals, Congress passed the *Bipartisan Campaign Reform Act* (known as *BCRA*, pronounced BICK-ra, or McCain-Feingold).[27] In order to cut off the soft-money "end run" around federal contribution limits, BCRA banned soft-money contributions to national parties. State and local parties can still accept money from individuals, corporations, and labor unions in amounts up to $10,000 per donor per year, and they can still collect unlimited donations for use in state elections.

BCRA also tried to shrink the issue ad loophole. If an issue ad mentioned a federal candidate, it would be termed an *electioneering communication* and would be regulated, even if it didn't use the "magic words" of express advocacy (such as "vote for," "elect," and "defeat"). These "electioneering" ads could not be aired within 60 days of a general election or 30 days of a primary unless they were funded entirely by federally regulated money or by soft money contributed only by individuals. Ads funded by corporations or unions could not be run during this "window," though they could still be aired at other times. The restriction applied only to broadcast media ads directed at targeted audiences, however, so advocacy groups could continue to use soft money for direct mail, phone banks, and voter registration during this time. Many groups did move their soft money into these activities.[28]

In addition, BCRA increased the individual contribution limit to $2,000 for federal campaigns, raised the overall limit on individual contributions to candidates, parties, and other political committees combined, and provided that these limits would rise with inflation. An even higher limit (called the "millionaires amendment") was set for candidates whose opponents could afford to spend unlimited amounts of their own money to run, but the Court struck down this provision in 2008 as limiting free speech.

Although most congressional Democrats voted for the bill, Democratic leaders worried that their party's fund-raising would be seriously undercut by BCRA. For decades, Republicans had been more successful than Democrats in raising hard money; many more of the individuals able to contribute $2,000 to a campaign are Republicans. Democrats had been able to narrow the fundraising gap by raising soft money from big donors such as labor unions. Within a year after the ban on soft money, the RNC had three times as much cash on hand as did the DNC.

More End Runs: 527 and 501(c) Advocacy Groups

After BCRA, then, Democrats looked for a new way to pour soft money into campaigns. They found it in a class of groups called *527s*. This odd name refers to the provision of the U.S. tax code that allows certain tax-exempt groups to accept unlimited contributions and spend without limit on election advocacy— as long as they do not expressly call for the election or defeat of specific candidates and do not coordinate their activities with federal candidates or parties. These groups could register voters, run get-out-the-vote drives, broadcast issue ads, send direct mail, and distribute voter guides, among other activities.

A small group of wealthy liberals formed several 527 groups in time for the 2004 campaign, including Americans Coming Together (ACT), The Media Fund, and the MoveOn.org Voter Fund. They hoped to raise soft-money contributions and run ads to support the Democratic presidential nominee when his or her funds ran low after the primaries.

Republicans had a harder time building their own network of 527s. Publicity about corporate scandals made business leaders uneasy about contributing to these groups. Finally, however, Republican 527s such as the Swift Boat Veterans for Truth and Progress for America geared up during the summer of 2004, raised tens of millions of dollars, and began putting up ads. All federal 527s combined raked in a total of $433 million in 2004, which replaced most but not all of the soft money the national parties had received in 2002.[29] Spending by 527s declined to about $200 million in 2008, but it was just as concentrated as in earlier years, with the bulk of the money provided by labor unions and contributors of at least $500,000 each. Some of the 527s' ads were among the most vicious attack ads of the campaign.

Congress required the 527s to disclose their contributors and expenses. Soon, the FEC further regulated their fund-raising, treating 527s funding federal candidates more like PACs. As a result, several organizations, including the U.S. Chamber of Commerce, moved their political activity from 527s into another category of groups organized as nonprofits. These groups, collectively called *501(c)s*, have an advantage over 527s: As long as federal campaign activity is not their "major purpose," 501(c)s do not need to disclose the names of their donors. Corporations in particular were attracted by this opportunity to avoid any consumer boycotts they might face if their names were publicly linked with controversial, partisan messages. Most 501(c)s got their funding in very large (often million-dollar) donations from a very few individuals or groups. These groups spent approximately $200 million in the 2008 election,[30] mainly to support Republican candidates and conservative causes.

Each of these channels is useful for certain kinds of fund-raising and spending. Thus, an organization might choose to set up several different types of groups: a 501(c) to run ads with money that the givers do not want to be disclosed, a 527 for advocacy ads and ground war activities, and a PAC to give direct but limited contributions to candidates.

The National Parties Survived BCRA

Although these nonparty groups replaced the national parties as movers of soft money, the parties found alternative ways of raising funds. Starting in 2006, more than a third of the money raised by the national party committees came in small contributions, three times as much as the total from contributors of $20,000 or more. Many of these small donations come via Internet fund-raising. A great benefit of the Internet is that contributions can be received immediately, with the click of a mouse, rather than weeks later as in the case of direct mail.[31] These small donations plus the larger contributions the parties could now raise (due to BCRA's higher limit on individual contributions) allowed the national parties to replace most of the soft money they had previously depended on.

State and local party organizations have not fared as well under BCRA as their national counterparts. After the ban on soft-money transfers from the national party organizations, state and local parties' fund-raising declined, especially that of Democratic Parties. As a result, many state parties reduced their broadcast activity, direct mail, and phone banking. In particular, state parties' broadcast ads for federal candidates nearly disappeared after BCRA. Many state parties helped to make up for these losses by increasing their own fund-raising efforts. But most found it challenging to comply with the complicated provisions of the new law.[32]

In short, BCRA did force the parties to change the ways they raised and spent money. They adapted by increasing their fund-raising and developing more intensive programs to reach small contributors. Donors can give much larger sums to joint fund-raising committees that benefit both the candidates and their national and state parties. And wealthy individuals, corporations, and labor unions are still allowed to contribute unlimited amounts to the national parties to help pay for the national conventions; donors gave $124 million to the parties for this purpose in 2008.

Bundling

By raising the limit on individual donations from $1,000 to at least $2,000, BCRA also encouraged greater use of a practice called *bundling*. Although individual contributions to a campaign are limited, an individual or group can solicit large numbers of these individual donors, combine ("bundle") their contributions, deliver them to a campaign, and take credit for a much more substantial donation. Groups such as the pro-choice EMILY's List and the antitax Club for Growth have given bundled donations totaling hundreds of thousands of dollars to a single candidate. Although bundling is clearly an end run around the contribution limits, it has not been ruled illegal.

In 2008, both presidential candidates asked each of their bundlers to raise at least $250,000 in donations and by mid-August, McCain had received $75 million from 534 bundlers, and Obama got $63 million from 561 bundlers,[33] over 100 of whom raised at least half a million dollars each. In preparation for 2012, the Obama campaign raised the target to $350,000 a year from each bundler in contributions to the campaign and the DNC. Most of the bundlers are corporate CEOs, lawyers, lobbyists, and developers who, like other big donors, have interests in federal policies.[34] Some restrictions were placed on bundling in 2008: lobbyists raising more than $15,000 for a candidate on two or more occasions must disclose their contributions.

Raising the individual contribution limit probably helped jump-start the campaigns of some lesser-known candidates as well. No one is seen as a "real" presidential candidate until he or she gains recognition by journalists and activists. When BCRA doubled the individual contribution limit, it became easier for long-shot candidates, such as Rick Santorum and Haley Barbour in 2010, to raise the funds needed to buy advertising that brought media attention. For most candidates, it was only after having passed this threshold of recognition that they could successfully raise money from small donors.

Citizens United and Super PACs

The Supreme Court helped to dismantle BCRA with rulings culminating in *Citizens United v. FEC* (2010), just as it had earlier opened up huge loopholes in FECA. The Court ruled in *Citizens United* that corporations and labor unions can spend as much as they'd like from their own treasuries on independent expenditures for speech that is an electioneering communication (see BCRA, above) or that expressly advocates the election or defeat of a presidential or congressional candidate. (Both of these types of speech are now referred to as independent spending.) Without this right, the Court's narrow majority argued, corporations' and other groups' free speech rights would be limited.

It was widely assumed that the *Citizens United* ruling would open the floodgates to massive corporate campaign spending. The mechanism for that spending quickly appeared. After a later ruling by a lower court, corporate-funded groups began setting up so-called *super PACs*[35] to fund ads. Super PACs can accept unlimited contributions, including from corporations, unions, and individuals, for the purpose of making independent expenditures; they can directly advocate the election or defeat of a candidate as long as they do not coordinate with candidates or parties. In 2011, the FEC allowed candidates and elected officials to raise money for super PACs (with restrictions). In fact, some super PACs were set up solely to promote the election of a single presidential candidate and led by the candidate's former staffers. Could these PACs' spending be truly independent of the candidate's campaign? If a donor can give millions of dollars to the candidate's super PAC, then what is the point of trying to limit contributions to candidates' campaigns?

Though they began to form only in the summer of 2010, super PACs quickly proliferated. Like all other PACs, super PACs are supposed to report who gave them money. But super PACs could spend money through 501(c) nonprofits, which do not have to report their donors. Corporations and individuals gave millions in 2010 to a conservative super PAC called American Crossroads and contributed additional, unreported sums to its 501(c) sister group, American Crossroads GPS. The super PAC alone pledged to raise $120 million in 2012.

These groups formed especially on the Republican side, paralleling the structure of the national party's campaign committees, because of the money troubles of the RNC. In 2010, conservative groups outspent liberal groups by more than two to one.[36] (See Table 12.5.) That helped Republicans make up for the slight Democratic advantage in candidates' fund-raising. Note, however, that fears of a corporate spending blitz were not realized in that election. As in previous years, the great majority of money spent in campaigns in 2010 came from candidates' campaigns and party organizations, not from outside groups.[37]

Democrats responded by forming several similar groups in 2011, including a 501(c), Priorities USA, and its super PAC, Priorities USA Action, aiming to raise $100 million in 2012. Although Obama had discouraged independent groups from raising and spending money in 2008, the rise of Republican-leaning groups

TABLE 12.5

The Top Spenders Among Outside Groups (on Independent Spending and Electioneering Ads in Federal Campaigns, 2009–2010)

Rank	Group (partisan leaning)	Type of Group	Spending (in millions of dollars)
1	U.S. Chamber of Commerce (Republican)	501(c)	32.9
2	American Action Network (Republican)	501(c)	26.1
3	American Crossroads (Republican)	Super PAC, 527	21.6
4	Crossroads Grassroots Policy Strategies (Republican)	501(c)	17.1
5	Service Employees International Union (Democratic)	527	16.0
6	American Federation of State, County, Municipal Employees (Democratic)	527	13.2
7	National Education Association (Democratic)	Super PAC, 527	10.2
8	American Future Fund (Republican)	501(c)	9.6
9	Americans for Job Security (Republican)	501(c)	9.0
10	National Association of Realtors (bipartisan)	Super PAC, 527	8.9

Source: Center for Responsive Politics, at www.opensecrets.org/outsidespending/index.php (accessed November 20, 2011).

in 2010 led the Democrats to switch gears and encourage liberal independent groups to form and help the 2012 Obama campaign.

Whether these groups will complement or supplant the party committees is not yet clear. The groups can be more nimble and flexible than the party committees, yet can tap big party contributors for their own fund-raising purposes. Most of their funds typically come from a few million-dollar donors, and they can operate very much like candidates' committees, but without the contribution limits. But if the Supreme Court lifts regulations on party fund-raising and spending as well, the party committees will reassert their fund-raising role.

State Regulation and Financing

Candidates for state office are governed by the 50 different sets of state regulations. The Watergate scandals triggered a reform movement in many states during the 1970s, focusing mainly on requiring public disclosure. The movement has broadened since then. When the federal government pushed a number of conflict-filled issues (abortion policy, for example) back to the states, interest group and PAC activity at the state level increased as a result, and so did efforts to regulate it. As of 2012, most states had rules limiting individuals', PACs', corporations', labor unions', and parties' contributions to campaigns.[38] Several states and even some cities (such as Portland, Oregon, and New York City) have provided optional public funding for at least some types of candidates for state and city office, though it typically covers only part of the campaign's costs.[39] But the Supreme Court has signaled that it may strike down some types of these programs, most of which are small and poorly funded.

HAS CAMPAIGN FINANCE REGULATION MADE A DIFFERENCE?

You have now read much more than you wanted to know about campaign finance reform. In some ways, the effort to reform the role of money in campaigns has had an effect. Compared with the "wild West" period of unregulated campaign finance before FECA, citizens (and candidates' opponents) now have a much greater opportunity to learn who is giving money to whom in campaigns. Transparency is not complete, of course, because 501(c) groups can still hide the names of their donors, and groups running independent spending ads can still form using names ("Citizens for the Future") that don't tell viewers who they really are. In 2004, according to one investigation, 98 percent of nonparty groups disclosed the names of donors who paid for their political ads, but in 2010, a much smaller percentage did so—and the sums spent have grown tremendously.[40]

But although contributions directly to candidates are still limited and reported, reformers have been frustrated by the ability of corporations, unions, other groups, and individuals to put much larger amounts of money into campaign ads that look very similar to the ads run by candidates. To those who support recent Supreme Court rulings, that is the way it should be; free speech, they feel, is more important than the effort to limit corruption.

As a consequence, however, many of the reformers' aims—to limit interested money and to slow the growth of campaign spending—are almost as far out of reach now as they were before FECA became law.[41]

MONEY IN AMERICAN POLITICS

Both before and after these reforms, money has played a bigger role in American elections than in those of most other democracies. The sheer size of many constituencies in the United States leads candidates to buy expensive mass media time. The large number of elected officials combined with frequent primary and general elections has produced a year-round election industry. Fund-raising occupies a great deal of the candidates' time even after they are elected, which takes public officials' time away from a thoughtful consideration of the public's needs and may give big contributors undue influence on public policy. And because many contributors have strong, even extreme views on issues, the polarization of the two parties in government is increased.

Campaign finance in Britain works very differently. British election campaigns run for only about 30 days, and candidates and parties cannot buy TV and radio time for ads during this period. Instead, British parties get free time on the government-run BBC network; each major party can air only five TV messages of five minutes in length, each shown only once. British campaigns are organized around their national party leaders, but there is considerable integration between the local parliamentary candidate and the leader rather than the largely separate campaigns of American congressional and presidential candidates. Campaign spending is pocket change by American standards; each party is permitted to spend no more than about $30 million during the campaign year, and candidates' spending is tightly limited as well. On the other hand, interested Britons have the opportunity to watch daily, and often contentious, news conferences by the parties' leaders.

The American system of campaign finance has its consequences. The fact that candidates dominate the fund-raising in American campaigns gives them greater independence from their party organizations once they take office. The parties are working hard to increase their role in the raising and spending of campaign money. Their ingenuity was sorely tested by FECA and BCRA and now by the *Citizens United* ruling, but both parties have shown a lot of resilience in adapting to these reforms.

After all this experience with reforms that fall short of their mark, is there any point in continuing to try to regulate campaign finance? Many would argue that it's a useless effort; interested money will always find its way into the pockets of power. On the other hand, although it is not unusual to see people break traffic laws, that is not normally used as an argument for ending regulations on driving. The lifting of all campaign finance rules would lead to unrestricted influence of big money on politics, even if the big money came from other nations or from organized crime. So the struggle to contain interested money will continue. Reform of campaign finance, like reform more generally, is always a work in progress.

The Party in Government

A letter arrived at the White House in June 2011 insisting that President Obama shut down a gun control program. The program in question was a "sting" operation in which gun dealers were allegedly encouraged to sell thousands of firearms to suspicious buyers. The 31 signers of the letter—all members of the U.S. House of Representatives—claimed that the Obama administration was not only using a questionable enforcement method but also keeping information from Congress about the program's operation.

Obama and every signer of the letter—most of them moderates who belong to a congressional group called the Blue Dog Democrats—are all members of the Democratic party in government. As you may recall from Chapter 1, the party in government includes *any elected or appointed public officials* who see themselves as belonging to that party. They are vitally important to the party as a whole because it is the members of the party in government who pass and enforce laws. They, rather than the party organization or the party electorate, are in a position to give life to the party's proposals on college student loans, pornography, abortion, and gun rights.

So if Obama and the Blue Dog Democrats are part of the same party in government, why did these letter signers attack the president on gun control? The Democratic Party in government, like its Republican counterpart, is a diverse group. In addition to the party in Congress, consisting of everyone elected to the House or the Senate as a Democrat, and the Democratic president, the Democratic Party in government includes Democrats who work for federal, state, and local administrative agencies; Democratic governors and state legislators; Democrats who serve in local elective and appointive offices; and even judges (and Supreme Court Justices) who see themselves as Democrats.

The design of the American political system works against a unified party in government. Because members of Congress are elected separately from the president, they do not need to act as a single Democratic or Republican "team." They represent different constituencies and pressures, so they may have different ideas from one another as to what their party in government should be doing. Congressional candidates are not chosen to run by their party organization; rather, they become the party's candidates by winning voter support in primary elections. Thus, the separation of powers, combined with federalism and the use of direct primaries, are formidable obstacles to the development of a united party working at all levels of government to achieve a coherent set of policy goals. In fact, in some cases, the House Democratic leadership encourages some Democratic representatives, elected from Republican-leaning districts, to vote against their party on a bill in order to please their constituents and win reelection.

For decades, reformers have dreamed of an alternative. One of the most discussed is the idea of *party government*, also called *responsible parties*. Its proponents suggest that American democracy would be improved if the parties were to offer clearer and fuller statements of their proposed policies, nominate candidates pledged to support those policies, and then see to it that their winning candidates enact those programs.[1] Voters would then choose not only between candidates but also, more importantly, between alternative sets of policies and be assured that the winning set would be put into effect. That would greatly strengthen the parties' role in American politics. Local, state, and national parties would work together as the main link between citizens and the uses of government power. Voters, the argument goes, would be better able to hold their government accountable.

Although we do see something close to party government in many other democracies, including Britain, it is not likely to develop fully in the United States without fundamental institutional change. Because of the separation of powers, Democrats can hold a majority in Congress while a Republican sits in the White House, or one party can dominate the House while the other controls the Senate. In fact, in the past half-century, divided control of government has been the norm at the national level and in most states. That makes it difficult for a party to implement all its preferred policies; instead, legislation is likely to involve compromise. Even at times when one party controls both Congress and the presidency, the legislative party might not always be in perfect agreement with its White House colleague, as an exasperated President Obama realized. The party organization can't guarantee that all the party's candidates, selected in primary elections in differing constituencies across the nation, will run on the party's platform. And the party electorate is still connected only loosely to the party organization.

However, the Democrats and the Republicans have been acting more like responsible parties in recent years. Congress and state legislatures now divide more along party lines than they have in decades. Partisanship has a major influence on the staffing of top executive offices and the appointment of judges. As more citizens are being attracted to party work because of particular issues that concern them, the pressure builds for greater party responsibility.

As a result, government policies change depending on which party is in charge of a branch of government. After the Democrats won the presidency and majorities in both houses of Congress in 2008, the national agenda was topped by proposals to increase government spending to stimulate the flagging economy, reform health insurance, and deal with climate change. Then in late 2010, when the Republicans won back the House, the emphasis shifted to cutting government spending and the climate change bill was declared dead. It would be too strong to call the result an American twin of British party government, but we are probably safe in describing it as a distant cousin.

Why have these changes occurred? What does this party polarization mean for American politics? The chapters in Part V address these questions of party influence in government. Chapters 13 and 14 examine the roles of the parties in the organization and operation of the legislature, the executive branch, and the courts. Chapter 15 looks at the degree to which party government can be said to exist in American politics.

Parties in Congress and State Legislatures

U nless Congress voted to raise the limit on the federal debt, economists warned, the U.S. government would have to begin shutting down. House Democrats fell in line with their party leadership and voted to raise the debt limit. John Boehner, the House Republican leader, strongly urged his party colleagues to do the same. A number of House Republicans refused, including many who were serving their first terms. They had been elected to reduce the government's debt, they told their leader, not to allow it to increase. An embarrassed Boehner was forced to modify the bill several times to avoid an economic crisis.[1]

This tense battle over the debt limit shows the dilemma faced by legislative party leaders. Both houses of Congress and almost all state legislatures are organized by party. Party leaders in these legislative bodies have more influence over their workings today than was the case during most of the 1900s. Each of the four congressional parties—the House Democrats, House Republicans, Senate Democrats, and Senate Republicans—is more unified internally, and legislative voting is more intensely partisan now, than it has been for decades. Congressional Republicans differ sharply on important issues from their Democratic colleagues.

Yet the parties' more central role in Congress has not come easily, and it remains conditional. To be effective, the congressional parties must fight an uphill battle against the system's design. One of the most basic rules of American politics, the separation of powers, undermines efforts at party unity. In a political system without a separation of powers—a parliamentary regime, such as that of Great Britain—the party that wins (or can put together a coalition of parties to win) a majority of seats in the legislature becomes the governing party; its leader becomes the prime minister, who in practice heads the executive as well as the legislative branch. If a majority of legislators vote that they have "no confidence" in the governing party's major policies, then either the governing cabinet must be reshuffled or the legislature must be dissolved and its members sent home to campaign for their jobs again. As a result, there is a strong incentive for the legislative party to remain united.

American legislators do not face these pressures. They can reject the proposals of a president, a governor, or a leader of their own legislative party without bringing down the government and having to face a new election. Their constituents probably will not punish them for doing so. But in Congress and many state legislatures in recent years, several forces are encouraging members of each legislative party to hang together.

To some analysts, these increasing levels of party unity don't reflect the power of *party* in legislative life. Rather, they suggest, legislators rely on their own preferences on issues when they vote, and to an increasing extent, conservative legislators have sorted themselves into the Republican Party and liberals into the Democratic Party.[2] However, there is ample evidence that changes in the parties outside of Congress, organizational reforms, and party leaders themselves have expanded the roles and power of the legislative parties.[3]

HOW THE PARTIES ARE ORGANIZED IN CONGRESS

Soon after the founding of the American government, members of Congress created political parties to serve their needs. Over time, these legislative parties came to coordinate ideas about public policy, set priorities, divide up the workload in moving legislation, try to get the party's bills passed, hold their leaders accountable, protect the party's reputation, and help party candidates get elected.[4] The congressional parties are independent of the national, state, and local party organizations but have ties to these organizations.

The members of each legislative party come together in meetings (called *caucuses* by the House Democrats and *conferences* by the Senate Democrats and both Republican parties) to select their party's leaders (see box "Party Leadership Positions in the House and Senate" on page 254). They also structure the chamber itself by nominating candidates for its presiding officer (the Speaker of the House of Representatives or president pro tempore of the Senate) and approving procedures for appointing party members to congressional committees.

The majority party dominates the organization of both houses. In the House, the majority party's elected leader, the Speaker, has extensive power over the chamber's operations. The majority party leadership controls the action in committees and on the floor and chooses the chairs of all the committees. Most of each committee's members come from the majority party, by a margin that is often larger than the majority's margin in the chamber. The Democrats held the House majority from the early 1950s until 1995 and again from 2007 to 2011. In the Senate, the majority leader manages floor action, to the degree that floor action can be managed in that highly individualistic institution. Democrats have held a Senate majority since 2007, but Republicans were in the majority from 1981 to 1987 and for most of the period from 1995 to 2007.

Party Leadership Positions in the House and Senate

Each party creates its own leadership structure in each house of Congress; the individual leaders are elected by the entire party membership of the chamber. At the top of the hierarchy is the party leader (called the *majority* or *minority leader*, depending on whether the party controls the chamber). In the House of Representatives, the *Speaker* ranks above the majority leader as the true leader of the majority party. These party leaders have assistants called *whips, and senior, deputy or assistant whips,* who tell members the party's position on bills, try to convince them to vote the way the party leadership wants, and keep a head count of each bill's supporters and opponents.

Each congressional party also has several specialized leadership positions. There is a *conference* or (among House Democrats) *caucus chair* to head the meeting of all party members. Other chairs are selected for the *Steering Committee,* which assigns party members to committees; the *Policy Committee,* which identifies the party's position on proposed legislation and sets issue priorities; the *Campaign Committee,* which provides campaign support to the party's congressional candidates; and any other committees the legislative party may create. Variations do occur; House Democrats, for example, have a single Steering and Policy Committee. ■

Changes in the Power of House Party Leaders

Congressional party leaders, especially those in the House, were very powerful a century ago, were weaker for most of the 1900s, and are now in a position of strength again. These changes reflect differences in the degree to which a party's members in Congress are willing to accept strong leadership. Because party leaders in Congress are chosen by the votes of all members of their legislative party, their power is, in effect, delegated to them by their party caucus (or conference), and they serve subject to its approval.[5]

The Revolt Against "Czar" Cannon Years ago, power in the House of Representatives was highly centralized in the hands of the Speaker. In the first decade of the 1900s, powerful Speaker Joe Cannon chaired the Rules Committee, the "traffic cop" through which he could control the flow of legislation to the floor. He appointed all standing committees and their chairs, putting his chief supporters in key positions, and generally had the resources and sanctions needed to enforce party discipline.[6]

In 1910, however, dissidents within his own party combined with the minority Democrats to revolt against "Czar" Cannon. For many decades after that, Speakers were not able to muster the kind of power that Cannon commanded. Instead, they had to operate in a much more decentralized House in which party discipline could be maintained only through skillful bargaining and strong personal loyalties. Successful Speakers during this era, such as Sam Rayburn and Tip O'Neill, were skilled negotiators rather than commanders.[7]

Growing Party Coordination For most of the 1900s, chairs of the standing committees that dealt with proposed legislation were selected using the *seniority rule:* The longest-serving member of the majority party on a committee automatically became its chair. Because of this rule, members of the majority party could win a chairmanship simply by being reelected to Congress many times, even if they did not support their party leadership's position on issues—in fact, even if they voted with the *other* party more often than with their own. That gave long-serving party members—many of them conservative southern Democrats—a base of power in Congress independent of the party leaders. Committee chairs could, and often did, use that power in an autocratic manner.

During the 1970s, under the prodding of the reform-minded Democratic Study Group and the wave of liberals elected in the wake of the Watergate scandals, Democrats took more serious steps toward greater policy coordination by strengthening the party caucus and then the party leadership. The growing number of liberals in the Democratic caucus pushed for several reforms to limit the independence of the committee chairs. First, the caucus weakened the seniority rule. It gave itself the right to vote by secret ballot on whether each committee chair would be retained. Soon after, the caucus did replace a few chairs with less senior Democrats whose views and behavior were more acceptable to liberals in the caucus.[8] The remaining committee chairs, and those who wanted to become chairs, saw that they needed to pay more attention to the views of the caucus. By reducing the chairs' autonomy, this reform expanded the power of their main competitors, the party leaders. And because the Democrats ran the House, it changed the structure of authority within the chamber as a whole.

The power to assign members to committees—a decision vital to members' careers—was moved to the new Steering and Policy Committee chaired by the Speaker. The Speaker was also allowed to choose, with the caucus's approval, the chair and other Democratic members of the Rules Committee, whose independence had formerly been a thorn in the side of the party leadership. Thus, the Speaker gained more power over other party legislators' futures and the fate of the bills that they wanted to pass. The whip system, a set of deputies responsible for informing their party colleagues about the party's stands and for finding out how many members are supporting those stands, was enlarged and made more responsive to party leaders.[9] The majority party leadership became not just a traffic cop but a major source of power and policy development.

The Gingrich Revolution

The Republican minority had had no input into the Democratic procedural reforms of the 1970s and 1980s. But in 1994, Republicans won a majority of House seats for the first time in 40 years, after a campaign centered on a set of conservative policy pledges called the "Contract with America." The election of a number of new conservative members made the House Republicans even more cohesive. Most of these newcomers had gotten campaign help from Representative Newt Gingrich, then the second-ranking Republican leader in the House, and credited him with engineering their party's unexpected takeover. They elected Gingrich Speaker and gave him unprecedented authority to push the Republican agenda.

To do so, Gingrich set aside the seniority rule entirely. The party leadership could now choose committee chairs on the basis of their commitment to bringing the party's desired bills to the floor. Each committee chair was limited to a six-year term. Why did the committee chairs agree to such a sharp reduction in their power? Republicans had only a slender majority in the House, and they faced a Democrat, Bill Clinton, in the White House. Perhaps GOP members were willing to accept strong party discipline to have a better chance of achieving the goals of the Contract.[10] Or perhaps the change reflected the chairs' personal loyalty to Gingrich, or even fear for their political careers if they resisted. It was a major step in the expansion of party power in the House, and Gingrich became the strongest Speaker since Cannon.[11]

The result, at least initially, was a level of party discipline with which "Czar" Cannon probably would have felt comfortable. When the 10 sections of the Contract with America came to a vote in the House, out of a possible 2,300 Republican voting decisions (10 provisions times 230 Republican House members), there were only 111 "no" votes; 95 percent of Republican votes supported the party leadership's position. To a greater extent than in almost a century, the majority party disciplined itself to achieve policy goals.

... And Later Shifts in Party Control

Gingrich's aura of invincibility started to crumble in late 1995. When a standoff on the national budget between President Clinton and House Republicans led to a shutdown of the government, Gingrich and his colleagues got the blame. The Speaker was dogged by charges of ethics violations and declining popularity ratings. House Republicans were frustrated by his uneven leadership style. An aborted effort to oust him from the Speakership in 1997 had quiet help from some other Republican leaders. Then, when the GOP lost a net of five House seats in the 1998 election, many House Republicans demanded new leadership, and Gingrich resigned.

The Republican leadership maintained control over the selection of House committee chairs after Gingrich stepped down. When the first term-limited chairs were due to be replaced in 2001, new chairs were chosen by the leadership-dominated Republican Steering Committee, which passed over several moderate Republicans to select conservatives who were less senior.[12]

Then the Republicans gained seats in the 2002 elections, and the new Majority Leader, Tom DeLay, was nicknamed "The Hammer" for his ironfisted use of power. The term limit on the Speaker was eliminated, seniority rules were undercut even more in order to move loyal leadership allies into powerful subcommittee chairs, and party leaders cracked down on Republicans who refused to follow the party's lead.[13] Democrats complained that they were being shut out of conference committees and prevented from offering amendments on bills. DeLay called on business lobbyists to help pressure Republican House members to support the party's positions. The Republican leadership was remarkably effective in pushing legislation through the House.

In the rapidly changing environment that has characterized Congress since DeLay was forced to resign in 2005, party leaders' power has had ups and downs, but the movement toward a more powerful party leadership has generally been sustained. Although the Democrats restored the practice of letting the party caucus choose committee chairs when the party won control of the House in 2007, and almost all the chairs chosen by the caucus were the most senior Democrats on their committees, incoming Speaker Nancy Pelosi imposed more party discipline on committee chairs than had previous Democratic Speakers. Chairs were now expected to act in support of the party leadership's aims and to raise a great deal of money for the party candidates' campaigns. And the Democratic Party leadership shut the minority Republicans out of the legislative process with as much partisan zeal as the Republicans under Gingrich and DeLay had shut out the Democrats.

Republicans' outrage at the Democratic leadership's use of its power produced frequent gridlock in the House during 2009–2010. When party control changed again in 2011, Republican Speaker John Boehner permitted a more open legislative process. More extensive floor debate and more amendments to bills were allowed. But the Republican leadership kept a strong hand on the working of the House, reinstated the term limit for committee chairs, and increased party control over the budget process.

Overall, then, the rules changes have made House members more dependent on their party leadership. If members want to pass legislation and advance in the House, they need to show considerable loyalty to their party and its leaders. And if they work hard on their party's behalf, they gain in the long run. To the extent that their efforts help their party gain or keep majority status in the House, members are much better able to achieve their individual goals.[14]

What Caused This Stronger Party Leadership?

One main reason why individual party members in the House have been more willing to accept strong party leadership since the 1970s is that the members of each party have become more ideologically cohesive—more inclined to agree with their party colleagues on issues.[15] As discussed in Chapter 7, white southern voters were leaving the Democratic Party in increasing numbers since the 1970s, and fewer conservative southern Democrats were being elected to Congress. Democratic House members, then, became more uniformly liberal than had been the case in many decades. The sharp gulf that had separated southern Democrats from northern Democrats during the mid-1900s had become an easily bridged creek. Because of the committee reforms, the remaining conservative southerners lost their strongholds of committee power.

Congressional Republicans were becoming more ideologically unified as well and were energized by the conservative policy leadership coming from President Ronald Reagan in the 1980s.

When a party is ideologically cohesive, the party caucus finds it easier to agree on a unified position on legislation. The members of a cohesive party can better trust that their leaders will share and promote their policy concerns and protect their reelection interests. In addition, the two congressional parties were more at odds with one another on issues during this period than they had been for some time. So the legislators of each party became more willing to grant power to their legislative party leaders, including the power to pressure straggling legislators to fall in line, to pass the party's legislation, and to keep the other party from winning votes.[16]

This account of the reasons for stronger party leadership is called *conditional party government*, or **CPG**. It stresses that as the two parties' supporting coalitions in the electorate become more *polarized*—the identifiers of a party become more similar to one another in their preferences and more different from those of the other party—the party members representing them in Congress become more polarized as well. Then, a party's legislators will grant their congressional party leaders more power to pursue those shared policy goals.[17] Party leaders, in turn, will work hard to protect their party's "brand" in order to get more party candidates elected, because they will gain power by doing so; majority leaders can get a lot more done than minority leaders can.[18]

Note that some party leaders have been more willing than others to make use of these new sources of power. Former Speaker Tom DeLay used and expanded the congressional reforms to become a highly assertive Republican leader. His successor, John Boehner, was not as comfortable with aggressive partisanship. Legislative party cohesion and party leaders' power, then, depends not only on party polarization but also on the skills and inclinations of individual party leaders.

Parties in the "Individualist" Senate

Clearly, the job of a House party leader is challenging, but the work of the Senate's party leaders is more like herding cats. By the mid-1970s, Barbara Sinclair explains,[19] the U.S. Senate had moved from an institution governed by elaborate "rules" of reciprocity, specialization, and apprenticeship, in which powerful committees dominated the legislative work, to a much more individualistic body with a more collegial distribution of power. Increasingly, and with avid media attention, members of the Senate established themselves as national spokespersons on various policy questions. Once they had become political "stars," these senators expected to participate more fully in the Senate's work, on their way, many hoped, to greater glory and higher office.

This change combined with institutional features of the Senate to produce the threat of stalemate. A leading institutional feature is the unique Senate rule of the filibuster—the right of extended debate, used to talk a bill or a nomination to death if the votes are not available to defeat it in any other way. It takes 60 votes to stop a filibuster, a number that is very difficult to achieve. As a result, even the threat of a filibuster is enough to stop legislation in its tracks. Members of the minority have been able to wrest control of the legislative agenda away from the majority by making more frequent use of such threats in the past two decades.

By this time, changes in southern politics had led to greater party polarization in the Senate, just as they had in the House. Issues reaching both houses of Congress were often contentious. Add to this a more partisan Senate and a set of rules that permitted any member to tie up the work of the institution for an indefinite period, and the result is a desperate need for a legislative traffic cop. Increasingly, it has been the party leadership in the Senate that has tried to direct the traffic. Individual senators have come to depend on their party leaders to promote the legislative party's interests, both inside and outside the Senate chamber. So even though the Senate majority leader still defers to committee chairs to a greater extent than his House counterpart (the Speaker) does, Senate party leaders have slowly expanded their power. Term limits were placed on committee chairs in 1995, and in 2005, the Majority Leader got the right to name half the membership of the most valued Senate committees without needing to follow seniority.

The Senate's rules make it harder for the majority to govern than is the case in the House; they do not allow as much centralization of power in the party leadership.[20] So the Senate's majority and minority party leaders consult extensively with their party colleagues, rather than command them, to build the unanimous consent agreements that allow bills to be brought to a vote without risking a filibuster by an unhappy senator. But even in the Senate's more individualistic environment, party leaders now play a more important role.[21]

Parties in the State Legislatures

As in Congress, the legislative parties organize the legislatures in almost every state.[22] They structure everything from the legislative leadership to its committees. The power of the legislative parties varies, however, depending in part on the legislature's rules and on the personal skills and resources of the party leaders. In a few state legislatures, daily caucuses and strong party leadership make for a party every bit as potent as in the recent U.S. House. In others, especially the traditionally one-party states, party organization is weaker than it was in Congress before the reforms of the 1970s.

Most state legislative party leaders have a lot of power over the day-to-day workings of the legislature. They do not usually have to defer to powerful committee chairs. The party leaders can appoint the members and chairs of these committees, often without having to consider the members' seniority. Thus, they can choose chairs and members on the basis of their support for the party leader personally or for their views on issues that the committee will consider. Party leaders also exercise their influence through the party caucus. In many states with strong two-party systems, party leaders call meetings to give members information about upcoming bills, learn whether their membership is united or divided on an issue, and encourage legislators to support the party's position. Leaders in a few of these states even try, occasionally, to get the caucus to hold a "binding" vote calling on all members to support the party's position on an important issue. Where the state parties are not as strong, it is more common for the party caucus simply to offer information or let leaders hear members' opinions but not to try to build consensus.[23]

In sum, although the parties' legislative organizations look similar across the states—their party leadership positions are fairly uniform—they differ in their behavior. Party leaders' power can vary even between the two houses of the same state legislature, as do the influence and effectiveness of the party caucus.[24]

METHODS OF PARTY INFLUENCE

How do legislative parties and their leaders exercise their power? What resources can they use to influence their members' behavior?

Carrots and Sticks

Congressional party leaders have a variety of tools available to affect the behavior of their party colleagues. They rely more on incentives than on punishments because the most effective punishments are limited in their use and occasionally have been known to backfire. The most powerful punishment would be to remove a maverick legislator from his or her seat in the House or Senate. Except in rare cases, however, such as that of Ohio Democrat James Traficant, who was in jail when the House expelled him in 2002, party leaders do not have that power. Only the legislator's constituents can do that, and they are not likely to serve as agents of the congressional party leadership. Thus, representatives and senators can normally vote against their party's leadership, or against major bills proposed by a president of their party, without fear of losing their jobs.

Even the in-your-face disloyalty of supporting the other party's presidential candidate has not been punished consistently in Congress. In 1965, the House Democratic caucus stripped committee seniority from two southern Democrats who had supported the Republican presidential candidate, Barry Goldwater, the year before. But Senate Democrats let Connecticut Senator Joe Lieberman keep his committee chairmanship in 2008, after he not only campaigned extensively for the Republican presidential nominee, John McCain, but also spoke for McCain at the Republican convention and ran for reelection to his own Senate seat as an independent. Democrats worried that punishing Lieberman might lead him to switch parties, which could endanger the Democrats' Senate majority.

Perhaps the most famous example of the weakness of party penalties is the story of Phil Gramm, elected as a Democratic representative from Texas in 1978. The House Democratic leadership gave Gramm, a conservative, a seat on the prestigious House Budget Committee in return for his promise to cooperate with party leaders. But in 1983, members of the Democratic caucus were infuriated to learn that Gramm had leaked the details of secret Democratic Party meetings on the Reagan budget to Republican House members. The caucus took away Gramm's seat on the Budget Committee.

Gramm did not accept his fate quietly. He resigned from the House and then ran—as a Republican—in the special election held to replace him. His constituents reelected him to the House and later to the Senate as a Republican. In fact, he was soon back on the House Budget Committee, courtesy of the Republican leadership! As long as legislative party leaders cannot keep a party maverick from being renominated and reelected and in districts where voters are not impressed by a legislator's party loyalty, party influence will be limited. Therefore, this step is taken very rarely.

In short, House and Senate party leaders have only a few punishments at their command when trying to unify their parties, and there is always the risk that punishing a legislator will cause him or her to defect, or lose his or her seat to the other party, or will give the party leadership a bad public image. Instead, party leaders tend to rely more on incentives to achieve party loyalty. They can offer or withhold desirable committee assignments, help in passing a member's bills, and promote federal projects in the member's district. They can give members useful information about the status of a bill on the legislative schedule. Some researchers find that junior members of Congress are more likely to vote with their party than are more senior members, perhaps because the newer legislators have greater need for the information or other resources that party leaders can provide.[25]

Party leaders can give speeches and raise money for a member's reelection effort. The parties' congressional campaign committees, with their campaign funds and services, have helped promote party cohesion on legislation.[26] Leaders can also use their personal relationships with party colleagues to cajole them through careful listening or more hard-edged persuasion. On a House vote on school vouchers, for example, a reporter described House Republican leaders surrounding a Kentucky Republican who had opposed the leadership on this bill the week before. A senior Democrat, "Representative David R. Obey (D-WI) took to the microphone. 'Is anyone from the office of the attending physician present?' he deadpanned. 'I understand someone's arm is being broken.'" The Republican did decide to vote for the bill.[27]

Agenda Control

According to *cartel theory*,[28] another vital source of party leaders' power is their ability to control the legislative agenda. When party leaders can control which bills will come up for a vote, they can derail legislation that could divide their party's members or damage the party's image, and they can forward bills that help the party keep its majority. In recent decades, both parties, when they held a House majority, have adopted rules that concentrate these powers of agenda control in the party leadership. Bills are normally debated under restrictive rules, set by a leadership-controlled Rules Committee, which often prevent involvement by the minority party's members. At times, legislation is combined into "omnibus" bills so broad in scope that individual members have to rely on the party leadership to understand their content. Conference committees, which previously included representatives of both parties to iron out differences between the House and Senate versions of a bill, are now held only rarely and often exclude the minority party. Party leaders negotiate the content of legislation at points in the process that they would not have controlled several decades ago.[29]

PARTY INFLUENCE ON LEGISLATIVE VOTING

When is this party influence most effective? In voting on a bill, a member of Congress could be swayed by any of several forces: not only party but also his or her beliefs about the proper size of government or about the issue at hand, or pressures from the president, campaign contributors, or constituents. Yet researchers have found that the parties in Congress play an important role in members' voting patterns, whether through the direct impact of party leaders' persuasion, the majority party's agenda control, or because of the ability of a member's partisanship to structure issues and create loyalties within his or her own mind.

How Unified Is Each Legislative Party?

Several measures can be used to determine how often members vote with their party. The first, the *party vote*, is the proportion of roll calls on which most Democrats vote one way on a bill and most Republicans vote the other way. The second, *party unity scores* (or *party support*), is the degree to which legislators vote with their party's majority on these party votes.

Party Votes Have Increased A very demanding test of party voting would be the percentage of all legislative roll calls in which at least 90 percent of one party's members vote yes and 90 percent or more of the other party vote no. By such a strict test, party discipline appears regularly in the British House of Commons and the German Bundestag, but not as often in American legislatures. Under Czar Cannon, about a third of all roll calls in the House met this standard of party discipline. From 1921 through 1948, that dropped to only 17 percent,[30] and it declined steadily below 10 percent in the 1950s and 1960s. During approximately the same period in the British House of Commons, this striking party division occurred on almost every roll call.

Since the late 1990s, however, there has been a notable increase in "90 percent votes" in Congress. Since 2009, for example, both houses have been almost perfectly divided by party on a number of major issues, including President Obama's massive economic stimulus spending program, climate change, and the federal budget (see Figure 13.1, Case 1). The most striking

Case 1: Should the EPA be prevented from regulating greenhouse gases to deal with climate change?

House of Representatives

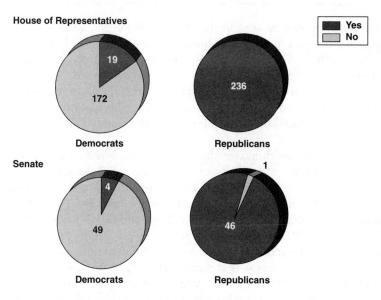

Senate

Case 2: Should the national debt limit be raised and federal spending cut?

House of Representatives

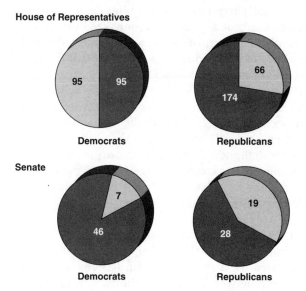

Senate

FIGURE 13.1
Congressional Party Unity and Disunity, 2011

Note: The figure shows the numbers of Democrats and Republicans in the Senate and House casting "yes" and "no" votes on the bills named. Senators Bernard Sanders (I-VT) and Joe Lieberman (I-CT) are counted as Democrats because they caucus with the Democrats.

Source: CQ Weekly, April 11, 2011, pp. 828 and 831 (regulation of greenhouse gases); August 8, 2011, pp. 1763 and 1768 (debt ceiling limit and spending cuts).

evidence of party voting can be seen in the big increase in *unanimous* party votes in the past decade—a remarkable demonstration of party solidarity.[31]

The 90 percent standard is too strict, however, for a look at the American legislative experience over time. So researchers have focused on a less demanding measure: the *party vote*, or the percentage of roll calls in which the *majority* of one party opposed a majority of the other. By this measure as well, the 1990s and 2000s produced the highest levels of congressional party voting in many years.

Let's start where senators think we should—with the Senate. During the late 1960s and early 1970s, a majority of Democrats opposed a majority of Republicans in less than 40 percent of all Senate roll call votes. By the mid-1990s, the figures bounced between 50 and about 65 percent. And when Democrats held a substantial Senate majority in 2009 and 2010, party voting hit a recent high: 72 and 79 percent, respectively.

Party voting has been even more prevalent in the House at times. In the late 1800s, congressional party voting was common (although still far below that of the British Parliament). This was a time when the parties were competitive in most congressional districts, party leaders wielded considerable legislative authority, and Congress was a much less professionalized institution. After 1900, following a decline in the party-based link among candidates for different offices and the development of a more professionalized Congress,[32] party voting decreased markedly. The start of the New Deal party system in the 1930s increased the frequency of party votes for a time, before it fell again to twentieth-century lows (of 27 percent) in 1970 and 1972.

Beginning in the mid-1980s, party voting in the House has reached levels not seen since the New Deal; a 50-year high of 73 percent was recorded in the rancorous 1995 session (see Figure 13.2). As with the Senate, these levels have bounced around since then, generally remaining in the 40 to 55 percent range through 2010. They rose with the new Republican majority in 2011. Overall, since the mid-1980s, "the only line of voting cleavage of any significance in this period was partisan,"[33] and the legislative agenda has been set largely by the White House and the House party leadership.

And So Has Legislators' Party Support To what extent do legislators support their party on party votes? From the late 1930s into the 1960s, conservative southern Democrats often crossed the aisle to vote with Republicans in the House and Senate, and their defections were tolerated by the decentralized party leadership of that time. This cross-party alliance, known as the *conservative coalition*, came together to oppose civil rights bills and Democratic labor and education proposals.

The reshaping of the Democratic Party's supporting coalition in the South seriously undercut the conservative coalition in the 1970s and 1980s. When the Voting Rights Act brought southern blacks into the electorate, the new southern Democratic constituency began to elect different types of representatives. Some conservative southern House members were defeated by moderate and liberal Democrats who could better appeal to black voters. Others retired or switched

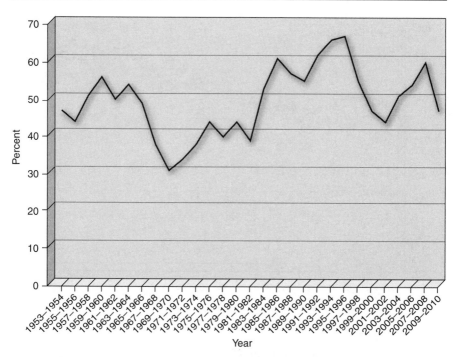

FIGURE 13.2
Party Voting in the House of Representatives, 1953–2010

Note: Entries are the percentage of roll call votes on which a majority of one party opposed a majority of the other party. Because party voting tends to decrease in the even-numbered years, as an election approaches, the data are averaged across the two sessions of each Congress.

Source: Calculated from *CQ Weekly,* January 3, 2011, p. 37.

parties. Most of the rest were unseated by the growing number of southern Republican House candidates. Thus, the Democratic Party in Congress lost most of its conservative wing.

The Republicans elected from the South beginning in the 1970s were more conservative than most of their new Republican colleagues. Since that time, non-southern Republicans have become more conservative as well.[34] As a result, congressional Democrats now tend to represent different types of districts from their Republican colleagues, face different pressures from party activists and organized interests, are recruited from different professions, and hold different views on big issues. As the conditional party government theory suggests, this produced a marked increase in party support, especially after Republicans won control of Congress in 1995 (see Figure 13.3). Party organizational reforms, discussed earlier in the chapter, made it easier for congressional party leaders to unite their party.[35]

The increase in party support has not been uniform. When Democrats regained control in 2007, Speaker Pelosi placed fewer demands for discipline on newly elected moderate Democrats. To retain its majority, the Democratic

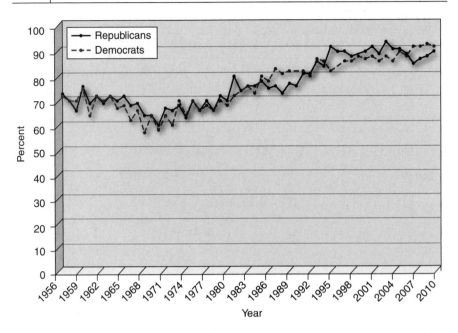

FIGURE 13.3
Average Party Unity Scores, 1956–2010

Note: Entries are the average percentages of members voting in agreement with a majority of their party on party votes—those in which a majority of one party voted against a majority of the other party. Figures for the House and Senate are averaged.

Source: Calculated from *CQ Weekly*, January 3, 2011, p. 37.

leadership needed these freshmen to be reelected in their suburban and exurban districts, which would require them to vote a more moderate line than the party leadership would otherwise push.[36] Many of these freshmen joined the "Blue Dog Coalition," a group of about 50 House Democrats from rural and small-town districts, typically in the South and West, who take moderate positions on issues including taxes and business concerns. Almost half of the Blue Dogs were defeated in the 2010 midterms. Again in 2011, then, both the Senate and House Democratic leadership encouraged vulnerable Democrats to vote against Democratic bills, criticize Obama—in short, do whatever it took to get reelected in a difficult political climate.

Similarly, some Republican moderates in the House (the "Tuesday Group," with 49 members in 2011) and a handful in the Senate continue to differ from their party on social issues such as abortion and civil unions, because their constituencies differ from those of most of their GOP colleagues. At the other end of the Republicans' ideological distribution, a substantial number of conservative Republicans broke with their party leadership on budget issues in 2011 (see Figure 13.1, Case 2), fearing that their district's Tea Party supporters would object that the proposed budget cuts were not deep enough. As long as the American parties cannot protect legislators from constituency pressures, and as long as what it means to be a Republican in New York differs from what it means to be a Republican in Mississippi, party cohesion will suffer.

These are the exceptions, however. Party support has been higher in recent years than it has ever been. In 2010, on party votes, House Republicans voted with their party's position 88 percent of the time, and Democrats did so 89 percent of the time. The comparable figures for the Senate were 89 percent for Republicans and 91 percent for Democrats. In the first four months of the new Congress in 2011, House Republicans voted with their party 93 percent of the time, and Democrats did so 88 percent of the time, much higher than the historical norm.[37] When the Americans for Democratic Action (ADA), a liberal group, examined how often legislators voted with the ADA's position on 20 key votes, the average score for Democratic House members in 2010 was 84 percent and that of Republicans was 5 percent. In the Senate, the comparable scores were 88 and 7 percent. Not a single Republican congressional leader got a liberalism score higher than zero.[38]

Note that roll call voting is only one indicator of the behavior of congressional parties, and the roll calls that get the greatest attention are generally those where party conflict is greatest.[39] To look at party leaders' influence, it is best to consider roll call patterns in combination with the increase in party leaders' other abilities to control the agenda of their legislative chamber, to get what they want in committee consideration, and other leadership tools.

Greater Polarization of the Congressional Parties

As indicators of the size of the gulf between the legislative parties, however, these patterns show that both the House and the Senate are more polarized by party now—Democrats grouped toward the left, Republicans toward the right—than they have been at any time since the late 1870s (see Figure 13.4). The center has shrunk; if all members of each chamber are arrayed along a scale from liberal to conservative, there is almost no overlap between Republicans and Democrats. In particular, each incoming class of Republican representatives has been more conservative than those who have left.[40] In fact, in the 2010 elections, even those Republicans who won formerly Democratic districts tended to be more conservative than the continuing Republican legislators.

One-party districts can add to this polarization. If a House district has been drawn to favor the incumbent's party, then the most likely source of a successful challenge is an ambitious candidate in the incumbent's party, running against him or her in a primary election. In primaries, Republican incumbents are most likely to be challenged from the right; for Democratic incumbents, challenges tend to come from the left. This encourages House members to move toward the extreme of their party rather than toward the center. One study finds that a credible primary challenge moves a typical

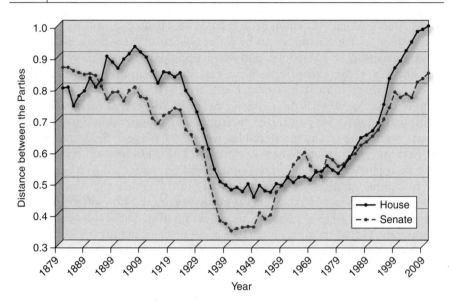

FIGURE 13.4
Party Polarization in Congress, 1879–2010

Note: Entries are the difference in mean DW-NOMINATE scores between the Democratic and Republican Parties in each house for each Congress. These scores estimate the position of each legislator on a liberal-conservative dimension by using the scaling of roll call votes; higher values (closer to 1.0) mean greater difference between the parties.

Source: Keith T. Poole, http://pooleandrosenthal.com/Polarized_America.htm#POLITICALPOLARIZATION (accessed November 21, 2011).

candidate for Congress fully 10 points along a 100-point conservative-to-liberal scale.[41] And as House members are elected to the Senate, that body has become more polarized as well.

The consequence is that these sharp party differences give most voters a clear choice when electing House members and senators. The Democratic-controlled Congress in 2009–2010 had the numbers to pass a remarkable tally of major pieces of legislation, ranging from health insurance reform and over-haul of the regulation of banks and financial services to a repeal of the "don't ask, don't tell" rule keeping gays from serving openly in the military and pas-sage of a new arms treaty with Russia. After the 2010 elections, when Demo-crats lost control of the House, that agenda came to a stop.

When Are the Parties Most Unified?

Students of Congress and state legislatures find that three types of issues are most likely to prompt high levels of party voting and party support: those touching the interests of the legislative party as a group, those involving support of or opposition to an executive program, and those that clearly divide the party's voters.

Issues That Touch the Interests of the Legislative Parties   produce the greatest party unity. Among the best examples are the basic votes to organize the legislative chamber. In Congress, for instance, it is safe to predict 100 percent party unity on the vote to elect the Speaker of the House. In 2011, when the 112th Congress began, Republican John Boehner got every other Republican member's vote for Speaker and lost every Democratic vote.

The parties also tend to be highly unified on issues affecting their numerical strength and on the procedures by which the legislature is run. Party discipline runs high in state legislatures on laws regulating parties, elections, and campaigning; the seating of challenged members of the legislature; and the redrawing of legislative district lines, all issues that touch the basic interests of the party as a political organization.

The Executive's Proposals   Legislators often rally around their party's executive or unite against the executive of the other party. This partisanship has been mounting. In the late 1960s, on average, members of a president's party in Congress voted about 60 percent of the time for issues that he clearly designated a part of his program. By the early 2000s, it was almost 90 percent. In 2010, Senate Democrats supported President Obama's position an unprecedented 94 percent of the time, and House Democrats voted for Obama's position 90 percent of the time in 2009 and 84 percent in 2010.

Conversely, the opposition party's support for a president's program has decreased steadily.[42] Since the 1980s, the opposition has supported the president's proposals only about one-third of the time, on average. The Clinton presidency is an excellent example of this party polarization with regard to the executive. In the early years of Clinton's first term, Democrats' support for their president was higher than it had been since the mid-1960s, and Republicans' support was low. The president became an even more powerful partisan trigger in 1998, when Clinton was impeached by the House for lying about his sexual relationship with a White House intern. Sparked by strongly antagonistic congressional party leaders on both sides of the aisle, the House vote to impeach and the Senate vote to acquit Clinton were close to being party-line votes. Gary Jacobson wrote, "On what everyone claimed was a conscience vote, 98 percent of Republican consciences dictated a vote to impeach the president, while 98 percent of Democratic consciences dictated the opposite."[43] In 2000, Clinton's last year as president, there was a difference of almost 50 percentage points between Republicans' and Democrats' support of the president's position.

When the president's party in Congress marches in lockstep with the president's proposals, it is important to ask whether Congress continues to play an independent role in the business of governing. The other party's united opposition can be a potential check on the executive, of course. But especially in the House, where even a slim majority can exercise a great deal of control, there have been periods of time when a highly partisan leadership has ceded congressional power to the executive branch.

Policies Central to the Party System   Legislative parties are also more unified on issues that fundamentally divide the parties in the electorate—the "label-defining" issues.[44] At the time of the Civil War, the questions of slavery and Reconstruction generated the greatest cohesion within each party and the clearest divisions between the two parties. These issues were displaced by conflicts between farm and industrial interests in the 1890s. Now the parties are most internally cohesive on the role of government in the economy and in people's personal lives, including taxes and the regulation of business. In many state legislatures, for instance, an attempt to limit or expand the rights of unions will pit one unified party against another, as will environmental issues and the rights of women and minority groups. In Congress, a similar set of issues—social welfare, environmental, and tax policy—has produced the most cohesive partisan voting.

The House Freshmen in 2011–2012: Team Players?

In a huge shift in the parties' fortunes, voters elected 88 new Republican members to the U.S. House during 2010. Their numbers alone—they made up more than a third of all House Republicans—would have given them a big impact on their congressional party. They were also viewed by journalists as a unified conservative voice and a strong force for slashing the federal budget. Many argued that they reflected the impatience of voters, "who, they say, are angry about big government and record budget deficits and want sweeping change right now."

Once in Congress, however, these "change now" freshmen painted a more mixed picture. Most supported their party almost unanimously on roll call votes that divided the two parties. But some pushed their party leaders to become agents of more dramatic change. Enthusiastic support from the freshmen stiffened the resolve of more senior conservatives to insist on trillions of dollars of cuts in federal spending. Several lobbied the Republican leadership to insist on deeper cuts in Medicaid and other social programs in the 2011 and 2012 budgets—cuts the Speaker felt might be too radical.

This threatened to expose a tension within the Republican Party. Republican congressional leaders have traditionally been oriented toward the business community, favoring low taxes and less regulation but also help for American industries. But Republican backbenchers increasingly favor draconian spending cuts, even at the expense of subsidies for businesses and highway funding, and their style can be more confrontational. Although the relationship between party leaders and members in Congress may often seem one-sided, with the leaders driving the discussions, in fact it is always two-way.

Sources: Alan K. Ota, "The House: New Majority, New Challenges," *CQ Weekly*, November 8, 2010, p. 2528; quotes from Bob Benenson, "In a Class of Their Own," *CQ Weekly*, May 2, 2011, p. 959.

COMPARING PARTY POWER IN CONGRESS AND STATE LEGISLATURES

In sum, based on what we know about the role of parties in the U.S. House and Senate and the state legislatures, we can draw some conclusions about the conditions most likely to produce strong legislative parties.

Party Polarization and Cohesion   When a party's legislators represent similar constituencies (for instance, when Republicans throughout the state or nation all get significant support from Christian conservatives and very little support from blacks), they are more likely to hold similar views, and party cohesion increases. This greater party cohesion, combined with greater distance between the two parties in the nature of their constituencies and their views on issues, encourages legislators to accept strong party leadership in order to translate those views into policy. Legislative party strength has long flourished in California and other states where the two parties have quite different bases of support—where Democratic strength is concentrated among union members and blacks in the big cities and Republican state legislators tend to represent suburban and rural districts that are largely white and conservative.[45] In most states, legislative parties have become more polarized in the past decade, though not to the same degree as Congress has. Increasing party polarization at the national level has been associated with an increase in party strength in Congress, especially in the House, whose rules, as we have seen, permit greater control by the leadership.

Greater Interparty Competition   There is an interesting relationship between the competitiveness of the two parties and the degree of party voting. At the level of the individual legislator, those from marginal districts, where the two parties have relatively equal shares of the electorate, are generally less likely to vote with their legislative party, and more likely to be responsive to their constituents' preferences, than are those from safer districts.[46] Two characteristics of marginal districts encourage a legislator to be highly sensitive to the constituency. First, both parties in marginal districts often have strong organizations and appealing candidates, so the opposition is a credible threat. Second, in many marginal districts, the groups that support Democrats or Republicans differ from those more typically associated with the party. When party voters in a district hold different views from the national or state party on a big issue, a representative will usually need to bend to constituency wishes in order to get reelected, even if that means opposing his or her legislative party's position.

As we have seen, party leaders may not insist on the member's party loyalty in such situations; they would rather have a legislator who will at least vote for the party's candidate for Speaker than a totally loyal legislator who is defeated for reelection because his or her constituents do not want what the national party is selling. Where constituency and party point in different directions, most legislators remember that their constituents, not their party leadership, gave them their job.

At the level of the legislature as a whole, however, close party competition can increase party voting. When the two parties in a legislature are relatively evenly balanced numerically, "the majority party must stick together to get legislation passed, and the minority party has some realistic chance of winning if it can remain cohesive."[47] Close party competition gives both parties an incentive to remain unified. By contrast, when a party wins a comfortable majority, it can become vulnerable to internal squabbles. That was true of many legislative parties in the South during the period of one-party Democratic rule. It is true today in state legislatures in which one party has a lopsided majority.

No Competing Centers of Power A legislature's standing committees may serve as sources of power rivaling those of the party leaders, as was the case in Congress when seniority was the only criterion for becoming a committee chair. When committee chairs are chosen on the basis of criteria other than party loyalty, the chairs owe less to their party leadership. Seniority is not used as often now in either Congress or state legislatures as a basis for appointing members to powerful positions. Moreover, other centers of power in some states—powerful business groups, labor unions, ideological groups, or other big contributors—are often closely allied with one party's leaders.

Other Needed Resources Where the party organizations have more to offer a legislator, he or she will be more inclined to follow the organization's lead in legislative voting. In Congress and many state legislatures, party leaders can use their power over the legislative agenda to help a member get a desired bill passed. Pork barrel projects in the member's home district can be moved up or down on the agenda by legislative party leaders to help to maintain the loyalty of their party colleagues, as happens in Congress and in at least some parliamentary democracies.[48] In some states, these material rewards, which also include patronage and other forms of governmental preference, are more abundant than in the national government.

The party organizations outside the legislature can also influence legislative voting if they control important resources. State parties' legislative campaign committees help fund legislative candidates in most states, and legislative party leaders' personal political action committees help in some.[49] Given the shortage of campaign funds at this level, many candidates look beyond the legislative campaign committees to the state parties themselves for campaign money and services. The state parties are better prepared to respond now than they have been in the past. Many states place no ceilings on party contributions to campaigns, so parties can make substantial investments, if they wish and can afford it. Another important resource is influence on the nominating process. The leaders of many state parties have become more active in recruiting legislative candidates, and some may be able to convince local activists to oppose the renomination of candidates disloyal to the party (although that ability can always be undermined by primary elections).

Lesser Legislative Professionalism Congress has evolved into a highly professional legislative body. Each member controls a sizable and well-paid personal staff and a considerable budget, which are used to meet the member's legislative and reelection needs. Serving in Congress is a full-time job with good pay and benefits. Although state legislatures have become more professional as well, very few provide ordinary members with levels of support that even approach those in the Congress. Staff and budget resources are usually minimal. Most state legislators are lucky to have as much as a private office and a personal secretary. Many state legislatures meet for only part of the year and pay so little that most members must hold other jobs and live only temporarily in the capital. With such limited personal resources, legislators in most states welcome party leaders' help in performing the tasks of legislative life. When a state legislator depends on the party leadership for needed resources, he or she is more likely to listen when a leader calls for party discipline.

Styles of Individual Leaders   Legislative party leaders in the states, like those in the U.S. House and Senate, vary in their willingness to take up the tools of strong leadership. Their leadership styles interact with the situation of their party—whether it is a powerful majority, a competitive party, or a weakened minority—to determine how effectively they function in uniting their party members and getting their bills passed.

THE POWER OF LEGISLATIVE PARTIES

The story that this chapter tells is complex. On the one hand, parties are at the very center of the legislative process. Some even view them as "legislative leviathans" that dominate the business of Congress in order to benefit their individual members.[50] Party affiliation does more to explain the legislative behavior of state legislators and Congress members than does any other single factor in their environment. There has been an increase in party voting and polarization in recent years in both the U.S. House and Senate.

Yet even now, most American legislative parties are not as unified as those of most other democracies. This is another instance in which the fragmenting institutions of American government have left their mark; because of the separation of powers, there is no institutional need for a party to remain internally cohesive, as there is in parliamentary systems.[51] Although the legislative parties in Congress and the states have been strengthened, the primary relationship in American legislatures is between representatives and their constituents rather than between legislators and their party leaders or party organizations (see box "Which Would You Choose?").

Under certain conditions, such as when the party's legislative constituencies are more alike in their preferences and more different from those of the other party, the legislative parties will be more unified and party voting will be common. That has been strikingly true in the U.S. Congress and many state legislatures in recent years. Increasing party polarization brought the views of legislative leaders and party voters into closer alignment, and members of Congress are not as likely to face a difficult choice between party and constituency. In the institutional world of American legislatures, however, party leaders can never take their power for granted.

Should Your Representative Listen More Closely to the Party or to the Constituents?

To the constituents: This sounds like a no-brainer. If we elect members of Congress, they ought to represent the interests of their constituents, right? We have a single-member district system with candidate centered campaigns; that encourages us to focus on the qualities of individual candidates rather than on the party's platform or plans. We vote for a candidate, and he or she goes to Washington and is then supposed to do whatever we ask. Why should the legislator listen to the party leadership?

To their party: This constituent centered approach sounds good, but it isn't realistic. How are members of Congress supposed to know what all of their 700,000 constituents want? Isn't it better for the two major parties to offer competing answers on issues, press their legislative party members to pass these policies, and then let voters decide whether they like the results? That asks less of us as voters and probably corresponds more closely to the (minimal) time that we are willing to spend on politics. Besides, by taking a longer view, the parties can look beyond local concerns to a broader national interest.

To both: As we have seen, when the various constituencies that a party's legislators represent become more similar in views and more different from those of the other party, most legislators don't have to choose between constituents and party. At these times, members can vote with their party colleagues and also speak for the interests and voters who, in their view, sent them to the legislature. So party and constituency are not necessarily in conflict. ■

The Party in the Executive and the Courts

If you sued your landlord to get your security deposit back, would you get a different ruling if your case was assigned to a Democratic rather than a Republican judge, or to a judge appointed by a Democratic rather than a Republican governor? It may surprise you to learn that in some places, the partisanship of the judge would make a difference.

Most Americans prefer to see courts as nonpartisan, just as we hope for nonpartisan behavior from police officers and the people who inspect restaurant kitchens. Yet, as we see in this chapter, American judges and executives (not just presidents and governors but also the people who head and work in government agencies) are partisans. Many presidents and governors behave like party leaders, and although the writers of the Constitution designed an independent federal court system with lifetime appointments, hoping to protect it from partisan controversy, it has never been possible to design judges who are free of party identification. Heated partisan battles over the nomination of Supreme Court judges show clearly that judicial appointments are matters of great partisan concern.

In many ways, partisanship has penetrated more deeply into the executive and judicial branches in the United States than in other Western democracies. As discussed in Chapter 2, the push for popular democracy led to the election of public officials who would be appointed to their jobs in most other nations, such as state school superintendents and local judges. When administrators and judges are elected, the door is open to party influence in their elections. Even when these officials are appointed, party affiliation is often a criterion for their appointment.

If partisanship affects their selection, wouldn't it also influence the ways in which administrators and judges use their powers? If so, does this reflect party organizations' efforts to influence the behavior of executives and judges? Or is it simply that most people feel closer to one party than the other, and people who consider themselves Democrats tend to share similar attitudes toward political issues, whether they are voters, police officers, or judges, and the same is true of those who identify as Republicans?

PRESIDENTS AND GOVERNORS AS PARTY LEADERS

Not all presidents have been highly partisan figures, but recent presidents have strongly affected their party's public standing. As the most visible members of the party in government, presidents often come to personify their party at the national level, just as many governors do within their states. A congressional aide explained, "The president becomes the face of your party,"[1] as Ronald Reagan was for Republicans during the 1980s and Barack Obama is now for many Democrats.

Several Republican presidents, in particular,[2] have become extensively involved in party activities by helping to recruit and campaign with party candidates and raise money for the party. These efforts have strengthened the bond between presidents and the party colleagues in Congress for whom they campaign. Especially in the current polarized atmosphere in Washington, and in many state capitals and when the party division in the legislature is close, executives nurture ties with their party's legislators to get the votes needed to pass their policies.

The President as Campaigner-in-Chief

Of all the ways in which presidents can help their parties, one of the most sought-after is that presidents are normally a big draw on the fund-raising circuit. George W. Bush was an unparalleled fund-raiser for Republican candidates, even after his own national popularity declined. Barack Obama has been a highly effective fund-raiser for his own campaigns, though many Democratic members of Congress have complained that Obama has been less inclined to do fund-raisers for other party candidates.

Presidents can do a great deal more for their party organizations as well. The state or national party organization often finds itself in the difficult position of trying to convince an attractive but reluctant prospect to run for a governorship, or urging an eager candidate not to oppose a party favorite in a primary. Presidents can be very persuasive recruiters or "decruiters." When the president of the United States calls to encourage the prospect to run, or not to run, that makes the party's job easier.

In 2009, for instance, the governor of New York appointed Democrat Kirsten Gillibrand to a vacant U.S. Senate seat. Gillibrand's poll ratings were not high, and Democratic leaders feared that her vulnerability and her moderate stands on issues would tempt other Democrats to enter the 2010 party primary against her. That would produce a costly intraparty struggle, which could drain funds from the general election race. So President Obama joined other Democratic Party leaders in clearing the primary field for Gillibrand. Her strongest potential Democratic challenger reported, "I spoke with President Obama today. He asked me that I not run for the U.S. Senate this year." The challenger complied.[3]

The President as the "Top of the Ticket"

Even when the president doesn't actively campaign for them, a president's actions and successes can affect the prospects of other party candidates.

Coattail Effects The most direct link between presidential success and party victories has been explained by the metaphor of *coattails*. Presidents ran "at the top of the ticket," the explanation goes, and the rest of the party ticket came into office clinging to their sturdy coattails. (Nineteenth-century dress coats did have tails.) This coattail effect was very common in the 1800s when the parties printed their own ballots, so a voter usually had to cast a ballot for an entire party ticket.

Coattail effects declined from the end of World War II through the 1980s.[4] Members of Congress became extremely good at cultivating their constituency by attending closely to its interests and providing services to individual constituents. This helped to insulate them from outside electoral forces, including presidential popularity.[5] Incumbents gained impressive advantages over their challengers in fund-raising and other campaign resources, especially in House races.

The relationship between presidential and congressional election results has reemerged since the early 1990s, as the parties have become more polarized,[6] though the size of the effect varies from one presidential candidate to the next.[7] Coattail effects can reach into nonfederal races as well.[8]

Coattails Even without the Coat Presidents can influence election results even when they are not on the ballot. Voters' approval of the president's job performance affects their support for candidates of the president's party in midterm congressional elections.[9] In the 2010 midterm, for instance, 37 percent of the respondents to an exit poll said their vote for Congress was meant to express opposition to the president, and 92 percent of this group voted Republican. Fewer voters (23 percent) said they were voting to express support for Obama, and 96 percent of them voted Democratic.[10] It was the strongest relationship between congressional voting and presidential approval in 40 years.

This helps explain why the president's party has almost always suffered a decline in its share of House seats in the midterm election.[11] Most presidents' public approval ratings have dropped by the midpoint of their terms, and the president's declining popularity can drag down congressional candidates of his or her party or discourage attractive party candidates from running.[12] Citizens who disapprove of the president's performance seem to vote in larger numbers in midterm elections than those who approve, and their disapproval can lead them to vote for the other party's candidates.[13]

The 1998 and 2002 elections broke this pattern of midterm losses by the president's party. In both years, voters' approval of the president was either holding steady or increasing. Although President Bush had begun his first term with fairly low approval ratings, his popularity soared to almost 90 percent after the September 11 terrorist attacks and remained consistently above 60 percent as the 2002 election approached. Observers reported that his 90 percent approval among Republicans, in particular, made a difference in close campaigns.[14] But the traditional pattern returned beginning in 2006.

In sum, whether or not they choose to act as party leaders, presidents' popularity and success can influence the likelihood that other candidates of their party will win their races. This happens especially if the candidates' advertising stresses their connection with the president and if the president campaigns actively for them. It gives presidents a potential source of influence over the legislative party colleagues they have helped elect.

PARTY LEADERSHIP AND LEGISLATIVE RELATIONS

To get their programs passed, presidents and governors must gain majority support in their legislature. That is not as easy as it sounds, even if the president's party holds the majority in both houses. To gain the needed support, executives can use their ability to attract media coverage, their public approval (if it is substantial), and the coattails and favors they may have provided to individual legislators. Chief executives also have legislative liaisons: staff people who work with party leaders and other members of Congress or state legislatures to encourage their support for the executive's proposals. A president's "legislative shop" can make a big difference in calming an angry committee chair or providing key information to a wavering supporter. It helps that members of the executive's party know that if they make him or her look weak, they might weaken their own reelection chances. This can encourage them to rally around the president or governor on important votes, even if they would prefer to vote differently.

Legislative Support for Executives

Popular support is a key resource for the chief executive in getting Congress to go along with his or her programs. President Bush's rise in public popularity after September 11 helped him to gain considerable success on the Hill, and his low public approval dragged down his success rate in 2007 and 2008 (see Figure 14.1). Presidents also do better when their party controls both houses of Congress; these periods of time—the early years of the Eisenhower, Kennedy and Johnson, Carter, George W. Bush, and Obama administrations—are typically the president's greatest opportunities for success on legislation. President Obama got historic levels of support from House Democrats in 2009 and 2010, when his party held the House majority—though part of his success stemmed simply from not taking clear positions on many bills until his congressional party had reached some agreement, and many of his victories came after long legislative battles.

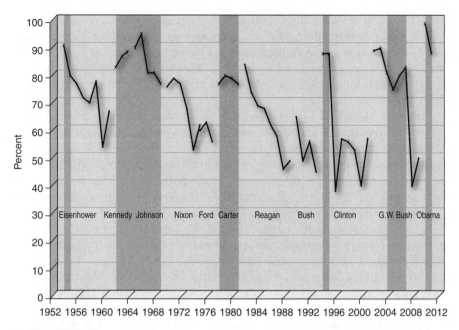

FIGURE 14.1

Presidential Success in the U.S. Congress, 1953–2010.

Note: The entry for each year is the percentage of time members of both the House and the Senate voted in support of the announced position of the president. Years that are shaded are those in which the president's party controlled both houses of Congress (unified government).

Source: CQ Weekly, January 3, 2011, p. 21.

Even unified party control of Congress does not *guarantee* success, however. Since the Bill Clinton years, a huge "public approval gap" has opened between Democratic and Republican identifiers' support of the president; the gap has often reached between 50 and 70 percent. Thus, legislators of the opposition party have every reason to vote "no" on the president's proposals, no matter how often they may praise bipartisanship, because the president is likely to be unpopular in their districts. As Chapter 13 showed, many of Obama's most important legislative accomplishments were passed with almost no Republican votes, thus requiring the president to rely heavily on legislators of his own party. But those party colleagues who represent "swing" districts, in which both parties are competitive, may endanger their reelections if they vote in lockstep with the president. The bigger the president's legislative majority, the more of his party's legislators are likely to come from swing districts.

In addition, the institutional rivalries designed into a separation of powers system help to insure that the president's party in Congress will not surrender all its powers to the co-partisan in the White House. As powerful House Democrat David Obey said in 2009, "I'm certainly willing to work with a Democratic president. But I work with him, not for him."[15]

Divided Control of Government Presidents generally get much less support, of course, when at least one house of Congress is in the hands of the opposing party. Unhappily for modern presidents, divided government has been the rule, not the exception, in the past five decades. During the same period, almost all of the states have also experienced divided party control of the legislature and the governorship.

In times of divided government, executives have two main choices. They can try to negotiate successfully with at least some legislators of the other party. In fact, some researchers find that divided government is as likely to produce significant policy change as is unified government.[16]Alternatively, they can try to brand the other party as the "party of no," the roadblock in the way of progress, hoping that voters will respond by giving the president's party a majority in the next election.

In times of both divided and unified party control, governors have some advantages over presidents in gaining support from their legislative party. In the state legislatures that do not use seniority rules, governors can take an active part in selecting committee chairs and party floor leaders. Most governors have greater control over party rewards and incentives than a president does. On the other hand, governors are not as visible as presidents are, so their coattails and prestige are normally less influential than those of presidents.

PARTY INFLUENCE IN EXECUTIVE AGENCIES

The president is the tip of an iceberg. Below the surface, huge and powerful, lies the rest of the executive branch. The administrators or bureaucrats who work in cabinet-level departments such as Defense and State and in other agencies such as the Environmental Protection Agency (EPA) are charged by the Constitution with carrying out the laws Congress passes. These executive agencies regulate vast areas of the economy—food safety, prescription drugs, and pollution, for example—under congressional mandates that require a lot of interpretation. The bureaucrats who implement these laws, then, shape policy by applying it. It is they who determine, for example, whether morning-after contraception will be available over the counter rather than by prescription only.

How might partisanship (or the chief partisan in the White House) affect the people who work in these executive agencies? Do we see evidence of partisan behavior in federal agencies?

How Is Presidential or Party Influence Exercised?

One major way in which partisan forces can affect federal agencies is that the heads of some of the largest agencies—the cabinet-level departments such as the Department of Health and Human Services and the Department of Justice—are appointed by the president and can be removed by the president as well. These agency heads have often had a long history of party activity. Most of President Obama's cabinet members are long-time Democratic loyalists, just as former President Bush's appointees were long-time Republican stalwarts.

Presidents no longer use these positions as rewards for loyal *party* service; instead, they look for loyalty to the president's *own* aims. Nevertheless, most presidential appointees have been active partisans whose values and political careers have been shaped to a significant degree by their party.

Modern presidents can make only a few thousand of these high-level political appointments, however—fewer appointive positions than some governors have—to try to gain control of an executive branch employing several million civilian employees. Many of these appointees are newcomers with little time to "learn the ropes" and little hope of gaining the necessary support of the career bureaucrats who serve under them.[17] Below this top level, agency officials are less likely to have party experience. These officials are most often chosen for their administrative skills and only secondarily for their political credentials. And most of the remaining agency employees are selected through civil service exams, not party screening procedures.

Another powerful segment of the executive branch is the large number of federal regulatory agencies such as the Food and Drug Administration (FDA) and the Federal Trade Commission (FTC), many of which were established during the Progressive era of the late 1800s and early 1900s. The Progressives worked hard to limit partisan influence in these agencies, including the influence of the president. For instance, the heads of agencies such as the FDA typically have terms of office longer than that of the president who appointed them, in order to block presidential control—and party control, through the president—of the agency's actions. Many agencies are required to be headed by commissions that include members of both parties.

These agencies, like the cabinet departments, deal with complex and very technical policy issues. To decide whether morning-after contraception will be available without prescription, for example, FDA staffers need to be able to read and evaluate complicated scientific literature on the medication's side effects and the public health implications of its widespread availability. Party loyalty does not provide this technical competence (though it may well affect an agency head's interpretation of the technical findings).

Another limit on presidential or party influence over the bureaucracy is that just as individual legislators try to meet the needs of their constituents, administrators have demanding constituencies as well. The EPA, for instance, works very closely with the many industries whose pollution it regulates as well as with a variety of professional and citizen groups.[18] If the EPA's rulings in applying the Clean Air Act outrage electric power companies or big environmental groups, the EPA will be in the political hot seat. Although presidents may try to give their agency heads protective cover at these times, they can't always counteract the impact of a well-financed constituency group.

Changing Partisan Perspectives in the Federal Bureaucracy

In spite of these limits on party and presidential control, the federal bureaucracy (and many state bureaucracies) does respond to partisan forces over the long run. As the federal government expanded in the 1930s, President Franklin Roosevelt drew people who were committed to his programs into the career bureaucracy. They then became a bulwark against later efforts to weaken these programs, especially as these dedicated New Dealers got promoted to more and more senior positions in their agencies.

This pro-Democratic slant could still be seen in the federal bureaucracy decades later. By 1970, Joel Aberbach and Bert Rockman found that nearly a majority of these career bureaucrats said they normally voted Democratic and only 17 percent usually voted Republican. In federal social service agencies, even the administrators who were not Democrats said that they favored liberal policies. So Republican President Richard Nixon, in office at that time, faced a federal bureaucracy that had little sympathy for his conservative agenda. His administration spent a lot of time trying to control the bureaucracy by appointing Nixon loyalists to top bureaucratic positions.[19]

By 1992, however, the bureaucratic environment had changed. In the intervening two decades, Republicans had held the White House for all but four years. When Aberbach and Rockman returned to interview career administrators in comparable positions to those they interviewed in 1970, they now found slight Republican pluralities, although the career executives were still much more Democratic and liberal than the Reagan and Bush political appointees. As older civil servants retired, a new generation, less committed to New Deal and Great Society programs, had been recruited into senior executive positions. Changes in civil service laws further allowed positions formerly reserved for career employees to be filled by political appointees who could be carefully screened by the White House. The bureaucracy was no longer as hostile to Republican initiatives.[20] The Reagan, Clinton, and George W. Bush administrations made serious efforts to put their own stamp on the federal bureaucracy's administration of the laws, sometimes resulting in complaints of partisan bias in federal agencies' activities.[21]

In short, there is evidence of party influence in the agencies of the executive branch. But most presidents and governors use their party leadership role to promote their own programs and reelection, not their party's programs. To the extent that the executive's goals are similar to those of his or her party, of course, the party's program benefits. For most American executives, however, the goals and interests of their party organization are secondary to their own policy goals and political careers.

TRACES OF PARTY IN THE COURTS

Courts and judges are affected by party politics as well. Most American judges—even most justices of the U.S. Supreme Court—are political men and women who took office after careers that involved them in some aspect of partisan politics (see box "The Partisan Backgrounds of U.S. Supreme Court Judges" on page 283). The appointment and election of judges has become increasingly partisan and contentious. Because of the nature of the judiciary, however, party influence can be subtle.

Judicial Voting along Party Lines

Hints of party influence appear when we examine the voting in American appellate courts. Judges appointed by Democratic presidents tend to be more liberal than those appointed by Republican presidents on issues such as civil liberties, labor issues, and regulation.[22] In a study of state and federal courts, in comparison with Republican judges, Democratic judges were found to decide more often in favor of the defendant in criminal cases, for the government in tax cases, for the regulatory agency in cases involving the regulation of business, and for the claimants in workers' compensation and unemployment compensation cases.[23] An environmental research group reported that federal judges appointed by Democratic presidents were much more likely to rule in favor of environmentalists than Republican-appointed judges were.[24] These are the kinds of differences that we would expect to find when comparing the views of Democrats and Republicans outside the courtroom.

The Partisan Backgrounds of U.S. Supreme Court Justices

Justices Appointed by Republican Presidents

John Roberts (*chief justice; appointed by G. W. Bush*) served as an aide to the attorney general and the White House counsel in the Republican Reagan administration and was the principal deputy solicitor general in the Republican G. H. W. Bush administration.

Antonin Scalia (Reagan) was named general counsel for the Office of Telecommunications Policy in the Republican Nixon administration and then assistant attorney general under Republican Gerald Ford.

Anthony Kennedy (Reagan) was a Republican activist and campaign donor in California and then became a legal adviser to Reagan as governor.

Clarence Thomas (G. H. W. Bush) served on the staff of Missouri's Republican attorney general and as assistant secretary for Civil Rights and director of the Equal Employment Opportunity Commission in the Republican Reagan administration. Thomas's wife was a senior aide to former House Republican Majority Leader Dick Armey.

Samuel A. Alito, Jr. (G. W. Bush) was assistant to the solicitor general and deputy assistant to the attorney general in the Republican Reagan administration.

Justices Appointed by Democratic Presidents

Ruth Bader Ginsburg (Clinton) had no formal party positions or appointments prior to her nomination to the Court.

Stephen G. Breyer (Clinton) was a special assistant to the assistant attorney general under Democratic President Lyndon Johnson, assistant special prosecutor in the Watergate investigation, and special counsel and then chief counsel to the Democratic-led Senate Judiciary Committee.

(continued)

(continued)

Sonia Sotomayor (Obama) served as a New York County assistant district attorney, appointed by a Democratic governor. She was recommended for a federal judgeship by a Democratic senator and nominated by both a Republican (G.H.W. Bush) president and a Democratic (Clinton) president.

Elena Kagan (Obama) was appointed U.S. Solicitor General by Democratic President Obama and as domestic policy adviser by the previous Democratic president, Bill Clinton. She clerked for Democratic justices and judges and interned for two Democratic U.S. House members. ■

Similarly, in redistricting cases, U.S. District Court judges have tended to uphold plans enacted by their party more than those enacted by the opposing party,[25] and court rulings on states' voter identification laws (see Chapter 8) closely reflect whether the court's majority was nominated by Democratic or Republican officials.[26] It is not easy to distinguish the impact of judges' partisanship from other influences, including their career considerations, law school training, and desire to protect their professional reputations. Judges show much less party cohesion than legislators do. Yet under some circumstances, Democratic judges rule differently from their Republican colleagues.

What Causes Partisan Behavior on the Courts?

Very little of this apparent partisanship is due to active efforts by Democratic and Republican Party leaders to influence court decisions. In most communities now, openly partisan activity by a judge or pressure by a party leader to decide a case in a certain way would be seen as violating the norms of the judicial system.

A much better explanation for the impact of party on judges' behavior is simply that laws do not interpret themselves; legislatures write laws using general language, and these general laws must be applied to specific cases with varying features. The judges who apply these laws, like the bureaucrats who administer them, have views on political issues and on how much interpretation is necessary or permissible in applying the law to particular situations.

Among the most fundamental of those views are party identifications. Just as the two parties reflect different sets of values, so do their identifiers, including those who become judges. Two judges might vote together on the regulation of business because of values they share about the proper role of government. Those values may have led them to identify with the same party years earlier or were developed out of experience in that party. Increasingly, these partisan values structure a judge's environment. Supreme Court justices, for instance, are now more likely to hire law clerks—lawyers who do much of the work of the Court and help shape its rulings—consistent with their partisanship: conservatives hiring Republican clerks and liberals hiring Democrats.[27] In other words, it is not usually the external pressure from a party leader but rather the party *in* the judge that can lead judges with similar partisan backgrounds to make similar decisions.

Those who appoint judges to their positions are well aware of the importance of judges' value systems. They know that judges have discretion in deciding some cases and that the choices they make may reflect, at least in part, the judge's own experiences and beliefs. This became a major issue in the confirmation hearings for Obama Supreme Court nominee Sonia Sotomayor, who had argued that her life experience as a Latina could add to the Court's breadth of understanding. So the selection of judges, especially for higher courts that receive the most challenging cases, has traditionally taken into account the values and attitudes of the possible nominees.[28]

Party and Judicial Appointments

Parties can affect the selection of judges in several ways. In many states, party leaders may advise on the nominations of prospective judges. That gives them a means to advance party goals by encouraging the appointment or election of judges who believe in the party's values. It also permits them to further the careers of lawyers who have served the party loyally. Even when party organizations don't have that opportunity, the nomination of judges by a governor or a president permits the influence of the party in government on judicial appointments.[29]

Federal Judges Presidents nominate candidates for federal judgeships; the Senate must confirm or reject them. Because prospective judges' party and ideology are important indicators of their attitudes and, thus, can affect their decisions in some kinds of cases, every American president for the past century has made at least 80 percent of his judicial appointments from within his own party; the average is higher than 90 percent.

President Reagan and both Bush administrations took special care to screen candidates for their dedication to conservative principles.[30] Thus, their appointees were even more ideologically distinctive (as well as more likely to have been active in party politics) than average among recent presidents— more than the Clinton administration, for instance.[31] As a result, appellate courts are often the site of bitter ideological battles between Bush-appointed conservative judges and liberal judges appointed by Democratic presidents. It has become routine for Democratic-appointed and Republican-appointed appeals court judges to attack one another's decisions in their own rulings with terms such as "unconscionable," "absurd," and "alarming."[32]

Senate action on the president's nominations to federal judgeships has become more partisan as well. Early shots were fired in the 1980s and early 1990s, when Senate Democrats and their allies waged major battles over the confirmation of two conservative nominees to the Supreme Court: Robert Bork and Clarence Thomas. (In fact, the former case gave rise to a new verb. When an intense, partisan campaign has been mustered against a nominee, he or she is said to have been "Borked.") By the end of the Clinton administration, the level of partisan animosity over judicial appointments was so high that Republican Senate leaders were refusing to schedule debate on some of the president's nominees.[33] The atmosphere surrounding judicial appointments has become more and more hostile as ideological groups of various kinds use these nominations to fire up their core supporters in the public.

State Court Judges State court judges, in contrast, are often elected rather than appointed—a practice used almost nowhere else in the world. Candidates for at least some types of judgeships must run in partisan elections in about a third of the states. Some states use a nonpartisan ballot for judges' races, though party organizations may still endorse their own candidates publicly. In these elections, candidates for judge routinely accept campaign contributions, often from lawyers and groups who will be bringing cases to their courts for a ruling. These contests are more and more costly and at times have become as acrimonious as those for the U.S. Supreme Court.

Even when judges are appointed to their posts, partisanship can still play a role. A number of states have moved toward a "merit appointment" system in which nominating commissions screen prospective judges or recommend a short list to the governor or another official. In these cases, the appointee usually has to run in a retention election within 4–12 years of his or her appointment (see box "Justice Wars" on this page). Reformers hoped that these long terms and the likelihood that the appointee would be reelected (thanks to incumbency) would free judges from party pressures, or even pressures from the governor or president. But partisanship is so often already internalized in the judge's values and preferences that a long-term judgeship merely allows them to flourish.[34]

Justice Wars

In 2010, three Iowa Supreme Court justices who joined a unanimous decision legalizing same-sex marriage were defeated for retention—thrown out of office— by Iowa voters. Retention elections have traditionally been low key; judges up for retention have no opponents and often do not campaign. But in the Iowa election, several out-of-state organizations opposed to same-sex marriage spent heavily on radio and TV ads and touted the results as a warning shot across the benches of other courts around the nation. Judges running for retention in several other states in 2010 found themselves in heated campaigns as well and had to raise large amounts of money to keep their posts—$3 million in the case of an Illinois retention election.

At least as contentious was a 2011 election to the Wisconsin Supreme Court. After newly elected state governor Scott Walker signed a bill greatly limiting the bargaining powers of public employees' unions in the state, the conservative chief justice whose court would hear appeals of the bill was opposed in an election by a liberal challenger. Labor unions and conservative groups raced into this "dogfight."

One Tea Party group sent out a fund-raising e-mail stating, "If radical liberal Joanne Kloppenburg wins, then Barack Obama and his union thug allies will have won." (Kloppenburg lost, but barely.) Judicial elections were publicly financed in Wisconsin at that time, but outside groups have the free-speech right to advertise in these races, and did—to the tune of $5 million. As a result, as one observer put it, the candidates have "almost become bystanders in their own election." ∎

Sources: A. G. Sulzberger, "Ouster of Iowa Judges Sends Signal to Bench," *New York Times*, November 4, 2010, p. A1; quotes from Kenneth P. Vogel, "Big Money, Union Fight Shape Wisconsin Court Race," *Politico*, April 4, 2011, at www.politico.com/news/stories/0411/52455.html (accessed November 19, 2011).

Many European countries choose judges differently. Someone prepares to be a judge through study, apprenticeship, and then by scoring well on a special exam. In the United States, in contrast, there is no special training process for judges—no exam to take, no advanced degree in "judgeship." Any lawyer can be a judge if he or she can win election or appointment to the job. But although the specialized training process required for judgeships in many European nations limits the impact of party organizations and partisan elections, those who become judges will still have political preferences, many of which will have been shaped by their partisanship.

THE PARTY WITHIN THE EXECUTIVE AND THE JUDGE

When we talk about party influence on executives and judges, then, the best explanation for this influence is that executives and judges are people who hold political beliefs, and those beliefs are often related to the individual's party affiliation. Democrats tend to hold different beliefs about government and the economy than Republicans do, and Democratic judges and bureaucrats, similarly, hold different views from Republican judges and bureaucrats. These party differences are reinforced by partisan aspects of the process by which presidents and governors, top executive officials, and most judges are chosen. And the fact that judges and administrators have to interpret laws when applying them allows these differences to be expressed. We rarely see much evidence of direct influence by the party organization on bureaucrats and courts. The parties don't have the means to enforce party discipline in the executive or judicial branches.

Reformers have tried to wring partisan considerations out of the selection process; one example is the use of the merit system to appoint officials. There is good reason to try. When citizens suspect that partisan forces are affecting courts and administrative agencies—for instance, when judges campaigning for reelection get big campaign contributions from lawyers and groups whose lawsuits they will later decide, public confidence in courts and administrative agencies can be undermined. But there is no way to eliminate individuals' beliefs and values, including their partisanship, from their selection as administrators or judges or from their behavior in office.

The Semi-Responsible Parties

In American politics, even when a party wins a majority in government, it still can't guarantee that its promises to the nation—the pledges it has made in its platform—will be carried out. Unified Republican control of Congress and the White House in the early 2000s brought the tax cuts promised by the Republican platform but not the limits on the growth of government spending. And in 2009–2010, when the Democrats controlled both the presidency and Congress, they delivered on their promises to expand access to health care and combat pay discrimination against women, but they could not carry out their pledges on climate change and immigration.

Parties are the most effective means we have of holding elected officials collectively responsible for their actions. If we are not able to hold the awesome powers of government accountable to the wishes of citizens, at least to a great extent, then democracy is at risk. If the American parties can't make elected officials keep their promises, then how can citizens protect their interests?

Some argue that the answer is to create a system of truly "responsible parties."[1] The governing party in this system would translate a coherent political philosophy into government action and would then be held responsible for the results. Others see a more limited problem with party politics. For decades, the American parties have been criticized for being too much alike in their platforms, too centrist, and not clear enough on big issues. Bloggers and other commentators have charged that both parties are under the control of moneyed special interests. The result, they argue, is that government serves well-financed minorities—corporations, labor unions, single-issue groups—rather than the people. These two sets of critics—the scholars who favor responsible parties and the ideologically oriented activists—have different perspectives, but at heart they make the same point. They both want the parties to offer clearer and more detailed stands on issues and for the winning party to put its promises to work in public policy.

To some extent, their demands have been met. The parties' stands on important issues now differ clearly from one another. The Democratic Party is more uniformly liberal today than it was a few decades ago, and the Republicans have followed a more consistently conservative path. In fact, many Americans think that the gulf between the parties has become *too* wide; in recent surveys, almost half of Americans describe the Democrats as "too liberal" and the Republican Party as "too conservative."[2] Have they become more like "responsible" parties, and does this improve their ability to serve the needs of a democracy?

THE CASE FOR RESPONSIBLE PARTY GOVERNMENT

The idea of *responsible parties*, also called *party government*, offers a vision of democracy very different from the traditional American commitment to limited government and the equally traditional American hostility to powerful political parties. Champions of party government believe that we need a strong and decisive government to solve social and economic problems. Our political institutions, they feel, may have been well suited to the limited governing of the early years of American history but do not serve us well today, when we need more vigorous government action against challenges ranging from terrorism to climate change.

However, the public must be able to keep this strong government under control. Individuals rarely have the time, information, or desire to play an active political role or even to find out what their elected representatives are doing. Candidate-centered elections can reduce public control as well; it is much harder for voters to monitor hundreds of different candidates than to judge the performance of one governing party.

How Would Party Government (Responsible Parties) Work?

To solve these problems, party government advocates say, we must restructure the political parties and let them hold elected officials accountable.[3] The parties would take the lead in organizing the government and would, in the process, reinvigorate the other institutions of popular democracy. Party government would work like this:

- Each party would draw up a clear, detailed statement of the principles and programs it favors. It would pledge to carry out those programs if the party wins.
- The parties would nominate candidates loyal to their party's program and willing to enact it into public policy if elected.
- Each party would run a campaign that clarifies the policy differences between the two parties, so voters would grasp these differences and vote on that basis.
- Once elected, the party would hold its officeholders responsible for carrying out the party program. Voters could then determine whether they liked the results and decide whether to keep or defeat the governing party at the next election.

In this system of responsible parties, then, winning elections would not be an end in itself. The party's main focus would be on the policies it has pledged to put into effect. Nominations and elections would become no more—and no less—than a means to achieve certain public policy goals. *For this to happen, all the elected branches of government would have to be controlled by the same party at a particular time.* The party would bind the divided institutions of government into a working whole, as happens in parliamentary democracies.

What qualifies the party to play this crucial role? A prominent party scholar wrote that "the parties have claims on the loyalties of the American people superior to the claims of any other forms of political organization.... The parties are the special form of political organization adapted to the mobilization of majorities."[4] So parties would hold a privileged position in politics compared with interest groups, their major rivals as intermediaries between citizens and government.[5]

Those who argue for party government do not always agree on the purposes they feel a strong federal government should serve. Many conservatives, once suspicious of a powerful central government, grew to like it better when conservative Presidents Reagan and Bush used their power to urge Congress to eliminate liberal programs. Similarly, liberals who were frustrated by the separation of powers developed greater enthusiasm for the principle when Congress proved capable of checking some of Reagan's and Bush's initiatives. It is easier to like party government, apparently, when your party is in charge. In any case, party government advocates feel that a government pulled together by strong parties would let citizens direct their government more effectively than they do now, with even less investment of citizens' time and effort.

THE CASE AGAINST PARTY GOVERNMENT

The proponents of party government are persuasive, but most American political scientists remain unconvinced. Their concerns about party government take two forms. One is the argument that party government would not produce desirable results. The other is that it simply would not work in the American context.[6]

It Would Increase Conflict

First, these skeptics fear that the nature of party government—its dedication to providing clear alternatives on major issues—would stimulate even more conflict in politics. Legislators, they say, would be bound to a fixed party position and would no longer be free to represent their own constituents and to negotiate mutually acceptable solutions. That would weaken the deliberative character of American legislatures.

Critics of party government also fear that a system that makes parties the main avenue of political representation could undercut the rich variety of interest groups that now exist. Without these other means of representing groups and views, the two major parties might be seriously overloaded.

Minor parties would pop up, further fragmenting American politics. In short, critics fear that legislatures would be dominated by rigid, dogmatic political parties unable to resolve problems.

It Wouldn't Work in American Politics

The second major argument against responsible parties is that the idea conflicts with the American government's design. The responsible parties model eases the path to majority rule. But the American founders set up a system that limits majority rule in important ways. They divided constitutional authority among the various levels and branches of government, using the principles of separation of powers and federalism, in order to prevent tyranny. The separation of powers allows voters to give control of the executive branch to one party and the legislative branch to the other. Federalism permits different parties to dominate in different states. Equal representation of states in the U.S. Senate advantages residents of the smaller states. Any change in these and other anti-majoritarian features of the American government would require fundamental revision of the Constitution.

American voters have made enthusiastic use of the separation of powers in recent years. Since 1950, in contrast with earlier times, we have had *divided government* most of the time, so that a president has faced at least one house of Congress controlled by the other party (see Table 15.1). This has been true of most state governments as well since the early 1980s.[7]

TABLE 15.1

Party Control of the Federal Government, 1951–2012

Party Control	Number of Years
Unified	*24*
Democrats control the presidency and both houses of Congress 1951–1952 (Truman), 1961–1968 (Kennedy, Johnson), 1977–1980 (Carter), 1993–1994 (Clinton), 2009–2010 (Obama)	18
Republicans control the presidency and both houses of Congress 1953–1954 (Eisenhower), 2003–2006 (G. W. Bush)	6
Divided	*38*
Democratic president, Republican House and Senate 1995–2000 (Clinton)	6
Republican president, Democratic House and Senate 1955–1960 (Eisenhower), 1969–1976 (Nixon, Ford), 1987–1992 (Reagan, G. H. W. Bush), 2007–2008 (G. W. Bush)	22

(*continued*)

TABLE 15.1 (CONTINUED)

Party Control	Number of Years
President's party controls one house of Congress 1981–1986 (Reagan), 2001–2002 (G. W. Bush)*, 2011–2012 (Obama)	10

Note: The names of the presidents during these years are in parentheses.

*The Senate was Republican controlled for the first five months of 2001 until Senator James Jeffords left the Republican Party and the Democrats gained majority control.

Source: Updated from Harold W. Stanley and Richard G. Niemi, *Vital Statistics on American Politics 1999–2000* (Washington, DC: CQ Press, 2000), pp. 34–38.

Divided government makes responsible party government impossible. When both Democratic-controlled and Republican-controlled parts of the government have their fingerprints on every major piece of legislation, voters find it difficult to figure out which party is responsible for bad policies. Without that ability, voters can't throw out the guilty party and replace it with the opposition.

To party government advocates, divided government helps to explain why the federal government has failed to respond effectively to a number of major concerns from economic downturn to campaign finance. The critics disagree. They contend that unified party government doesn't necessarily produce more significant legislative action, that the federal government has a lot of practice in coping with shared party power,[8] and even that American voters prefer it that way.[9]

The Gingrich Experiment: A Temporarily Responsible Party

Americans have gotten at least a whiff of party responsibility starting in the mid-1990s. In a move spearheaded by House Republican minority leader Newt Gingrich, the great majority of Republicans running for House seats in 1994 signed a statement they called a "Contract with America." In it, they pledged that if the voters would give Republicans a House majority, they would guarantee a vote on each of ten pieces of legislation, all embodying conservative principles, within the first one hundred days of the next Congress. The statement concluded, in words that would gladden the hearts of party government advocates: "If we break this contract, throw us out. We mean it."

The Republicans did win a majority of House seats in 1994. They delivered on their promise; once in office, the new Republican leadership used its iron control of the House agenda to vote on each of the bills before the self-imposed deadline. The House Republicans were more unified on these bills than they had been in decades. That, however, is when party government stalled. The Senate Republican majority had not committed itself to the Contract with America and did not feel bound to consider these bills promptly or to pass them. The House Republicans' efforts were further stymied by divided government; a Democratic president had the power to veto any legislation that made it through both houses.

What can we learn from this experiment? As we have seen, the separation of powers is a mighty roadblock in the path of responsible parties. Even the commitment of a legislative party to a set of clear and consistent principles is not enough to produce responsible party government, as long as the president and the other house of Congress are not willing to go along. There is reason to doubt, as well, that most voters appreciated the experiment; although Republicans kept their House majority in the next election year, so did the Senate Republicans who had not signed the Contract with America, and the Democratic president was reelected as well. So when House Republicans in 2010 announced a strongly conservative agenda titled "A Pledge to America," party leaders advised their candidates to emphasize it in their campaigns only if they thought it would help them win.

Even when the same party controls the White House and both houses of Congress, there are obstacles to achieving party government. Because the parties' candidates are chosen by voters in primary elections, parties cannot insist that their candidates remain loyal to the party's program; candidates who break with their party on important issues can still run, and win, as long as their constituents keep voting for them. Critics of the responsible parties model have also argued that American voters are not issue oriented enough to see politics only through ideological lenses, that the major parties are not centralized enough to enforce a single set of ideals on all their officeholders, and that Americans distrust parties too much to let them try. In short, the idea of responsible parties seems to its critics to ask too much of the voters, the parties, and the institutions of American government.

PARTY COHESION AND IDEOLOGY

Although genuine party government is unlikely in the United States, it is still possible to nudge the parties in the direction of greater accountability. Some observers suggest that this is happening now, in the only way that would be consistent with the American system of separated powers: The party in government, party voters, and the party organization have become more willing to agree voluntarily on a clear party program. But there are limits to the parties' cohesiveness on issues.

Are the American Parties Ideological?

An *ideological party* is one with clear and consistent principles on a wide range of issues, from the purpose of government to the essence of human nature. Examples include the old-style Communist parties and the Muslim fundamentalist parties that have arisen in Middle Eastern nations. The principles of an ideological party offer answers to questions such as these: What values should a government try to achieve? Who deserves to have power, and under what conditions do they forfeit that right?

Throughout their long histories, however, the American parties have tended to be more pragmatic than ideological, focusing on concrete problems rather than on the purity of their principles. Ever since their founding, each party has been a blend of its own original tradition (the egalitarian tradition of the Democrats and the Republican tradition of order and industrial capitalism) with those of other groups that associated with it because of personal ties, geographic nearness, or simple expectations of political gain.[10]

Why have the major American parties rarely been ideologically "pure"? Most important, there are only two of them to divide up a tremendous array of interests in American politics. In a system with several parties, a party can cater to one ideological niche in the voting public and still hope to survive. In a diverse two-party system, with many different interests and people to represent, such specialized appeals can be made only by minor parties—or by a major party intent on self-destruction.

Do They At Least Offer Clear Choices?

Yet even though the two major parties are not as ideological as are those in many other democracies, they have come to differ markedly in their stands on specific issues, and this can increase voters' ability to hold them responsible. We can see these differences in the platforms they adopt every four years at their national conventions (see box "Party Differences on Major Issues: The 2008 Party Platforms" on pages 294–96) and in the policies they pursue when they win. It would have been hard, for example, to mistake the stands taken by the Republican presidential candidates in 2012 on health care, poverty, and the environment from those expressed by President Obama and other Democrats. "Republicans mostly believe that the role of government is to foster greater individual economic achievement, even if it leads to more economic inequality," one perceptive analyst writes. "The Democratic philosophy is that the government should provide a safety net, even if it leads to economic inefficiency."[11] These differences, most notably the Democratic commitment to fund federal social programs and the Republican desire to limit them, have energized the two parties since the New Deal.

Party Differences on Major Issues: The 2008 Party Platforms

Abortion

Democrats: "The Democratic Party strongly and unequivocally supports *Roe v. Wade* and a woman's right to choose a safe and legal abortion, regardless of ability to pay, and we oppose any and all efforts to weaken or undermine that right."
Republicans: "We...affirm that the unborn child has a fundamental individual right to life which cannot be infringed."

(continued)

(continued)

Affirmative Action

Democrats: "We support affirmative action, including in federal contracting in higher education...."
Republicans: "Precisely because we oppose discrimination, we reject preferences, quotas, and set-asides, whether in education or in corporate boardrooms."

Education

Democrats: "The Democratic Party firmly believes that graduation from a quality public school and the opportunity to succeed in college must be the birthright of every child—not the privilege of the few."
Republicans: "We support choice in education for all families ... whether through charter schools, vouchers or tax credits for attending faith-based or other non-public schools, or the option of home schooling.... We will energetically assert the right of students to engage in voluntary prayer in schools and to have equal access to school facilities for religious purposes."

Environment

Democrats: "We will reinvigorate the Environmental Protection Agency.... We will restore the 'polluter pays' principle to fund the cleanup of the most polluted sites, so that those who cause environmental problems pay to fix them."
Republicans: "In caring for the land and water, private ownership has been the best guarantee of conscientious stewardship, while the world's worst instances of environmental degradation have occurred under governmental control."

Global Climate Change

Democrats: "We need a global response to climate change that includes binding and enforceable commitments to reducing emissions, especially for those that pollute the most: the United States, China, India, the European Union, and Russia."
Republicans: "Republicans support technology-driven, market-based solutions that will decrease emissions....Republicans caution against the doomsday climate change scenarios peddled by the aficionados of centralized command-and-control government."

Gun Control

Democrats: "We believe that the right to own firearms is subject to reasonable regulation."
Republicans: "We uphold the right of individual Americans to own firearms."

Health Care

Democrats: "The government should insure that health insurance is affordable and provides meaningful coverage."

(continued)

(continued)

Republicans: "Republicans support the private practice of medicine and oppose socialized medicine in the form of a government-run universal health care system."

Iraq

Democrats: "We will be as careful getting out of Iraq as we were careless in getting in. We can safely remove our combat brigades at the pace of one to two per month and expect to complete redeployment within sixteen months."

Republicans: "To those who have sacrificed so much, we owe the commitment that American forces will leave that country in victory and with honor. That outcome is too critical to our own national security to be jeopardized by artificial or politically inspired timetables that neither reflect conditions on the ground nor respect the essential advice of our military commanders."

Labor Unions

Democrats: "We will strengthen the ability of workers to organize unions... We will continue to vigorously oppose 'Right-to-Work Laws'..."

Republicans: "We affirm both the right of individuals to voluntarily participate in labor organizations and bargain collectively and the right of states to enact 'Right to Work' laws."

Same-Sex Marriage

Democrats: "We support the full inclusion of all families, including same-sex couples, in the life of our nation, and support equal responsibility, benefits, and protections.... We oppose the Defense of Marriage Act."

Republicans: "A Republican Congress enacted the Defense of Marriage Act, affirming the right of states not to recognize same-sex 'marriages' licensed in other states."

Taxes

Democrats: "We will shut down the corporate loopholes and tax havens and use the money so that we can provide an immediate middle-class tax cut that will offer relief to workers and their families."

Republicans: "We support a major reduction in the corporate tax rate so that American companies stay competitive with their foreign counterparts and American jobs can remain in this country." ■

Note: You can find the full text of the platforms at http://www.democrats.org/about/party_platform (for the Democrats) and www.gop.com/2008Platform/ (for the Republicans)

Each major party has become more unified in its stands during the past few decades as well as more different from the other party. A major contributor was the issue of civil rights. As questions of racial justice emerged as an important focus of national policy in the 1960s, white southerners deserted the Democratic Party in increasing numbers and took with them their more conservative views on many other issues. (This story is told more fully in Chapter 7.) This lowered the biggest barrier to unity within the Democratic Party on several issues.[12]

The Ronald Reagan presidency during the 1980s further polarized the parties. Reagan, who was strongly identified with the religious, neoconservative wing of the Republican Party, demonstrated the appeal of a simple vision based on one major idea: less government. His assault on the role of government as it had developed since the New Deal gave a more ideological tone to American politics than had been seen in decades. Since then, more issue-oriented leaders have been selected in both parties,[13] and political issues—purposive incentives—have become more prominent in bringing people into party activism. As Chapter 13 showed, both congressional parties vote more cohesively on issues now than they have in decades. State parties tend to divide along issue lines as well, with Democratic parties more liberal, especially when there is real party competition in the state.[14]

But Internal Divisions Remain

These clear differences on major issues, however, do not add up to the kinds of all-encompassing political philosophies that are found in genuinely ideological parties. Consider, for instance, the interesting relationship between each party's stand on economic policy and its position on issues such as abortion and pornography. Democrats have long stood for an activist federal government in promoting individuals' social welfare but very limited government power over individuals' decisions on abortion. Republicans generally want to loosen the federal government's grip on the economy and environmental regulation but argue for government activism in banning abortion. Nimble advocates could probably construct a rationale as to why these sets of positions are actually consistent. But in reality, these stands coexist within each party's platform because the major parties, as they always have, adjust their policy positions to attract groups of potential supporters—in this case, when Republicans found common cause with conservative Christians and Democrats reached out to pro-choice women—even at the cost of internal consistency.

In addition, because the major American parties are pragmatic and vote seeking above all, neither party has stayed completely true to the principles it articulates.[15] For instance, the Republican platform has long pledged to bring smaller government. Yet after winning control of Congress in 1994 and the presidency in 2000, Republicans in Congress promoted a number of big government programs, from a huge ($500 billion) expansion of Medicare entitlements to a major boost in pork barrel spending. Their aim was to hold the votes of constituents who value tangible economic benefits more than abstract principles. A conservative group tracking the 30 Republicans first elected to the House in 1994 who were still serving there in 2004 found that in their first term, most had sponsored bills that would have had a net effect of cutting federal spending, whereas in 2004, all but two sponsored legislation that would have a net effect of increasing spending.[16] And both parties continue to deal with internal dissent.[17]

What about party voters? Is it true, as some ideologues charge, that most Americans are committed to ideological principles and want the Democrats and Republicans to provide more clearly defined choices? Or are party voters bored with, or even alienated by, the programmatic concerns of many party activists?

IDEOLOGY AND THE AMERICAN VOTER

Media reports of election results frequently use the terms "liberal" and "conservative" to describe voters' choices. The question is more complicated for political scientists, who have long debated the nature and structure of citizens' political attitudes.

How Ideological Is the American Public?

An ideological voter, like an ideological party, would not just hold clear attitudes toward some individual issues but would also connect those attitudes into a coherent structure. However, careful study of American political attitudes raises serious doubt that most voters can be described as "ideological" or even as very consistent in their political beliefs.

Analysts have found that many individuals with conservative attitudes on, say, government spending may express moderate or liberal attitudes on other issues, such as gay rights or the environment.[18] We do not necessarily hold a set of fixed stands, such as an unqualified "yes" on abortion rights and a firm "no" on taxes. Rather, we might feel that taxes are a great burden *and* that they can be necessary at times. We can be pulled toward one of these views under some conditions and toward another view under other conditions. Thus, most people react to issues with a degree of ambivalence[19]—a sharp contrast with a more ideological thinker.

This ambivalence permits many of us to hold sets of beliefs that might drive an ideologue to drink. For instance, large numbers of survey respondents say that they want a smaller government with lower taxes *and* a government that provides more services in areas such as antiterrorism, health care, and education. That is understandable; most people would like to pay less while getting more. But it is not a likely foundation for consistent thinking.[20]

Even in elections when voters are offered clearly contrasting choices, many voters tend to focus on more pragmatic considerations instead. Reagan campaigned for president in 1980 as a principled conservative, yet many voters supported him in spite of his conservative policy positions, rather than because of them. In fact, in both 1980 and 1984 most voters preferred the policy stands that Reagan's opponent stood for, though Reagan won both elections handily.[21] Voters' judgments turned more on their *retrospective evaluations* of presidential performance—their feelings as to whether the most recent presidency had turned out well—than on Reagan's ideological stance.

Because many voters tend to be results oriented, parties and candidates try to stitch together winning coalitions by appealing to a range of qualities— candidates' personal characteristics, group interests, and feelings about the party in power—rather than by stressing ideological differences.

It is important to note, however, that ideology has played a bigger role in recent elections. Analysts disagree on the nature of the change. Some argue that Americans have become more extreme in their views, with fewer moderates and more conservatives and liberals.[22] Others claim that voters remain as pragmatic and nonideological as ever, but that political debate *appears* to be more ideological now because the sides are more clearly drawn. A "partisan sorting" has occurred in which most liberal Republicans have switched to the Democratic Party and most conservative Democrats have become Republicans.[23]

There is no doubt that partisan sorting has taken place. We saw in Chapter 7 the remarkable degree to which conservative whites in the South and liberals in the Northeast and West have moved to the "correct" party since the 1960s. Figure 15.1 shows the extent to which Democrats now call themselves liberals and Republicans consider themselves conservatives. These terms are closely related to people's voting choices as well. In 2008, CNN's exit poll found

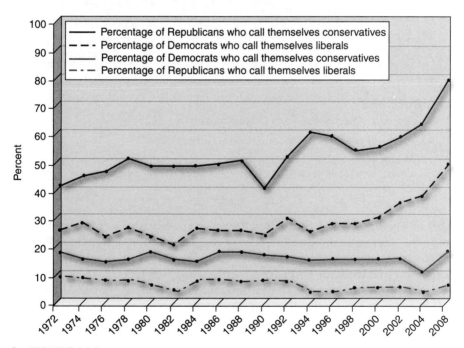

FIGURE 15.1

Increasing Polarization of Democrats and Republicans, 1972–2008.

Note: Lines are the percentages of Democrats and Republicans (including "leaners") who classify themselves as liberal (1–3 on a 1–7 liberal to conservative scale) or conservative (5–7) in each year listed.

Source: 2008 American National Election Study, University of Michigan; data made available by the Inter-University Consortium for Political and Social Research.

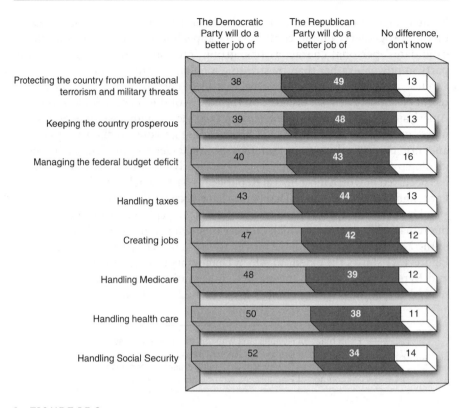

FIGURE 15.2

Percentage of Voters Seeing Party Differences on Issues, 2011.

Note: Rows do not always add up to 100 percent because of rounding error.

Source: AP-GfK Polls conducted June 16–20, and May 5–9, 2001, at www.pollingreport.com/prioriti.htm and Gallup Poll conducted September 5–9, 2011, at www.gallup.com/poll/149783/americans-give-gop-edge-handling-nation-problems.aspx (both accessed November 19, 2011).

that voters who termed themselves liberal or conservative were very likely to pick the "correct" candidate (89 percent of liberals selecting Democrat Barack Obama, 78 percent of conservatives choosing Republican John McCain). Differences between the two parties' activists are even greater.[24]

Much of this "sorting" is a response to changes in the parties' behavior. More polarized party leaders and platforms remind voters of these party differences.[25] Americans are more likely now to see a distinction between the parties on big issues (see Figure 15.2) and to divide by party in their attitudes toward candidates and issues.[26] They are more likely to view their own party's ideology as very similar to their own and the other party's ideology as quite different (see Figure 15.3).

Changes in the media have made a difference too. The wider range of available media outlets allows political junkies to choose programs and blogs that support their own beliefs.[27] Conservatives who watch Fox News and liberals who read

Democratic Identifiers:

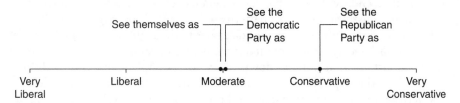

Republican Identifiers:

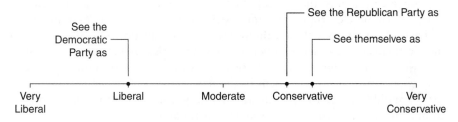

FIGURE 15.3

Party Identifiers Feel Close to Their Party Ideologically and Distant from the Other Party, 2011.

Note: Identifiers include strong and weak partisans and leaners.

Source: Pew Research Center for The People & The Press, "Views of Parties' Ideologies," September 12, 2011, at http://people-press.org/files/legacy-pdf/9-12-11%20Party%20Ideology_1.pdf (accessed November 19, 2011).

the *Huffington Post* can trust that most of what they watch and read will agree with their views. The overwhelming majority of those who read political blogs seek out bloggers from only their own side of the ideological fence.[28]

But the change is not limited to partisan sorting. The proportion of people in the American National Election Studies calling themselves conservative or extremely conservative, and liberal or extremely liberal, rose from 19 percent in 1972 to a high of 43 percent in 2008. These voters tend to be more interested and engaged in politics, so we can guess that these terms have some meaning for them. These changes improve many voters' ability to meet the demands of the responsible parties model.[29]

Even so, a lot of Americans have managed to sit out this polarization so far. Paul Allen Beck refers to "two electorates—one partisan and about evenly divided, the other estranged from party politics."[30] Is the polarized portion of the electorate big enough to sustain a movement toward more responsible parties?

Differences among Voters, Activists, and Candidates

Party activists and leaders take more extreme positions on many issues than do party voters.[31] Studies of delegates to the national parties' nominating conventions have consistently found Democratic activists on the liberal end of the liberal-conservative continuum and Republican activists on the conservative end, with both parties' voters closer to the center. You can find a dramatic illustration of these patterns in Table 10.2, on page 197–198. The table shows that a full 94 percent of delegates to the 2008 Democratic National Convention believed that providing health care coverage to all Americans is more important than holding down taxes, for example, compared with only 7 percent of the Republican convention delegates. More generally, people who are actively involved in campaigns and politics are more likely to be liberal or conservative rather than moderate. The division between the parties' voters is not as dramatic.

Some candidates and officeholders find themselves caught in between: closer to the left or right than the party's voters but not as extreme as its activists. That can put these candidates in a difficult position. If they try to muffle their conservative or liberal views, they risk alienating their party's activists.[32] But if they express those views candidly, more moderate voters may choose not to support them in the next election.[33] It is no wonder that many candidates prefer to remain ambiguous when asked about issues in their campaigns, at least when they speak to general audiences.

These differences can aggravate the tensions among the party organization, the party in government, and the party's voters. Ideologues in both parties complain about the moderation of at least some parts of the party in government. Liberal Democrats objected to what they saw as President Obama's "sellout" on climate change and budget cuts, and Tea Party conservatives felt betrayed by some Republican House leaders' reluctance to cut federal spending as deeply as they had allegedly promised. Bipartisan behavior in a politician seems to turn off strong partisans (who are most likely to vote), whereas weak identifiers and independents claim to reward bipartisanship in their elected officials.[34]

The dilemma of ideology, then, is not whether the American parties can become genuinely ideological parties. That is not likely. The problem is whether the increasing ideological commitment of their activists and of many of their officeholders can be sustained without alienating their more pragmatic supporters. The parties already face a deep well of public suspicion. Much of the public feels alienated from the parties' attachment to organized interests, their affinity for negative campaigns, and their failure to keep their promises.[35] As one writer put it, moderates may become more convinced that "politics no longer speaks to them, that it has become a dialogue of the deaf, a rant of uncompromising extremes."[36]

WHEN IS PARTY GOVERNMENT MOST LIKELY?

Responsible parties are hard to achieve. Even the British Parliament, so often cited as a model of party government, has not always had the cohesion and the binding party discipline that a "pure" responsible party government would require.[37] Under what conditions have the American parties come closest to the ideal of responsible parties?

When There Is Strong Presidential Leadership

At times, a strong president—Ronald Reagan and George W. Bush in his first term are good examples—has been able to push Congress to enact important parts of the platform on which he ran for office. That is especially likely, of course, when the president's party controls both houses of Congress. Party-oriented presidents can also draw voters' attention to party differences. But the result is likely to be "presidential government" rather than party government; voters are likely to respond to the president's performance rather than that of the party as a whole.

In Times of Crisis

At critical times in American history, the parties have divided in ways that were, if not truly ideological, at least very policy oriented. In the 1936 presidential election, for example, the Democrats and the Republicans offered dramatically different solutions to a nation devastated by the Great Depression. The hardships of that economic collapse probably focused voter attention to an unusual degree on the possible remedies that government could provide. Combined with a campaign centered on the pros and cons of the Roosevelt program for economic change, this may well have produced something close to a mandate in the election for both the president and Congress. When strong presidential leadership is combined with crisis conditions, then a degree of responsible party government might be achieved, at least until the crisis ends.

When the Parties' Supporting Coalitions Are Reshaped

At times when the parties' supporting coalitions of social groups have undergone real change—often called "realignments"—American politics seems to have most closely approached the requirements for party government. At these times, the parties have tended to divide more clearly on a single, riveting set of issues, and party leaders, activists, and voters have reached high levels of agreement with one another and major differences with the other party (see Chapter 7).

These changes in the party system typically produce a unified federal government, with the same party controlling both houses of Congress, the presidency, and a judiciary that, through the president's appointment power, comes to reflect the new majority. On only five occasions in American history has one party enjoyed control of Congress and the presidency continuously for more than a decade, and each time, this control was first established during a realignment. Party cohesion in Congress is especially high at the beginning of a new party system. So it is not surprising that major bursts of comprehensive policy change have followed the realignments of the parties' coalitions after the Civil War and during the 1930s.

Even at these times, the American version of party government has been a pale imitation of its European counterparts. The party change of the 1930s, for example, produced a majority Democratic Party by linking a liberal northern wing, attracted to the party because it represented the hopes of disadvantaged groups and championed the developing welfare state, and a conservative southern wing that often opposed both of these goals. The president at the time, Franklin D. Roosevelt, had a congressional majority large enough to achieve many of his policy goals, but he faced opposition within his own party throughout his long career in the White House. In short, even when they have been most unified around a single political agenda, the American parties have still typically contained differing interests and goals.

PARTY GOVERNMENT AND POPULAR CONTROL

In sum, the idea of party government, or responsible parties, has continuing appeal to many analysts. When parties stand for clear principles and voters are offered clear choices in elections, it is easier for citizens to hold government responsible for the policies it produces. That may make for a stronger and more vibrant democracy.

The major American parties are not ideological parties like many in other nations. But the congressional parties and, to some extent, the parties in the electorate have become more cohesive in the past two decades than they have been in a very long time. At the federal level and in many states, there is a marked difference between the parties on basic principles of public policy.

Yet, if the parties are to become more accountable, more like responsible parties in a system of party government, these differences on issues and greater organizational strength are not enough. There must be some set of basic principles that can connect different issues into a single logical structure for each party, some means by which voters and leaders are able to distill the large number of policy issues into one major dimension or a few, so that voters can easily understand and predict the party's stands.

That much structure and coherence will be harder and perhaps impossible to achieve. Too many powerful forces stand in the way. Even if party organizations gain immense new resources, they still won't be able to choose their own candidates; prospective officeholders will still have to attract voter support in primary elections. Thus, candidates will still need to run their own campaigns and raise most of their own campaign money. Primaries give candidates greater independence from their parties than the increase in party resources can counteract. And no amount of party money can buy an exception to the rules of federalism and the separation of powers.

It is not likely, then, that the American parties and voters can meet the demands of the responsible parties model. To many people, that is great news. Others would remind us that, in a system of government as fragmented as that of the United States, semi-responsible parties make it even harder to accomplish one of the basic tasks of a democracy: holding public officials accountable for their actions.

The Place of Parties in American Politics

The American political parties leave their mark on the substance of every national election, every major public policy, and therefore on the life chances of college students and their families. The parties have grown into different types of organizations than they once were, but in this changed form, they remain a fundamental part of the American political landscape.

To conclude this look at the American parties, this chapter will sum up these changes in relation to a simple but important truth: Political parties are powerfully shaped not only by the people who lead and participate in them but also by the environment in which they act. They are profoundly affected by election and campaign finance rules, interest groups, citizens, legislatures, and courts, just as they influence these forces. Thus, to understand the changes in party power and functions over time, we need to explore the relationships between parties and their environment.

PARTIES AND THEIR ENVIRONMENT

Political parties affect their environment in a variety of ways. They promote public policies in response to citizens' beliefs, demands, and fears. They recruit individuals into active roles in politics and government. Through their communications and performance, parties affect public attitudes about the Democrats and the Republicans and about politics more generally. Party organizations and the parties in government structure their own environment even more directly as well: They make the rules governing how the parties' candidates will be nominated and financed and who will have the opportunity to choose them.

In turn, their environment helps to shape the parties' nature, activities, and effectiveness. Three types of environmental forces have been especially important in influencing the American parties as well as those in other Western democracies: the nature of the electorate, the nation's basic governmental institutions and rules, and the forces that affect the broader society (Table 16.1).[1]

313

> ## TABLE 16.1
>
> ### Environmental Forces that Influence the American Parties
>
> | Types of Influences | Examples |
> | --- | --- |
> | Nature of the electorate | Expansion of the right to vote, citizens' political interest and knowledge, social characteristics of the electorate (age, race, income) |
> | Political institutions and rules | |
> | (a) Institutions | Federalism, separation of powers, nature of the presidency, single-member districts |
> | (b) Electoral processes | Direct primary, nonpartisan elections |
> | (c) Laws and regulations | Laws governing campaign finance, structure of party organization, patronage |
> | Social forces | |
> | (a) National events and conditions | State of the economy, war |
> | (b) Other political intermediaries | Types of other organized interests, media, independent consultants |
> | (c) Political culture | Attitudes toward parties and politics |

The Nature of the Electorate

The nature and concerns of the voting population are vital influences on a party system. The societal "fault lines" that divide the electorate into opposing groups—race is one of the clearest and most persistent examples in American politics—help to define the parties' issue agendas. So do the social characteristics that make some groups more likely to vote than others.

The right to vote has expanded enormously in the United States. From an extremely limited suffrage—the small proportion of white male adults who owned property—it now includes the great majority of citizens over the age of 18. Political information has expanded as well. Mass media and computers have made information about politics much more accessible, and more citizens have the advantage of higher education, which helps them find and understand the information. Voters have gained unprecedented opportunities to take part in political decisions through primary elections, referenda, recall elections, and Internet access to public officials. Yet people's interest in politics and their feelings of political effectiveness and trust have not increased. So at the same time that these opportunities for participation expanded, voter turnout dropped. Even though it has since rebounded, turnout in the United States remains lower than in most other industrialized democracies.

Turnout did not decline to the same degree among all groups in the population. There has been a steeper decline among lower-income Americans than among those with greater wealth.[2] And as we saw in Chapter 8, the turnout rate of college-age Americans, though it rose in 2004 and 2008, still remains substantially lower than the turnout rate of adults over 65. It should come as no surprise, then, that Social Security and Medicare are much more frequent campaign issues than are college loans. Those who participate are more likely to be heard.

Political Institutions and Rules

The second cluster of environmental influences on the parties includes the nation's basic framework of political institutions: whether the government is federal or unitary, whether it is parliamentary or has separated powers, and how its positions of power are structured. Then there are the laws that regulate the parties, ranging from the secret ballot and state laws governing the makeup of party committees to federal laws regulating campaign spending.

American political institutions differ in many ways from those of most other democracies.[3] Most democratic nations do not divide governmental powers so insistently among different branches and levels of government. Few other democracies choose most of their leaders in single-member districts with plurality rules for electing officials, or stagger the terms of different types of officials. The direct primary limits the party organization's role in the selection of candidates to a degree unknown in most other democracies. The American party organizations are regulated more heavily than are parties in other nations, and American state laws defining the party organizations have no parallel in the democratic world. The effect of this regulation—and in most cases its aim—is to restrict the development of the party organizations. An unintended effect is to boost the power of the party in government relative to that of the party organization.

As a result, the major American parties differ in some important ways from parties in most other democracies. In particular, the American parties are more decentralized; just as state and local governments have powers independent of the national government, so do state and party organizations relative to the national party. The two-party system is due in large part to the impact of American political institutions. The strength of the party in government means that the party organization's leaders have few effective tools to keep party legislators and other elected officials acting in accord with the party's stands. To survive independent of a strong party organization, candidates must raise much larger sums of money from private interests and spend much more on campaigns than do their counterparts in other democracies. With the important exceptions of the direct primary and the secret ballot, however, these rules have changed less dramatically over time than has the nature of the electorate, so they are less well able to explain changes in the parties.

Societal Forces

A third set of environmental influences refers to events and trends in the larger society that affect politics at a particular time. The horrors of the September 11 attacks, the relocation of American industries to Mexico and China, and the changes in women's roles and family structures have had powerful effects on the nation's agenda. Thus, they have become part of the parties' agenda as well and affect the parties' platforms, campaign appeals, and supporting coalitions.

These societal forces also include the number and character of organized interests in the nation, the nature and behavior of the media, and other means of representing interests. If individuals find alternative ways to pursue their political goals that seem more effective than the parties, they will use them. If the "hot line" of a local newspaper is better able to track down a reader's Social Security check or if an interest group is more vocal in opposing abortion, then why should the individual try to achieve her political aims through a party? The nature of the parties at any given time, then, depends in part on the available alternatives to parties and the competition among them.

All these elements of their environment have contributed to the unique character of the American parties. Thus, as this chapter summarizes the dramatic changes that have occurred in the parties' structure, supporting coalitions, and strength during the past four decades, let us pay special attention to the effects of their environment and above all to changes in the electorate.

PARTY DECLINE IN THE 1960s AND 1970s

A basic feature of the American parties is that the three party sectors are bound together only loosely. The party organization has not been able to involve large numbers of party identifiers in its structure and activities, nor has it been able to direct the campaigns or the policy making of the party in government. The party decline that was becoming apparent in the 1960s affected the three sectors very differently.

The Parties in the Electorate

During a time of upheaval in many of aspects of American life, voters' loyalty to the parties weakened noticeably in the late 1960s and 1970s. More people began to think of themselves as independent "leaners" rather than as strong party identifiers. Those who remained attached to a party no longer took their party's advice in elections as much as they once did. The parties, then, found themselves with smaller numbers of less loyal identifiers.

One result was a surge in ticket splitting. By 1968, almost half of the respondents in national surveys said they had voted for more than one party's candidates in state or local elections, and in 1974 that figure topped out at 61 percent. At the aggregate level, the number of congressional districts selecting a presidential candidate of one party and a congressional candidate of the other party exceeded 30 percent for the first time in history in 1964 and reached 44 percent early in the next decade.[4]

As education levels increased, some voters became more responsive to the issue-oriented candidacies of the time. The campaigns of Barry Goldwater in 1964, Eugene McCarthy and George Wallace in 1968, and George McGovern in 1972 spurred many people's awareness of political issues. As television came to be used more widely in campaigns, viewers were drawn to candidates' media images. The attractive faces and ready smiles that television screens convey evoked some of the support that party symbols once commanded.

To a greater extent than they had in the past, then, voters became more inclined to respond to candidates as individuals than as members of a party. Independent candidates for president and governor gained some success. Because candidates and issues change far more often than parties, the result was a less stable pattern of voting.

Party Organizations

The last of the great party machines were fading by the 1960s and 1970s. The famous Daley machine in Chicago was ripped apart in a series of tumultuous struggles. Party organizations could no longer depend on the patronage and preferments that once were so vital in recruiting party activists. Instead, more people were being drawn into party activism because of their commitment to particular issues. These were better-educated people, and they demanded greater participation in the party's decisions. Some of these new activists felt that compromise was a dirty word; to them, standing on principle was more important than winning an election. If their party did not satisfy their ideological goals, they stood ready to leave it for other groups—candidates' campaigns and single-issue organizations—which were more narrowly targeted to meet their needs.

Other aspects of the party organization were under stress as well. As the direct primary came to dominate presidential nominations, party organizations gave up their control over nominations to whoever voted in the primary. By the time a primary season had ended, the party's presidential nominee had been determined, so its nominating convention no longer had much of an independent role. As grassroots activists came to expect a bigger say within the party organization, its own internal decision making was no longer under the party leaders' control. This was particularly true of the Democrats, who in 1972 and 1976 nominated presidential candidates who were well outside the mainstream of their own party.

In addition to their declining influence over nominations, by the 1960s and 1970s the party organizations had lost their central role in campaigns more generally. To run in primaries, candidates now had to build their own campaign organizations, raise their own campaign money, and judge how to spend it. The campaign assets that they once received from their local party organizations—fund-raising, volunteers, information about public opinion—could now be obtained directly from pollsters, issue-oriented activists, or campaign consulting firms that were, in effect, "rent-a-party" agencies. Campaign finance reforms gave candidates an incentive to raise nonparty money at a time when the technologies for doing so were becoming more effective and widely available.

In fact, the campaign skills that local party organizations could offer their candidates were fairly primitive at that time, especially in comparison with the skills of many independent consultants. The national parties began to develop expertise in newer campaign technologies during the 1970s and to share their resources with state and local parties, but consultants had already established a beachhead. Even in the face of new vigor in the national committees, the party organizations in the 1970s remained more decentralized than did life and politics in the United States. Voters were looking more and more to national political leaders and symbols, but the party organizations still tended to be collections of state and local activists.

The Party in Government

In the 1960s and 1970s, elected officials came to depend more than ever on direct appeals to voters. Officeholders had been freed from reliance on the party organization by the direct primary, their direct access to the media, and the money and volunteers they could attract independent of the party's efforts. Because of split-ticket voting, candidates could not rely as much on party identification to generate support. Through personal style, personal appeals, and personally raised funds, they developed a "personal vote" independent of party.[5]

It became harder than ever to unseat an incumbent, especially in Congress. The cycle perpetuated itself. Because there was not as much chance of beating an elected official, serious challengers did not appear as frequently. When they did, party organizations were not vigorous enough to provide challengers with the campaign resources they so desperately needed. Holding public office became more of a profession—a lifetime career—even at the state and local levels, where political professionals had formerly been rare.

As incumbents became more secure electorally (even though many did not feel that way), members of Congress gained greater freedom from the party organizations. Legislative party leaders found it harder to marshal their members on behalf of the legislative party's bills or the programs of the party's president. The Democratic Party in Congress was especially diverse, divided between southern conservatives and northern moderates and liberals. Thus, congressional Democrats were initially reluctant to grant much power to their legislative party leaders; neither the southern nor the northern Democrats could trust that leaders selected from the other group would act to serve the needs of all members of the congressional party. Senate and House Republicans were a varied group as well. So party-line voting in Congress fell to a new low at this time. However, it was a perverse kind of freedom. Protected from the demands of party leaders, legislators were more exposed to other pressures, mainly from growing numbers of interest groups.

With little competition from the legislative parties, presidents and governors could exercise greater leadership. Presidents did not depend on their party organizations for much; in fact, with the help of federal campaign money after 1974, presidential candidates were able to run their campaigns free of obligation to the party organization at any level. By that time, however, divided government had become the norm. That undercut executives' power by permitting the opposition party to block their initiatives.

Shifting Power Centers within the Parties

These changes had produced a major shift of power within the parties. The party organizations had lost power not only to the individual members of the party in government but also to other political intermediaries, especially interest groups and the media. Party organizations and their leaders became even more vulnerable to suspicions that they were run by bosses plotting in smoke-filled rooms. Visions of "boss rule" were as much alive in the 1960s and 1970s as they were in the early 1900s, even though, ironically, the resources that the party organizations had in the early 1900s, which could have justified the charge of boss rule at that time, were largely eroded by the 1960s.

The result was a peculiar kind of political party. A party organization is the only sector of the party whose interests go beyond winning individual elections. It is the party organization that sustains the party when its candidates lose their races. It is the organization that links the party's officeholders and office seekers; it can call them to collective action of the type that parties were created to achieve. Without it, party candidates are individual entrepreneurs seeking individual goals in a political system that requires collective decisions. The decline of the party organizations was a major force in the decline of the parties more generally.

PARTY RENEWAL

This marked decline was not the end of the story, however. The American parties responded to these challenges, just as they have adapted to changing circumstances at other times. The steady decay of the parties was stopped and reversed, but some of the changes that took place in the 1960s and 1970s continue to leave their imprint even now. The parties have had to adjust to new roles in American politics.

Change in the Parties' Electoral Coalitions

The slow, steady change in the parties' supporting coalitions since the 1960s (see Chapter 7) has been significant enough to alter the nature of the party system. The most striking elements of this coalitional change have been the movement of white southerners into the Republican Party, which led to a dramatic decline of Democratic strength in the South (see Figure 16.1) and the growth of almost uniform Democratic identification among black Americans. Other demographic characteristics not normally associated with the party division have taken on a partisan tinge as well. Religious conservatives, both Catholic and Protestant, have become a major force within the GOP. Marital status and sexual identity have become important to partisanship; unmarried people (especially women) and gay people now identify preponderantly as Democrats.

These changes have transformed a Democratic-dominated political environment into close party competition. Republicans won both the presidency

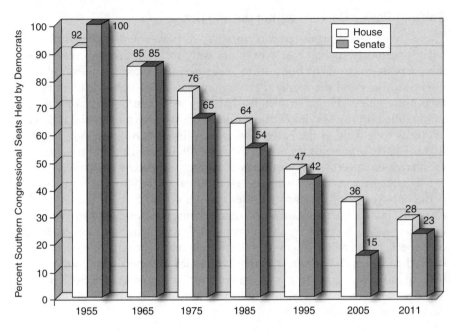

FIGURE 16.1

Eroding Democratic Strength in the South: U.S. House and Senate Seats, 1955–2011.

Note: Data points are the percentage of U.S. senators and House members from the 13 southern states (Alabama, Arkansas, Florida, Georgia, Kentucky, Louisiana, Mississippi, North Carolina, Oklahoma, South Carolina, Tennessee, Texas, Virginia) who are Democrats.

Source: Data for 1955–1995 from *Congressional Quarterly Weekly Report,* November 12, 1994, p. 3231. Data for 2005 from *CQ Weekly,* November 6, 2004, pp. 2664–2666, and December 11, 2004, p. 2931. Data for 2011 compiled by the author, as of June 24, 2011.

and the Senate in 1980 and gained control of both the House and Senate in 1994—the first time since 1954 that there was a Republican majority in both Houses of Congress. In the 1990s and at times in the 2000s, Republicans came closer to parity with the Democrats in both party ID and election results than they had since the 1930s. And after the 2010 midterms, Republicans won back the House, held more state legislative seats than at any point since 1929, and controlled a majority of state legislatures.

Which Party Will Gain the Advantage?

The close party division at the national level has combined with a series of dramatic events to make the past decade highly volatile. After their victories in 2002 and 2004, Republican candidates lost big in 2006 and 2008. Even in the South, Barack Obama won many suburban counties in North Carolina and Virginia, where educational levels are rising and high-technology jobs make up an increasing share of the economy. The ability of Democratic candidates to increase their margins among more educated and upper-income voters in all regions and to attract large majorities of the fastest-growing segments of the electorate–young people and Latinos in particular–led to claims that the Republican Party was in serious trouble.[6]

These changes led to a feverish debate among Republicans as to what went wrong. Conservative Republicans charged that their party had sacrificed its principles (small government in particular) when it gained power, and pandered to voters' short-term desire for tangible benefits in order to win a lasting Republican majority. The declining number of moderate Republicans disagreed. Many warned that the party's hard-line stands on social issues, dear to the hearts of white evangelical Christians, were limiting the party's attractiveness to independents. To expand the Republican base, they said, would require making the party into a more inclusive organization by finding ways to enlist the support of young people, Latinos, and suburbanites. That is the plan the Democrats followed in 2006 and 2008 to regain strength; although the Democratic revival was due in part to Republican missteps, it was led by more centrist Democratic candidates who were promoted by the party in moderate and conservative congressional districts.

The challenge for the Republicans is that a more inclusive, "big tent" appeal could alienate the remaining Republican base. The base has been energized by the small-government enthusiasts of the Tea Party, driven by outright hostility toward President Obama and all of his major legislative initiatives. It expressed itself powerfully in the 2010 midterms, contributing to the biggest Republican House majority in 60 years. In the period of divided party government that followed, Tea Party supporters pressed Republican congressional leaders to shun even the appearance of cooperation with Obama or other Democrats as a means of cementing their majority. But the groups that now form the Republican base—married white Christians—are shrinking as a proportion of the total electorate. The nonwhite share of the voting public grew from 13 percent in 1992 to 26 percent in 2008,[7] and tends to be more supportive of government social programs and services. Unless the Republican base is expanded, or unless young people, Latinos, and blacks drop out of the electorate even more, a "base strategy" will soon put the Republicans at risk.

Even if Democratic dominance is later restored, however, there is good evidence that we are now in a different party system from that of the New Deal. This sixth party system emerged differently from the New Deal party system. In contrast with the political changes that accompanied the Depression of the 1930s, the more recent shifts in party coalitions have developed over several decades and continue to evolve. Election results have been mercurial. Neither party has dominated for long. Polls show very little public enthusiasm for the major parties or, for that matter, many other aspects of American politics.

Thus, the events of the 1960s and 1970s resulted in a continuing challenge to party loyalties. Large numbers of voters now rely on sources other than the parties, such as cable TV, blogs, and single-issue groups, for their political information. Sometimes these sources reinforce partisan views; in other cases, they don't.[8] Even with this formidable competition, however, parties remain important landmarks on most people's political maps. Levels of party identification rebounded in the 1990s, and partisanship is at least as strong an influence on people's voting now as it was before the 1960s.[9] Split-ticket voting, especially as measured by the number of districts voting for a presidential candidate of one party and a congressional candidate of the other, recently hit a 50-year low.[10]

The Rise of More Cohesive Parties in Government

Well before the current revival of partisanship among voters—and a likely cause of it—the parties in government had begun a revival of their own. By the mid-1970s, the long decline in party unity in Congress had stopped and the organizational seeds had been sown for greater party strength. By the 1980s, the congressional parties were becoming more cohesive than they had been in a century. Their cohesion was enhanced by the coalitional changes within the party electorates. The slow, steady movement from the Democratic "solid South" to a largely Republican South left both congressional parties more homogeneous, which in turn made it easier for each party to offer clear alternatives on big issues. In many states, as well, legislative parties were becoming more unified and taking clearer positions on issues.

Parties also took on greater importance in the executive branch. The Reagan administration came into office in 1981 as the most ideologically committed and the most partisan in decades. Reagan's leadership placed conservative principles at the top of the GOP's agenda and solidified the hold of his brand of conservatives on the party. The Democrats became more unified in response. By the mid-1990s, there was intense partisan conflict between a programmatically committed, Republican-led Congress and an activist Clinton White House. The battles have continued, resulting in a level of incivility that can threaten congressional effectiveness. Consider one House member's recollection of a new member orientation program in which a Democratic leadership staff member suggested the importance of getting to know Republican legislators. One of the new Democrats replied, "Why would we want to do that?"[11]

The New "Service Parties"

The party organizations have revived just as dramatically. Facing an environment of candidate centered campaigns, both parties retooled their national organizations to provide services to the party's candidates. They have used their increased funding and staffing to help state and local parties, recruit candidates, offer them more resources, and thus step up their role in campaigns, compared with the 1960s and 1970s.

The new service party, however, differs a great deal from the grassroots organizations of earlier years. Because its main role is to support candidates, it is not very visible to voters, nor can it always make a major impact on campaigns. In the big-spending world of campaign finance, party organizations do not often bring enough money to the table to be able to dominate political campaigning or at times even to be heard very clearly. The service party is one of many forces trying to win the attention of candidates, influence elected officials, and mobilize citizens.

The party organizations, in short, are more vigorous now than they have been in years. There is a greater balance of power between the national and state and local parties now than ever existed before. Party organizations have adapted to new conditions by taking on a new form: the service party. However, as service parties, the party organizations are no longer as distinctive as they used to be in the sense of providing campaign resources that no other group could deliver.

THE FUTURE OF PARTY POLITICS IN AMERICA

These trends are vital to us because political parties are vital to us. Parties have the potential to do a great deal of good for a democracy. They can enable political leaders to work together in achieving shared interests over time. They can provide cues that permit voters to make decisions on candidates and issues with relatively little effort. Parties can bring voters to the polls, which helps to legitimize a democracy. Perhaps most important, parties organize majorities, which are necessary for governing. Interest groups can effectively represent intense minorities, but there are not many alternatives to the parties for organizing lasting and predictable majorities.

A Changing Intermediary Role

Elections require voters to make large numbers of choices, even though most voters don't know much about most candidates. Parties serve as efficient guides. The value of the party label in elections is probably greatest when a mass electorate has just begun to develop and has serious need for information. As the electorate matures, its needs change. One explanation for American voters' decreased reliance on party loyalties in the 1960s and 1970s was that voters had become better educated than was the case in the early 1900s, and could sift through a broader range of political messages without the need for party labels as a guide.[12]

It is interesting, then, that although education levels have continued to increase since the 1960s, party identification has reasserted itself as an influence on many voters' choices. Why should partisanship help citizens who have so many other sources of information about candidates and issues? Perhaps *because* they are exposed to so much information. Without this simple guide, the blizzard of political communication could serve as a source of confusion rather than as a helpful tool. At the same time, the fact that the two major parties have drawn farther apart from one another on important issues lends even more value to the party labels for politically engaged citizens. Added to the heightened party competition in the 2000s and the resulting intensity of campaign advertising, changes in the political environment can make an individual's partisanship even more meaningful to him or her.

Granted, the parties' traditional dominance in politics has been eroded by competition from organized interests and the media. A century ago, someone concerned about environmental quality would probably have had to pursue his or her goals through a political party; not many groups focused specifically on resource conservation or pollution control. Now, however, along with the growing reach of government into most aspects of private life, a huge array of organized interests has developed that permit individuals to establish a "designer link" with the political system. If someone prefers to see politics entirely from the perspective of environmental rights, or property rights, several groups exist to make that possible. There is no need to compromise or support a coalition of other groups' needs and a range of candidates, as a party loyalty would encourage.

In this fractured political world, parties become even more important as a means of broadening individuals' perspectives and improving their ability to hold elected officials accountable. The parties have long struggled with hostile environmental forces, from a system of separated powers that is inhospitable to strong parties to a political culture suspicious of all parties. However, as we have seen throughout this book, the parties are adaptable. They are not the intermediaries they were in 1900 or 1950, but for large numbers of Americans and for the policy-making process, the major parties remain the most important intermediaries.

The Need for Strong Parties

Although we need parties, we don't like them. We don't even like to admit that they influence us. Most of us claim that issues and candidates' personal qualities have the biggest impact on our votes. Yet it's clear that partisanship is closely related to our attitudes toward issues and candidates and is the source of much of their influence.

Democracy is unworkable without parties.[13] The United States has probably come closer to testing that principle than any other democracy; much of American local politics has been, at least officially, nonpartisan for some time. But when parties are reduced to playing a smaller role in politics, the quality of democracy is weakened.

Consider the role strong parties can play in Congress and state legislatures. As a representative body, Congress is structured to permit legislators to give their constituents what they want: short-term, tangible benefits such as disaster relief, expanded Medicare benefits, and jobs on pork-barrel projects. Legislators facing reelection seek the Holy Grail of constituent service: a project such as a new dam or highway that provides tangible benefits to their own constituents but whose costs are paid by taxpayers all over the country. But if the individual voter and the individual legislator are motivated to pay close attention to the benefits they can get for their district, who is motivated to pay attention to the collective cost? Very few voters support the idea of raising their own taxes in order to pay for benefits to others, or even to pay for benefits to themselves.

Strong legislative parties have an incentive to take responsibility for the collective costs.[14] Some legislative party members can gain personal career advantages by becoming leaders of their congressional party. When the party's members in Congress are elected from similar districts and hold similar views, they can afford to trust these legislative party leaders with greater power to structure the choices they will make. Members realize that although their own reelection needs are primary, they also need coordination within the legislature in order to pass bills and to help with the endless tasks of legislative life.

By using the carrots and sticks discussed in Chapter 13, legislative party leaders can induce their party colleagues to make truly national policy, not just "Christmas tree" legislation that consists of pork-barrel ornaments for each congressional district. By holding their legislators to this party program, they can create a favorable brand name for their party in elections, which voters can come to recognize and associate with their own district's candidate. In the absence of strong parties, it is difficult to imagine where this collective responsibility might come from. Without strong parties, individual members of Congress and state legislatures have every reason to behave in ways that conflict with their collective interest and that of their constituents.[15]

In a society dominated by interest groups and other intermediaries, most people would not be as well represented. Among the many links between citizens and government, only the parties have the incentive to create majorities in order to win a wide range of elections over a long period. In turn, that gives the parties, to a greater extent than interest groups or even elected officials, a reason to pay attention to those citizens who are not activists or big campaign contributors. As political scientist Walter Dean Burnham has written, parties are the only devices that can "generate countervailing collective power on behalf of the many individually powerless against the relatively few who are individually—or organizationally—powerful.[16]

It is the parties that can mobilize sheer numbers against the organized minorities that hold other political resources. The parties do so in the one political arena where sheer numbers count most heavily: elections. Because of that, parties traditionally have been the means by which newly enfranchised but otherwise powerless groups gained a foothold in American life. The old-style urban machines, for example, provided the instrument with which recent immigrants won control of their cities from the more established Anglo-Saxon Protestant elites.

In a less party-driven politics, well-organized minorities with critical resources—money, insider knowledge, and technological expertise—would probably have even greater advantages than they do now. As we have seen from research on nonpartisan elections, eliminating the party symbol often makes it tougher for citizens to hold their representatives responsible.[17] That may be one reason why participation has declined more sharply in recent decades among poorer and less educated Americans; they may feel less represented by a politics in which the parties are no longer preeminent.[18]

Finally, weakened parties would rob the political system of an effective means of governing. Without at least moderately strong parties, it is harder to mobilize majorities in support of policies. Individual candidates, freed from party loyalties, would have to recreate majorities for every new legislative proposal. The result could be even greater gridlock, in which legislatures splinter into conflicting and intransigent groups. The "game of chicken" that characterized Congress' response to the debt ceiling crisis in 2011 might suggest to many observers that even the parties are not capable of dealing with such difficult issues. But in practice, it is hard to imagine 535 House members and senators reaching any such agreement without parties. Laws and policies could continue to be made only by shifting coalitions of elected officials, campaign contributors, and interest groups. Because these coalitions would be less permanent and less identifiable to the public, they would be much harder for citizens to hold accountable.

How to Make the Parties Stronger

Because parties bring so much value to American democracy, some analysts have considered ways to expand the parties' role in political life. The most potent solutions—abolishing the separation of powers, the direct primary, and the antiparty sentiment engrained into the political culture—are not on the table, of course. But there are less dramatic ways in which the parties might be strengthened.

One survey showed that most respondents would like the parties to be more active in helping people deal with government. Its authors propose, among other ideas, that party organizations could create "mobile units" to help citizens in areas where the U.S. (and perhaps the state) representative is from the other party. That would allow the party organization, not just members of the party in government, to perform constituent service. They note that this idea was especially attractive to respondents who described themselves as alienated from politics.[19]

By providing attractive nonpolitical benefits such as low-cost health insurance, as many interest groups do now, parties could help to build long-term loyalty among their volunteers.[20] Parties could also renew their connection with citizens by airing campaign ads promoting the party as a whole, rather than just individual candidates. These ads could strengthen the meaning of party by stressing the link between the party's stands and individuals' daily lives.

CONCLUSION: THE PARTIES' PROSPECTS

The American parties have never lacked interesting challenges. The electorate has become more and more varied. Some traditional group ties have broken down. New groups, from antiabortion to animal liberation, are tilling the ground that the major parties once owned. Most voters still identify with a party, but they also respond to candidates, issues, and national trends. The result is a more diverse, complicated politics that frustrates elected officials, party leaders, voters, and nonvoters.

The parties can't meet every political need. We can't expect the parties in government to get along if we elect candidates who are proud of their refusal to compromise. Parties find it hard to offer policy alternatives in campaigns without engaging in the conflict that many Americans find so distasteful. It is difficult for parties to unite their office holders and office seekers on a single agenda while giving candidates the independence to choose their own appeals and meet their own districts' needs. Parties can't provide accountability to a public that wants to choose candidates individually.

We will continue to challenge the parties with these conflicting expectations and criticisms. The parties' distinctive character has sustained them longer than any other tool of democratic politics. For the sake of representation, effective policy making, and accountability in governance, even the most independent-minded citizens have a stake in sustaining vigorous party politics in the United States.

END NOTES

FOREWORD

1. Frank J. Sorauf, *Party and Representation, Legislative Politics in Pennsylvania* (New York: Atherton Press, 1963).
2. See, for example, Frank J. Sorauf, *Money in American Elections* (Glenview, IL: Scott Foresman/Little, Brown College Division, 1988) or *Inside Campaign Finance: Myths and Realities* (New York: Yale University Press, 1992).
3. He has written a great deal on this subject. One illustration that has long been one of my favorites is his "A Socialization Theory of Partisan Realignment," which was originally published in *The Politics of Future Citizens*, edited by Richard Niemi (San Francisco, CA: Jossey-Bass, 1974, pp. 199–219), and reprinted in *Classics in Voting Behavior*, edited by Richard Niemi and Herbert Weisberg (Washington, DC: CQ Press, 1992).
4. See especially her books, *Running for Office: The Political Education of Campaigners* (Chatham, NJ: Chatham House, 1984) and *The Making of Campaign Strategy* (Lexington, MA: D.C. Heath-Lexington, 1974).
5. An especially interesting account of the ways the political parties reacted to female suffrage can be found in Anna L. Harvey, *Votes without Leverage: Women in American Electoral Politics, 1920–1970* (Cambridge: Cambridge University Press, 1998).
6. See, for example, "Constructing Explanations for U.S. State Governors' Races: The Abortion Issue and the 1990 Gubernatorial Elections," *Political Communication* 17 (July–September 2000): 239–262; "The Meaning of a Mandate: Interpretations of 'Mandate' in 1984 Presidential Election Coverage," *Polity* (Winter 1995): 225–254; and "Support for Political Women: Sex Roles," in John C. Pierce and John L. Sullivan, eds., *The Electorate Reconsidered* (Beverly Hills, CA: Sage, 1980), pp. 179–198.
7. http://nationaljournal.com/member/magazine/top-gop-priority-make-obama-a-one-term-president-20101023 (accessed November 29, 2011).
8. Larry M. Bartels, "Partisanship and Voting Behavior, 1952–1996," *American Journal of Political Science* 44 (2000): 35–50. Donald Green, Bradley Palmquist, and Eric Schickler, *Partisan Hearts and Minds: Political Parties and the Social Identities of Voters* (New Haven: Yale University Press, 2002).
9. See the discussion of poll reports in the height of the debate over this concern (July 14, 2001) at http://people-press.org/2011/07/14/the-debt-ceiling-showdown-%E2%80%93-where-the-public-stands (accessed November 29, 2011).
10. Keith Krehbiel, *Pivotal Politics: A Theory of U.S. Lawmaking* (Chicago: University of Chicago Press, 1998); David W. Brady and Craig Volden, *Revolving Gridlock: Politics and Policy from Jimmy Carter to George W. Bush* (Boulder, CO: Westview Press, 2006).
11. David R. Mayhew, *Divided We Govern: Party Control, Lawmaking, and Investigations, 1946–1990* (New Haven: Yale University Press, 1991) and *Partisan Balance: Why Political Parties Don't Kill the U.S. Constitutional System* (Princeton: Princeton University Press, 2011).
12. Robert S. Erikson, Michael B. MacKuen, and James A. Stimson, *The Macro Polity* (Cambridge, UK: Cambridge University Press, 2002).
13. Alan I. Abramowitz, *The Disappearing Center: Engaged Citizens, Polarization and American Democracy* (New Haven: Yale University Press, 2010); Morris P. Fiorina, *Culture War: The Myth of a Polarized America*, 3rd ed., with Samuel J. Abrams and Jeremy C. Pope (New York: Longman, 2011) and *Disconnect: The Breakdown of Representation in American Politics* with Samuel J. Abrams (Norman, OK: University of Oklahoma Press, 2009).

PART I PARTIES AND PARTY SYSTEMS

1. This is the title of Harold Lasswell's pioneering book, *Politics: Who Gets What, When, How* (New York: McGraw-Hill, 1936).
2. See Regina Smyth, *Candidate Strategies and Electoral Competition in the Russian Federation* (Cambridge: Cambridge University Press, 2006); and Henry E. Hale, *Why Not Parties in Russia?* (Cambridge: Cambridge University Press, 2006).

3. Austin Ranney, *Curing the Mischiefs of Faction* (Berkeley: University of California Press, 1975).

CHAPTER 1 WHAT ARE POLITICAL PARTIES?

1. Alan I. Abramowitz, *The Disappearing Center* (New Haven: Yale University Press, 2010), p. 112.
2. From calculations by Adam Bonica in "Ideological Cartography," November 5, 2010, at ideologicalcartography. com/2010/11/05/Introducing-the-112th-congress (accessed October 29, 2011).
3. In *The Party Decides* (Chicago: University of Chicago Press, 2008), Marty Cohen, David Karol, Hans Noel, and John Zaller argue that these interest groups and other social groups are part of the party coalition itself. Many other scholars see these groups as external to parties but a vital part of their environment.
4. These definitions come from Edmund Burke, "Thoughts on the Cause of the Present Discontents (1770)," in *The Works of Edmund Burke* (Boston: Little, Brown, 1839), vol. I, pp. 425–426; Anthony Downs, *An Economic Theory of Democracy* (New York: Harper & Row, 1957), p. 24; William Nisbet Chambers, "Party Development and the American Mainstream," in Chambers and Walter Dean Burnham, eds., *The American Party Systems* (New York: Oxford University Press, 1967), p. 5; John H. Aldrich, *Why Parties? A Second Look* (Chicago: University of Chicago Press, 2011), p. 297; and V. O. Key, Jr., *Politics, Parties, and Pressure Groups* (New York: Crowell, 1958), pp. 180–182.
5. V. O. Key, Jr., used this "tripartite" conception to organize his classic text, *Politics, Parties, and Pressure Groups*. Key attributed the concept of party in the electorate to Ralph M. Goldman, *Party Chairmen and Party Factions, 1789–1900* (Ph.D. diss., University of Chicago, 1951).
6. See Denise L. Baer and David A. Bositis, *Elite Cadres and Party Coalitions* (Westport, CT: Greenwood Press, 1988), pp. 21–50.
7. See Joseph A. Schlesinger, "The Primary Goals of Political Parties," *American Political Science Review* 69 (1975): 840–849.
8. This image is Joseph A. Schlesinger's in "The New American Political Party," *American Political Science Review* 79 (1985): 1152–1169.
9. State legislative elections in Nebraska are nonpartisan, although the candidates' partisan ties are obvious to many voters, and statewide officials (such as the governor and attorney general) are elected on a partisan ballot.

10. See Cohen et al., *The Party Decides*.
11. See William N. Chambers, *Political Parties in a New Nation* (New York: Oxford University Press, 1963).
12. Quoted in David Von Drehle, "Origin of the Species," *Washington Post*, July 25, 2004, p. W12.
13. Aldrich, *Why Parties?*, p. 83.
14. See John H. Aldrich and Ruth W. Grant, "The Antifederalists, the First Congress, and the First Parties," *Journal of Politics* 55 (1993): 295–326.
15. Chilton Williamson, *American Suffrage* (Princeton: Princeton University Press, 1960).
16. Neal R. Peirce and Lawrence D. Longley, *The People's President* (New Haven: Yale University Press, 1981).
17. See Aldrich, *Why Parties?*, Chapter 4; and A. James Reichley, *The Life of the Parties* (Lanham, MD: Rowman & Littlefield, 1992), Chapter 5.
18. See Reichley, *The Life of the Parties*, Chapters 6–11.
19. On party reform, see Austin Ranney, *Curing the Mischiefs of Faction* (Berkeley: University of California Press, 1975); and Richard Hofstadter, *The Age of Reform* (New York: Vintage Books, 1955).
20. See Mark A. Smith, *The Right Talk* (Princeton: Princeton University Press, 2000).
21. Frank Newport and Lydia Saad, "Republicans Negative, Democrats Positive in Describing Unions," Gallup Poll, March 11, 2011 at www.gallup.com/poll/146588/ Republicans-Negative-Democrats-Positive-Describing-Unions.aspx (accessed October 29, 2011).
22. Frank Newport, "On Economy, Republicans Trust Business; Dems Trust Gov't," Gallup Poll, March 12, 2009, at www.gallup.com/ poll/116599/Economy-Republicans-Trust-Business-Dems-Trust-Gov.aspx (accessed October 29, 2011).
23. See Leon Epstein, *Political Parties in the American Mold* (Madison: University of Wisconsin Press, 1986), pp. 155–199.
24. Jeffrey M. Jones, "Republican, Democratic Party Images Equally Negative," Gallup Poll, September 30, 2011, at www.gallup. com/poll/149795/Republican-Democratic-Party-Images-Equally-Negative.aspx (accessed October 29, 2011). Distrust of parties is common in other nations as well; see Ingrid van Biezen and Michael Saward, "Democratic Theorists and Party Scholars," *Perspectives on Politics* 6 (2008): 21–35.
25. See Larry M. Bartels, *Unequal Democracy* (Princeton: Princeton University Press, 2008).

CHAPTER 2 THE AMERICAN TWO-PARTY SYSTEM

1. Arend Lijphart, *Electoral Systems and Party Systems* (New York: Oxford University Press, 1994).
2. See John F. Bibby and L. Sandy Maisel, *Two Parties—Or More?*, 2nd ed. (Boulder, CO: Westview, 2003), p. 46.
3. Charles S. Bullock III, "It's a Sonny Day in Georgia," in Larry J. Sabato, ed., *Midterm Madness* (Lanham, MD: Rowman & Littlefield, 2003), p. 177.
4. Interparty competition refers to competition between the parties, as opposed to competition within a particular party ("intra-party"). The index was first presented in Austin Ranney, "Parties in State Politics," in Herbert Jacob and Kenneth Vines, eds., *Politics in the American States* (Boston: Little, Brown, 1965), p. 65. For alternative indices, see Thomas M. Holbrook and Emily Van Dunk, "Electoral Competition in the American States," *American Political Science Review* 87 (1993): 955–962; and James W. Ceaser and Robert P. Saldin, "A New Measure of Party Strength," *Political Research Quarterly* 58 (2005): 245–256.
5. See Peverill Squire, "Uncontested Seats in State Legislative Elections," *Legislative Studies Quarterly* 25 (2000): 131–146. Data from *Ballot Access News*, October 1, 2010, at www.ballot-access.org (accessed October 29, 2011).
6. Data are from the Center for Responsive Politics at www.opensecrets.org/bigpicture/reelect.php. On the influence of incumbency on elections, see Gary C. Jacobson, *The Politics of Congressional Elections*, 7th ed. (New York: Longman, 2008), Chapter 3; Stephen Ansolabehere, James M. Snyder, Jr., and Charles Stewart III, "Old Voters, New Voters, and the Personal Vote," *American Journal of Political Science* 44 (2000): 17–34; and Scott W. Desposato and John R. Petrocik, "The Variable Incumbency Advantage," *American Journal of Political Science* 47 (2003): 18–32.
7. John M. Carey, Richard G. Niemi, and Lynda W. Powell, "Incumbency and the Probability of Reelection in State Legislative Elections," *Journal of Politics* 62 (2000): 671–700.
8. Stephen Ansolabehere and James M. Snyder, Jr., "The Incumbency Advantage in U.S. Elections," *Election Law Journal* 1 (2002): 315–338. See also David W. Romero, "What They Do *Does* Matter," *Political Behavior* 28 (2006): 241–258.
9. John R. Alford and David W. Brady, "Personal and Partisan Advantage in U.S. Congressional Elections, 1846–1990," in Lawrence C. Dodd and Bruce I. Oppenheimer, eds., *Congress Reconsidered*, 5th ed. (Washington, DC: CQ Press, 1993), p. 147.
10. Gary C. Jacobson, "The Congress," in Michael Nelson, ed., *The Elections of 2004* (Washington, DC: CQ Press, 2005), pp. 166–167.
11. Bruce I. Oppenheimer, "Deep Red and Blue Congressional Districts," in Dodd and Oppenheimer, eds., *Congress Reconsidered*, 8th ed. (Washington, DC: CQ Press, 2005), pp. 135–157.
12. Bill Bishop with Robert G. Cushing, *The Big Sort* (New York: Houghton Mifflin, 2008).
13. Alan I. Abramowitz, Brad Alexander, and Matthew Gunning, "Incumbency, Redistricting, and the Decline of Competition in U.S. House Elections," *Journal of Politics* 68 (2006): 75–88.
14. See Robert S. Erikson and Gerald C. Wright, "Voters, Candidates, and Issues in Congressional Elections," in Dodd and Oppenheimer, eds., *Congress Reconsidered*, 9th ed. (Washington, DC: CQ Press, 2009), p. 83.
15. Maurice Duverger, *Political Parties* (New York: Wiley, 1954). See also Octavio Amorim Neto and Gary W. Cox, "Electoral Institutions, Cleavage Structures, and the Number of Parties," *American Journal of Political Science* 41 (1997): 149–174.
16. In 1955, 58 percent of all American state legislative districts were multimember; this number had declined to 10 percent by the 1980s. See Richard Niemi, Simon Jackman, and Laura Winsky, "Candidates and Competitiveness in Multimember Districts," *Legislative Studies Quarterly* 16 (1991): 91–109.
17. James D. King, in "Single-Member Districts and the Representation of Women in American State Legislatures," *State Politics and Policy Quarterly* 2 (2002): 161–175 found that a change from multimember to single-member districts also decreases the representation of women in state legislatures.
18. See A. James Reichley, *The Life of the Parties* (Lanham, MD: Rowman & Littlefield, 2002), p. 4.
19. Leon Epstein, *Political Parties in the American Mold* (Madison: University of Wisconsin Press, 1986), pp. 129–132.
20. V. O. Key, Jr., *Politics, Parties, and Pressure Groups*, 5th ed. (New York: Crowell, 1964), pp. 229ff.
21. Marjorie Randon Hershey, "How American Election Law and Institutions Cripple Third Parties," in Matthew

J. Streb, ed., *Law and Election Politics* (New York: Routledge, 2012).

22. See Ronald B. Rapoport and Walter J. Stone, *Three's a Crowd* (Ann Arbor, MI: University of Michigan Press, 2005) on Republican successes in appealing to Ross Perot supporters in 1994 and 1996; and Shigeo Hirano and James M. Snyder, Jr., "The Decline of Third Party Voting in the U.S.," *Journal of Politics* 69 (2007): 1–16.

23. Brian Schaffner, Matthew J. Streb, and Gerald C. Wright, "A New Look at the Republican Advantage in Nonpartisan Elections," *Political Research Quarterly* 60 (2007): 240–249.

24. Brian F. Schaffner, Matthew J. Streb, and Gerald C. Wright, "Teams without Uniforms," *Political Research Quarterly* 54 (2001): 7–30.

25. Gerald C. Wright and Brian F. Schaffner, "The Influence of Party," *American Political Science Review* 96 (2002): 367–379.

26. J. David Gillespie, *Politics at the Periphery* (Columbia: University of South Carolina Press, 1993).

27. Holly A. Heyser, "Minnesota Governor," in Sabato, ed., *Midterm Madness*, pp. 233–245.

28. Among the best books on American third parties are Steven J. Rosenstone, Roy L. Behr, and Edward H. Lazarus, *Third Parties in America*, 2nd ed. (Princeton: Princeton University Press, 1996); Paul S. Herrnson and John C. Green, *Multiparty Politics in America*, 2nd ed. (Lanham, MD: Rowman & Littlefield, 2002); John F. Bibby and L. Sandy Maisel, *Two Parties—Or More?*, 2nd ed. (Boulder, CO: Westview, 2003); Scot Schraufnagel, *Third Party Blues* (New York: Routledge, 2011); and Rapoport and Stone, *Three's a Crowd*.

29. Joseph M. Hazlett II, *The Libertarian Party* (Jefferson, NC: McFarland and Company, 1992). Minor parties' Web sites can be found at www.politics1.com/parties.htm.

30. As evidence, almost all third-party presidential candidates since 1900 have received less support on Election Day than they did in preelection polls; see Rosenstone, Behr, and Lazarus, *Third Parties in America*, p. 41.

31. Rosenstone, Behr, and Lazarus, *Third Parties in America*, p. 162.

32. See Paul R. Abramson, John H. Aldrich, and David W. Rohde, *Change and Continuity in the 1992 Elections* (Washington, DC: CQ Press, 1994).

33. This is called "fusion." See Howard A. Scarrow, *Parties, Elections, and Representation in the State of New York* (New York: New York University Press, 1983).

34. See *Ballot Access News* at www.ballotaccess.org, and issues of the *Election Law Journal*.

35. Orit Kedar, "When Moderate Voters Prefer Extreme Parties," *American Political Science Review* 99 (2005): 185–199.

36. James E. Campbell, "The 2002 Midterm Election," *PS* 36 (2003): 203–207.

PART II THE POLITICAL PARTY AS AN ORGANIZATION

1. See Alan Ware, ed., *Political Parties* (New York: Basil Blackwell, 1987).

CHAPTER 3 THE STATE AND LOCAL PARTY ORGANIZATIONS

1. Andrew M. Appleton and Daniel S. Ward, *State Party Profiles* (Washington, DC: CQ Press, 1997), Appendix.

2. A public utility is a government-regulated provider of services, such as a gas or a water company. Leon Epstein, *Political Parties in the American Mold* (Madison: University of Wisconsin Press, 1986), pp. 155–199.

3. The cases are *Tashjian v. Republican Party of Connecticut* (1986), *Eu v. San Francisco County Democratic Central Committee et al.* (1989), and *California Democratic Party v. Jones* (2000). See David K. Ryden, "The Good, the Bad, and the Ugly," in John C. Green and Daniel M. Shea, eds., *The State of the Parties*, 3rd ed. (Lanham, MD: Rowman & Littlefield, 1999), pp. 50–65.

4. V. O. Key, Jr., *Politics, Parties and Pressure Groups* (New York: Crowell, 1964), p. 316.

5. Samuel J. Eldersveld, *Political Parties: A Behavioral Analysis* (Chicago: Rand McNally, 1964).

6. The organization of American political parties differs from what Robert Michels calls the "iron law of oligarchy"—that organizations are inevitably controlled from the top. See Robert Michels, *Political Parties* (Glencoe, IL: Free Press, 1949).

7. M. Craig Brown and Charles N. Halaby, "Machine Politics in America, 1870–1945," *Journal of Interdisciplinary History* 17 (1987): 587–612.

8. See David Mayhew, *Placing Parties in American Politics* (Princeton: Princeton University Press, 1986), pp. 19–21.

9. See Kenneth Finegold, *Experts and Politicians* (Princeton: Princeton University Press, 1995).

10. Steven P. Erie, *Rainbow's End* (Berkeley: University of California Press, 1988); but see John F. Bibby, "Party Organizations 1946–1996," in Byron E. Shafer, ed., *Partisan Approaches to Postwar American Politics* (New York: Chatham House, 1998), pp. 142–185.

11. Anne Freedman, *Patronage: An American Tradition* (Chicago: Nelson-Hall, 1994), Chapter 5.

12. Kenneth R. Mladenka, "The Urban Bureaucracy and the Chicago Political Machine," *American Political Science Review* 74 (1980): 991–998.

13. Michael Johnston, "Patrons and Clients, Jobs and Machines," *American Political Science Review* 73 (1979): 385–398. On the impact of patronage on party success over time, see Olle Folke, Shigeo Hirano, and James M. Snyder, Jr., "Patronage and Elections in U.S. States," *American Political Science Review* 105 (2011): 567–585.

14. James L. Gibson, Cornelius P. Cotter, John F. Bibby, and Robert J. Huckshorn, "Whither the Local Parties?" *American Journal of Political Science* 29 (1985): 139–160.

15. Cornelius P. Cotter, James L. Gibson, John F. Bibby, and Robert J. Huckshorn, *Party Organization in American Politics* (New York: Praeger, 1984), pp. 49–53.

16. See Cotter et al., *Party Organization in American Politics*, p. 54, for 1964–1980. On 1984: James L. Gibson, John P. Frendreis, and Laura L. Vertz, "Party Dynamics in the 1980s," *American Journal of Political Science* 33 (1989): 67–90. On 1988: Charles E. Smith, Jr., "Changes in Party Organizational Strength and Activity 1979–1988," unpublished manuscript, Ohio State University, 1989. See also Samuel J. Eldersveld, "The Party Activist in Detroit and Los Angeles," in William J. Crotty, ed., *Political Parties in Local Areas* (Knoxville: University of Tennessee Press, 1986), pp. 89–119.

17. Douglas D. Roscoe and Shannon Jenkins, "State and Local Party Organizations in the 21st Century," paper presented at the 2010 annual meeting of the American Political Science Association, pp. 34–36.

18. Daniel M. Shea and John C. Green, "Local Parties and Mobilizing the Vote," in John C. Green and Daniel J. Coffey, eds., *The State of the Parties*, 5th ed. (Lanham, MD: Rowman & Littlefield, 2007), pp. 222 and 224.

19. Carol S. Weissert, "Michigan," in Appleton and Ward, *State Party Profiles*, pp. 153–160.

20. Melody Crowder-Meyer, "The Party's Still Going," in Green and Coffey, eds., *The State of the Parties*, 6th ed. (Lanham, MD: Rowman & Littlefield, 2010), p. 120.

21. L. Sandy Maisel, "American Political Parties," in Jeffrey E. Cohen, Richard Fleisher, and Paul Kantor, eds., *American Political Parties: Decline or Resurgence?* (Washington, DC: CQ Press, 2001), pp. 112–114.

22. Gary F. Moncrief, Peverill Squire, and Malcolm E. Jewell, *Who Runs for the Legislature?* (Upper Saddle River, NJ: Prentice Hall, 2001).

23. John J. Coleman, "The Resurgence of Party Organization?" in Shea and Green, eds., *The State of the Parties* (Lanham, MD: Rowman & Littlefield, 1994), pp. 282–298.

24. A. James Reichley, *The Life of the Parties* (Lanham, MD: Rowman & Littlefield, 2000), pp. 129–130.

25. Malcolm E. Jewell and Sarah M. Morehouse, *Political Parties and Elections in American States*, 4th ed. (Washington, DC: CQ Press, 2001), p. 4.

26. Jewell and Morehouse, *Political Parties and Elections*, p. 1.

27. See James L. Gibson, Cornelius P. Cotter, John F. Bibby, and Robert J. Huckshorn, "Assessing Party Organizational Strength," *American Journal of Political Science* 27 (1983): 193–222.

28. Jewell and Morehouse, *Political Parties and Elections*, p. 52; and John H. Aldrich, "Southern Parties in State and Nation," *Journal of Politics* 62 (2000): 655–659.

29. Jewell and Morehouse, *Political Parties and Elections*, p. 211.

30. Anthony Gierzynski, *Legislative Party Campaign Committees in the American States* (Lexington: University Press of Kentucky, 1992).

31. Robert E. Hogan, "Candidate Perceptions of Political Party Campaign Activity in State Legislative Elections," *State Politics and Policy Quarterly* 2 (2002): 66–85.

32. Raymond J. La Raja, "State Parties and Soft Money," in John C. Green and Rick Farmer, eds., *The State of the Parties*, 4th ed. (Lanham, MD: Rowman & Littlefield, 2003), pp. 132–150.

33. Anthony Corrado, "Political Party Finance under BCRA: An Initial Assessment," Brookings Institution paper, 2004, at www.brookings.edu/views/papers/corrado20040311_paper.pdf (accessed July 3, 2011).

34. Sarah M. Morehouse and Malcolm E. Jewell, "State Parties," in Green and Farmer, eds., *The State of the Parties*, p. 151. The budget estimates come from Robert J. Huckshorn and John F. Bibby, "State Parties in an Era of Political Change,"

in Joel L. Fleishman, ed., *The Future of American Political Parties* (Englewood Cliffs, NJ: Prentice-Hall, 1982), pp. 70–100; and Aldrich, "Southern Parties," p. 656.

35. Derek Willis, "State Parties Adjust to McCain-Feingold," Center for Public Integrity press release, Washington, DC, August 26, 2004.

36. See Aldrich, "Southern Parties," pp. 656–657.

37. Aldrich, "Southern Parties," Table 7, pp. 656–657.

38. See Ari Berman, "The Prophet," *The Nation*, January 5, 2009, at www.thenation.com/article/prophet (accessed November 4, 2011).

39. Kimberly H. Conger, *The Christian Right and Republican State Politics* (New York: Palgrave MacMillan, 2009).

40. See Marty Cohen, David Karol, Hans Noel, and John Zaller, *The Party Decides* (Chicago: University of Chicago Press, 2008); and Seth Masket, *No Middle Ground* (Ann Arbor, MI: University of Michigan Press, 2011).

41. John H. Kessel, "Ray Bliss and the Development of the Ohio Republican Party During the 1950s," in John C. Green, ed., *Politics, Professionalism, and Power* (Lanham, MD: University Press of America, 1994), pp. 48–61.

42. See Jewell and Morehouse, *Political Parties and Elections*, p. 36. See also Edward G. Carmines and James A. Stimson, *Issue Evolution* (Princeton: Princeton University Press, 1989); and Joseph A. Aistrup, *The Southern Strategy Revisited* (Lexington: University Press of Kentucky, 1996).

43. Charles Prysby, "North Carolina," and Anne E. Kelley, "Florida," in Appleton and Ward, *State Party Profiles*, pp. 234–243 and 62–64.

44. See the articles in John A. Clark and Charles Prysby, eds., "Grassroots Party Activists in Southern Politics, 1991–2001," *American Review of Politics* 24 (Spring and Summer 2001), pp. 1–223.

45. Aldrich, "Southern Parties," p. 655.

46. Walter Dean Burnham, *Critical Elections and the Mainsprings of American Politics* (New York: Norton, 1970), p. 72.

47. Alan Ware, *The Breakdown of the Democratic Party Organization 1940–80* (Oxford, UK: Oxford University Press, 1985).

CHAPTER 4 THE PARTIES' NATIONAL ORGANIZATIONS

1. Cornelius P. Cotter and Bernard C. Hennessy, *Politics without Power: The National Party Committees* (New York: Atherton, 1964).

2. See Philip A. Klinkner, *The Losing Parties: Out-Party National Committees, 1956–1993* (New Haven: Yale University Press, 1994).

3. James W. Ceaser, "Political Parties—Declining, Stabilizing, or Resurging," in Anthony King, ed., *The New American Political System* (Washington, DC: American Enterprise Institute, 1990), p. 115. See also Sidney M. Milkis, *The President and the Parties* (New York: Oxford University Press, 1993).

4. Jo Freeman, *A Room at a Time* (Lanham, MD: Rowman & Littlefield, 2000).

5. David B. Magleby, "Electoral Politics as Team Sport," in John C. Green and Daniel J. Coffey, eds., *The State of the Parties*, 6th ed. (Lanham, MD: Rowman & Littlefield, 2010), pp. 81–100.

6. John C. Green, ed., *Politics, Professionalism, and Power: Modern Party Organization and the Legacy of Ray C. Bliss* (Lanham, MD: University Press of America, 1994).

7. See Austin Ranney, *Curing the Mischiefs of Faction* (Berkeley: University of California Press, 1975); William J. Crotty, *Decisions for the Democrats* (Baltimore: Johns Hopkins University Press, 1978); and Byron E. Shafer, *The Quiet Revolution* (New York: Russell Sage Foundation, 1983).

8. John F. Bibby, "Party Renewal in the Republican National Party," in Gerald M. Pomper, ed., *Party Renewal in America* (New York: Praeger, 1981), pp. 102–115.

9. See Paul S. Herrnson, "The Revitalization of National Party Organizations," in L. Sandy Maisel, ed., *The Parties Respond*, 2nd ed. (Boulder, CO: Westview, 1994), pp. 45–68.

10. See Marian Currinder, *Money in the House* (Boulder, CO: Westview, 2009), pp. 34–39.

11. Emily Cadei, "Incumbents Feed the Party Coffers," *CQ Weekly*, October 6, 2008, p. 2642.

12. Gary C. Jacobson, "Congress: The Second Democratic Wave," in Michael Nelson, ed., *The Elections of 2008* (Washington, DC: CQ Press, 2009), pp. 107–108.

13. See Paul S. Herrnson, *Party Campaigning in the 1980s* (Cambridge, MA: Harvard University Press, 1988), p. 47.

14. See David B. Magleby and J. Quin Monson, eds., *The Last Hurrah?* (Provo, UT: Center for the Study of Elections and Democracy, 2003).

15. Daniel A. Smith, "Strings Attached," in Magleby and Monson, eds., *The Last Hurrah?*, p. 194.

16. Jacobson, "Congress," p. 107.

17. Elaine C. Kamarck, "Assessing Howard Dean's Fifty State Strategy and the 2006 Midterm Elections," *The Forum* 4 (2006),

at www.bepress.com/forum/vol4/iss3/art5 (accessed November 7, 2011).

18. Ari Berman, "The Prophet," *The Nation*, January 5, 2009, at www.thenation.com/article/prophet (accessed November 7, 2011).

19. Adam Nagourney, "Dean Seeks Some Respect (and Credit) for Obama's Victory," *New York Times*, November 11, 2008, at www.nytimes.com/2008/11/12/us/politics/12web-nagourney.html (accessed November 7, 2011).

20. James W. Ceaser, Andrew E. Busch, and John J. Pitney, Jr., *Epic Journey* (Lanham, MD: Rowman & Littlefield, 2009), p. 46.

21. Timothy P. Nokken, "Ideological Congruence Versus Electoral Success," *American Politics Research* 31 (2003): 3–26.

22. Leon D. Epstein, *Political Parties in the American Mold* (Madison: University of Wisconsin Press, 1986), p. 200.

23. John J. Coleman, "The Resurgence of Party Organization?" in Daniel M. Shea and John C. Green, eds., *The State of the Parties* (Lanham, MD: Rowman & Littlefield, 1994), pp. 311–328.

CHAPTER 5   PARTY ACTIVISTS

1. Peter B. Clark and James Q. Wilson, "Incentive Systems: A Theory of Organizations," *Administrative Science Quarterly* 6 (1961): 129–166.

2. See A. James Reichley, *The Life of the Parties* (Lanham, MD: Rowman & Littlefield, 2000), pp. 72, 118, 128–130, 174–176; and Martin Shefter, *Political Parties and the State* (Princeton: Princeton University Press, 1994).

3. The 1976 case is *Elrod v. Burns*; the 1980 case is *Branti v. Finkel*, and the 1990 case is *Rutan v. Republican Party of Illinois*.

4. On the case for patronage, see the dissenting opinions to the Supreme Court's *Elrod, Branti,* and *Rutan* decisions. The case against patronage is well put in Anne Freedman, *Patronage: An American Tradition* (Chicago: Nelson-Hall, 1994), Chapter 5.

5. Cornelius P. Cotter, James L. Gibson, John F. Bibby, and Robert J. Huckshorn, *Party Organizations in American Politics* (New York: Praeger, 1984), p. 42; and Robert J. Huckshorn, *Party Leadership in the States* (Amherst: University of Massachusetts Press, 1976), p. 37.

6. See Sidney Verba, Kay Lehman Schlozman, and Henry E. Brady, *Voice and Equality* (Cambridge, MA: Harvard University Press, 1995), pp. 112–121.

7. John H. Aldrich, *Why Parties? A Second Look* (Chicago: University of Chicago Press, 2011), p. 188.

8. Samuel J. Eldersveld, "The Party Activist in Detroit and Los Angeles," in William Crotty, ed., *Political Parties in Local Areas* (Knoxville: University of Tennessee Press, 1986), Chapter 4.

9. John A. Clark, John M. Bruce, John H. Kessel, and William Jacoby, "I'd Rather Switch than Fight," *American Journal of Political Science* 35 (1991): 577–597; and Dorothy Davidson Nesbit, "Changing Partisanship among Southern Party Activists," *Journal of Politics* 50 (1988): 322–334.

10. Verba, Schlozman, and Brady, *Voice and Equality*, p. 121.

11. See M. Margaret Conway, *Political Participation in the United States*, 3rd ed. (Washington, DC: CQ Press, 2000).

12. See Clark and Wilson, "Incentive Systems." Note that the term "professional," as used here, does not necessarily refer to someone who is paid for party work.

13. See Marty Cohen, David Karol, Hans Noel, and John Zaller, *The Party Decides* (Chicago: University of Chicago Press, 2008), pp. 88–91, 178 (quote on p. 89).

14. Michael A. Maggiotto and Ronald E. Weber, "The Impact of Organizational Incentives on County Party Chairpersons," *American Politics Quarterly* 14 (1986): 201–218.

15. Robert D. Putnam, *Bowling Alone* (New York: Simon & Schuster, 2000).

16. Verba, Schlozman, and Brady, *Voice and Equality*, Chapter 3. This seems to be true in other democracies as well; see Paul F. Whiteley, "Is the Party Over?" *Party Politics* 17 (2011): 21–44.

17. American National Election Studies, University of Michigan; data made available by the Inter-University Consortium for Political and Social Research.

18. See Paul Allen Beck and M. Kent Jennings, "Updating Political Periods and Political Participation," *American Political Science Review* 78 (1984): 198–201; and Steven E. Finkel and Gregory Trevor, "Reassessing Ideological Bias in Campaign Participation," *Political Behavior* 8 (1986): 374–390.

19. See Verba, Schlozman, and Brady, *Voice and Equality*, pp. 15–16 and Chapters 9–14.

20. Henry E. Brady, Kay Lehman Schlozman, and Sidney Verba, "Prospecting for Participants," *American Political Science Review* 93 (1999): 153–168.

21. Verba, Schlozman, and Brady, *Voice and Equality*, pp. 135 and 139–144.

22. See, for example, Patrick R. Cotter, Samuel H. Fisher III, and Patrick Fuller, "Alabama: Maturing Party Competition," *American Review of Politics* 24 (2003): 26.

23. See Verba, Schlozman, and Brady, *Voice and Equality*, p. 190, Chapters 7 and 12, for campaign activists; Kyle L. Saunders and Alan I. Abramowitz, "Ideological Realignment and Active Partisans in the American Electorate," *American Politics Research* 32 (2004): 285–309, for party activists more generally; Ronald B. Rapoport, Alan I. Abramowitz, and John McGlennon, *The Life of the Parties* (Lexington: University of Kentucky Press, 1986), Chapter 3, for state convention delegates; Samuel J. Best and Brian S. Krueger, "Analyzing the Representativeness of Internet Political Participation," *Political Behavior* 24 (2005): pp. 183–216, for online activists; Chapter 10 of this book for national convention delegates, and American Political Science Association Task Force, "American Democracy in an Age of Rising Inequality," *Perspectives on Politics* 2 (2004): 655 on protest activity.

24. See Michael Margolis and Raymond E. Owen, "From Organization to Personalism," *Polity* 18 (1985): 313–328.

25. Marjorie Randon Hershey, Nathaniel Birkhead, and Beth C. Easter, "Party Activists and Political Polarization," in Mark D. Brewer and L. Sandy Maisel, eds., *The Parties Respond*, 5th ed. (Boulder, CO: Westview Press, 2012).

26. Verba, Schlozman, and Brady, *Voice and Equality*, pp. 84–91.

27. Ibid., pp. 220–225.

28. Edward G. Carmines and James Woods, "The Role of Party Activists in the Evolution of the Abortion Issue," *Political Behavior* 24 (2002): 361–377; and Larry M. Bartels, "Base Appeal: The Political Attitudes and Priorities of Core Partisans," paper presented at the 2010 annual meeting of the American Political Science Association, Washington, DC.

29. Alan I. Abramowitz, *The Disappearing Center* (New Haven: Yale University Press, 2010), pp. 47–48.

30. Saunders and Abramowitz, "Ideological Realignment and Active Partisans in the American Electorate."

31. Geoffrey C. Layman, Thomas M. Carsey, John C. Green, Richard Herrera, and Rosalyn Cooperman, "Activists and Conflict Extension in American Party Politics," *American Political Science Review* 104 (2010): 324–346.

PART III   THE POLITICAL PARTY IN THE ELECTORATE

1. See Angus Campbell, Philip E. Converse, Warren E. Miller, and Donald E. Stokes, *The American Voter* (New York: Wiley, 1960), Chapter 6.

2. Steven E. Finkel and Howard A. Scarrow, "Party Identification and Party Enrollment," *Journal of Politics* 47 (1985): 620–642.

CHAPTER 6   PARTY IDENTIFICATION

1. Party identification is developing in newer democracies such as Russia and the Ukraine as well, even in the face of overwhelmingly negative attitudes toward political parties. See Ted Brader and Joshua A. Tucker, "The Emergence of Mass Partisanship in Russia, 1993–1996," *American Journal of Political Science* 45 (2001): 69–83.

2. For a summary of these approaches, with an argument for party identification as social identity, see Donald Green, Bradley Palmquist, and Eric Schickler, *Partisan Hearts and Minds* (New Haven: Yale University Press, 2002), Chapter 5. See also Thomas M. Carsey and Geoffrey C. Layman, "Changing Sides or Changing Minds?" *American Journal of Political Science* 50 (2006): 464–477.

3. Alternative forms of measurement have been suggested by John R. Petrocik, "An Analysis of the Intransitivities in the Index of Party Identification," *Political Methodology* 1 (1974): 31–47; and Herbert F. Weisberg, "A Multidimensional Conceptualization of Party Identification," *Political Behavior* 2 (1980): 33–60. See also Green, Palmquist, and Schickler, *Partisan Hearts and Minds*, Chapter 2.

4. Jeremy Zilber, *Why Mommy Is a Democrat* (Madison, WI: Jeremy Zilber, 2006); and David W. Hedrick, *The Liberal Claus* (Camas, WA: Freedoms Answer, 2010).

5. Paul Allen Beck and M. Kent Jennings, "Family Traditions, Political Periods, and the Development of Partisan Orientations," *Journal of Politics* 53 (1991): 742–763.

6. Paul Allen Beck, Russell J. Dalton, Steven Greene, and Robert Huckfeldt, "The Social Calculus of Voting," *American Political Science Review* 96 (2002): 57–73.

7. Richard G. Niemi and M. Kent Jennings, "Issues and Inheritance in the Formation of Party Identification," *American Journal of Political Science* 35 (1991): 970–988.

8. Green, Palmquist, and Schickler, *Partisan Hearts and Minds*, pp. 7–8.

9. Duane F. Alwin and Jon A. Krosnick, "Aging, Cohorts, and the Stability of Sociopolitical Orientations over the Life Cycle," *American Journal of Sociology* 97 (1991): 185–187.

10. See William Clagett, "Partisan Acquisition vs. Partisan Intensity," *American Journal of Political Science* 25 (1981): 193–214.

11. Logan Dancey and Paul Goren, "Party Identification, Issue Attitudes, and the Dynamics of Political Debate," *American Journal of Political Science* 54 (2010): 686–699.

12. James E. Campbell, "Sources of the New Deal Realignment," *Western Political Quarterly* 38 (1985): 357–376; and Warren E. Miller, "Generational Changes and Party Identification," *Political Behavior* 14 (1992): 333–352.

13. The seminal report of these studies is Angus Campbell, Philip E. Converse, Warren E. Miller, and Donald E. Stokes, *The American Voter* (New York: Wiley, 1960).

14. See Luke Keele and Jennifer Wolak, "Value Conflict and Volatility in Party Identification," *British Journal of Political Science* 36 (2006): 671–690.

15. See Paul Allen Beck, "The Dealignment Era in America," in Russell J. Dalton, Scott C. Flanagan, and Paul Allen Beck, eds., *Electoral Change in Advanced Industrial Democracies* (Princeton: Princeton University Press, 1984), pp. 244–246.

16. Philip E. Converse and Gregory B. Markus, "Plus ça change …: The New CPS Election Study Panel," *American Political Science Review* 73 (1979): 32–49. See also Donald Philip Green and Bradley Palmquist, "How Stable Is Party Identification?" *Political Behavior* 16 (1994): 437–466; and Paul Goren, "Party Identification and Core Political Values," *American Journal of Political Science* 49 (2005): 881–896.

17. Russell Dalton, "The Decline of Party Identification," in Russell J. Dalton and Martin P. Wattenberg, eds., *Parties without Partisans* (Oxford, UK: Oxford University Press, 2000), pp. 19–36. On split-ticket voting, see Barry C. Burden and David C. Kimball, *Why Americans Split Their Tickets* (Ann Arbor, MI: University of Michigan Press, 2002).

18. Martin P. Wattenberg, *The Decline of American Political Parties, 1952–1994* (Cambridge, MA: Harvard University Press, 1996), p. ix.

19. See James H. Kuklinski, Paul J. Quirk, Jennifer Jerit, and Robert F. Rich, "The Political Environment and Citizen Competence," *American Journal of Political Science* 45 (2001): 410–424.

20. Jeffrey M. Stonecash, "Changing American Political Parties," in Stonecash, ed., *New Directions in American Political Parties* (New York: Routledge, 2010), p. 4.

21. James W. Ceaser and Andrew E. Busch, *Red Over Blue* (Lanham, MD: Rowman & Littlefield, 2005), p. 136.

22. See John R. Petrocik, "Measuring Party Support: Leaners Are Not Independents," *Electoral Studies* 28 (2009): 562–572.

23. Jeffrey M. Jones, "Number of Solidly Democratic States Cut in Half From '08 to '10," Gallup Poll, February 21, 2011, at www.gallup.com/poll/146234/Number-Solidly-Democratic-States-Cut-Half.aspx (accessed November 8, 2011). Note that those who say they lean toward one party are counted as party identifiers.

24. Pew Research Center for the People & the Press, "GOP Makes Big Gains Among White Voters," July 22, 2011, at people-press.org/2011/07/22/gop-makes-big-gains-among-white-voters/ (accessed November 8, 2011).

25. David Madland and Ruy Teixeira, "New Progressive America: The Millennial Generation," May 13, 2009, at www.americanprogress.org/issues/2009/05/millennial_generation.html (accessed November 8, 2011).

26. See, for example, Alan S. Gerber, Gregory A. Huber, and Ebonya Washington, "Party Affiliation, Partisanship, and Political Beliefs," *American Political Science Review* 104 (2010): 720–744.

27. Jeffrey M. Jones, "Republicans, Democrats Shift on Whether Gov't Is a Threat," October 18, 2010, at www.gallup.com/poll/143717/Republicans-Democrats-Shift-Whether-Gov-Threat.aspx (accessed November 8, 2011).

28. The poll data are from Green, Palmquist, and Schickler, *Partisan Hearts and Minds*, p. 127. They see these poll results, however, as evidence that the two groups of partisans are using different standards of evaluation rather than as an indicator of perceptual bias.

29. See Alan S. Gerber and Gregory A. Huber, "Partisanship, Political Control, and Economic Assessments," *American Journal of Political Science* 54 (2010): 153–173; and Michael W. Wagner, "Think of It This Way," Ph.D. dissertation, Indiana University, 2006.

30. "Beyond Red vs. Blue," Pew Research Center for the People & the Press, May 4, 2011, at http://pewresearch.org/pubs/1982/political-typology-2011-ideological-extremes-diverse-center (accessed November 8, 2011).

31. Alan I. Abramowitz, *The Disappearing Center* (New Haven: Yale University Press, 2010), pp. 44–45.

32. Andy Baker, Barry Ames, and Lucio R. Renno, "Social Context and Campaign Volatility in New Democracies," *American Journal of Political Science* 50 (2006): 382–399.

33. See, for example, Larry M. Bartels, "Partisanship and Voting Behavior, 1952–1996," *American Journal of Political Science* 44 (2000): 35–50.

34. Paul Allen Beck, Lawrence Baum, Aage R. Clausen, and Charles E. Smith, Jr., "Patterns and Sources of Ticket Splitting in Subpresidential Voting," *American Political Science Review* 86 (1992): 916–928.

35. Kyle L. Saunders, Alan I. Abramowitz, and Jonathan Williamson, "A New Kind of Balancing Act," *Political Research Quarterly* 58 (2005): 69–78.

36. Barry C. Burden and David C. Kimball, "A New Approach to the Study of Ticket-Splitting," *American Political Science Review* 92 (1998): 533–544.

37. Scott Basinger and Howard Lavine, "Ambivalence, Information, and Electoral Choice," *American Political Science Review* 99 (2005): 169–184.

38. See Morris P. Fiorina, *Retrospective Voting in American National Elections* (New Haven: Yale University Press, 1981); and Michael B. MacKuen, Robert S. Erikson, and James A. Stimson, "Macropartisanship," *American Political Science Review* 83 (1989): 1125–1142.

39. And on which the individual sees differences between the parties; see Carsey and Layman, "Changing Sides or Changing Minds?"

40. See Paul R. Abramson, John H. Aldrich, and David W. Rohde, *Change and Continuity in the 2008 and 2010 Elections* (Washington, DC: CQ Press, 2012), Chapter 8.

41. These figures are much higher than those presented in Chapter 8 because respondents to the American National Election studies often overreport their levels of voter turnout.

42. Sidney Verba and Norman H. Nie, *Participation in America* (Chicago: University of Chicago Press, 1987), Chapter 12.

43. David B. Magleby, Candice J. Nelson, and Mark C. Westlye, "The Myth of the Independent Voter Revisited," in Paul M. Sniderman and Benjamin Highton, eds., *Facing the Challenge of Democracy* (Princeton: Princeton University Press, 2011), pp. 238–263.

44. V. O. Key, Jr. (with Milton C. Cummings), *The Responsible Electorate* (Cambridge, MA: Harvard University Press, 1966).

45. See David Nather, "Courting the Independents," *CQ Weekly*, June 16, 2008, p. 1610.

46. Todd Donovan, "A Goal for Reform," *PS: Political Science and Politics* 40 (2007): 683.

47. See Paul R. Abramson, John H. Aldrich, and David W. Rohde, *Change and Continuity in the 1992 Elections* (Washington, DC: CQ Press, 1995), p. 245.

48. See Martin P. Wattenberg, *The Rise of Candidate-Centered Politics* (Cambridge, MA: Harvard University Press, 1991).

CHAPTER 7 PARTY COALITIONS AND PARTY CHANGE

1. See Edward G. Carmines and James A. Stimson, *Issue Evolution* (Princeton: Princeton University Press, 1989); and Paul M. Sniderman and Thomas Piazza, *The Scar of Race* (Cambridge, MA: Harvard University Press, 1995).

2. See, for example, Jerome M. Clubb, William H. Flanigan, and Nancy H. Zingale, *Partisan Realignment* (Boulder, CO: Westview Press, 1990), Chapter 3.

3. See John H. Aldrich, *Why Parties? A Second Look* (Chicago: University of Chicago Press, 2011), pp. 281–287.

4. See V. O. Key, Jr., "A Theory of Critical Elections," *Journal of Politics* 17 (1955): 3–18; Walter Dean Burnham, *Critical Elections and the Mainsprings of American Politics* (New York: Norton, 1970); and James L. Sundquist, *Dynamics of the Party System* (Washington, DC: Brookings Institution, 1973).

5. These events typically unfold over a period of time, but for convenience, the beginning of each party system is located in the year in which the new majority party coalition first took office.

6. Michael Holt, *The Rise and Fall of the American Whig Party* (New York: Oxford University Press, 2003).

7. The third party system actually contained two distinct periods. From the end of the Civil War in 1865 through 1876, Democratic voting strength in the South was held in check by the occupying Union army and various Reconstruction policies and laws. So to reflect the true party balance during this time, it is helpful to differentiate between 1861–1876 and the 1877–1896 period.

8. A. James Reichley, *The Life of the Parties* (Lanham, MD: Rowman & Littlefield, 2000), p. 104.

9. See Jeffrey M. Stonecash, "Class in American Politics," in Stonecash, ed., *New Directions in American Political Parties* (New York: Routledge, 2010), pp. 110–125.

10. James Madison, *The Federalist No. 10*, November 22, 1787.

11. See Larry Bartels, *Unequal Democracy* (Princeton: Princeton University Press, 2008).

12. See Paul R. Abramson, John H. Aldrich, and David W. Rohde, *Change and Continuity in the 2008 and 2010 Elections* (Washington, DC: CQ Press, 2011), pp. 203–204.

13. Jeffrey M. Stonecash, *Class and Party in American Politics* (Boulder, CO: Westview Press, 2000), pp. 13 and 139, and Chapter 4.

14. On the change in upper-income people's attitudes toward the Republican Party, see Mark D. Brewer, *Party Images in the American Electorate* (New York: Routledge, 2009), pp. 25–26.

15. See Donald C. Baumer and Howard J. Gold, *Parties, Polarization, and Democracy in the U.S.* (Boulder, CO: Paradigm, 2010), pp. 164–165.

16. Henry E. Brady, "Trust the People: Political Party Coalitions and the 2000 Election," in Jack N. Rakove, *The Unfinished Election of 2000* (New York: Basic Books, 2001), p. 55.

17. See Frank Newport, "Democrats Do Best Among Generation Y and Baby Boomers," Gallup Poll, May 8, 2009, at www.gallup.com/poll/118285/Democrats-Best-Among-Generation-Baby-Boomers.aspx?CSTS=alert (accessed November 10, 2011).

18. Frank Newport, "Blacks as Conservative as Republicans on Some Moral Issues," Gallup Poll, December 3, 2008, at www.gallup.com/poll/112807/Blacks-Conservative-Republicans-Some-Moral-Issues.aspx (accessed November 10, 2011).

19. See David E. Campbell, John C. Green, and Geoffrey C. Layman, "The Party Faithful," *American Journal of Political Science* 55 (2011): 42–58.

20. Frank Newport, "Republicans Remain Disproportionately White and Religious," Gallup Poll, September 1, 2010, at www.gallup.com/poll/142826/Republicans-Remain-Disproportionately-White-Religious.aspx (accessed November 10, 2011).

21. See David C. Leege and Lyman A. Kellstedt, eds., *Rediscovering the Religious Factor in American Politics* (Armonk, NY: M. E. Sharpe, 1993).

22. This was also the result of anti-immigrant ballot propositions sponsored by California Republicans in the 1990s and in other states since then; see Shaun Bowler, Stephen P. Nicholson, and Gary M. Segura, "Earthquakes and Aftershocks," *American Journal of Political Science* 50 (2006): 146–157.

23. CNN exit poll data at www.cnn.com/ELECTION/2008/results/polls/#USP00p1 (accessed November 10, 2011).

24. See Torben Iversen and Frances Rosenbluth, "The Political Economy of Gender," *American Journal of Political Science* 50 (2006): 1–19.

25. Janet M. Box-Steffensmeier, Suzanna De Boef, and Tse-Min Lin, "The Dynamics of the Partisan Gender Gap," *American Political Science Review* 98 (2004): 515–528; and Karen M. Kaufman and John R. Petrocik, "The Changing Politics of American Men," *American Journal of Political Science* 43 (1999): 864–887.

26. Kira Sanbonmatsu, *Democrats, Republicans, and the Politics of Women's Place* (Ann Arbor, MI: University of Michigan Press, 2002), Chapter 3; see also Christina Wolbrecht, *The Politics of Women's Rights* (Princeton: Princeton University Press, 2000); and Brian Schaffner, "Priming Gender," *American Journal of Political Science* 49 (2005): 803–817.

27. Calculated from *CQ Weekly*'s profiles of House freshmen, November 8, 2010, pp. 2586–2616 and updates.

28. Calculated from www.cnn.com/ELECTION/2008/results/polls/#val=USP00p3 (accessed November 10, 2011).

29. Mark D. Brewer and Jeffrey M. Stonecash, *Dynamics of American Political Parties* (Cambridge: Cambridge University Press, 2009), Chapter 11.

30. Greg D. Adams, "Abortion: Evidence of an Issue Evolution," *American Journal of Political Science* 41 (1997): 718–737.

31. Quoted in Thomas B. Edsall, "Political Party Is No Longer Dictated By Class Status," *Washington Post*, November 9, 2000, p. A37.

32. See Geoffrey C. Layman, *The Great Divide* (New York: Columbia University Press, 2001).

33. Matthew Levendusky, *The Partisan Sort* (Chicago: University of Chicago Press, 2009).

34. Seth C. McKee, *Republican Ascendancy* (Boulder, CO: Westview Press, 2010).

35. Nicholas A. Valentino and David O. Sears, "Old Times There Are Not Forgotten," *American Journal of Political Science* 49 (2005): 673.

36. Jeffrey M. Stonecash, *Political Parties Matter* (Boulder, CO: Lynne Rienner, 2006), Chapter 4.

37. Merle Black, "The Transformation of the Southern Democratic Party," *Journal of Politics* 66 (2004): 1001–1017.

38. Valentino and Sears, "Old Times There Are Not Forgotten," p. 676. See also Earl Black and Merle Black, *Divided America* (New York: Simon & Schuster, 2007), pp. 32–39 and 74–91.

39. Associated Press, "White Southern Democrats All But Gone," *Hoosier Times*, November 7, 2010, p. E2.

40. Gary Miller and Norman Schofield, "The Transformation of the Republican and Democratic Party Coalitions in the U.S.," *Perspectives on Politics* 6 (2008): 433–450.

41. John R. Petrocik, "Party Coalitions in the American Public," in John C. Green and Daniel J. Coffey, *The State of the Parties*, 5th ed. (Lanham, MD: Rowman & Littlefield, 2007), p. 285.

42. Martin P. Wattenberg, *The Decline of American Political Parties 1952–96* (Cambridge, MA: Harvard University Press, 1998).

43. Donald Green, Bradley Palmquist, and Eric Schickler, *Partisan Hearts and Minds* (New Haven: Yale University Press, 2002), pp. 141 and 158.

44. Helmut Norpoth, "Under Way and Here to Stay: Party Realignment in the 1980s?" *Public Opinion Quarterly* 51 (1987): 376–391; and Warren E. Miller, "Party Identification, Realignment, and Party Voting," *American Political Science Review* 85 (1991): 557–570.

45. See Earl Black and Merle Black, *The Rise of Southern Republicans* (Cambridge, MA: Harvard University Press, 2002); Michael F. Meffert, Helmut Norpoth, and Anirudh V. S. Ruhil, "Realignment and Macropartisanship," *American Political Science Review* 95 (2001): 953–962; and Paul Frymer, "The 1994 Electoral Aftershock," in Philip A. Klinkner, ed., *Midterm* (Boulder, CO: Westview Press, 1996), pp. 99–113.

46. Alan Cooperman and Thomas B. Edsall, "Evangelicals Say They Led Charge for the GOP," *Washington Post*, November 8, 2004, p. A1.

47. See Alan I. Abramowitz, "The Incredible Shrinking Republican Base," *Sabato's Crystal Ball* 6 (May 1, 2009).

48. David R. Mayhew, *Electoral Realignments* (New Haven: Yale University Press, 2002); see also Carmines and Stimson, *Issue Evolution*; Byron E. Shafer, ed., *The End of Realignment?* (Madison: University of Wisconsin Press, 1991); and Samuel Merrill III, Bernard Grofman, and Thomas L. Brunell, "Cycles in American National Electoral Politics, 1854–2006," *American Political Science Review* 102 (2008): 1–17.

49. Carmines and Stimson, *Issue Evolution*.

50. See Paul Allen Beck, "A Tale of Two Electorates," in John C. Green and Rick Farmer, eds., *The State of the Parties*, 4th ed. (Lanham, MD: Rowman & Littlefield, 2003), pp. 38–53.

CHAPTER 8 PARTIES AND VOTER TURNOUT

1. See Pippa Norris, *Electoral Engineering* (Cambridge: Cambridge University Press, 2004).

2. The term "suffrage" means the right to vote. See Alexander Keyssar, *The Right to Vote* (Boulder, CO: Basic Books, 2009).

3. Ticket splitting at the local level did occur prior to the secret ballot; see Alan Ware, *The Democratic Party Heads North, 1877–1962* (Cambridge: Cambridge University Press, 2006), p. 21.

4. Stephen M. Nichols and Gregory A. Strizek, "Electronic Voting Machines and Ballot Roll-off," *American Politics Quarterly* 23 (1995): 300–318.

5. Paul Kleppner, *Continuity and Change in Electoral Politics, 1893–1928* (Westport, CT: Greenwood, 1987), pp. 165–166.

6. Peverill Squire, Raymond E. Wolfinger, and David P. Glass, "Residential Mobility and Voter Turnout," *American Political Science Review* 81 (1987): 45–65.

7. Walter Dean Burnham, "Theory and Voting Research," *American Political Science Review* 68 (1974): 1002–1023.

8. The Supreme Court finally ended the white primary in *Smith v. Allwright* (1944).

9. See V. O. Key, Jr., *Southern Politics in State and Nation* (New York: Knopf, 1949).

10. Chandler Davidson and Bernard Grofman, eds., *Quiet Revolution in the South* (Princeton: Princeton University Press, 1994).

11. The landmark Supreme Court cases are *Baker v. Carr* (1962); *Reynolds v. Sims* (1964); and *Wesberry v. Sanders* (1964).

12. The Supreme Court declined to ban partisan gerrymandering most recently in the case of *Vieth v. Jubelirer* (2004).

13. Thomas B. Edsall, "Parties Play Voting Rights Role Reversal," *Washington Post*, February 25, 2001, p. A1. See also Kevin A. Hill, "Does the Creation of Majority Black Districts Aid Republicans?" *Journal of Politics* 57 (1995): 384–401.

14. The cases are *Miller v. Johnson* (1995) and *Easley v. Cromartie* (2001), respectively. On majority–minority districts, see David T. Canon, *Race, Redistricting, and Representation* (Chicago: University of Chicago Press, 1999).

15. See Jeff Manza and Christopher Uggen, "Punishment and Democracy," *Perspectives on Politics* 2 (2004): 491–505.

16. See Robert L. Dudley and Alan R. Gitelson, *American Elections: The Rules Matter* (New York: Longman, 2002), pp. 7–15.

17. See Benjamin Highton and Raymond E. Wolfinger, "Estimating the Effects of the National Voter Registration Act of 1993," *Political Behavior* 20 (1998): 79–104.

18. Glenn E. Mitchell and Christopher Wlezien, "The Impact of Legal Constraints on Voter Registration, Turnout, and the Composition of the American Electorate," *Political Behavior* 17 (1995): 179–202.

19. Nathaniel Persily, testimony before the U.S. Senate Committee on Rules and Administration, March 11, 2009.

20. Raymond E. Wolfinger and Jonathan Hoffman, "Registering and Voting with

Motor Voter," *PS: Political Science and Politics* 34 (2001): 85–92; and Michael D. Martinez and David Hill, "Did Motor Voter Work?" *American Politics Quarterly* 27 (1999): 296–315.

21. See the symposium "Voter Identification," *PS: Political Science & Politics* 42 (2009): 81–130. The case is *Crawford v. Marion County Election Board* (2008).

22. Michael R. Alvarez, Stephen Ansolabehere, Adam Berinsky, Thad Hall, Gabriel Lenz, and Charles Stewart III, "2008 Survey of the Performance of American Elections," May 5, 2008, p. 2, at http:// vote.caltech. edu/drupal/files/report/2008%20Survey% 20of%20the%20Performance%20of% 20American%20Elections%20Executive% 20Summary.pdf (accessed November 11, 2011).

23. Peter Wallsten, "In States, Parties Clash Over Voting Laws That Call for IDs," *Washington Post,* March 7, 2011, p. A1. In 2011, the Texas legislature, for example, voted that licenses to carry concealed handguns, but not student ID cards, are a valid form of voter ID.

24. Henry E. Brady and John E. McNulty, "Turning Out to Vote," *American Political Science Review* 105 (2011): 115–134 find that reducing the number of polling places in Los Angeles in 2003 led to a decline in voter turnout.

25. Ian Urbina, "Reports of Intimidation and Electronic Problems Surface at Polls Across the U.S.," *New York Times*, November 3, 2010, p. P8.

26. See Justin Buchler, Matthew Jarvis, and John E. McNulty, "Punch Card Technology and the Racial Gap in Residual Votes," *Perspectives on Politics* 2 (2004): 517–524.

27. David C. Kimball and Martha Kropf, "The Street-Level Bureaucrats of Elections," *Review of Policy Research* 23 (2006): 1257–1268.

28. See Michael Tomz and Robert P. Van Houweling, "How Does Voting Equipment Affect the Racial Gap in Voided Ballots?" *American Journal of Political Science* 47 (2003): 46–60.

29. Abby Goodnough, "Lost Record of Vote in '02 Florida Race Raises '04 Concern," *New York Times*, July 28, 2004, p. 1.

30. Ian Urbina, "Hurdles to Voting Persisted in 2008," *New York Times*, March 11, 2009, at www.nytimes.com/2009/03/11/us/ politics/11vote.html (accessed November 11, 2011).

31. Because of the difficulties in estimating American turnout, many "official" turnout figures *underestimate* it. The percentages here and in Figure 8.3 correct for this underestimation. Their denominator is an effort to estimate the *eligible* population: the voting-age population minus the number of noncitizens living in the United States. The numerator of the turnout fraction is the number of voters who cast a vote for president or for the office with the highest vote in midterm elections. See Walter Dean Burnham, "The Turnout Problem," in A. James Reichley, ed., *Elections American Style* (Washington, DC: Brookings, 1987), pp. 97–133; and Michael McDonald, "Voter Turnout," at http://elections.gmu.edu/voter_ turnout.htm (accessed November 11, 2011).

32. Unless otherwise indicated, turnout figures are those of the U.S. Census Bureau.

33. Exit poll data from http://elections.nytimes. com/2008/results/president/national-exit-polls.html (accessed November 11, 2011).

34. Walter Dean Burnham, "The Changing Shape of the American Political Universe," *American Political Science Review* 59 (1965): 7–28.

35. Richard A. Brody, "The Puzzle of Participation in America," in Anthony King, ed., *The New American Political System* (Washington, DC: American Enterprise Institute, 1978), pp. 287–324.

36. See John H. Aldrich, "Rational Choice and Turnout," *American Journal of Political Science* 37 (1993): 246–278.

37. Rachel Milstein Sondheimer and Donald P. Green, "Using Experiments to Estimate the Effects of Education on Voter Turnout," *American Journal of Political Science* 54 (2010): 174–189; and Robert A. Jackson, "Clarifying the Relationship between Education and Turnout," *American Politics Quarterly* 23 (1995): 279–299.

38. See Rebecca B. Morton, *Analyzing Elections* (New York: Norton, 2006), pp. 53–55.

39. See Sidney Verba, Norman H. Nie, and Jae-On Kim, *Participation and Political Equality* (Cambridge: Cambridge University Press, 1978).

40. Cliff Zukin, Scott Keeter, Molly Andolina, Krista Jenkins, and Michael X. Delli Carpini, *A New Engagement?* (Oxford: Oxford University Press, 2006).

41. Karl T. Kurz, Alan Rosenthal, and Cliff Zukin, "Citizenship: A Challenge for All Generations," 2003, at www.cpn.org/topics/ youth/k12/pdfs/NCSL_Citizenship.pdf (accessed November 11, 2011).

42. See Zukin et al., *A New Engagement?*, Chapter 6.

43. Lawrence Bobo and Franklin D. Gilliam, Jr., "Race, Sociopolitical Participation, and Black Empowerment," *American Political Science Review* 84 (1990): 377–393.

44. Scott D. McClurg, "The Electoral Relevance of Political Talk," *American Journal of Political Science* 50 (2006): 737–754.

45. Nancy Burns, Kay Lehman Schlozman, and Sidney Verba, "The Public Consequences of Private Inequality," *American Political Science Review* 91 (1997): 373–389.

46. See Steven J. Rosenstone and John Mark Hansen, *Mobilization, Participation, and Democracy in America* (New York: Longman, 2003), pp. 141–156.

47. Lyn Ragsdale and Jerrold G. Rusk, "Who Are Nonvoters?" *American Journal of Political Science* 37 (1993): 721–746.

48. Paul R. Abramson, John H. Aldrich, and David W. Rohde, *Change and Continuity in the 2004 and 2006 Elections* (Washington, DC: CQ Press, 2007), p. 97.

49. Robert A. Jackson, "The Mobilization of U.S. State Electorates in the 1988 and 1990 Elections," *Journal of Politics* 59 (1997): 520–537.

50. David K. Levine and Thomas R. Palfrey, "The Paradox of Voter Participation?" *American Political Science Review* 101 (2007): 143–158.

51. Gerald M. Pomper, "The Presidential Election," in Michael Nelson, ed., *The Elections of 2008* (Washington, DC: CQ Press, 2009), p. 47. See also Michael P. McDonald, "The Return of the Voter," *The Forum* 6 (2008), at www.bepress.com/forum/vol6/iss4/art4 (accessed November 11, 2011).

52. See Donald P. Green and Alan S. Gerber, *Get Out the Vote!* (Washington, DC: Brookings Institution, 2004); and Kevin Arceneaux and David W. Nickerson, "Who Is Mobilized to Vote?" *American Journal of Political Science* 53 (2009): 1–16.

53. Thomas Patterson, press release from the Vanishing Voter Project, John F. Kennedy School of Government, Harvard University, November 11, 2004.

54. McDonald, "The Return of the Voter."

55. Brad T. Gomez, Thomas G. Hansford, and George A. Krause, "The Republicans Should Pray for Rain," *Journal of Politics* 69 (2007): 649–663.

56. Jack Citrin, Eric Schickler, and John Sides, "What If Everyone Voted?" *American Journal of Political Science* 47 (2003): 75–90.

57. See, for example, Andrea Louise Campbell, "Parties, Electoral Participation, and Shifting Voting Blocs," in Paul Pierson and Theda Skocpol, eds., *The Transformation of American Politics* (Princeton: Princeton University Press, 2007), pp. 68–102.

58. Adriel Bettelheim, "Youth's Long-Term Role in Politics," *CQ Weekly*, November 10, 2008, p. 2973.

59. APSA Task Force Report, "American Democracy in an Age of Rising Inequality," *Perspectives on Politics* 2 (2004): 658.

60. Paul S. Martin, "Voting's Rewards," *American Journal of Political Science* 47 (2003): 110–127.

CHAPTER 9 HOW PARTIES CHOOSE CANDIDATES

1. See Alan Ware, *The American Direct Primary* (Cambridge: Cambridge University Press, 2002); and John M. Carey and John Polga-Hecimovich, "Primary Elections and Candidate Strength in Latin America," *Journal of Politics* 68 (2006): 530–543.

2. Stephen J. Wayne, *The Road to the White House 2008* (Belmont, CA: Wadsworth, 2008), pp. 6–8.

3. Charles E. Merriam and Louise Overacker, *Primary Elections* (Chicago: University of Chicago Press, 1928).

4. Robert M. La Follette, *La Follette's Autobiography* (Madison, WI: R. M. La Follette, 1913), pp. 197–198.

5. Some states allow third parties to nominate their candidates through conventions.

6. See L. Sandy Maisel and Mark D. Brewer, *Parties and Elections in America*, 5th ed. (Lanham, MD: Rowman & Littlefield, 2008), pp. 204–205.

7. The National Conference of State Legislatures lists the states' various primary election systems at www.ncsl.org/default.aspx?tabid=20112 (accessed November 11, 2011).

8. For one typology, see Thomas M. Holbrook and Raymond J. LaRaja, "Parties and Elections," in Virginia Gray, Russell L. Hanson, and Thad Kousser, eds., *Politics in the American States*, 10th ed. (Washington, DC: CQ Press, 2012), Table 3-3. Note that experts disagree on these definitions and on the dividing line between an "open" and a "closed" primary.

9. A 1986 Supreme Court decision (*Tashjian v. Republican Party of Connecticut*) upheld the Connecticut party's efforts to establish an open primary by overriding the state's closed primary law. This decision affirmed the authority of the party, rather than the state, to control its own nomination process. However, many state parties would prefer a closed primary to an open one.

10. Researchers differ as to whether closed primaries are more likely to produce ideologically extreme candidates. Compare Karen M. Kaufmann, James G. Gimpel, and Adam H. Hoffman, "A Promise Fulfilled?" *Journal of Politics* 65 (2003): 457–476; with David W. Brady, Hahrie

Han, and Jeremy C. Pope, "Primary Elections and Candidate Ideology," *Legislative Studies Quarterly* 32 (2007): 79–106.

11. The case was *California Democratic Party v. Jones* (2000). On blanket primaries, see Bruce E. Cain and Elisabeth R. Gerber, eds., *Voting at the Political Fault Line* (Berkeley: University of California Press, 2002).

12. Lynn Vavreck, "The Reasoning Voter Meets the Strategic Candidate," *American Politics Research* 29 (2001): 507–529; and Philip Paolino and Daron R. Shaw, "Lifting the Hood on the Straight-Talk Express," *American Politics Research* 29 (2001): 483–506.

13. Gary D. Wekkin, "Why Crossover Voters Are Not 'Mischievous' Voters," *American Politics Quarterly* 19 (1991): 229–247.

14. See the monthly newsletter *Ballot Access News* at www.ballot-access.org (accessed November 11, 2011).

15. See, for instance, Thomas A. Reitz and Rebecca B. Morton, "Majority Requirements and Minority Representation," *NYU Annual Survey of American Law* 63 (2008): 691–725.

16. V. O. Key, Jr., *American State Politics: An Introduction* (New York: Knopf, 1956), p. 195.

17. John G. Geer and Mark E. Shere, "Party Competition and the Prisoner's Dilemma," *Journal of Politics* 54 (1992): 741–761.

18. See, for example, Malcolm E. Jewell and Sarah M. Morehouse, *Political Parties and Elections in American States*, 4th ed. (Washington, DC: CQ Press, 2001), p. 123.

19. Priscilla L. Southwell, "The Effect of Nomination Divisiveness on the 2008 Presidential Election," *PS: Political Science & Politics* 43 (2010): 255–258. See also Marjorie Randon Hershey, "The Media: Coloring the News," in Michael Nelson, ed., *The Elections of 2008* (Washington, DC: CQ Press, 2009), pp. 128–129.

20. Paige L. Schneider, "Factionalism in the Southern Republican Party," *American Review of Politics* 19 (1998): 129–148.

21. Matt Bai, "Fight Club," *New York Times Magazine*, August 10, 2003, pp. 24–27.

22. Gary F. Moncrief, Peverill Squire, and Malcolm E. Jewell, *Who Runs for the Legislature?* (Upper Saddle River, NJ: Prentice Hall, 2001), p. 39.

23. Sarah McCally Morehouse, *The Governor as Party Leader* (Ann Arbor, MI: University of Michigan Press, 1998), pp. 22–23.

24. Jewell and Morehouse, *Political Parties and Elections in American States*, pp. 109–110.

25. L. Sandy Maisel, Linda L. Fowler, Ruth S. Jones, and Walter J. Stone, "Nomination Politics," in L. Sandy Maisel, ed., *The Parties Respond* (Boulder, CO: Westview Press, 1994), pp. 155–156.

26. See Jewell and Morehouse, *Political Parties and Elections in American States*, pp. 118–120; and Jay Goodliffe and David B. Magleby, "Campaign Finance in U.S. House Primary and General Elections," in Peter F. Galderisi, Marni Ezra, and Michael Lyons, eds., *Congressional Primaries and the Politics of Representation* (Lanham, MD: Rowman & Littlefield, 2001), pp. 62–76.

27. Malcolm E. Jewell, "Northern State Gubernatorial Primary Elections: Explaining Voting Turnout," *American Politics Quarterly* 12 (1984): 101–116.

28. Jewell and Morehouse, *Political Parties and Elections in American States*, pp. 124–125.

29. See Alan Abramowitz, "Don't Blame Primary Voters for Polarization," *The Forum* 5 (2008) at www.bepress.com/forum/vol5/iss4/art4 (accessed November 13, 2011).

30. James Adams and Samuel Merrill III, "Candidate and Party Strategies in Two-Stage Elections Beginning with a Primary," *American Journal of Political Science* 52 (2008): 344–359.

CHAPTER 10 CHOOSING THE PRESIDENTIAL NOMINEES

1. Marjorie Randon Hershey, "Shedding Light on the Invisible Primary," in Larry J. Sabato, ed., *Get in the Booth! The Presidential Election of 2004* (New York: Longman, 2004), pp. 27–47.

2. Marty Cohen, David Karol, Hans Noel, and John Zaller, *The Party Decides* (Chicago: University of Chicago Press, 2008), especially Chapter 9.

3. See John S. Jackson III and William J. Crotty, *The Politics of Presidential Selection*, 2nd ed. (New York: Longman, 2001), Chapters 3 and 4.

4. See Larry M. Bartels, *Presidential Primaries and the Dynamics of Public Choice* (Princeton: Princeton University Press, 1988), pp. 17–21.

5. Byron E. Shafer, *Bifurcated Politics* (Cambridge, MA: Harvard University Press, 1988), pp. 181–184.

6. William G. Mayer and Andrew E. Busch, *The Front-Loading Problem in Presidential Nominations* (Washington, DC: Brookings Institution Press, 2004), pp. 24–25.

7. James W. Ceaser, Andrew E. Busch, and John J. Pitney, Jr., *Epic Journey* (Lanham, MD: Rowman & Littlefield, 2009), p. 22.

8. See John H. Aldrich, *Before the Convention* (Chicago: University of Chicago Press, 1980); and Paul-Henri Gurian and Audrey A. Haynes, "Campaign Strategy in Presidential Primaries," *American Journal of Political Science* 37 (1993): 335–341.

9. John M. Broder, "Show Me the Delegate Rules and I'll Show You the Party," *New York Times*, February 17, 2008, Week in Review, p. 1.
10. Proportional representation doesn't always slow down the Democratic nomination race. If one candidate gains early momentum, as has happened in most recent Democratic races, then the party can settle on a nominee quickly. But when the leading candidates are closely matched in support, PR can prolong their competition.
11. For an interesting analysis, see Jonathan Weisman, Shailagh Murray, and Peter Slevin, "Strategy Was Based on Winning Delegates, Not Battlegrounds," *Washington Post*, June 4, 2008, p. A1.
12. Justin M. Sizemore, "How Obama Did It," *Sabato's Crystal Ball* 6 (June 5, 2008).
13. Ibid.
14. See Richard Herrera, "Are 'Superdelegates' Super?" *Political Behavior* 16 (1994): 79–92. The Republicans send a smaller number of unpledged delegates, including state party chairs, to their national convention.
15. See Patrick J. Kenney and Tom W. Rice, "Voter Turnout in Presidential Primaries," *Political Behavior* 7 (1985): 101–112; and Barbara Norrander and Gregg W. Smith, "Type of Contest, Candidate Strategy, and Turnout in Presidential Primaries," *American Politics Quarterly* 13 (1985): 28–50.
16. Barbara Norrander, *The Imperfect Primary* (New York: Routledge, 2010), p. 63.
17. Mark J. Wattier and Raymond Tatalovich, "Gods, Generals, and the Confederate Flag," The Citadel Symposium on Southern Politics, Charleston, 2004.
18. See Scott Keeter and Cliff Zukin, *Uninformed Choice* (New York: Praeger, 1983); and John G. Geer, *Nominating Presidents* (New York: Greenwood Press, 1989).
19. Samuel L. Popkin, *The Reasoning Voter* (Chicago: University of Chicago Press, 1991), Chapters 6–8.
20. Bartels, *Presidential Primaries and the Dynamics of Public Choice*, Chapter 4.
21. Paul R. Abramson, John H. Aldrich, Phil Paolino, and David W. Rohde, " 'Sophisticated' Voting in the 1988 Presidential Primaries," *American Political Science Review* 86 (1992): 55–69.
22. See Walter J. Stone, Ronald B. Rapoport, and Alan I. Abramowitz, "Candidate Support in Presidential Nomination Campaigns," *Journal of Politics* 54 (1992): 1074–1097.
23. Michael G. Hagen and William G. Mayer, "The Modern Politics of Presidential Selection," in William G. Mayer, ed., *In Pursuit of the White House 2000* (New York: Chatham House, 2000), pp. 17–21.

24. See Lee Sigelman and Paul J. Wahlbeck, "The 'Veepstakes'," *American Political Science Review* 91 (1997): 855–864.
25. L. Sandy Maisel, "The Platform-Writing Process," *Political Science Quarterly* 108 (1993–1994): 671–699.
26. Gerald M. Pomper, "Party Responsibility and the Future of American Democracy," in Jeffrey E. Cohen, Richard Fleisher, and Paul Kantor, eds., *American Political Parties: Decline or Resurgence?* (Washington, DC: CQ Press, 2001), pp. 170–172.
27. These data and those cited in the rest of the chapter come from the *New York Times*/CBS News Polls of Democratic and Republican National Convention delegates.
28. Warren E. Miller and M. Kent Jennings, *Parties in Transition* (New York: Russell Sage Foundation, 1986), Chapters 7–9.
29. See John W. Soule and Wilma E. McGrath, "A Comparative Study of Presidential Nomination Conventions," *American Journal of Political Science* 19 (1975): 501–517.
30. Denise L. Baer and David A. Bositis, *Elite Cadres and Party Coalitions* (New York: Greenwood Press, 1988), Chapter 7.
31. Shafer, *Bifurcated Politics*, Chapter 8; and Costas Panagopoulos, ed., *Rewiring Politics* (Baton Rouge: Louisiana State University Press, 2007).
32. See Emmett H. Buell, Jr., "The Changing Face of the New Hampshire Primary," in William G. Mayer, ed., *In Pursuit of the White House 2000* (New York: Chatham House, 2000), pp. 87–144.
33. Nelson W. Polsby, *The Consequences of Party Reform* (Oxford: Oxford University Press, 1983).
34. See Norrander, *The Imperfect Primary*, especially Chapters 3 and 4; and Caroline Tolbert and Peverill Squire, eds., "Reforming the Presidential Nominating Process," *PS: Political Science and Politics* 42 (2009): 27–79.

CHAPTER 11   THE GENERAL ELECTION

1. See Paul S. Herrnson, *Congressional Elections*, 5th ed. (Washington, DC: CQ Press, 2008); and Marjorie Randon Hershey, *Running for Office* (Chatham, NJ: Chatham House, 1984).
2. This has been the case since World War II; see Gary C. Jacobson, *The Politics of Congressional Elections*, 7th ed. (New York: Longman, 2009).
3. Edward I. Sidlow, *Challenging the Incumbent* (Washington, DC: CQ Press, 2003).
4. See Herrnson, *Congressional Elections*, pp. 221–244.

5. John R. Petrocik, William L. Benoit, and Glenn J. Hansen, "Issue Ownership and Presidential Campaigning, 1952–2000," *Political Science Quarterly* 118 (2003): 599–626.

6. See, for example, David A. Dulio, *For Better or Worse* (Albany, NY: SUNY Press, 2004).

7. James A. Thurber and Candice J. Nelson, eds., *Campaign Warriors* (Washington, DC: Brookings, 2000).

8. See Darrell M. West, *Air Wars*, 5th ed. (Washington, DC: CQ Press, 2009).

9. See Doris A. Graber, *Mass Media and American Politics*, 8th ed. (Washington, DC: CQ Press, 2009), Chapter 4.

10. Dave Barry, "Scandal Sheep," *Boston Globe Magazine*, March 15, 1998, pp. 12–13.

11. Jeff Valenzuela, "Midwest Local TV Newscasts Devote 2.5 Times as Much Air Time to Political Ads as Election Coverage," press release, Joyce Foundation, November 21, 2006.

12. Markus Prior, "News vs. Entertainment," *American Journal of Political Science* 49 (2005): 577–592.

13. Stephen E. Frantzich, "E-Politics and the 2008 Presidential Campaign," in William J. Crotty, ed., *Winning the Presidency 2008* (Boulder, CO: Paradigm, 2009), p. 146.

14. Aaron Smith, "The Internet's Role in Campaign 2008," at http://pewresearch.org/pubs/1192/internet-politics-campaign-2008 (accessed November 13, 2011).

15. Richard J. Semiatin, *Campaigns in the 21st Century* (Boston: McGraw Hill, 2005), p. 178.

16. Allison Dale and Aaron Strauss, "Don't Forget to Vote," *American Journal of Political Science* 53 (2009): 787–804.

17. Aaron Smith, "Twitter and Social Networking in the 2010 Midterm Elections," Pew Internet & American Life Project, January 27, 2011, at http://pewresearch.org/pubs/1871/internet (accessed November 13, 2011).

18. Exit poll data at www.cnn.com/ELECTION/2008/results/polls/#val=USP00p2 (accessed November 13, 2011).

19. Erika Franklin Fowler and Travis N. Ridout, "Advertising Trends in 2010," *The Forum* 8 (2010): 10–11, at www.bepress.com/forum/vol8/iss4/art4 (accessed November 13, 2011).

20. See Richard R. Lau and Gerald M. Pomper, "Effectiveness of Negative Campaigning in U.S. Senate Elections," *American Journal of Political Science* 46 (2002): 47–66; and John G. Geer, *In Defense of Negativity* (Chicago: University of Chicago Press, 2006). On its use by challengers, see James N. Druckman, Martin J. Kifer, and Michael Parkin, "Campaign Communications in U.S. Congressional Elections," *American Political Science Review* 103 (2009): 343–366.

21. Yanna Krupnikov, "When Does Negativity Demobilize?" *American Journal of Political Science* 55 (2011): 797–813.

22. Paul R. Abramson, John H. Aldrich, and David W. Rohde, *Change and Continuity in the 2000 and 2002 Elections* (Washington, DC: CQ Press, 2003), pp. 261–262.

23. Christopher F. Karpowitz, J. Quin Monson, Kelly D. Patterson, and Jeremy C. Pope, "Tea Time in America?" *PS: Political Science & Politics* 44 (2011): 303–309.

24. Calculations by Nate Silver, "Health Care, Bailout Votes May Have Hurt Democrats," November 16, 2010, FiveThirtyEight.com.

25. Alan Abramowitz, "Terrorism, Gay Marriage, and Incumbency," *The Forum* 2 (2004), at www.bepress.com/forum/vol2/iss4/art3 (accessed November 13, 2011).

26. Shira Toeplitz, "Angle's Campaign Sank Candidate," *Politico,* November 21, 2010, at www.politico.com/news/stories/1110/45463.html (accessed November 13, 2011).

27. See Robert Huckfeldt and John Sprague, "Political Parties and Electoral Mobilization," *American Political Science Review* 86 (1992): 70–86; Peter W. Wielhouwer, "The Mobilization of Campaign Activists by the Party Canvass," *American Politics Quarterly* 27 (1999): 177–200; and Thomas M. Holbrook and Scott D. McClurg, "The Mobilization of Core Supporters," *American Journal of Political Science* 49 (2005): 689–703.

28. Donald P. Green and Alan S. Gerber, *Get Out the Vote!* (Washington, DC: Brookings Institution Press, 2004), pp. 92–93.

29. David W. Nickerson, "Quality Is Job One," *American Journal of Political Science* 51 (2007): 269–282.

30. John P. Frendreis, James L. Gibson, and Laura L. Vertz, "The Electoral Relevance of Local Party Organizations," *American Political Science Review* 84 (1990): 225–235.

31. Daron R. Shaw, "The Effect of TV Ads and Candidate Appearances on Statewide Presidential Votes, 1988–96," *American Political Science Review* 93 (1999): 345–361.

32. Alan S. Gerber, James G. Gimpel, Donald P. Green, and Daron R. Shaw, "How Large and Long-lasting Are the Persuasive Effects of Televised Campaign Ads?" *American Political Science Review* 105 (2011): 135–150.

33. Daron R. Shaw, "A Study of Presidential Campaign Effects from 1952–1992,"

Journal of Politics 61 (1999): 387–422; and Adam Simon, *The Winning Message* (Cambridge: Cambridge University Press, 2002).

34. See Paul Freedman, Michael Franz, and Kenneth Goldstein, "Campaign Advertising and Democratic Citizenship," *American Journal of Political Science* 48 (2004): 723–741; and Paul Gronke, *The Electorate, the Campaign, and the Office* (Ann Arbor, MI: University of Michigan Press, 2000).

35. D. Sunshine Hillygus and Simon Jackman, "Voter Decision Making in Election 2000," *American Journal of Political Science* 47 (2003): 583–596; and Matthew A. Baum, "Talking the Vote," *American Journal of Political Science* 49 (2005): 213–234.

36. Shanto Iyengar and John R. Petrocik, "'Basic Rule' Voting," in James A. Thurber, Candice J. Nelson, and David A. Dulio, eds., *Crowded Airwaves* (Washington, DC: Brookings, 2000), p. 142.

37. See Joanne M. Miller and Jon A. Krosnick, "News Media Impact on the Ingredients of Presidential Evaluations," *American Journal of Political Science* 44 (2000): 295–309.

38. David A. M. Peterson, "Campaign Learning and Vote Determinants," *American Journal of Political Science* 53 (2009): 445–460.

39. Russell J. Dalton, Paul A. Beck, and Robert Huckfeldt, "Partisan Cues and the Media," *American Political Science Review* 92 (1998): 111–126.

40. See Robert Huckfeldt and John Sprague, "Networks in Context," *American Political Science Review* 81 (1987): 1197–1216; and Paul Allen Beck, "Voters' Intermediation Environments in the 1988 Presidential Contest," *Public Opinion Quarterly* 55 (1991): 371–394.

41. Project for Excellence in Journalism, "The New Washington Press Corps," at http://journalism.org/print/14678 (accessed November 13, 2011).

42. The classic is Paul Lazarsfeld, Bernard Berelson, and Hazel Gaudet, *The People's Choice* (New York: Columbia University Press, 1948).

43. John H. Aldrich, *Why Parties? A Second Look* (Chicago: University of Chicago Press, 2011), pp. 266–269.

44. See Holbrook and McClurg, "The Mobilization of Core Supporters."

45. See Paul S. Herrnson and Diana Dwyre, "Party Issue Advocacy in Congressional Election Campaigns," in John C. Green and Daniel M. Shea, eds., *The State of the Parties*, 3rd ed. (Lanham, MD: Rowman & Littlefield, 1999), pp. 86–104.

CHAPTER 12 FINANCING THE CAMPAIGNS

1. Unless otherwise noted, all figures cited in this chapter come from Federal Election Commission reports, at times (and so noted) via the Center for Responsive Politics at www.opensecrets.org. For excellent analyses of campaign finance, see Michael J. Malbin, ed., *The Election after Reform* (Lanham, MD: Rowman & Littlefield, 2006); and Marian Currinder, *Money in the House* (Boulder, CO: Westview Press, 2009).

2. Calculated from FEC data at www.fec.gov/press/2010_Full_summary_Data.shtml: 2009-2010 Financial Activity of Senate and House General Election Campaigns (accessed November 20, 2011).

3. Data from the New Jersey Election Law Enforcement Commission, at www.elec.state.nj.us/ELECReport/EntityListing-DetailView.aspx?Report=NonPac&Type=G&Year=2007&Office=1 (accessed November 16, 2011).

4. Data from James Sample et al., "The New Politics of Judicial Elections, 2000–2009," Brennan Center for Justice, at www.brennancenter.org/content/resource/the_new_politics_of_judicial_elections (accessed November 16, 2011). See also James L. Gibson, "Challenges to the Impartiality of State Supreme Courts," *American Political Science Review* 102 (2008): 59–75.

5. See John J. Coleman and Paul F. Manna, "Congressional Campaign Spending and the Quality of Democracy," *Journal of Politics* 62 (2000): 757–789.

6. Gary C. Jacobson, *The Politics of Congressional Elections*, 7th ed. (New York: Pearson-Longman, 2009), p. 45.

7. See these articles in the *American Journal of Political Science*: Donald Philip Green and Jonathan S. Krasno, "Salvation for the Spendthrift Incumbent," 32 (1988): 884–907; Gary C. Jacobson, "The Effects of Campaign Spending in House Elections," 34 (1990): 334–362; and Kenneth Benoit and Michael Marsh, "The Campaign Value of Incumbency," 52 (2008): 874–890.

8. Peter Francia, John C. Green, Paul S. Herrnson, Lynda W. Powell, and Clyde Wilcox, *The Financiers of Congressional Elections* (New York: Columbia University Press, 2003).

9. Dan Eggen and T. W. Farnam, "Despite Tea Party Energy, Outside Groups Funded by Swift Boaters, Other Old Hands," *Washington Post*, October 22, 2010, p. A1.

10. Frank J. Sorauf, *Inside Campaign Finance* (New Haven: Yale University Press, 1992), Chapter 4.

11. Gregory Wawro, "A Panel Probit Analysis of Campaign Contributions and Roll-Call Votes," *American Journal of Political Science* 45 (2001): 563–579.

12. See Richard L. Hall and Frank W. Wayman, "Buying Time," *American Political Science Review* 84 (1990): 797–820.

13. FEC *Record*, July 2011, p. 13, at www.fec.gov/pdf/party_guide_supp.pdf (accessed July 22, 2011).

14. See Anthony J. Corrado, Michael J. Malbin, Thomas E. Mann, and Norman J. Ornstein, *Reform in an Age of Networked Campaigns* (Washington, DC: Campaign Finance Institute, American Enterprise Institute, and Brookings Institution, 2010), Table 4.

15. On public funding, see Michael J. Malbin, "Small Donors, Large Donors and the Internet," at www.cfinst.org/president/pdf/PresidentialWorkingPaper_April09.pdf (accessed November 16, 2011).

16. The case was decided in 1976. See Thomas E. Mann, "Linking Knowledge and Action," *Perspectives on Politics* 1 (2003): 69–83.

17. The cases are *Colorado Republican Federal Campaign Committee v. Federal Election Commission* (1996), known as "Colorado I," and *McConnell v. Federal Election Commission* (2003).

18. From the record in *McConnell v. Federal Election Commission*, quoted in Adam Cohen, "Buying a High-Priced Upgrade on the Political Back-Scratching Circuit," *New York Times*, September 15, 2003, p. A22.

19. See Anthony Corrado, Sarah Barclay, and Heitor Gouvea, "The Parties Take the Lead," in John C. Green and Rick Farmer, eds., *The State of the Parties*, 4th ed. (Lanham, MD: Rowman & Littlefield, 2003), pp. 97–114.

20. For a different view of the partisan impact of soft money, see Raymond J. LaRaja, *Small Change* (Ann Arbor, MI: University of Michigan Press, 2008).

21. John Kenneth White and Daniel M. Shea, *New Party Politics* (Belmont, CA: Wadsworth, 2004), p. 258.

22. Paul S. Herrnson, "The Congressional Elections," in Gerald M. Pomper, ed., *The Election of 2000* (New York: Chatham House, 2001), p. 170.

23. Mark J. Rozell, Clyde Wilcox, and David Madland, *Interest Groups in American Campaigns*, 2nd ed. (Washington, DC: CQ Press, 2005), pp. 146–147.

24. Michael J. Malbin, "Political Parties Under the Post-*McConnell* Bipartisan Campaign Reform Act," *Election Law Journal* 3 (2004): 183.

25. Raymond J. La Raja, "State Parties and Soft Money," in Green and Farmer, eds., *The State of the Parties*, 4th ed., pp. 132–150.

26. Jonathan Krasno and Kenneth Goldstein, "The Facts About Television Advertising and the McCain-Feingold Bill," *PS Political Science & Politics* 35 (2002): 210.

27. Raymond J. LaRaja, "State and Local Political Parties," in Malbin, ed., *The Election after Reform*, Chapter 4.

28. Michael M. Franz, Joel Rivlin, and Kenneth Goldstein, "Much More of the Same," in Malbin, ed., *The Election after Reform*, Chapter 7.

29. IRS data as of October 3, 2007.

30. Steve Weissman, "Soft Money Political Spending by 501(c) Nonprofits Tripled in 2008 Election," February 25, 2009, at www.cfinst.org/pr/prRelease.aspx?ReleaseID=221 (accessed November 16, 2011).

31. See Robert C. Boatright, "Fundraising—Present and Future," in Richard J. Semiatin, ed., *Campaigns on the Cutting Edge* (Washington, DC: CQ Press, 2008), pp. 10–26.

32. Joseph E. Sandler and Neil P. Reiff, "State and Local Parties Must Tread Carefully Through the Campaign Finance Minefield," *Campaigns & Elections* 25 (2004): 50–51.

33. Michael Malbin, "Reality Check: Obama Received About the Same Percentage from Small Donors in 2008 as Bush in 2004," CFI press release, November 24, 2008, at www.cfinst.org/Press/PReleases/08-11-24/Realty_Check_-_Obama_Small_Donors.aspx (accessed November 16, 2011).

34. President George W. Bush's propensity to give many of his biggest contributors appointments to high-level government jobs was not matched by President Obama, but even so, several big Obama bundlers were nominated for ambassadorships.

35. These are known officially as "independent expenditure-only committees." See Dan Eggen and T. W. Farnam, "New 'Super PACs' Bringing Millions into Campaigns," *Washington Post*, September 28, 2010, p. A1.

36. Estimate by the Campaign Finance Institute.

37. Michael M. Franz, "The *Citizens United* Election?" *The Forum* 8 (2010): 22, at www.bepress.com/forum/vol8/iss4/art7 (accessed November 16, 2011).

38. See the National Conference of State Legislatures at www.ncsl.org/programs/legismgt/about/ContribLimits.htm (accessed November 16, 2011).

39. See Michael Miller, "Gaming Arizona," *PS: Political Science and Politics*

61 (2008): 527–532. The Campaign Finance Institute has examined several state and city programs for public financing; see, for example, Michael Malbin and Peter W. Brusoe, "Why New York City Could Be a Model for the Nation and States," working paper, Campaign Finance Institute, December 1, 2010, at www.cfinst.org/smalldonors/nyc_as_model.aspx (accessed November 16, 2011).

40. Mike McIntire, "The Secret Sponsors," *New York Times,* October 2, 2010, at www.nytimes.com/2010/10/03/weekinreview/03mcintire.html?hpw (accessed November 16, 2011). The investigation was done by Public Citizen, an interest group.

41. Raymond J. LaRaja, "From Bad to Worse," *The Forum* 6 (2008) at www.bepress.com/forum/vol6/iss1/art2 (accessed November 16, 2011).

PART V   THE PARTY IN GOVERNMENT

1. See the report of the Committee on Responsible Parties of the American Political Science Association, *Toward a More Responsible Two-Party System* (New York: Rinehart, 1950).

CHAPTER 13   PARTIES IN CONGRESS AND STATE LEGISLATURES

1. See Richard E. Cohen and Joseph J. Schatz, "Debt Dispute Goes Down to the Wire," *CQ Weekly,* August 1, 2011, pp. 1690–1691.

2. Keith Krehbiel, "Where's the Party?" *British Journal of Political Science* 23 (1993): 225–266.

3. Gary W. Cox and Keith T. Poole, "On Measuring Partisanship in Roll-Call Voting," *American Journal of Political Science* 46 (2002): 477–489; and Gerald C. Wright and Brian F. Schaffner, "The Influence of Party," *American Political Science Review* 96 (2002): 367–379.

4. Steven S. Smith, *Party Influence in Congress* (Cambridge: Cambridge University Press, 2007).

5. D. Roderick Kiewiet and Mathew D. McCubbins, *The Logic of Delegation* (Chicago: University of Chicago Press, 1991).

6. Even Cannon faced limits, however; see Eric D. Lawrence, Forrest Maltzman, and Paul J. Wahlbeck, "The Politics of Speaker Cannon's Committee Assignments," *American Journal of Political Science* 45 (2001): 551–562.

7. Steven S. Smith and Gerald Gamm, "The Dynamics of Party Government in Congress," in Lawrence C. Dodd and Bruce I. Oppenheimer, eds., *Congress Reconsidered*, 9th ed. (Washington, DC: CQ Press, 2009), p. 149.

8. Gary W. Cox and Mathew W. McCubbins, *Legislative Leviathan,* 2nd ed. (Berkeley: University of California Press, 1993), pp. 279–282.

9. Barbara Sinclair, "Evolution or Revolution?" in L. Sandy Maisel, ed., *The Parties Respond,* 3rd ed. (Boulder, CO: Westview Press, 1998).

10. Barbara Sinclair, *Unorthodox Lawmaking,* 2nd ed. (Washington, DC: CQ Press, 2000), pp. 103–106.

11. C. Lawrence Evans and Walter J. Oleszek, *Congress Under Fire* (Boston: Houghton Mifflin, 1997); and Lawrence C. Dodd and Bruce I. Oppenheimer, "A Decade of Republican Control," in Dodd and Oppenheimer, eds., *Congress Reconsidered,* 8th ed. (Washington, DC: CQ Press, 2005), Chapter 2.

12. David Rohde and John Aldrich, "Consequences of Electoral and Institutional Change," in Jeffrey M. Stonecash, ed., *New Directions in American Political Parties* (New York: Routledge, 2010), pp. 234–250.

13. Mike Allen, "GOP Leaders Tighten Their Grip on House," *Washington Post,* January 9, 2005, p. A5.

14. Marian Currinder, *Money in the House* (Boulder, CO: Westview Press, 2009), Chapter 2 and p. 203.

15. David W. Rohde, *Parties and Leaders in the Postreform House* (Chicago: University of Chicago Press, 1991). See also Barbara Sinclair, *Legislators, Leaders, and Lawmaking* (Baltimore: Johns Hopkins University Press, 1995).

16. See, for example, William T. Bianco and Itai Sened, "Uncovering Evidence of Conditional Party Government," *American Political Science Review* 99 (2005): 361–371.

17. See John H. Aldrich, *Why Parties? A Second Look* (Chicago: University of Chicago Press, 2011), Chapter 7.

18. Rohde and Aldrich, "Consequences of Electoral and Institutional Change."

19. Barbara Sinclair, "The New World of U.S. Senators," in Dodd and Oppenheimer, eds., *Congress Reconsidered,* 9th ed., pp. 1–22.

20. Smith and Gamm, "The Dynamics of Party Government in Congress," pp. 141–164.

21. See Nathan W. Monroe, Jason M. Roberts, and David W. Rohde, eds., *Why Not Parties?* (Chicago: University of Chicago Press, 2008).

22. The main exception is Nebraska, which is officially nonpartisan.
23. Malcolm E. Jewell and Sarah M. Morehouse, *Political Parties and Elections in American States,* 4th ed. (Washington, DC: CQ Press, 2001), pp. 236–238.
24. Keith E. Hamm and Robert Harmel, "Legislative Party Development and the Speaker System," *Journal of Politics* 55 (1993): 1140–1151; and Malcolm E. Jewell and Marcia Lynn Whicker, *Legislative Leadership in the American States* (Ann Arbor, MI: University of Michigan Press, 1994).
25. Thomas Stratmann, "Congressional Voting over Legislative Careers," *American Political Science Review* 94 (2000): 665–676. This depends, of course, on whether the junior legislator's district is similar in views to those of the typical district of his or her party.
26. Paul S. Herrnson, *Congressional Elections,* 5th ed. (Washington, DC: CQ Press, 2008); and Kathryn Pearson, "Congressional Party Discipline," paper delivered at the 2002 Annual Meeting of the Midwest Political Science Association.
27. Juliet Eilperin, "House GOP Practices Art of One-Vote Victories," *Washington Post,* October 14, 2003, p. A1.
28. See Gary W. Cox and Mathew D. McCubbins, *Setting the Agenda* (Cambridge: Cambridge University Press, 2005).
29. Barbara Sinclair, "Orchestrators of Unorthodox Lawmaking," *The Forum* 6 (2008), at www.bepress.com/forum/vol6/iss3/art4 (accessed November 19, 2011).
30. Julius Turner, *Party and Constituency,* rev. ed., Edward V. Schneier, ed. (Baltimore: Johns Hopkins University Press, 1970), pp. 16–17.
31. "Republicans Lift Unanimity Trend," *CQ Weekly,* January 3, 2011, p. 34. See Jason M. Roberts and Steven S. Smith, "Procedural Contexts, Party Strategy, and Conditional Party Voting in the U.S. House of Representatives, 1971–2000," *American Journal of Political Science* 47 (2003): 305–317.
32. Nelson W. Polsby, "The Institutionalization of the United States House of Representatives," *American Political Science Review* 62 (1968): 144–168; and Walter Dean Burnham, *Critical Elections and the Mainsprings of American Politics* (New York: Norton, 1970), pp. 91–134.
33. Aldrich, *Why Parties?,* p. 243.
34. Roberts and Smith, "Procedural Contexts."
35. Rohde, *Parties and Leaders in the Postreform House,* Chapter 3. See also M. V. Hood III, Quentin Kidd, and Irwin L. Morris, "Of Byrd[s] and Bumpers,"

American Journal of Political Science 43 (1999): 465–487; and Stanley P. Berard, *Southern Democrats in the U.S. House of Representatives* (Norman, OK: University of Oklahoma Press, 2001).
36. On Pelosi's Speakership, see Kathryn Pearson and Eric Schickler, "The Transition to Democratic Leadership in a Polarized House," in Dodd and Oppenheimer, *Congress Reconsidered,* 9th ed., pp. 165–188.
37. Stephen Gettinger, "Return of the Floor Vote," *CQ Weekly,* May 2, 2011, p. 961.
38. "The ADA 2010 Voting Record," May 25, 2011 at www.adaction.org/media/votingrecords/2010.pdf (accessed November 19, 2011).
39. See Frank R. Baumgartner, Jeffrey M. Berry, Marie Hojnacki, David C. Kimball, and Beth L. Leech, *Lobbying and Policy Change* (Chicago: University of Chicago Press, 2009), Chapter 5.
40. Gary C. Jacobson, "Explaining the Ideological Polarization of the Congressional Parties Since the 1970s," in David W. Brady and Mathew D. McCubbins, eds., *Party, Process, and Political Change in Congress,* vol. 2 (Stanford: Stanford University Press, 2007), pp. 91–101.
41. Barry Burden, "Candidate Positioning in U.S. Congressional Elections," *British Journal of Political Science* 34 (2004): 211–227.
42. Mark A. Peterson, *Legislating Together* (Cambridge, MA: Harvard University Press, 1990); and Cary R. Covington, J. Mark Wrighton, and Rhonda Kinney, "A 'Presidency-Augmented' Model of Presidential Success on House Roll Call Votes," *American Journal of Political Science* 39 (November 1995): 1001–1024.
43. Gary C. Jacobson, *The Politics of Congressional Elections,* 7th ed. (New York: Pearson-Longman, 2009), p. 255.
44. C. Lawrence Evans and Claire E. Grandy, "The Whip Systems of Congress," in Dodd and Oppenheimer, 9th ed., p. 210.
45. Boris Shor and Nolan McCarty, "The Ideological Mapping of American Legislatures," *American Political Science Review* 105 (2011): 530–551.
46. See John D. Griffin, "Electoral Competition and Democratic Responsiveness," *Journal of Politics* 68 (2006): 911–921.
47. Jewell and Morehouse, *Political Parties and Elections,* p. 244.
48. David Denemark, "Partisan Pork Barrel in Parliamentary Systems," *Journal of Politics* 62 (2000): 896–915.
49. Anthony Gierzynski, *Legislative Party Campaign Committees in the American States* (Lexington: University of Kentucky Press, 1992); and Daniel M. Shea,

Transforming Democracy (Albany: SUNY Press, 1995).

50. Cox and McCubbins, *Legislative Leviathan.*

51. See Gary Cox, *The Efficient Secret* (New York: Cambridge University Press, 1987).

CHAPTER 14 THE PARTY IN THE EXECUTIVE AND THE COURTS

1. Quoted in Adam Clymer, "Not So Fast," *New York Times*, April 1, 2001, sec. 4, p. 1.

2. See Daniel J. Galvin, *Presidential Party Building* (Princeton: Princeton University Press, 2010).

3. Elizabeth Benjamin, "At Obama's Request, Steve Israel Stands Down," www.nydailynews.com/blogs/dailypolitics/2009/05/at-obamas-request-steve-israel.html (accessed November 19, 2011).

4. James E. Campbell, "Predicting Seat Gains from Presidential Coattails," *American Journal of Political Science* 30 (1986): 164–183.

5. See Bruce Cain, John Ferejohn, and Morris Fiorina, *The Personal Vote* (Cambridge, MA: Harvard University Press, 1987).

6. Paul R. Abramson, John H. Aldrich, and David W. Rohde, *Change and Continuity in the 2004 and 2006 Elections* (Washington, DC: CQ Press, 2007), pp. 261–263; but see Ray C. Fair, "Presidential and Congressional Vote-Share Equations," *American Journal of Political Science* 53 (2009): 55–72.

7. See, for instance, Paul S. Herrnson, *Congressional Elections*, 5th ed. (Washington, DC: CQ Press, 2008), p. 24.

8. See James E. Campbell, "Presidential Coattails and Midterm Losses in State Legislative Elections," *American Political Science Review* 80 (1986): 45–63.

9. Robin F. Marra and Charles W. Ostrom, Jr., "Explaining Seat Change in the U.S. House of Representatives, 1950–86," *American Journal of Political Science* 33 (1989): 541–569.

10. Paul R. Abramson, John H. Aldrich, and David W. Rohde, *Change and Continuity in the 2008 and 2010 Elections* (Washington, DC: CQ Press, 2012), p. 294.

11. The classic statement is Angus Campbell, "Surge and Decline: A Study of Electoral Change," in Angus Campbell, Philip E. Converse, Warren E. Miller, and Donald E. Stokes, eds., *Elections and the Political Order* (New York: Wiley, 1966), pp. 40–62.

12. See James E. Campbell, "The Midterm Landslide of 2010," *The Forum* 8 (2010) at www.bepress.com/forum/vol8/iss4/art3 (accessed June 5, 2011).

13. Richard Born, "Surge and Decline, Negative Voting, and the Midterm Loss Phenomenon," *American Journal of Political Science* 34 (1990): 615–645.

14. See Abramson, Aldrich, and Rohde, *Change and Continuity*, p. 196.

15. David Baumann, "At the Top of His Game," *CQ Weekly*, May 18, 2009, pp. 1142–1143.

16. See David R. Mayhew, *Divided We Govern*, 2nd ed. (New Haven: Yale University Press, 2005).

17. Hugh Heclo, *A Government of Strangers* (Washington, DC: Brookings Institution, 1977).

18. Hugh Heclo, "Issue Networks and the Executive Establishment," in Anthony King, ed., *The New American Political System* (Washington, DC: American Enterprise Institute, 1979), pp. 87–124.

19. Joel Aberbach and Bert A. Rockman, "Clashing Beliefs Within the Executive Branch," *American Political Science Review* 70 (1976): 456–468.

20. Joel D. Aberbach and Bert A. Rockman, "The Political Views of U.S. Senior Federal Executives, 1970–1992," *Journal of Politics* 57 (1995): 838–852.

21. Sanford C. Gordon, "Assessing Partisan Bias in Federal Public Corruption Prosecutions," *American Political Science Review* 103 (2009): 534–554.

22. Robert A. Carp and Ronald Stidham, *Judicial Process in America* (Washington, DC: CQ Press, 2001), p. 292.

23. Stuart S. Nagel, "Political Party Affiliations and Judges' Decisions," *American Political Science Review* 55 (1961): 843–850. See also Jeffrey A. Segal and Harold J. Spaeth, *The Supreme Court and the Attitudinal Model* (Cambridge: Cambridge University Press, 1993).

24. Juliet Eilperin, "Environmental Group Cites Partisanship in the Judiciary," *Washington Post*, October 9, 2004, p. A2.

25. See Randall D. Lloyd, "Separating Partisanship from Party in Judicial Research," *American Political Science Review* 89 (1995): 413–420.

26. See Robert Barnes, "Partisan Fissures Over Voter ID," *Washington Post*, December 25, 2007, p. A1.

27. Adam Liptak, "Clerks Highlight Supreme Court's Polarization," *New York Times*, September 6, 2010, p. A1.

28. Elisha Carol Savchak, Thomas G. Hansford, Donald R. Songer, Kenneth L. Manning, and Robert A Carp, "Taking It to the Next Level," *American Journal of Political Science* 50 (2006): 485–486.

29. See Amy Goldstein and Dan Eggen, "Immigration Judges Often Picked Based on GOP Ties," *Washington Post*, June 11, 2007, p. A1.

30. Sheldon Goldman, "The Bush Imprint on the Judiciary," *Judicature* 74 (1991), 294–306.

31. Sheldon Goldman, Elliot Slotnick, Gerard Gryski, and Gary Zuk, "Clinton's Judges," *Judicature* 84 (2001): 244, 249.

32. R. Jeffrey Smith, "The Politics of the Federal Bench," *Washington Post*, December 8, 2008, p. A1.

33. Daniel J. Parks, "Senate Judicial Nominations Spat Again Frustrates Appropriators," *CQ Weekly*, October 20, 2001, pp. 2470–71. See also Sarah A. Binder and Forrest Maltzman, "Senatorial Delay in Confirming Federal Judges, 1947–1998," *American Journal of Political Science* 46 (2002): 190–199.

34. See Melinda Gann Hall, "State Supreme Courts in American Democracy," *American Political Science Review* 95 (2001): 315–330.

CHAPTER 15   THE SEMI-RESPONSIBLE PARTIES

1. Committee on Political Parties of the American Political Science Association, *Toward a More Responsible Two-Party System* (New York: Rinehart, 1950).

2. Jeffrey M. Jones, "Near-Record 49% Say Democratic Party 'Too Liberal,' " June 14, 2010, at www.gallup.com/poll/139877/Near-Record-Say-Democratic-Party-Liberal.aspx (accessed November 19, 2011).

3. See Austin Ranney, *The Doctrine of Responsible Party Government* (Urbana: University of Illinois Press, 1964), Chapters 1 and 2.

4. E. E. Schattschneider, *Party Government* (New York: Rinehart, 1942), p. 208.

5. E. E. Schattschneider, *The Semi-Sovereign People* (New York: Holt, Rinehart, and Winston, 1960).

6. See John Kenneth White and Jerome M. Mileur, eds., *Challenges to Party Government* (Carbondale: Southern Illinois University Press, 1992).

7. See Malcolm E. Jewell and Sarah M. Morehouse, *Political Parties and Elections in American States*, 4th ed. (Washington, DC: CQ Press, 2001), p. 222; and Morris Fiorina, *Divided Government* (New York: MacMillan, 1992), Chapter 3.

8. John J. Coleman, "Unified Government, Divided Government, and Party Responsiveness," *American Political Science Review* 93 (1999): 821–835; and

David R. Mayhew, *Divided We Govern*, 2nd ed. (New Haven: Yale University Press, 2005).

9. Richard Born, "Split-Ticket Voters, Divided Government, and Fiorina's Policy-Balancing Model," *Legislative Studies Quarterly* 19 (1994): 95–115.

10. A. James Reichley, *The Life of the Parties* (Lanham, MD: Rowman & Littlefield, 2000), Chapter 6.

11. David E. Rosenbaum, "Bush to Return to 'Ownership Society' Theme in Push for Social Security Changes," *New York Times*, January 16, 2005, p. 20.

12. Edward G. Carmines and James A. Stimson, *Issue Evolution* (Princeton: Princeton University Press, 1989); see also Geoffrey C. Layman and Thomas M. Carsey, "Party Polarization and 'Conflict Extension' in the American Electorate," *American Journal of Political Science* 46 (2002): 786–802.

13. Jason M. Roberts and Steven S. Smith, "Procedural Contexts, Party Strategy, and Conditional Party Voting in the U.S. House of Representatives, 1971–2000," *American Journal of Political Science* 47 (2003): 305–317. See also Barbara Sinclair, *Party Wars* (Norman, OK: University of Oklahoma Press, 2006).

14. Charles Barrilleaux, Thomas Holbrook, and Laura Langer, "Electoral Competition, Legislative Balance, and American State Welfare Policy," *American Journal of Political Science* 46 (2002): 415–427.

15. See David Karol, *Party Position Change in American Politics* (New York: Cambridge University Press, 2009).

16. Sheryl Gay Stolberg, "The Revolution That Wasn't," *New York Times*, February 13, 2005, section 4, p. 1. Data are from the National Taxpayers Union.

17. Robin Kolodny, "Moderate Party Factions in the U.S. House of Representatives," in John C. Green and Daniel M. Shea, eds., *The State of the Parties*, 3rd ed. (Lanham, MD: Rowman & Littlefield, 1999), pp. 271–285; and Nicol C. Rae, "Party Factionalism, 1946–1996," in Byron E. Shafer, ed., *Partisan Approaches to Postwar American Politics* (New York: Chatham House, 1998), pp. 41–74.

18. The seminal study is Philip E. Converse, "The Nature of Belief Systems in Mass Publics," in David Apter, ed., *Ideology and Discontent* (New York: Free Press, 1964), pp. 206–261.

19. John Zaller and Stanley Feldman, "A Simple Theory of the Survey Response," *American Journal of Political Science* 36 (1992): 579–616.

20. Kathleen A. Frankovic and Monika L. McDermott, "Public Opinion in the 2000 Election," in Gerald M. Pomper, ed., *The Election of 2000* (New York: Chatham House, 2001), pp. 76–78 and 88–89.

21. Paul R. Abramson, John H. Aldrich, and David W. Rohde, *Change and Continuity in the 1984 Elections* (Washington, DC: CQ Press, 1986), Chapter 6.

22. Alan I. Abramowitz, *The Disappearing Center* (New Haven: Yale University Press, 2009).

23. See Matthew Levendusky, *The Partisan Sort* (Chicago: University of Chicago Press, 2009); and Morris P. Fiorina with Samuel J. Abrams and Jeremy C. Pope, *Culture War*, 3rd ed. (New York: Longman, 2011).

24. Kyle L. Saunders and Alan I. Abramowitz, "Ideological Realignment and Active Partisans in the American Electorate," *American Politics Research* 32 (2004): 293.

25. Jacob S. Hacker and Paul Pierson, "Abandoning the Middle," *Perspectives on Politics* 3 (2005): 33–53.

26. Marc J. Hetherington, "Resurgent Mass Partisanship," *American Political Science Review* 95 (2001): 619–631.

27. See Markus Prior, *Post-Broadcast Democracy* (New York: Cambridge University Press, 2007).

28. Eric Lawrence, John Sides, and Henry Farrell, "Self-Segregation or Deliberation?" *Perspectives on Politics* 8 (2010): 141–157.

29. David R. Jones and Monika L. McDermott, "The Responsible Party Government Model in House and Senate Elections," *American Journal of Political Science* 48 (2004): 1–12.

30. Paul Allen Beck, "A Tale of Two Electorates," in John C. Green and Rick Farmer, eds., *The State of the Parties*, 4th ed. (Lanham, MD: Rowman & Littlefield, 2003), pp. 38–53.

31. For example, see Seth E. Masket and Hans Noel, "Serving Two Masters," *Political Research Quarterly* 64 (2011): 1–20. See also Marjorie Randon Hershey, Nathaniel Birkhead, and Beth C. Easter, "Party Activists and Political Polarization," in Mark D. Brewer and L. Sandy Maisel, eds., *The Parties Respond*, 5th ed. (Boulder, CO: Westview Press, forthcoming).

32. See Seth E. Masket, "It Takes an Outsider," *American Journal of Political Science* 51 (2007): 482–497.

33. See Brandice Canes-Wrone, David W. Brady, and John F. Cogan, "Out of Step, Out of Office," *American Political Science Review* 96 (2002): 127–140.

34. Laurel Harbridge and Neil Malhotra, "Electoral Incentives and Partisan Conflict in Congress," *American Journal of Political Science* 55 (2011): 494–510.

35. John R. Hibbing and Elizabeth Theiss-Morse, "Process Preferences and American Politics," *American Political Science Review* 95 (2001): 145–153.

36. David Von Drehle, "Political Split Is Pervasive," *Washington Post*, April 25, 2004, p. A1.

37. Leon D. Epstein, "What Happened to the British Party Model?" *American Political Science Review* 74 (1980): 9–22.

CHAPTER 16   THE PLACE OF PARTIES IN AMERICAN POLITICS

1. See Robert Harmel and Kenneth Janda, *Parties and Their Environments* (New York: Longman, 1982).

2. See Ruy A. Teixeira, *The Disappearing American Voter* (Washington, DC: Brookings Institution, 1992), Chapter 3.

3. See Stephen K. Medvic, *Campaigns and Elections* (Boston: Wadsworth, 2010), pp. 312–314.

4. Harold W. Stanley and Richard G. Niemi, *Vital Statistics on American Politics 1999–2000* (Washington, DC: CQ Press, 2000), pp. 44 and 133.

5. Bruce E. Cain, John Ferejohn, and Morris P. Fiorina, *The Personal Vote* (Cambridge, MA: Harvard University Press, 1987).

6. Philip A. Klinkner and Thomas Schaller, "LBJ's Revenge," *The Forum* 6 (2008), at www.bepress.com/forum/vol16/iss4/art9 (accessed June 25, 2011).

7. Alan I. Abramowitz, "Beyond 2010," *Sabato's Crystal Ball*, March 11, 2010, at www.centerforpolitics.org/crystalball/articles/aia2010031101 (accessed June 25, 2011).

8. See Robert Huckfeldt and Paul Allen Beck, "Contexts, Intermediaries, and Political Activity," in Lawrence C. Dodd and Calvin Jillson, eds., *The Dynamics of American Politics* (Boulder, CO: Westview Press, 1994), Chapter 11. On the other hand, organized interests have become more polarized by party since the Reagan years; see Jack L. Walker, Jr., *Mobilizing Interest Groups in America* (Ann Arbor, MI: University of Michigan Press, 1991), Chapter 8, and media coverage frequently refers to party; see Marjorie Randon Hershey, "If 'The Party's in Decline,' Then What's That Filling the News Columns?" in Nelson W. Polsby and Raymond E. Wolfinger, eds., *On Parties* (Berkeley: Institute of Governmental Studies, 1999), pp. 257–278.

9. Larry M. Bartels, "Partisanship and Voting Behavior, 1952–1996," *American Journal of Political Science* 44 (2000): 35–50.

10. Gary C. Jacobson, *The Politics of Congressional Elections*, 7th ed. (New York: Pearson-Longman, 2009), p. 163.

11. Rep. Daniel Lipinski, "Navigating Congressional Policy Processes," in Lawrence C. Dodd and Bruce I. Oppenheimer, eds., *Congress Reconsidered*, 9th ed. (Washington, DC: CQ Press, 2009), p. 344.

12. See Ronald Inglehart, *Culture Shift* (Princeton: Princeton University Press, 1990), Chapters 10 and 11.

13. John H. Aldrich, *Why Parties? A Second Look* (Chicago: University of Chicago Press, 2011), p. 3; and Nancy L. Rosenblum, *On the Side of the Angels* (Princeton: Princeton University Press, 2008).

14. David R. Mayhew, *Congress: The Electoral Connection* (New Haven: Yale University Press, 1974), especially pp. 141–149.

15. See Marjorie Randon Hershey, "Political Parties as Mechanisms of Social Choice," in Richard S. Katz and William Crotty, eds., *Handbook of Party Politics* (London: Sage, 2005), pp. 75–88.

16. Walter Dean Burnham, *Critical Elections and the Mainsprings of American Politics* (New York: Norton, 1970), p. 133.

17. See Gerald C. Wright and Brian F. Schaffner, "The Influence of Party," *American Political Science Review* 96 (2002): 367–379.

18. See Steven J. Rosenstone and John Mark Hansen, *Mobilization, Participation, and Democracy in America* (New York: Macmillan, 1993), Chapter 8.

19. Larry J. Sabato and Bruce Larson, *The Party's Just Begun* (New York: Longman, 2002), pp. 156–157.

20. Ibid., pp. 159–160.

INDEX